THE UNEXPECTED SHAW

OTHER BOOKS BY STANLEY WEINTRAUB

Private Shaw and Public Shaw:
    A Dual Portrait of Lawrence of Arabia and G.B.S.
Beardsley: A Biography
The Last Great Cause:
    The Intellectuals and the Spanish Civil War
Journey to Heartbreak: Bernard Shaw 1914–1918
Whistler: A Biography
Four Rossettis: A Victorian Biography
The London Yankees:
    Portraits of American Writers and Artists in London, 1894–1914

EDITED BY STANLEY WEINTRAUB

An Unfinished Novel by Bernard Shaw
Shaw: An Autobiography 1856–1898
Shaw: An Autobiography 1898–1950
    The Playwright Years
Bernard Shaw's Nondramatic Literary Criticism
Saint Joan; Fifty Years After—1923/24–1973/74
The Portable Bernard Shaw
Modern British Dramatists 1900–1945

THE UNEXPECTED SHAW

Biographical Approaches to G.B.S. and His Work

Stanley Weintraub

FREDERICK UNGAR PUBLISHING CO.
New York

Copyright © 1982 by Stanley Weintraub
Printed in the United States of America
Design by Tom Christopher

Library of Congress Cataloging in Publication Data

Weintraub, Stanley, 1929–
  The unexpected Shaw.

  Includes index.
  1. Shaw, George Bernard, 1856–1950. 2. Dramatists,
Irish—20th century—Biography.   I. Title.
PR5366.W43   1982   822′.912   82-40250
ISBN 0-8044-2974-X

for Warren Sylvester Smith

CONTENTS

Preface:
The Unexpected Shaw

I can still recall my surprise, as a graduate student hunting through the library stacks, that the author of *Man and Superman* and other plays had begun his career as a writer with a series of unsuccessful yet strikingly lively and characteristic novels. The G.B.S. I would continue to discover was as full of paradoxes as his plays, which themselves appear hidden in embryo in the unsalable and commercially lifeless novels of his nonage. He was an amateur boxer who afterward inserted memories of pugilism into his plays. He was a self-made director whose experience as an actor was minimal and almost completely amateur. He had been an art critic, briefly, because he needed the money rather than because he knew much about art, but art would then percolate through his plays in dramatically suggestive ways. He became a literary critic for similar pecuniary reasons, proceeding afterward to couch almost all the literary criticism he ever wrote in economic and social perspectives, defending even the art-for-art's-sake school through a logic of social good which must have perplexed the turn-of-the-century decadents.

Although he hungered for commercial as well as artistic success as a playwright, Shaw (who felt the future in him) unpredictably urged the management he was quietly backing to take off his plays at the box-office peak of their runs in order to experiment with innovative new plays by other, less commercial, writers; and the profits from his successes not only subsidized the others but proved the possibilities of the repertory system in England and of an English national theater. Lavishly, he would feed the demand for information about himself and his background from would-be biographers, but it was at least in part because he thought that a surfeit of data would put writers off trails he preferred to leave untraversed. He permitted romantic stories about how he was inspired to write plays like *Saint Joan*—perhaps his greatest—while the actual development of the play was far less simple and far more fascinating. He even railed publicly against the idolatry of Shakespeare while being not only a great Shakespeare critic but one of the playwrights most creatively influenced by Shakespeare—so much so that he confessed (in his nineties) that one of his finest works, *Heartbreak House*, had been conceived as his *King Lear*.

He seems to have toyed for years with the idea of writing a play about the Unknown Soldier while denying it all the time and leaving little written record of what had become almost an obsession. When he did tell the truth about the background of one of his major plays, *Caesar and Cleopatra*—that it was cribbed not from Plutarch and the other obvious historians of Rome but from the romantic German history of Mommsen—even the German critics largely ignored the clues and misunderstood why certain "facts" and scenes were the way they were. He wrote a play which he lightly referred to as "[Gilbert] Murray's Mother-in-Law," alluding to the original of Lady Britomart Undershaft, and then intended to call it "Andrew Undershaft's Profession," suggesting the dealing in death of Major Barbara's father. Yet it turns out to have immensely complex ramifications which make the lordly industrialist the composite of many shapers of contemporary history as well as the inheritor of Shaw's reading, from Plato to the present. And in real life the model for the Salvation Army major would marry a man who might have been Barbara Undershaft's father.

Then there is the paradox that Shaw's Irish countrymen, disenchanted with his clowning at their expense and his incessant search for compromise solutions which would leave the land of his birth united with the despised other island, should find in his unlikely person the makings of a staunch and outspoken Irish patriot. One outspoken Irishman even became the symbol of another Shavian paradox. For most people, Shaw was always a tight-fisted codger who resisted putting his hand to his checkbook to benefit any cause, no matter how deserving; yet he was constantly (and quietly) helping people financially and professionally, and he became the person whom Sean O'Casey first leaned upon for inspiration and then counted on for financial support as a fellow exile in England. Conversely, Shaw was at his worst as a friend to the increasingly down-and-out Frank Harris, once his editor at the *Saturday Review* when G.B.S. (as he then signed himself) was becoming the leading drama critic in London. One sees, in Shaw's toying with the old pirate in the very act of befriending him, an unsatisfactory side of Shaw—an element of unrecognized cruelty in the underside of benevolence.

Finally, among unexpected facets of Shaw, one will see that when he spoke of himself as old-fashioned and left behind by other hands, the critics were quick to believe him, although he had pioneered avant-garde and absurdist techniques that resemble what was being considered innovative in Beckett, Brecht, and Ionesco in the year of Shaw's centenary.

The paradoxes which made up the G.B.S. persona became the subject of much of my exploration of Shaw and—through the man—his writings. Over the years some of the articles developed into books, and some of the ideas became prefaces to other books. Some suppositions have since been proved accurate by later writers or by my own later research, and many other findings can now be fleshed out by new information and new perspectives I have brought to the pieces myself. No part of this book appears in its original form. Some of these essays are extensively revised, rewritten, and augmented, and others coalesce several related pieces. Much of what was the unexpected Shaw when first published is now everybody's Shaw; however, it was not possible to leave even those sections unamended, for in a few cases I have seized the opportunity to change my mind, and in some others too much new information has surfaced to permit early essays to remain the same. Perhaps there will always be something of the unexpected in Shaw.

To furnish a background for the exploration which follows I have begun with the familiar cocky Irishman, "Everybody's Shaw." Still relatively unknown at forty-four, with grey already infiltrating his reddish beard, he had not yet had a box-office success in London. Nor had he even begun *Man and Superman*. Nevertheless he could write confidently to critic William Archer, in January 1900, "As a matter of fact I am by a very great deal the best English-language playwright since Shakespear, and considerably *his* superior on a good many points." This is the G.B.S. one expects. And as we shall see, he was not far off the mark.

University Park, Pennsylvania
June 1982

1 Everybody's Shaw

The G.B.S. of popular reputation was a playwright and polemicist of multifarious activities and prodigious energies. A long life—his fatal accident, a broken hip, occurred when he was pruning a tree in his garden at ninety-four—made it all possible, for he was handicapped by a decade-long false start in fiction and even more by the circumstances of his upbringing. Born George Bernard Shaw in Dublin on July 26, 1856, he was the third and youngest child and only son of George Carr and Lucinda Elizabeth Gurly Shaw. Technically he belonged to the Protestant "ascendancy"—the landed Irish gentry—but his father (first a sinecured civil servant and then an unsuccessful corn merchant) was too impractical and intemperate to sustain anything more than a "downstart" atmosphere of genteel impecuniosity, an atmosphere which his son felt was more humiliating than to be born poor and have pretensions to nothing more. After being tutored by a clerical uncle, he attended—briefly—both Protestant and Catholic day schools (the latter an experience repugnant to him in the extreme), and before he was sixteen he was working in a land agent's office, having derived his most useful education outside the classroom.

Bookkeeping about rents, especially those of the very poor, and having to go out to collect some of them constituted an early confrontation with economic injustice and the poverty of opportunity. Books—after working hours—compensated for office tedium, especially Dickens, Bunyan, and Charles Lever; and he discovered Blake, Byron, and Shelley—all rebels and all to be read with some degree of furtiveness. Theater was a joy. Although Dublin productions consisted largely of adaptations of French melodrama and watered-down Shakespeare, Shaw was captivated by the plays of Dion Boucicault, an Irishman who had gone to England and then America to make his fortune. For art there was the National Gallery of Ireland, poor in works of any consequence but an initiation nevertheless to a young man whose earliest culture hero was Michelangelo and who had first thought seriously about an artist's vocation.

Music pervaded the Shaw household. His mother had turned for consolation not only to music but to her music teacher, George John Vandeleur Lee, a mesmeric figure in Dublin music circles. By 1866 Lee shared, at the least, a house in Dublin with the Shaws and a cottage on Dalkey Hill, overlooking the bay, which provided the young Shaw with the beginnings of a love for nature which Synge Street and Harrington Street could not have inspired. (It would rarely emerge in an explicit way in his writings, but he would always love the countryside, even its less-tamed aspects, and until he was well along in years would relish long walking holidays.) As Lee trained singers in his studio in the shared home and conducted operas and oratorios in Dublin halls, Shaw absorbed what he could, often accompanying on the piano or assisting in other ways. Meanwhile, at the estate office of Uniacke Townshend, Shaw sang arias to himself to relieve the boredom, realizing at his ledgers that the job augured a joyless future.

Opportunity to escape came when his mother and sisters left George Carr Shaw in Ireland and followed Lee to London in 1875. Determined to somehow make his way in literature, young Shaw followed the next year. He was twenty.

For Shaw, 1876–84 were years of frustration and poverty. Briefly he produced ghostwritten musical criticism for Lee (some of it reproduced in *How to Become a Musical Critic* [1960]). He experimented with short fiction and with drama, even beginning a blank-verse satirical portrayal of Jesus at home, with Mary as a termagant mother (1878); it was published posthumously as *A Passion Play* (1971). Late in 1879, through an aunt, he obtained employment with the Edison Telephone Company of London, but he seized the opportunity of its consolidation with a competing firm to leave in mid-1880. It was his last nonliterary employment. Living with his mother and elder sister Lucy (Agnes had died in 1876), he depended upon their pound a week—from a family bequest—mailed from Dublin by George Carr Shaw and his mother's earnings as a music teacher. He spent his days in the British Museum Reading Room, writing novels and reading what he had missed at school, and his nights in search of additional self-education in the form of the lectures and debates which characterized contemporary middle-class London intellectual ferment.

His fiction failed utterly. The semiautobiographical and aptly titled *Immaturity* (1879; published 1930) was both reminiscent of Dickens and anticipatory of Gissing. Its sometimes sober, sometimes satirical evocation of mid-Victorian England put off every publisher in London. Not until the Collected Edition of 1930–31 was opus 1 published. The next four novels, similarly rejected, soon padded out propagandist magazines edited by Shaw's socialist friends. *The Irrational Knot* (1880; serialized 1885–87; in book form 1905) Shaw later pronounced a forerunner of the Ibsen of whom he had not yet heard, for the hero marries at the beginning and walks out on the heroine at the end. Its characters, hardly more than animated theories, were each endowed with an "original morality" publishers' readers found "disagreeable," "perverse," and "crude." With halfhearted job hunting still fruitless, he began *Love Among the Artists* (1881; serialized 1887–88; in book form 1900), which reflected, in the neglect of the novel's hero, "a British Beethoven" among dilettantes and mediocrities, his passionate belief in his own talents and his bitterness at being thwarted. Midway through the manuscript he was stricken during the 1881 smallpox outbreak in London; he then stubbornly completed the unsalable novel and the next year began another, *Cashel Byron's Profession* (1882; serialized 1885-86; in book form from magazine plates 1886). Its exuberance belied Shaw's lack of success, and its core ("immoral" and "retrograde" professions—in this case, prizefighting—as an indictment of society) anticipated such early plays as *Mrs Warren's Profession*. In 1901 Shaw satirized his own novel in a burlesque Elizabethan blank-verse adaptation, *The Admirable Bashville* (staged in 1903).

The socialism in *Cashel Byron* was an afterthought, most of it daubed in for its magazine appearance after Shaw had been converted by an 1882 Henry George lecture which spurred him to a reading of Marx. Meanwhile the new gospel was the stimulus for his last novel, *An Unsocial Socialist* (1883; serialized 1884; in book form 1887). Intended as a "gigantic grapple with the whole social problem," it broke down under the weight of its incongruities, which included a runaway husband, a finishing school for girls, and ponderous paraphrases from *Capital* among passages of sparkling Shavian dialogue. A fragment, posthumously published as *An Unfinished Novel* in 1958 (but written 1887-88) was his final false start in fiction, begun after years of resentment he felt as novel reviewer (mostly at the *Pall Mall Gazette*) at the claptrap forced upon him.

Despite his failure in fiction, the 1880s were the decade in which Shaw found himself. He became a vegetarian, a socialist, a spellbinding orator, a polemicist, and even, tentatively, a playwright. He became the driving force behind the newly founded (1884) Fabian Society, a middle-class socialist group which aimed at the transformation of English society not through revolution but through "permeation" (in Sidney Webb's term) of the nation's intellectual and political life. Adept at committee work, Shaw involved himself in every aspect of Fabian activities, most visibly as editor of what proved to be one of the classics of British socialism, *Fabian Essays* (1889), to which he also contributed two sections. Through the Fabians, too, he assisted at the birth of the Labour Party (1893) and helped Fabian-supported candidates contest municipal and parliamentary elections.

A pamphleteer and platform speaker of rare dialectical skill, he spoke to crowds of any size, often as frequently as three times a week and always without compensation. The experience forged the forceful prose of his missionary books *The Quintessence of Ibsenism* (1891; published 1913), *The Perfect Wagnerite* (1898), *The Sanity of Art* (1895; enlarged 1908), *The Common Sense of Municipal Trading* (1904, 1908—the result of his years, from 1897-1903, as vestryman and borough councillor of St. Pancras Parish, London), and the later *Common Sense About the War* (1914), *The Intelligent Woman's Guide to Capitalism and Socialism* (1928), and *Everybody's Political What's What?* (1944) as well as the challenging prefaces to, and debating dialogue of, his plays. His journalism itself, beginning via friendship with drama critic William Archer, ranged at the time from bread-and-butter book reviews in the *Pall Mall Gazette* (1885–88) and art criticism in the *World* (1886–90) to brilliant (and often brilliantly digressive) musical columns in the *Star* (as "Corno di Bassetto"—basset horn) from 1888–90 and in the *World* (as "G.B.S.") from 1890–94. His aim as music critic had been to write such readable copy about music that even "deaf stock-brokers" would consume his columns. They are still reprinted and still read; however, they were more than entertainments. "People have pointed out evidences of personal feeling in my notices," he wrote in 1890, "as if they were accusing me of a misdemeanor, not knowing that a criticism written without personal feeling is not worth reading. It is the capacity for making good or bad art a personal matter that makes a man a critic. . . . When people do less than their best, and do that less at once badly and self-complacently, I hate them, loath them, detest them. . . . When my critical mood is at its height, personal feeling is not the word: it is passion: the passion for artistic perfection—for the noblest beauty of sound, sight, and action, that rages in me. The true critic, I repeat, is the man who becomes your personal enemy on the sole provocation of a bad performance, and will only be appeased by good performances." When he was an art critic, he wrote in 1892, he downgraded the Academics and promoted

the Impressionists. "It is just the same in music. I am always electioneering.
. . . I desire certain reforms, and in order to get them, I make every notable performance an example of the want of them. . . . Never in my life have I penned an
impartial criticism; and I hope I never may. As long as I have a[n artistic] want,
I am necessarily partial to the fulfillment of that want, with a view to which I
must strive with all my wit to infect everyone else with it."

Recruited by Frank Harris to the *Saturday Review* as a theater critic
(1895–98), he carried on in its columns a campaign to displace the artificialities
and hypocrisies of the Victorian stage ("Sardoodledom" to Shaw) with a theater of vital ideas. With the talk about a "New Drama" threatening to end in
the humiliating admission that in England, at least, it was "only a figment of
the revolutionary imagination," Shaw had already determined that the condition could not be endured: "I had rashly taken up the case; and rather than let it
collapse I manufactured the evidence." That effort became his primary activity
during the 1890s. The strain—for his critical and political work went on unabated—sapped his strength to such an extent, however, that a minor illness
became a major one; and in 1898, during the process of recuperation (while still
on crutches from necrosis of the bone), he married his unofficial nurse, Charlotte
Payne-Townshend, an Irish heiress and friend of Beatrice and Sidney Webb. It
was an unusual marriage, for at Charlotte's insistence it excluded a sexual side.
(That the marriage remained unconsummated is suggested by internal evidence
in Shaw's postmarriage plays.) The couple remained childless but for a series of
surrogate-parent relationships, such as with actors Granville Barker and Robert Loraine and writer-soldier T. E. Lawrence, which satisfied the otherwise
unfulfilled need. As Shaw confessed to Frank Harris, he had been financially
unable as a young man to maintain a mistress or a marriage; but after his sexual
initiation at twenty-nine, he had had a number of affairs (two simultaneous ones
self-satirized in his play *The Philanderer* in 1893; performed 1905). Eventually
his passions cooled and concentrated themselves into female friendships which
were mostly epistolary, the chief exception being his relationship with Mrs.
Stella Patrick Campbell (1865–1940), the Eliza Doolittle of his *Pygmalion* in
1914, which nearly wrecked his marriage. Otherwise, his emotional relationships with women remained largely on paper, from an almost fatherly flirtation
with American actress Molly Tompkins when Shaw was in his sixties and sev-
enties to a near-brotherly one (in every sense of the word) with Dame Laurentia
MacLachlan, a Benedictine nun, which ended only with Shaw's death. As he
wrote in the preface to a volume of his correspondence with actress Ellen Terry
(1931), "only on paper has mankind ever yet achieved glory, beauty, truth,
knowledge, virtue and abiding love."

The Shaws' marriage lasted their lives. When Charlotte died of a lingering
illness in 1943, G.B.S., frail and feeling the effects of World War II privations,
made permanent his retreat from his apartment in bomb-wrecked London to
his country home at Ayot St. Lawrence, a village in Hertfordshire in which he
had lived since 1906. He died there at ninety-four on November 2, 1950, having
continued to write and to maintain the famous G.B.S. persona to the end. He
had lived to see himself acknowledged as the most significant English playwright since the seventeenth century (although the theater was only one of his
many careers) and as more than the best comic dramatist of his time, for some
of his greatest work for the stage—*Caesar and Cleopatra* , the "Don Juan in
Hell" episode of *Man and Superman, Major Barbara, Heartbreak House,* and

Saint Joan—have a high purpose and prose beauty unmatched by his most serious stage contemporaries. Among his other careers, he had become the most trenchant pamphleteer since Swift, the most readable music critic in English, the best theater critic of his generation, a prodigious lecturer and essayist on politics, economics, and sociological subjects, and the most prolific letter writer in literature.

"The Celebrated G.B.S.," its creator once wrote, "is about as real as a pantomime ostrich. . . . I have played my game with a conscience. I have never pretended that G.B.S. was real: I have over and over again taken him to pieces before the audience to shew the trick of him." The real Shaw, according to J. B. Priestley, "was courteous, kind, generous, shy rather than imprudent, physically strong and courageous, yet rather timid and prudish in his relations with the world of food and drink, sex or hearty male companionship or conviviality, no dramatist for the Mermaid Tavern." But G.B.S. to the outside world was ruthless as a critic, devastating in wit, irreverent about people, careless of feelings, imprudent toward convention, iconoclastic toward institutions, hyperbolic for effect, cold-blooded about politics, inconsistent as a debater, secondhand as a thinker—a Mephistopheles-Machiavelli (as one of his characters is charged) who boasted that he was better than Shakespeare. Few understood the humane vision that articulated what Shaw wrote and did better than his friend and ideological opposite G. K. Chesterton, who still early in Shaw's career wrote, "Here was a man who could have enjoyed art among artists, who could have been the wittiest of the flaneurs; who could have made epigrams like diamonds and drunk music like wine. He has instead labored in a mill of statistics and crammed his mind with all the most dreary and most filthy details, so that he can argue on the spur of the moment about sewing-machines or sewage, about typhus fever or twopenny tubes. . . ."

Shaw had been experimenting in the drama since his early twenties, but not until William Archer suggested a collaboration in 1884 (Archer to supply the plot, Shaw the dialogue) did serious work result. Even then the project was abandoned when Shaw used up all the projected plot; but seven years later, in 1892, Shaw completed it on his own for J. T. Grein's fledgling Independent Theatre. *Widowers' Houses* created a newspaper sensation all out of proportion to its two performances, for it was a dramatized socialist tract on slumlandlordism redeemed in part by what Shaw had learned about ironic comedy from Ibsen and Dickens. The romantic predicament of the lovers (who find that both their incomes derive from the exploitation of the poor) becomes an economic one, and the "happy ending" in which they embrace the monstrosity could not please an audience expecting the threadbare conventions exploited even by the most daring new playwrights.

Unafraid to satirize himself or even the new movements he championed, Shaw next in *The Philanderer* invented an "Ibsen Club" and ironically portrayed the "New Woman." No one was willing to produce the play, but Shaw, undeterred, began a third, *Mrs Warren's Profession* (1893; performed 1902). This time the Lord Chamberlain as Censor of Plays refused it a license, although its ostensible subject, organized commercial prostitution, was treated remorselessly and without the titillation afforded by fashionable comedies about "fallen women" which long had been the West End's stock in trade. To make that certain, his Mrs. Warren is drawn as a vulgarly flashy woman who once found that being proprietor of her own body was more advantageous than sweating for a pittance in a factory or a pub and turned her discovery into a chain of profitable brothels. Her daughter, Vivie, whose discovery of the facts behind her fashionable Newnham College education brings the problem into focus, is an apparently cold-blooded creature unlikely to look sentimentally for very long at daughterly duty or economic rationalizations. The result is a sardonic high comedy built on the paradox of a form of prostitution meant to symbolize not only social and economic guilt but all the ways in which human beings prostitute their humanity for gain. Labeling as "unpleasant" the first three plays in his first collection, *Plays, Pleasant and Unpleasant* (1898), Shaw explained that "their dramatic power is being used to force the spectator to face unpleasant facts. No doubt all plays which deal sincerely with humanity must wound the monstrous conceit which it is the business of romance to flatter."

The "pleasant" plays of the companion volume represented Shaw's attempt to find the producers and audiences his mordant comedies put off. "To me," he explained in the preface to the second volume, both the "tragedy and comedy of life lie in the consequences, sometimes terrible, sometimes ludicrous, of our persistent attempts to found our institutions on the ideals suggested to our imaginations by our half-satisfied passions, instead of on a genuinely scientific natural history." *Arms and the Man* (performed 1894), in a spoof-Balkan setting, satirized romantic falsifications of love, war, and upward mobility, and was itself romanticized (unauthorized by Shaw) in the Oscar Straus operetta *The Chocolate Soldier* (1909). *Candida* (1894; performed 1897) seemed to be a conventional comedy-drama about a husband, wife, and young interloper, complete to happy ending in which the sanctity of the hearth is upheld and the interloper ejected into the night. Beneath the surface, however, the wife—who represents herself in a tour de force "auction scene" as being compelled to choose between her clergyman husband (a well-meaning Christian Socialist) and a hysterical and immature young poet—chooses the best of all possible worlds for herself, and the poet renounces what Shaw later called "the small beer of domestic happiness" for the larger creative purpose he senses within himself. The two other "pleasant" plays were of lighter weight. The one-act *The Man of Destiny* (1895; performed 1897) Shaw described as a "bravura piece to display the virtuosity of two performers," but it was more than that. Shaw's antidote to the "older, coarser Napoleon" of previous plays, it was his first study in greatness. In *You Never Can Tell* (1896; performed 1899) Shaw played out his themes about parent-child relationships, the equality of women in society, and the power of the sex instinct—the latter bringing together a would-be lover of uncertain confidence and an impregnably rational New Woman. Valentine, the young and amorous dentist, who plays the Benedick to the Beatrice of Gloria Clandon, claims "lightness of heart" as his signal attribute, and the same might be said of the play. The most refreshingly spirited of Shaw's early plays, it is only now coming into its own as a stage vehicle after nearly a century of being misunderstood.

Three Plays for Puritans (1901) packaged Shaw's continued output, again with what became the traditional Shavian preface: an introductory essay in an electric prose style dealing as much with the themes suggested by the plays as with the plays themselves. The texts of the plays, made available to the wider reading public to whom his plays were generally inaccessible even when produced, included—a Shaw innovation—stage directions and descriptions in narrative form rather than in the brevity of directorial jargon. *The Devil's Disciple*

(1896; performed 1897), a play set in New Hampshire during the American Revolution (a New England about as realistic as the Bulgaria of *Arms and the Man*) and written as an inversion of traditional Adelphi Theatre melodrama, has been accepted by most audiences, eager to fulfill expectations, as the real thing. Dick Dudgeon, however, the black sheep of his family because he rejects Puritan masochism and hypocrisy, is represented as heroically taking the place of a rebel minister whom the English condemn to the gallows, but Dudgeon does the right things for the wrong reasons. He acts, not in Sydney Carton fashion (Shaw's Dickensian inspiration for the scene) out of love for the Reverend Anderson's wife—as she supposes—but spontaneously, out of some instinctive imperative. As with Caesar and other significant later Shavian characters, virtue is a quality, not an achievement.

Caesar and Cleopatra (1898; performed 1901) was Shaw's first attempt at a play of Shakespearean scope for a heroic actor (Sir Johnston Forbes-Robertson). By choosing a sixteen-year-old Cleopatra as opposed to Shakespeare's thirty-eight-year-old temptress of Antony, and a Caesar in Egypt not yet enticed into the domestic demagoguery against which Brutus reacts, Shaw seemingly evades the "Better than Shakespear?" challenge of his preface. His feline Cleopatra, however, is a logical precursor to Shakespeare's; and G.B.S.'s Caesar, as much philosopher as soldier in this mentor-disciple play, is meant to be a study in credible magnanimity and "original morality" rather than a superhuman hero on a stage pedestal—in Shaw's words, a hero "in whom we can recognize our own humanity." A seriocomic chronicle play which rises to prose-poetic eloquence and wisdom, it may be the best theatrical work written in English in the nineteenth century. Its companion piece in *Three Plays for Puritans*, *Captain Brassbound's Conversion* (1899; performed 1900), is subtitled "An Adventure" and appears to be little more than that. Here too, however, are serious themes, particularly that of revenge as perverted justice, lurking amid the musical-comedy plot of an aristocratic and charismatic Englishwoman (a role written for Ellen Terry) among brigands in turn-of-the-century Morocco.

In *Man and Superman* (1901-02; published 1903; performed 1905) Shaw "took the legend of Don Juan in its Mozartian form and made it a dramatic parable of Creative Evolution. But being then at the height of my invention and comedic talent, I decorated it too brilliantly and lavishly. I surrounded it with a comedy of which it formed only one act, and that act was so episodical (it was a dream which did not affect the action of the piece) that the comedy could be detached and played by itself. . . . Also I supplied the published work with an imposing framework consisting of a preface, an appendix called The Revolutionist's Handbook, and a final display of aphoristic fireworks. The effect was so vertiginous, apparently, that nobody noticed the new religion in the centre of the intellectual whirlpool." Although Henri Bergson's *Creative Evolution* (1907) was still unwritten, Shaw used the term to describe the purposeful and eternal movement toward ever-higher organisms which he saw as a more satisfactory explanation of the nature of things than "blind" Darwinian evolution and which, besides, restored a sense of divinity to the universe. Subtitled "A Comedy and a Philosophy," the play on the surface is Shaw's equivalent to Congreve's *The Way of the World* (1700), even to a brilliant last-act proposal scene, a comedy of manners about the relations between the sexes in which a resourceful young woman, Ann Whitefield, determines to capture her man, the reluctant John Tanner, a social philosopher and socialist propagandist. The action provides the basis for a series of interlocking debates and discussions in which Shaw explored the intellectual climate of the new century. It provides, too, the frame for the nonrealistic third-act "Don Juan in Hell" dream scene, often played separately and independently, in which mythic counterparts to four characters in *Man and Superman*—Don Juan Tenorio, Dona Ana, Commander (Ana's father), and the Devil—play out a dramatic quartet that is spoken theater at its most operatic. Shaw's early operatic education at the hands of his mother and of Lee never left him, nor did his music critic years, and he often not only cast his own plays via the timbre of voice needed but shaped his scenes into recitatives, arias, and vocal ensembles. In the duets and arias of the Devil and Don Juan, twentieth-century literature for the stage reached a point, in its first years, that it would seldom touch again.

John Bull's Other Island (written and performed 1904; published 1907) was written at Yeats's request for the Abbey Theatre, Dublin, but the Abbey directors, concerned about audience reaction to the honesty of its picture of Ireland, used the excuse of casting difficulties to avoid producing it, although Shaw had deliberately placed in his play of contemporary Anglo-Irish relations, for exhibition to an Irish audience, a comic Englishman as absurd as the comic Irishman so often seen at that time on the London stage. However its politics have dated, the play when performed as a period piece remains insightful about the Irish character as well as being one of Shaw's most amusing comedies; while in the minor but exquisitely drawn character of the unfrocked priest Father Keegan, it is one of his earliest explorations of the religious rebel as saint. "Every dream is a prophecy," says Keegan, and "every jest is an earnest in the womb of Time." Unlike the self-styled commonsense Englishman, Thomas Broadbent, Keegan confesses to not feeling "at home in the world," which he sees as "a place of torment and penance, a place where the fool flourishes and the good and wise are hated and persecuted; a place where men and women torture one another in the name of love; where children are scourged and enslaved in the name of parental duty and education; where the weak in body are poisoned and mutilated in the name of healing, and the weak in character are put to the horrible torture of imprisonment, not for hours but for years, in the name of justice. It is a place where the hardest toil is a welcome refuge from the horror and tedium of pleasure, and where charity and good works are done only for hire to ransom the souls of the spoiler and the sybarite. Now, sir, there is only one place of horror and torment known to my religion; and that place is hell. Therefore it is plain to me that this earth of ours must be hell. . . ."

Broadbent finds it "rather a jolly place, in fact" and recommends, "Try phosphorus pills. I always take them when my brain is overworked."

While performances of Shaw's earlier plays in central Europe had already begun to establish him on the Continent as a major dramatist, it was the Vedrenne-Barker London production of *John Bull* including a command performance for Edward VII which belatedly made Shaw's stage reputation in England. He had backed John Vedrenne and Harley Granville Barker's management of the Royal Court Theatre, Sloane Square, not only with his own capital but with his own plays; and in the years of their association (1904–07), with Barker also acting and directing, a skilled repertory group grew up which gave Shavian drama many of its finest moments. His plays soon attracted box-office receipts to such an extent that the Court management, while experimenting with the work of other dramatists, found it necessary to produce Shaw 701 times (via eleven plays) in 988 total performances.

In *Major Barbara* (written and performed 1905; published 1907), also produced at the Court, Shaw continued, through the medium of high comedy, to explore the religious consciousness and to point out society's complicity in its own evils. Barbara Undershaft, a major in the Salvation Army, discovers that her estranged father, a munitions manufacturer, may be a dealer in death but that his principles and practice, however unorthodox, are religious in the highest sense, while those of the Salvation Army require the hypocrisies of often-false public confession and the cynical, self-serving donations of the distillers and the armorers against which it inveighs. Indebted to Plato *(The Republic)* and Euripides *(The Bacchae)* as well as to dozens of other sources, including the lives of such contemporary armaments makers as Nobel and Krupp, it is one of Shaw's most intellectually complex plays yet ironically one of his most moving, particularly in its second-act Salvation Army shelter scene (peopled with Dickensian characters), in which Barbara recants her adopted faith. Reviewing the first production, Desmond MacCarthy thought that it was the first play he had ever experienced in which the conflict was "between two religions in one mind." Critic Max Beerbohm, previously skeptical about the theatrical qualities of Shaw's plays, feeling that their freight of intellectual content made them unstageable, publicly revised his opinions after the production. Despite its philosophical density, *Major Barbara* (G.B.S. first intended titling it "Andrew Undershaft's Profession") is also accessible as high comedy and remains one of the most frequently revived of Shaw's plays.

With his place in the English theater now secure, Shaw began shifting after *Major Barbara* to theatrical experiments already foreshadowed in earlier plays. In *The Doctor's Dilemma* (written and performed 1906; published with *The Shewing-up of Blanco Posnet* and *Getting Married* in 1911), he produced a comedy with a seriocomic death scene and a satire on the medical profession (representing the self-protection of professions in general) and on both the artistic temperament and the public's inability to separate it from the artist's achievement. If, in the tubercular and double-dealing painter Louis Dubedat, Shaw failed to create a convincing artistic genius, it may be not that he could not depict one but that he aimed rather at depicting the self-advertising frauds who use the license of "genius" to bilk a world baffled by the artistic temperament. (It still remains for criticism to apply itself to Shaw's deliberate dramatic ambiguities in character and situation.) Other plays of the prewar period ranged from self-described potboilers to an attempt to create a discussion-drama which might best be described as serious farce. *Getting Married* (1907–08; performed 1908), *Misalliance* (1909; performed 1910; published with *Fanny's First Play* and *The Dark Lady of the Sonnets* in 1914), and *Fanny's First Play* (1911) are examples of the genre—dramatized debates on marriage, parents and children, and women's rights, respectively. *Misalliance* has since shown remarkable vivacity in revival as a period farce, while the thinner *Fanny's First Play* set a first-run box-office record unequaled by any other Shavian play—622 performances. *The Shewing-up of Blanco Posnet* (1909), set in an improbable American "Wild West," and aptly subtitled "A Sermon in Crude Melodrama," concerned the conversion of a horse thief. The play was banned by the Lord Chamberlain on grounds of heresy and immorality, whereupon Shaw took it to the Abbey Theatre in Dublin, beyond the lawful reach of the censor, where it played in August 1909 to capacity audiences. When the play was published, Shaw included a preface which incorporated a statement he had offered to a parliamentary hearing on stage censorship. "I am not an ordinary playwright in general practice," he declared. "I am a specialist in immoral and heretical plays. My reputation has been gained by my persistent struggle to force the public to reconsider its morals. . . . I write plays with the deliberate object of converting the nation to my opinion in these matters." The declaration was deliberate hyperbole, yet Shaw was not far wrong. Only a few years later, when St. John Ervine, then a young playwright, was introducing Shaw at a lecture, he confided jokingly that sometimes he passed on to G.B.S. ideas for plays he was unable to write himself, including a play about God. "The suggestion that I write a play about God," Shaw responded as he began, "is one I rather resent, because I have never written a play on any other subject; and as a matter of fact that is the subject of these lectures, as you will find when I get to the end of them."

Androcles and the Lion (written 1912 performed 1913; published with *Overruled* and *Pygmalion* in 1916), more successfully than *Blanco Posnet*, handled true and false religious exaltation, combining the traditions of miracle play and Christmas pantomime in turning the fable of the Greek slave and the Roman lions into a philosophical farce about early Christianity. Its central theme—recurrent in Shaw—was that one must have something worth dying for—an end outside oneself—in order to make life worth living. Lavinia, its heroine, is—like Keegan and Barbara before her—a step toward Shaw's Joan of Arc. *Pygmalion* (1912; performed 1913) was claimed by Shaw to be a didactic play about phonetics, and its anti-heroic hero, Henry Higgins, is a phonetician; however, the play is a high and humane comedy about love and class, the story of a Cockney flower girl trained to pass as a lady and the repercussions of the experiment's success. Possibly Shaw's comedic masterpiece and certainly his funniest and most popular play, it is never absent from the stage somewhere in the world and has been both filmed (1938), winning an Academy Award for Shaw for his screenplay, and musicalized (as *My Fair Lady*, 1956).

The play's London success in 1914 outraged as well as delighted Shaw. Sir Herbert Beerbohm Tree, the Henry Higgins of the production, having played a lifetime of romantic endings, had devised a way to distort Shaw's ironic and ambiguous conclusion without altering a word. In the interval between the last lines of the play and the last lowering of the curtain, he would provide by demonstrative affection for Eliza a broad hint that matrimony was in store for the professor and his pupil. Shaw was furious at the Cinderella suggestion and wrote to Tree, telling him what he thought of the performance. "My ending makes money; you ought to be grateful," Tree answered smugly. Shaw fired back, "Your ending is damnable: you ought to be shot." And to prevent future fairy-tale endings, Shaw wrote an unsentimental short-story epilogue for the published play which "proved" that Eliza would marry the weak Freddy Eynsford Hill and open a successful flower shop with money proffered by Colonel Pickering. "It does not follow in the least," Shaw defended himself to his Edinburgh printer, William Maxwell, nearly twenty years later, "that Liza and Higgins were sexually insensible to each other, or that their sensibility took the form of repugnance . . . but the fact stands that their marriage would have been a revolting tragedy and that the marriage with Freddy is the natural and happy ending to the story." But no one acts an undramatized prose epilogue, and Shaw's bittersweet ending to the actual play leaves the Higgins-Eliza relationship more dramatically at its appropriate—and unsettled—point.

The 1914–18 war, which followed immediately upon the success of *Pygmalion*, was a watershed for Shaw. At first he ceased writing plays, producing instead a lengthy Swiftian pamphlet, *Common Sense about the War* (*New Statesman*, supplement, November 14, 1914), which called Britain and its allies equally culpable with the Germans and argued for negotiation and peace. It sold more than seventy-five thousand copies and made him internationally notorious. "It is an established tradition," he wrote years afterward, that he was "a pro-German, a Pacifist, a Defeatist, a Conscientious Objector, and everything that an enemy of his country can be without being actually shot as a traitor. Nothing could be more absolutely wide of the truth." The common sense of his, and similar, arguments prevailed only when the nation was ground down by astronomical—and futile—casualties and home front austerities, but meanwhile unreason reigned, even to some of his antiwar speeches being erased from history by newspaper censorship and his being ejected from the Dramatists' Club, although he was its most distinguished member. As the tide of public opinion turned, the government's measure of Shaw's usefulness shifted as well, and in early 1917 he was even invited to Flanders to report from the front (*Daily Sketch*, March 6–8, 1917, reprinted in *What I Really Wrote About the War* in 1931). By war's end he was not that persecuted but proud figure, a major prophet whom his own people refused to honor, but a confirmed oracle, a prophet who had survived into his own time. Explaining the Shavian apotheosis, T. S. Eliot afterward remarked that "it might have been predicted that what he said then would not seem so subversive or blasphemous now. The public has accepted Mr. Shaw not by recognizing the intelligence of what he said then, but by forgetting it; we must not forget that at one time Mr. Shaw was a very unpopular man. He is no longer the gadfly of the commonwealth; but even if he has never been appreciated, it is something that he should be respected."

The unforgetful Shaw translated his experience of 1914–18 into a dozen plays, sometimes defiantly, sometimes unobtrusively. *Heartbreak House* (written 1916–17; published 1919: performed 1920) became the classic Shavian presentation of the spiritual bankruptcy of the generation responsible for the war, a departure for Shaw in that he combined high discursive comedy with a new symbolism, producing a somber vision owing much in mood to Chekhov's *Cherry Orchard* while its elderly leading figure, as well as much else, derived in part from Shakespeare's *Lear*. Captain Shotover is eighty-eight and half mad; although he tries to recall the heroine from a cynical despair induced by disillusioned love, his own sense of foreboding (he warns that the country must "learn navigation") is expressed in his having turned his skills as an inventor to military uses. At the end there is an air raid which causes casualties and destruction, but there is no other sign (except for a character playing several bars of "Keep the Home Fires Burning" on his flute in the last act) that the action takes place in wartime. The drama's culminating horror lies, however, not in exploding bombs but in the comments of two jaded women at the curtain, with one saying, "But what a glorious experience! I hope theyll come again tomorrow night," and the other ("*radiant at the prospect*," in Shaw's stage directions) agreeing, "Oh, I hope so." Thanatos has replaced Eros.

Back to Methuselah (1918–20; performed 1922) was Shaw's attempt to keep from falling into "the bottomless pit of an utterly discouraging pessimism." A cycle of five linked plays (*In the Beginning, The Gospel of the Brothers Barnabas, The Thing Happens, The Tragedy of an Elderly Gentleman*, and *As Far as Thought Can Reach*), it created a parable of Creative Evolution which moved through time from the Garden of Eden to A.D. 31,920, a "Metabiological Pentateuch" which drew imaginatively upon Genesis, Plato, Swift, and dozens of other sources, including the war in progress (only the last part was begun after the war), with the aim of creating a work on the order of Wagner's *Ring*. The first play, through Adam and Eve (and the Serpent), Cain and Abel, dramatizes the need to overcome death by the renewal of birth and the need to have aspirations beyond mere subsistence. (Serpent: "You see things; and say 'Why?' But I dream things that never were; and I say 'Why not?' ") Having killed his brother, and resenting his plodding father, Cain discovers that he does not know what he wants, "except that I want to be something higher and nobler than this stupid old digger." "Man need not always live by bread alone," says Eve. "There is something else." Finding the something else—and the means—motivates the cycle. The second part takes place in the years just after World War I and is an indictment of the generation which made the war ("Burge" is Lloyd George, and "Lubin" is Asquith). But in it, too, Conrad Barnabas makes the discovery that sufficient longevity to learn from experience—perhaps three hundred years—might be willed. The Shavian superman is here no longer thought of as attainable through eugenic breeding, his earlier thesis. He comes with a leap in the third play. Two undistinguished characters from the second play prove to be still alive in A.D. 2170, and longevity has given them wisdom. In the fourth play, in A.D. 3000, an elderly gentleman from the shrinking race of short-livers confronts the conflicting manners and motives of the passionless and ascetic long-livers, who possess extraordinary powers over nature, but to the Gentleman—no soul. Still, he wants to remain in the land of his ancestors (the scene is the shore of Galway Bay), although he is warned that he will very likely die of discouragement. "If I go back," he pleads, like Gulliver among the Houyhnmnms, "I will die of disgust and despair. . . . It is the meaning of life, not of death, that makes banishment so terrible to me." He stays and dies. In the remote fifth play, humans are born, fully developed, from eggs and live lives of contemplative ecstasy achieved through creative use of intellect after a brief adolescent phase of physical pleasure. Using satire which ranges from bright to bleak, Shaw speculates through his futuristic characters about the values of escaping from "this machinery of flesh and blood." An uneven work, it is compounded of the prosaic as well as the poetic, and it is dated as well as enlarged by the topical references in the middle plays. *Back to Methuselah* is nevertheless ennobling in vision although awkward as a total theater experience.

Thinking that the long cycle had exhausted his creative energies, Shaw anticipated at sixty-seven that he had concluded his career as a playwright; however, the canonization of Joan of Arc in 1920 had reawakened within him ideas for a chronicle play about her which had never quite been dormant.* For G.B.S. it would not have been enough to depict Joan as the sentimental heroine of a melodrama arrayed against a stageful of stock villains. Neither the militant nor the martyr in Joan was as important to him as her symbolizing the possibilities of

---

*For a more detailed exploration of the genesis of *Saint Joan*, see Chapter 15.

the race. A species that could beget Joans could have greater aspirations for itself than getting and spending. It could, in fact, aspire to the acceptance of its Joans as part of the natural order of things. Thus for Shaw, the Maid is not only Catholic saint or martyr but Shavian saint and martyr, a combination of practical mystic, heretical saint, and inspired genius. For this reason Shaw made the conflict irreconcilable in the sense of Sophocles' *Antigone*. To make Joan's greatness of soul credible, he had to make her adversaries credible, which meant that Shaw—with more courage than the Vatican itself—had to rehabilitate Bishop Peter Cauchon and his clerical colleagues who found her guilty of heresy, much as Joan herself had to be rehabilitated nearly five centuries earlier. As Hegel—whom Shaw had read—had suggested, the truly tragic is not to be found in the conflict between right and wrong but in that between right and right. Joan as the superior being (in the Inquisitor's words) "crushed between those mighty forces, the Church and the Law" is the personification of the tragic heroine, but to Shaw it was not sufficient for his theme. Tragedy was not enough; thus the epilogue, in which a twentieth-century Joan, newly canonized, is rejected once again, moves inexorably from satire to litany, and transforms the play from a tragedy of inevitability to the embodiment of the paradox that humankind fears—and often kills—its saints and its heroes and will go on doing so until the very qualities it fears become the general condition of man.

Being Shavian, the play could not be entirely somber, and the fantasy, farce, and faith of the epilogue very likely came first in order of conception. Even the opening "No eggs?" scene, in which the first alleged miracle attributed to the still-unseen Joan turns out to be homely and humorous yet moving in its simplicity, surprises—certainly one of the most unusual openings ever written for a play intended to have, from the beginning, the fatality of tragedy. Shaw's supporting characters are drawn in a range of wit from sharp satire to sheer farce, and even those given lofty eloquence often have wry lines which rescue them from pomposity. Joan herself, despite a "heart high and humble," is pert, proud, and impatient, and inevitably lonely and lost until she determines to follow her voices to the end.

Acclaim for *Saint Joan* (written and performed 1923; published 1924) resulted in a Shavian apotheosis. Even the Nobel Prize committee could no longer look away, and Shaw received the Nobel Prize for Literature in 1925, an honor almost certainly owed to *Joan*. To the consternation of the grantors, he wrote to "discriminate between the award and the prize." The money, he said, in refusing it, was "a lifebelt thrown to a swimmer who has already reached the shore in safety." At Shaw's request, an Anglo-Swedish Literary Foundation was funded with the prize money.

Although the dream epilogue to *Saint Joan* continued Shaw's explorations into tragicomic and nonrealistic symbolism, his last fourteen plays intensified this aspect of his work, which involved broad, caricatured impersonations, sometimes of Aristophanic extravagance, on which Shaw based a theater of disbelief—characterizations deliberately designed to destroy Ibsenesque verisimilitude by regularly reminding the audience that these were performances in a theater, not life in a three-walled room or realistic exterior. After a six-year theatrical silence (during which he worked on his Collected Edition of 1930–38 and the encyclopedic *Intelligent Woman's Guide*), he produced the Platonic "political extravaganza" *The Apple Cart* (1928; performed 1929), a futuristic high comedy which emphasized Shavian inner conflicts between his lifetime of radical politics and his essentially conservative mistrust of the common man's ability to govern himself. Later plays included apocalyptic imagery, with Shaw warning that 1914–18 was about to be repeated. The deliberately absurd *Too True to Be Good* (1931; performed 1932) is a dream fantasy, including a Bunyanesque prophet, a Lawrence of Arabia caricature, and a burglar turned preacher who (as the curtain closes upon him) suggests Shaw confronting his own obsolescence. *On the Rocks* (written and performed in 1933) predicts the collapse of parliamentary government in a proto-fascist, depression-ridden England. *The Simpleton of the Unexpected Isles* (1934; performed 1935), in a futuristic South Seas setting, satirizes a eugenic solution to human problems and ends with a Day of Judgment. *The Millionairess* (1932–34; performed 1936), a "Jonsonian comedy" according to the subtitle, is a knockabout farce which probes the human type of "born boss," while *Geneva* (1936–38; performed 1938) translates the problem into contemporary political terms, lampooning the futile League of Nations and dictators Hitler, Mussolini, and Franco, all of whom appear on the stage under nearly invisible disguises. That the despots are treated so lightly suggest that Shaw's flirtation with dictatorships which arose out of the 1914–18 disillusionment with democracies was slow in dying, with the one involving Stalin stubbornly enduring to the end. *In Good King Charles's Golden Days* (1938–39; performed 1939), his last prewar play, is a throwback to the mood of *The Apple Cart*, a warm yet discursive high comedy in which Charles II, Newton, Fox, Nell Gwynn, and others in "a true history which never happened" debate leadership, science, art, and religion. Eloquent, humorous, and intermittently moving, it dwells further upon the major preoccupation of Shaw's final period. "The riddle of how to choose a ruler is still unanswered," says Charles, "and it is the riddle of civilization."

After a wartime hiatus Shaw produced several plays in his nineties. *Buoyant Billions* (begun 1936–37; completed 1945–47; performed 1948), subtitled "a comedy of no manners," concerned the peregrinations of Junius, a self-styled "world-betterer." *Farfetched Fables* (1948; performed 1950) is a farce in six short scenes, in which Shaw attempted to see into a timeless future which, in his postatomic outlook, is much different than that envisioned in the *As Far as Thought Can Reach* play of *Back to Methuselah*. *Shakes versus Shav* (written and performed in 1949) is a brief puppet play in which the two playwrights confront each other and challenge the greatness of each other's works, with Shaw reaffirming his once-shaken evolutionary optimism in the face of Shakespeare's alleged pessimism. A last playlet, *Why She Would Not* (1950), a fantasy with flashes of the earlier Shaw in evidence, combines the "born boss" theme with the duel of sex but has more historic than dramatic interest. As G.B.S. had written in the preface to *Buoyant Billions*, "As long as I live I must write." He did.

Shaw's last major work may have been his lengthy *Last Will and Testament*, which after directing his trustees to publish his works as "by Bernard Shaw" (thus forever eliminating the "George" from his authorized writings) and distributing small legacies, directed that the major portion of his estate be used via a charitable trust in an effort to revamp the English alphabet into a phonetic one of forty letters. Since the estate at his death was announced as amounting to £367,233 (then $1,028,252.40) and expanded attractively with accruing royalty income, the residuary legatees (named by Shaw should this clause be invalidated)—the British Museum, the Royal Academy of Dramatic Art, and the National Gallery of Ireland—sued in Chancery to break the alphabet trust.

In December 1957, a settlement gave token recognition to alphabet reform by setting aside a small sum (£8,300) for a competition for a new alphabet in which, at Shaw's direction, an edition of *Androcles and the Lion* was printed (1962). The balance remained with the residuary legatees, who continue to derive substantial income from Shaw works in copyright.

Shaw left no school of playwrights as such, although much of the drama of his time and after was in his debt. His invention of a drama of moral passion and of intellectual conflict and debate, his revivifying the comedy of manners, his ventures into symbolic farce and into a theater of disbelief all helped shape the theater of his time and after. And his application of a bold new critical intelligence to his many other areas of interest helped mold the political, economic, and sociological thought of three generations.

2 Sketches for a Self-Portrait

When Bernard Shaw was a young man, he observed from the safety of an anonymous book review that an autobiography was "usually begun with interest by reader and writer alike, and seldom finished by either. Few men care enough about their past to take the trouble of writing its history. Braggarts like Benvenuto Cellini, and morbidly introspective individuals like Rousseau, are the exceptions that prove the rule." A generation later—although he was guilty himself by then of perpetrating scattered pieces of memoir—he had not changed his mind. As autobiographer, he gibed to Frank Harris, he was "like a dog returning to his own vomit" or "a conscientious snake . . . collecting all his cast skins for a museum." Serious memoirists, he thought, proved the weakness of the form by avoiding themselves in their histories. Goethe, for example, found it necessary to retreat from the subject of himself to write about uninteresting and otherwise-forgotten friends of his youth, while Wagner wrote more vividly about his musical associates than himself, and even Rousseau faded out of his own confessions as his favorite subject became an adult. He understood the reaction, Shaw told Harris. "I find I can't go over my autobiographical stuff again, not only from lack of time, but from loathing."

Whatever the reasons, G.B.S. resisted the urge to fashion a formal autobiography and waited until his nineties to piece together a scrappy substitute out of his own confessions. Building upon *Shaw Gives Himself Away,* a thin volume of essays and extracts privately printed (in three hundred copies) in 1939, he produced a trade-edition parallel, *Sixteen Self Sketches* (1949). Few of the sketches were new, while some of the sixteen were no more than unannounced revisions of essays published as much as fifty years before. Obviously Shaw, over the years, had had much more to say about himself and had done so elsewhere and at great length, but even with a curious concluding section of padding labeled "Biographers' Blunders Corrected," the *Sketches* ran to only 134 pages. Why the passed-over pieces escaped inclusion he failed to explain, but why all of them were originally written was made carefully clear: "Only when I can make a case of myself, economic, artistic, sociologic, or what not, can I make literary use of myself. . . ." Shaw made literary use of himself—and wrote his autobiography—all his life.

Always a believer in the utilitarian function of the writer's art, he saw no valid aesthetic or psychological excuse for memoir production and condemned as misguided any reader interest in the private life of an author—"because the actual facts of an author's life are for the most part mere accidents, and have no more to do with his genius than the shape of his nose; less, in fact." It was the reason why, he said, when people asked him why he did not write his own life he would reply, "I am not at all interesting biographically. . . . Nothing very unusual has happened to me." Amid the protestations, Shaw nevertheless continued to write several very different kinds of self-portraits, identifying the most public of himself as the subtle and not always subconscious autobiography one can read between the lines of his novels and plays. "Things have not happened to me: on the contrary, it is I who have happened to them," he explained, underplaying himself, "and all my happenings have taken the form of books and plays. Read them, or spectate them; and you have my whole story: the rest is only breakfast, lunch, dinner, sleeping, wakening and washing. . . ."

Elsewhere, too, Shaw confessed as much. To Frank Harris he had pointed out that he never would have thought of the idea of Joey Percival, the boy with three fathers in *Misalliance* (1909), had he not had three fathers himself. The three of them, we learn in the play, "took charge of Joey's conscience. He used to hear them arguing like mad about everything. . . . Between the lot of them Joey got cultivated no end." In Dublin, Shaw had his legal father, his medical Uncle Walter and his unofficial musical mentor "Professor" Lee. Lee even lived in the Shaw house in Hatch Street, and when Uncle Walter came to visit, the three men gossipped and argued into the morning—and young G.B.S. listened. There is even a naive young clerk in the play, employed, like the teenage Shaw in Dublin, as a cashier proud of never being a farthing wrong in his accounts.

Shaw's clerkship was first fictionalized in his first novel, *Immaturity* (1879), in which there is little unsupported by early Shavian experience—his hero's encounters with employers, preachers, artists, romantic and rationalistic women, with the Chelsea and South Kensington locales in which he prowled, solitarily, full of extravagant thoughts about his future. Both "Smith" and Shaw perform the barren drudgery of their clerkships conscientiously, despise their employers, loathe their servility, and retain so much of the vocation after their resignations that each writes in the best commercial style, painstakingly perfected in large canvas-covered ledgers.

The young genius in London, frustrated by the rejection of his early fiction by every publisher to which he took his manuscripts and defensively cultivating within himself a defiant self-sufficiency, is magnified by Shaw in his third novel into a turbulent British Beethoven. Unwilling to bow to popular taste for cheap success Owen Jack, of *Love Among the Artists* (1881), insists, "I must make my own music, such as it is or such as I am. . . ." So with Shaw, although he narrowly missed popular success with *Cashel Byron's Profession* (1882), a novel of ideas based broadly upon his own experiences as amateur boxer and reader of *Bell's Life.* Shaw's last completed novel, *An Unsocial Socialist* (1883), was another self-portrait, this time of the young Marxist missionary who, like his hero Sidney Trefusis, was beginning to discover that while he ran from women who had designs upon him, he was still fascinatedly drawn to them. "Poverty and fastidiousness" kept him from "a concrete love affair" until he was twenty-nine, he wrote Frank Harris, but "the five novels I wrote before that . . . show much more knowledge of sex than most people seem to acquire after bringing up a family of fifteen."

Even Shaw's critical columns—literary, artistic, musical and dramatic—are given extra gusto by Shavian reminiscences about his Dublin and Dalkey childhood, curious relatives, inadequate schooling, informal musical and artistic education, idiosyncratic tastes and lifestyle. As "Corno di Bassetto" in *The Star* he invented a persona, complete to nonexistent wife; however Bassetto's musical adventures are Shaw's own, as are Bassetto's relatives. "I believe that a taste for brass instruments is hereditary," he confided (in 1889). "My father destroyed his domestic peace by immoderate indulgence in the trombone, and my uncle played the ophicleide—very nicely, I must admit—for years, and then perished by his own hand." Shaw's father's indulgences came more in a glass than in brass, yet the reviews were a public confession box in which Shaw exposed the colorful side of a family he often privately deprecated. Even in so obscure a paper as *The Hawk*, edited by George Moore's feisty brother Augustus, Shaw (under the pseudonym of "Reuter"—German for "Red") would write, the same year, about visiting Bayreuth, "The first time I ever heard a note of Wagner's music was in my small boy days, when I stumbled on a military band playing the Tannhäuser march. I will not pretend that I quite rose to the occasion; in fact I said . . . that it was a plagiarism from the famous theme in Der Freischütz. But a little after this bad beginning I picked up a score of Lohengrin and before I had taken in ten bars of the prelude I was a confirmed Wagnerite."

Covert confessions and sly self-portraits turn up in many of his plays. The No. 1 Hatch Street *ménage à trois* of George Carr Shaw, Lucinda Shaw, and George John Lee is suggested in the 1908 comedy *Getting Married.* G.B.S.'s philanderings with widow Jenny Patterson and actress Florence Farr, which led to a hair-pulling match over him, became the basis for an altercation between the two female leads in *The Philanderer* (1893), while Charteris, the hero, is a variation upon the author. Even before that, in an 1887 sketch Shaw refrained from publishing at the time, "Don Giovanni Explains," he described in detail—in supposed fiction—his seduction by the fortyish Mrs. Jane Patterson:

> At last a widow lady at whose house I sometimes visited, and of whose sentiments towards me I had not the least suspicion, grew desperate at my stupidity, and one evening threw herself into my arms and confessed her passion for me. The surprise, the flattery, my inexperience and her pretty distress, overwhelmed me. I was incapable of the brutality of repulsing her; and indeed for nearly a month, I enjoyed without scruple the pleasure she gave me, and sought her company whenever I could find nothing better to do. It was my first consummated love affair.

Shaw's infatuation with phonetic language is translated into Professor Higgins of *Pygmalion* (1913), while his infatuation with the play's first Eliza, Mrs. Patrick Campbell (which led to her once trying to physically restrain him from leaving her to meet his wife), is translated into the closely parallel amatory interlude in *The Apple Cart* (1929). Even his prosaically happy marriage with Charlotte has its parallels in the dowdy but devoted and practical queens of *The Apple Cart* and *In Good King Charles's Golden Days* (1939), while additional Shavian self-portraits appear in the articulate young revolutionary John Tanner of *Man and Superman* (1903) and in Captain Shotover, the aging postwar prophet of *Heartbreak House* (1920). "The best autobiographies are confessions," he observed in his last years, "but if a man is a deep writer, all his works are confessions."

Shaw's earliest confessional work was his diary, at first an irregular scrappy collection of jottings begun in a tuppence notebook in 1872, when he was a teenage clerk in the Dublin office of Charles Uniacke Townshend. But for some cryptic personal references, such as to youthful infatuations, it was a careful record of expenditures and encounters, suggesting erroneously that the young man was temperamentally well-suited to the ledger and the cashier's stool. As his life became more complex, so did some of the entries, which recorded—in the London continuation of his notes—beginnings of fads, friendships, and attempts at fiction writing, experiences with vegetarianism, smallpox, speechmaking, French verbs, and German economics. The journal faded out in 1884, and in the following year Shaw began a different kind of diary—more informative because it detailed not only his multifarious professional and social activities but what he ate and how he slept, yet paradoxically less informative than before, because he kept the diary in his own idiosyncratic version of Pitman shorthand, an appropriate medium for an eccentric life of erratic hours, irregular food, occasional income, and unusual friends. Enthusiasm for the journal often flagged, but Shaw persisted with it, sometimes catching up omissions with extended *ex post facto* entries. But by 1894 it had become more engagement book than diary, and by the end of 1897 his diary was blank, a victim of his increasingly complicated juxtaposition of careers.

Although the diaries were personal rather than public documents, meant for an audience of one, Shaw later returned to the journal form as a deliberately autobiographical method, meant for publication, noting on the third day of the new venture, "I am going to try to keep [the diary] for a year, as a sample slice of my life." But the notes, begun with gusto on January 1, 1917, faltered to nothing in a fortnight. With the experiment abandoned, there was always other personal writing he could turn to, especially his private letters, although there too he appeared to be writing for the small audience of the recipient and himself. Still, when Shaw, in midcareer, recorded portions of his outer and his inner life in the many thousands of his letters, he had long since reached certainty that his letters—even the most terse of his postcards—would be preserved by his friends, treasured by his admirers, hoarded by library archivists, and sold and resold by manuscript dealers. Once he had become a public figure, his private letters, whether or not he desired it so, were largely destined for posterity. He could not help but write for it.

Some of Shaw's letters were deliberately and calculatedly confessional—the hundreds of them he wrote to interviewers and biographers, in a generally successful effort to satisfy them beyond their desire to search further than he cared to have them probe, to throw them off—if necessary—troublesome scents, to establish a persona consistent with his public image. Yet at the same time, the writing of them was often a considerable and a considerate effort to provide facts. In many cases, grateful biographers used Shaw's words verbatim and at great length. One of his many long letters to his first biographer Archibald Henderson—then a young mathematics professor in North Carolina—ran to fiftyfour pages. (Frugally, Shaw later cribbed heavily from his copy of the letter when writing the autobiographical preface to *London Music*.) Shaw not only came close to writing the first Henderson biography (of three) himself, he offered suggestions for its construction and even for its promotion. Keep on the lines, he recommended, "of Boswell's Johnson and Lockhart's Scott, not to mention Plutarch. . . . If you really want an introduction, better let *me* write it." Shaw was more serious than Henderson could have imagined, for when Frank Harris and Hesketh Pearson began their Shavian biographies, their subject not only provided much of the information in interviews and letters but rewrote

large sections of the text himself—assistance far more elaborate than the furnishing of an introduction.

G.B.S would have done the same in other cases, if given the opportunity, but
usually was sufficiently generous by mail. One scholar even more obscure than
Henderson at the time Shaw authorized his biographical researches—Henderson had a recent doctorate from Chicago, albeit in mathematics—was Thomas
Denis O'Bolger, whose queries elicited eager offerings of autobiography from
Shaw, in letters primarily about the Dublin years. O'Bolger was an Irishman
resident in Philadelphia, writing a doctoral dissertation on the most famous living Irishman, and Shaw found it difficult to refuse a fellow émigré. Letter after
letter crossed the Atlantic, with details about Shaw's Dublin relatives and
about the curious *ménage à trois* in Hatch Street, where young George had two
fathers in residence, a phlegmatic, alcoholic legitimate one, and a fascinating,
musical surrogate one. But when O'Bolger drew disturbing inferences from the
household arrangements, G.B.S. prevented O'Bolger's biography from being
published. Eventually Shaw published some of the letters mildly altered. But
even earlier he had drawn upon the material himself for the autobiographical
preface to the belated first publication of his first novel. He had kept, he confided to Frank Harris in 1918, copies of many of the autobiographical letters
("notes" he called them) he had sent to Henderson and O'Bolger, and it had
occurred to him to look up the file "and publish a recast of it as my own, on a
plan of my own." The fact that he had carefully retained copies and drafts of the
lengthy confessional correspondence may only have been Shaw's usual businesslike behavior, but it may also be a clue as to how long the writing of his own
autobiography (in a substantial manner) had been in the back of his mind.

Although—as we shall see in more detail later*—Shaw was just as calculatedly helpful to Frank Harris, he had more logical reasons to help him than he
had to provide an unknown young mathematics professor or an even more obscure doctoral candidate in literature with the crucial original materials likely
to create an academic or authorial reputation for the recipient. He felt twinges
of old journalistic loyalties toward the disreputable Harris, who had made for
himself a shaky new career as a memoirist, not only with the censorable *My Life
and Loves* but more legitimately by way of a series of biographical magazine
pieces he labeled "Contemporary Portraits." Near the end of his financial rope
as well as the end of his life, Harris had seized desperately upon a commission
from an American publisher to do a biography of Shaw. Knowing Harris's pen-
chant for scandal, G.B.S. reluctantly agreed to supply material to the down-
and-out ex-editor for whose magazine a generation before he had written his
famous theater columns. Even that failed, for Harris completed only sixty-five
faltering pages before his health cracked altogether and ghostwriter Frank
Scully took over, completing the job by the use of paid researchers and Shaw's
letters. Harris saw the proofs before he died but never saw Shaw's later corrections and additions. As far as Shaw was concerned, it was mostly his book,
although Scully had told him after examining the printed version that the
text was really seventy-two percent Scully (often through rewriting Shaw's
letters), twenty-two percent Shaw, and two percent Harris. In any case,
Harris's widow got the royalties, and Shaw had his autobiographical way with
another biography.

---

*"The Playwright and the Pirate: Bernard Shaw and Frank Harris," Chapter 17.

Earlier, in 1919, Shaw had already practiced the Harris style. His "How Frank Ought to Have Done It" was a self-portrait in the third person which parodied Harris's biographical method. Its purpose may have been sheer spoofery, yet its effect was to reduce to absurdity some of the tales about his life Shaw did not want taken seriously. Harris, grateful for something salable in his drab, declining years, published it in an otherwise lame volume of his *Contemporary Portraits*, but—Shaw thought—"I cannot believe he ever read it." No praise of Shaw was ever more fulsome—or more obviously ironic.* No disparaging anecdote then printable was left out. "Dramatizing myself from an objective point of view," Shaw observed, was a "method (which) came natural to me. . . ." (Pursuing the illusion of objectivity, he later used third-person headings for all the pieces he included in *Shaw Gives Himself Away*, suggesting that an editor, rather than the subject, had chosen and arranged the selections; but afterward, in a belated burst of honesty, he penciled into the printer's proofs a "me" or an "I" to replace each "Shaw.")

Since Harris relished writing about his subjects' sex lives, Shaw furnished what Harris might have discovered—or invented—concluding with a tale involving Beerbohm Tree and Mrs. Patrick Campbell:

> Shaw's gallantries are for the most part non-existent. He says, with some truth, that no man who has any real work in the world has time or money for a pursuit so long and expensive as the pursuit of women. . . . Nobody knows the history in this respect, as he is far too correct a person to kiss and tell. To all appearances he is a model husband; and in the various political movements in which his youth was passed there was no scandal about him. Yet a popular anecdote describes a well known actor manager as saying one day at rehearsal to an actress of distinguished beauty, "Let us give Shaw a beefsteak and put some red blood into him." "For heaven's sake don't!" exclaimed the actress: "he is bad enough as it is; but if you give him meat, no woman in London will be safe."

"How Frank Ought to Have Done It" was one of many autobiographical effusions Shaw produced in the third person, most of them taking the less formal form of self-interviews purporting to be live and spontaneous give-and-take. But there were also elaborate third-person attempts, some serious efforts to control his history, others only private jokes, such as the elaborate one he created for Cyril Maude. In November 1902, Shaw wrote—for Maude's *History of the Haymarket Theatre*—a good-humored chapter (XXVII) describing the disastrous rehearsals there for a production of *You Can Never Tell*. The comedy had never come off, because of differences between the author and the management as to how it was to be handled. As Shaw had the exaggeratedly dour actor-manager tell the story, the crisis became inevitable when the playwright turned up at rehearsals in his curious limp one-piece health suit manufactured by Dr. Jaeger. "Nobody," the author chronicled, "who had not seen Mr. Shaw sitting there day after day in a costume which the least self-respecting carpenter would have discarded months before, could possibly have understood the devastating effect of the new suit on our minds. . . ." The clash of personalities ended, "Maude" explained, when it was agreed to withdraw the play; but he had nevertheless retained great admiration for Shaw's talents in other fields than the theatrical. "In any other walk of life than that of a dramatic author, I should expect

---

*Oscar Wilde said of him, Shaw wrote (as "Harris"), "He has not an enemy in the world; and none of his friends like him." As "Harris" he added, "If I cannot say that Shaw touches nothing that he does not adorn, I can at least testify that he touches nothing that he does not dust and polish and put back in its place much more carefully than the last man who handled it."

him to achieve a high measure of success. I understand that he has made considerable mark as a vestryman (for the London borough of St. Pancras) collecting dust with punctuality, and supervising drainage with public-spirited keenness. . . ."

Forty years later Shaw spent months rewriting and adding to Hesketh Pearson's biography, first making penciled corrections and interpolations Pearson could rewrite and rub out, and red-inked comments meant for background rather than for publication. Pearson, who had received fifteen times his usual publisher's advance on the strength of Shaw's consent to let the book be done, tried to hurry the elaborate corrections and amplifications, but Shaw shrugged off the importunities with, "You don't know how long this takes." Turning over the last installment, he assured Pearson that he could have written three plays in the time that it took him to revise and emend the information based on the so-called authorities Pearson had consulted. "Posterity," Pearson replied with as much sarcasm as he felt he could get away with, "will be grateful to me." The wit was not lost on Shaw, whose reaction, Pearson afterward thought, "lacked restraint."

The problem for the biographer was that he had been saddled, both for better and for worse, with the autobiographer as his collaborator. Trying to devise a way to emphasize as an attractive feature of his book what his insistent partner, Shaw, had referred to as the "unique private history" he had contributed, Pearson came up with the suggestion that all the Shavian additions and revisions be identified in the printed text between square brackets or by setting them off as quotations in the usual manner, via indentations. "Not on your life, Hesketh!" Shaw exploded. "What I have written I have written in your character, not in my own. As an autobiographer I would have written quite differently. There are things that you may properly say which would come less gracefully from me." Pearson could, Shaw conceded, acknowledge personal help from his subject, including consultation on points of fact. "But if a word is said to connect me with the authorship of the book . . . I shall be driven to the most desperate steps to disclaim it. If you are not prepared to father my stuff, you can rewrite it; but you must not publish it as mine. . . ." Pearson took the hint and sent the copy to the printer unchanged. But Shaw had more to say, sending on several additional pages with recommendation that they not be de-Shavianized out of concern that "readers—least of all the critics—will spot any difference between your stuff and mine. They won't. In the Harris book they didn't. If the story carries them along they won't start detective work; and, anyhow, my style won't disgrace you."

The press of potential Boswells compelled Shaw to tell more than one prospective chronicler that he had exhausted himself as a subject for books: "Everything about me that is of the smallest public interest has been told, and very well told by myself. . . ." Much of potential public interest he found useful to evade, disguise or ignore, but such prefaces as those to *Plays Pleasant and Unpleasant* (1898), *Immaturity* (1930), and *London Music* (1937) he had written substantially as memoirs. Less noticeable autobiography was written into his drama and music criticism: a leaflet entitled *Trade Unionism for Clerks*; introductions or afterwords to books by or about such political or theatrical colleagues as Sydney Olivier, Lillah McCarthy, William Archer, Ellen Terry, and Henry Salt; BBC talks; Fabian essays and lectures; City Temple sermons; periodical and newspaper journalism—even to letters to the editor—and other publications which lent themselves to personal statements and asides. This overt telling of his own story, of memoirs written as such, in prefaces and articles and reviews, in political tracts, pamphlets, and polemical essays, in sermons, self-interviews, and speeches, was his fourth variety of autobiography and the only one written in the spirit of true autobiography. It had been a task often urged upon Shaw, but not in the piecemeal, occasional way he supplied it. "What one really wishes," J. C. Squire had appealed in 1915, "is that Mr. Shaw would write his own biography. The numerous small portions of it which he has produced have given us a great thirst for the whole. If he cannot find time to write it, let him hire a corps of typists and dictate it."

In time Shaw largely fulfilled Squire's hopes, for however much he was an ascetic in other ways, he was seldom guilty of self-denial as an autobiographer; and in his own defense he had provided justification for this side of his writing early in his career. "It is quite true," he wrote Henderson in 1904, "that the best authority on Shaw is Shaw. My activities have lain in so many watertight compartments that nobody has yet given anything but a sectional and inaccurate account of me except when they have tried to piece me out of my own confessions." Accordingly, for forty-six more years—the second half of his long life— he continued to produce pages of additional "confessions," the raw material for what is very likely one of the great biographies in the English language.

In preference to putting down his personal history yet again for yet another biographer, Shaw protested to Frank Harris in 1916, "I had rather die misunderstood: a doom that has no terrors for me as far as my mere personal history (which I have never admitted as more than the merest accident) is concerned." But rather than be misunderstood—after all, he was a playwright who insisted on putting prefaces before all his plays—he gave Harris what he wanted and more. One can only conclude that in Shaw's proliferation of self-sketches is the man as he wanted the world to remember him—not the only G.B.S. but perhaps the most likable and entertaining G.B.S., and close enough to the real thing that, like Hamlet with Yorick's skull, Shaw could look on the result and own that he knew the subject well.

3   The Novelist in Spite of Himself

"There is an end to all things," Shaw once wrote, "even to stocks of un-published manuscript." The occasion was his letter, "the Author to the Reader," a preface dated September 1, 1887, to the fourth of his novels to reach magazine publication. The journal was the November 1887 number of Annie Besant's personal organ, *Our Corner*, in which all her crotchets—religious, so-cial, and economic—were aired. "It may be a relief to you," Shaw went on to *Our Corner's* handful of subscribers, "to know that when this 'Love among the Art-ists' shall have run its course, you need apprehend no more furbished-up early attempts at fiction from me. I have written five novels in my life; and of these there will remain then unpublished only the first—a very remarkable work, I assure you, but hardly one which I should be well advised in letting loose whilst my livelihood depends on my credit as a literary workman."

What he left unsaid was that in addition to his first work of fiction—much later published as *Immaturity* (1931)—he had carefully laid aside his sixth (and last), begun only a few months before. Soon, in spite of pious protestations that he had given up novel writing, he was to pick it up again. For a young man weaned on Dickens, Thackeray, Trollope, Eliot, Lever, and Reade, novel writing was a difficult habit to break.

From 1879 to 1888, Shaw was a novelist in spite of himself, traveling in his fashion the traditional Victorian novel-writing path toward success in litera-ture but finding that it led him nowhere. From his superficially mid-nineteenth-century first novel to the imaginative radicalism of his fifth, his fiction was unpalatable to publishers. If any trend at all was evident, it was that the more he wrote, the more uncommercial his work became. Although he publicly deni-grated the nearly stillborn novels of his nonage, he carefully preserved the mice-chewed manuscripts for decades and belabored publishers about them even after he had loudly declared them dead.

That Shaw wrote novels at all is no more strange than that Alexander Pope wrote satires. In the England of the three-decker novel, the novel was the road to literary glory: not the high road of conscious art so much as the shortcut to the fame and fortune of magazine publication and Mudie's circulating library. But Shaw, having drafted his first novel, was forced to conclude, in a letter to a prospective employer late in 1879: "My only reason for seeking commercial em-ployment is a pecuniary one. I know how to wait for success in literature, but I do not know how to live on air in the interim. . . ."[1] He was then twenty-three.

Through his cousin, Mrs. Cashel Hoey (the minor novelist Fanny Johnstone), Shaw obtained a job with the Edison Telephone Company of London that November, and began paying sixpences to Messrs. Carter, Paterson and Co., carriers, for shunting the heavy brown parcel containing *Immaturity* from one reluctant publisher to another.

The novel was Shaw's own *David Copperfield*, with a flavor both reminiscent of Dickens and anticipatory of Gissing. Robert Smith, the drab, melancholy, inhibited clerk, was something new to publishers' readers used to the more dashing, gentlemanly species of hero. Like his creator at that time, he was egotistical, proud, pontifical, and inhibited. Like most successful fiction of the time, the novel carefully observed all the Victorian decencies, but there was neither conventional hero nor heroine. Instead, the heroines were a faded Italian music-hall dancer who never meets her timid admirer, a rationalistic, irreligious dressmaker, and a flirtatious socialite who had recently been converted to Roman Catholicism. The hero was hardly calculated to set female hearts palpitating, inspire sales of a three-volume edition, or create a demand at Mudie's. Instead he was an obscure clerk in the counting room of Figgis and Weaver, rug merchants, one who was defiantly agnostic, poked fun at street-corner evangelism, read Shelley, Mill, and Ruskin, and was overshadowed in shyness only by his priggishness.

Smith, the tentative Shaw, was a more autobiographical portrait than the author was willing to admit in the piecemeal revelations of his later prefaces and self-sketches. Yet *Immaturity* is more than a prentice novelist's spiritual catharsis. It remains a remarkable work, one which might have affected the course of the English novel had it been successfully published when first written in 1879, for it might have tempered the gloomy realism that was to come by its often-sober, sometimes-satirical evocation of the atmosphere of London in the 1870s. "I have given more than the usual attention to this M.S.," said the Macmillan reader, "for it has a certain quality about it—not exactly of an attractive kind, but still not common. It is the work of a humourist and a realist, crossed, however, by veins of merely literary discussion. There is a piquant oddity about the situations now and then: and the characters are certainly not drawn after the conventional patterns of fiction. It is dry and ironic in flavour. . . . It is undoubtedly clever. . . ."[2] Rejecting the novel, a Macmillan editor sent Shaw a reader's report, which concluded that readers would find the work too long, too unattractive, and too empty of emotion. Shaw agreed:

> Gentlemen
>   My MS has arrived safely with a very kind letter from you, and a critical description of my book which could not, I believe, be more accurate.
>   The flatness of the novel was so involved by its design, that in writing it, I did not propose to myself to save it from appearing dull to a reader who should seek for excitement in it. This design was, to write a novel scrupulously true to nature, with no incident in it to which everyday experience might not afford a parallel, and yet which should constantly provoke in [a] reader full of the emotional ethics of the conventional novel, a sense of oddity and unexpectedness. In short, not to be ironic, but to deal with those ordinary experiences which are a constant irony on sentimentalism, at which the whole work is mainly directed. . . .[3]

Only Blackwood and Sons nibbled at the long, meticulously handwritten manuscript before the mice (which later ate the ends from two *cahiers*); however, they withdrew their interest before Shaw suffered any delusions of imminent fame. *Immaturity*, publishers concluded, displayed exactly that. Not until a half century later was it finally published.

Jumped to Way-Leave manager at twice his salary by February, Shaw quickly acquired a notion of what the rationalistic man of science was like from the American electrical engineers he observed. The result was Edward Conolly, the engineer hero of his second novel, *The Irrational Knot*. But Shaw, beginning by writing about something he knew well through personal experience, changed in midcourse to writing about marriage (his "irrational knot"), concerning which he knew little. Unperturbed by such a thing as ignorance, the young novelist— who had not yet heard of the still-untranslated Ibsen his novel seemed to fore-shadow—attacked the "villainous institution" with all the brashness and iconoclasm of which he was capable. His Victorian heroine, unlike the usual va-riety in popular fiction, further inverted the expected by marrying the hero at the beginning and losing him at the end. Adding to the novel's unsalability, the characters were animated theories, each endowed with an "original morality" which publishers' readers unanimously found "disagreeable," "perverse," and "crude." It was a work, the Macmillan reader concluded, "of a man writing about life, when he knows nothing of it." But he judged it to be the writing "of a man with a certain originality and courage of mind."

Readers wanted familiarity, not originality, and Smith, Elder as well as Bentley soon joined Macmillan in refusing the novel. Shaw investigated pub-lishing it at his own expense but gave that up. He had no job and no income. In mid-1880 the telephone company had merged with another, and Shaw was of-fered the opportunity to continue work. Instead, he escaped back into full-time writing. Unemployment had its benefits. He would now have all the time he needed for reading and writing. He spent much of it in the British Museum's vast, newly electrified reading room. Fortunately for Shaw, as his finances were becoming increasingly precarious, the museum provided free ink and blotting paper. The pound a week still came from his father in Dublin, but his mother's music pupils had dwindled as the depression of the 1880s worsened; and Mrs. Shaw and her son (daughter Lucy being often away as a soprano in a light opera company) moved with regularity from a cottage in the suburbs to less and less fashionable quarters and finally to a second floor in shabby Fitzroy Square.

When Shaw later wrote, "I employed myself in novel writing because nobody would employ me in any other sort of writing," he was apparently referring to more than jobs in journalism or criticism. Even the clerkships he loathed seemed then beyond reach. He had earlier taught himself Pitman shorthand as a literary shortcut. Now, although he had been writing to prospective employers that he was not expert in it, desperation forced him to answer classified adver-tisements for shorthand clerks. He lacked even the money to post the heavy packages of manuscript fiction to additional publishers.

Novel writing proved as fruitless as job hunting. Shaw seemed to spend as much time writing letters soliciting publishers to read his increasing crop of manuscript novels as he did writing the novels themselves. *Love Among the Artists*, his third attempt in fiction, reflected Shaw's passionate belief in his own talents and his bitterness at being thwarted, in the neglect of the novel's hero, "a British Beethoven." The composer Owen Jack, an original genius, is not only an early Shavian man of destiny but a Pygmalion figure anticipating Liza Doolittle's mentor, Henry Higgins. In one of the parallel plots of the novel, Jack, formerly "professor of music and elocution" at Alton College, trains

Madge Brailsford in voice, elocution, and poise. She proves so adept a pupil that she eventually rises to star billing as an actress. After her success, she seeks affection (and perhaps matrimony) from him, having fallen in love in spite of his rudeness and abusiveness as a teacher and as a person. However, the tutor is too immersed in the interests of his own life and rejects the notion of love or marriage.

Love Among the Artists, a conversation novel, is less plot than Shaw on music, painting, drama, and artistic genius, with the attitudes toward each personified in satirically etched characters. It is also a series of brilliant scenes and sermons which reiterate the author's optimism about his eventual vindication as an artist. So the youthful Shaw, certainly with himself in mind as he wrote the lines, had a cynical dowager question her piano virtuoso daughter about Owen Jack: "My child, they seek to deceive you. This *Monsieur Jacques*, with whose music you are to make your *début* here, is he famous in England?"

The reply of Aurelie, one of the finest female characterizations Shaw ever drew, was firm and confident: "Be tranquil, mother. He will not long be unknown." Publishers were less certain.

The firm of Bentley, rejecting the novel, informed Shaw that it lacked interest for the "general reader." Shaw responded with Owen Jack-like undiplomacy. "Your reader," he retorted, "either underrates the capacity of 'the general reader,' or applies the term to a class of persons who—like himself—read little else but newspapers, and whom therefore a novelist is not concerned to please."[4] Yet Shaw had the confidence in himself to send his next novel to Bentley, and Bentley took it seriously enough to have it read by three readers before finally rejecting it, too.

One a year, Shaw would produce five novels between 1879 and 1883, with the fourth, *Cashel Byron's Profession*, being the result of his interest in pugilism. With boxing as a springboard, Shaw told of Cashel Byron, who runs away from his public school to Australia and returns to England a champion prizefighter. His physique attracts Lydia Carew, a priggish young millionairess of determined and unorthodox views. Possessed by some primitive Shavian anticipation of the Life Force, she determines—for eugenic reasons—to marry the already-smitten Cashel, explaining to a bewildered, unsuccessful suitor, "I believe in the doctrine of heredity; and as my body is frail and my brain morbidly active, I think my impulse towards a man strong in body and untroubled in mind a trustworthy one. You can understand that: it is a plain proposition in eugenics." In this manner the "romance" is concluded in the antiromantic vein Shaw never ceased to mine.

The exuberance of *Cashel Byron's Profession* was hardly justified by its author's success up to that time. It was replete with comic absurdity of incident in the best tradition of the later plays: Cashel's impromptu speech at a Sunday soirée, in which he expounds on Beethoven and Wagner in pugilistic argot; one of the most memorable prizefights in English literature, in which the guest of honor is a visiting Zulu chieftain; a love scene between a blue stockinged intellectual and an unsophisticated Adonis, in which as John Mackinnon Robertson commented in *Our Corner* (May 1886), "When the hero actually comes to the point of embracing the heroine . . . he is ashamed of it; and that is just how the reader feels. It is as if you had seen something humiliating, some distressing exposure. . . ."

The socialism in *Cashel Byron* was an afterthought, much of it daubed in when Shaw offered his unsalable novels to obscure radical journals as padding. Late in 1882 he had been converted to socialism, first by a Henry George lecture and then by his reading Marx. He was ready to become a disciple but found difficulty in selecting a radical group to which he could pledge allegiance, possibly because (as the first four novels indicated) he was suffering from acute intellectual indigestion, the result of incomplete assimilation of nineteenth-century idols and idol breakers: Byron, Shelley, Disraeli, Goethe, Mill, Peacock, Darwin, Tyndall, Spencer, Ruskin, and Bradlaugh, followed by the prophets of *Progress and Poverty* and *Capital.*

Meanwhile his new gospel was the stimulus of his last completed novel, *An Unsocial Socialist.* Intended as a "gigantic grapple with the whole social problem," the novel broke down under the weight of its incongruities. Sidney Trefusis, the hero of the title, was an impossible combination of Sidney Webb, Bernard Shaw, and Annie Oakley, and the plot's axis was a runaway husband and a finishing school for girls. The gaily paradoxical Shaw had overreached himself, attempting to erect his economic edifice on a foundation of whipped cream.

The major weakness of Sidney Trefusis is his weakness for pulchritude; and his lack of effectiveness as a socialist missionary is due not to his being unsocial but rather to his being an excessively social socialist, particularly toward women of no use to his cause. Unfortunately for an otherwise witty novel, Shaw made his hero mouth large gobs of Marxist gospel, inserting ponderous paraphrases from *Capital* among passages of sparkling Shavian dialogue.

After his fifth fiasco, Shaw directed his writing energies elsewhere. Literary journalism paid poorly, but the income was regular. Meanwhile the heavy brown parcels of longhand manuscript kept returning unaccepted. "Surely," the author of *An Unsocial Socialist* had written in appeal to one publisher in 1885, "out of thirty millions of copyright persons (so to speak) there must be a few thousand who would keep me in bread and cheese for the sake of my story-telling, if you would only let me get at them." But publishers responded that they were in business to supply what the public wanted to read. It was mistakenly clear to them that the English public would not purchase books which ridiculed its most cherished ideals, traditions, and institutions.

The professed subject *was* unpalatable, as Shaw recognized when he sent his inquiry to the firm of Kegan Paul, Trench & Company. They were, Shaw suggested, "less likely to be repelled by the appearance of a few economic considerations in a novel than firms who deal chiefly in popular fiction."[5] But the novel would get into print only as padding for the splinter socialist magazine *To-Day* in 1884. "The title of this novel finished me with the publishers," Shaw wrote when he was ninety, in presenting the manuscript to the National Library of Ireland. Having made his hero a Marxist was "beyond endurance. . . . A Red, an enemy of civilization, a universal thief, atheist, adulterer, anarchist and apostle of the Satan he disbelieved in!! And presented as a rich young gentleman, eccentric but not socially unpresentable!!! Too bad." Shaw was clearly incapable of accommodation to the requirements of commerce.

While the novels were first emerging as padding in ephemeral radical magazines, Shaw had become a stalwart of the Fabian Society, preaching its brand of socialism in parks, on street corners, in shabby basement workmen's clubs, and through the printed page. Although financially unremunerative, Fabian pamphleteering and debate sharpened his verbal facility and inspired some of the journalistic work William Archer helped him obtain in the mid-1880s.

Possibly the small success of *Cashel Byron* reinforced his determination to make a go of fiction. In America, Harper had refused the novel as of "no use" and then published it in 1886 in the "Harper's Handy Series" and offered Shaw £10 in satisfaction, as there was no copyright protection for him in the United States. Also in 1886 a cheap English edition of a thousand copies, printed from plates used in its serial publication, sold well. Later he would say that he barely escaped the fate of becoming a popular novelist; yet he appears— briefly—to have sought it actively. He began a sixth novel in May 1887. At the end of March 1887, Shaw had closed his accounts on a pecuniarily successful year, his earnings of nearly £136 representing a gain of £25 from the previous year. The increase was undoubtedly due more to work as a critic than to publication of two novels. Although most of the thousand *Cashel Byron*s printed had been sold, their full price had been only a shilling a copy. Pirated editions, though indicative of popularity, earned the author nothing. As late as 1897, Shaw was writing, "It is my private belief that half the book-selling trade in London consists in the sale of unauthorised *Cashel Byron*s."

Selling poorly, but also finally published—in an error-ridden edition by Swan Sonnenschein, Lowrey and Co.—was *An Unsocial Socialist*. On the verso of the title page appeared "Some Opinions of the Press"—by whom the book had been received politely. The stimulus to produce another work of fiction may not have come from publication, but in early 1887 it was again there.

On May 14, 1887, Shaw had dinner at eight with Dr. J. Kingston Barton of St. Bartholomew's Hospital. At nine o'clock Barton was summoned "to a long case" (as Shaw put it in his diary), and the evening was unexpectedly over. He entrained home and "began a new novel and sat up till 3 at it. Hooray!" The three pages he managed to write were indicative of the troubles he would have sustaining the enterprise. On May 15, 1928, forty-one years later to the day, he wrote to Maurice Holmes, who was then at work on a bibliography of the Shavian novels, "My secretary has just unearthed a beginning of a novel in 1888 which, were not my own handwriting against me, I could swear I never wrote, saw, conceived, nor heard of in my life."[6]

Nothing more was heard about the manuscript until 1946, when Shaw presented it, along with other manuscripts of his novels (except *Love Among the Artists*, once disposed of as trash by his mother and now scattered among private and library collections), to the National Library of Ireland. The first page bore no title originally, but Shaw added one later: "An Unfinished Novel." Appended in 1946 was a preface inviting "who will and can" to finish the novel begun almost sixty years before.

By June 1, 1887, Shaw had sat down to work on the manuscript on eight different days but had only reached Chapter 2 and completed twenty-six pages. After three further attempts, the last on June 14, he abandoned it, to pick it up again briefly the following year. In a month only thirty-three pages had been written—in contrast to the five pages of fiction he had once forced himself to produce daily while turning out his earlier novels.

The abandonment of the novel left no visible gap in Shaw's crowded calendar; between platform appearances for the Fabians, he managed to find time for the writing of book reviews, art criticism, socialist propaganda, essays, music columns, literary spoofs, and short fiction. His own meticulously kept scrapbooks of cuttings show dozens of pieces of pseudonymous and unsigned journalism as well as writings under his own name, and his diaries are crowded with lectures, meetings, concerts, exhibitions, and a tangled web of involvements with women.

His review of Samuel Butler's anti-Darwinian treatise *Luck or Cunning?* appeared in the *Pall Mall Gazette* on May 31, and on June 9 appeared his review of a humorous novel by an old acquaintance, George R. Sims, who had once (in 1879, when *Immaturity* was being completed) paid him fifteen shillings for the jejune essay "Christian Names." The review of *Mary Jane's Memoirs*, another comic variation on the Pamela theme, was entitled "An Autobiography from the Kitchen" and signed "By an English Mistress." The reviewer affected to be scandalized by the book and by journalists and authors in general.

Shaw also wrote seriously of books, and in the *Pall Mall Gazette* that summer he reviewed (and condemned) George Moore's short naturalistic novel *A Mere Accident*, objecting to its timid reticence and amorality. In August he spent three consecutive weekly issues of the *National Reformer* reviewing Marx's *Capital*. Closing the long critique on August 21, he wrote of the volume with the highest praise he could summon—the autobiographical endorsement: "I must now leave the subject with a confession that I never took up a book that proved better worth reading than 'Capital.'" Also dated that August was his most memorable short work of fiction, "Don Giovanni Explains," his first treatment of the Don Juan legend, apparently based more on his affair with Jenny Patterson than on the legend.

Autumn 1887 was filled with political and economic agitation, and Shaw was in the middle of it, forgetting his work as a novelist, although others did not. William Morris, in writing about the socialist agitators arrested regularly at Hyde Park in 1887, commented that the " 'rioters' being brought up before Mr de Rutzen, were prosecuted by the Government jackal, Mr Poland, the farcical nature of whose opening speech no one, now Dickens is dead—more's the pity— need attempt to render."[7] Here the sage of Kelmscott added the note, alluding to the Shavian novel he had reviewed in his *Commonweal* the year before: "I don't know, though: the author of *Cashel Byron*, though he wouldn't do it with the richness of Dickens, might deal with such a case—why doesn't he?"[8] Whether Morris ever mentioned the subject's possibilities to Shaw is unknown, but Shaw never took literary advantage of it.

In November he was involved in the "Bloody Sunday" fiasco in Trafalgar Square, during which marchers from various radical groups, exhorted by Shaw, Morris, Mrs. Besant, W. T. Stead, and others, defied the police prohibition of processions briefly and then disintegrated into headlong flight. In the relative calm which followed, Shaw found time to think again about novel writing, as there was then a steady correspondence passing between him and the publisher of his *Unsocial Socialist*, Swan Sonnenschein. In order to stimulate lagging sales, Sonnenschein had suggested that Shaw write a preface for it or that the novel be remaindered in paper wrappers at a shilling—possibly appealing to impecunious but fervent socialists in the cheap edition. Shaw countered by suggesting an appendix in the form of a letter to the author from the hero of the novel. Several letters later, after Shaw had admitted feeling "sorry to have let Sonnenschein in for this book," the publisher replied in an apparently sincere letter of praise. After politely confirming that sales of the novel had been poor "this half year," Sonnenschein concluded with prophetic words of encouragement:

> I felt rather keen on the book when I read it, which was before we took it: and I
> still think it as clever a novel as we have bought. If you were to stick to novels,
> or go in for plays (which are even more suited to you, in my opinion), I believe
> this book, in common with all your others if there are more than "Byron,"
> would work into a good circulation. I certainly don't regret the small sum of
> money we probably have in "U.S." still; and shall not do so unless you choose to
> drop your pen, or die, or do something else foolish.[9]

Shaw had heard words of encouragement before, but usually in letters of con-
dolence from publishers rejecting his novels. Sonnenschein's surprising letter
was a declaration of faith. Perhaps it accounts for Shaw's sudden renewal of
interest in the novel manuscript he had abandoned the previous June. On January 23, 1888, he added two pages to it and then added one more page on each of
the two days that followed. He also wrote a leader for the *Star*, self-taught himself some algebra and German, lectured at the Lee and Lewisham Radical Club
on "Practical Socialism," visited several friends, went at his arrears of correspondence, wrote two additional pieces for the *Star*, attended the Hampstead
Historical Club and the Bedford Debating Society and a meeting of the Fabian
Executive, and had himself fitted for two pairs of trousers at his favorite (and
only) clothing supplier, Jaeger's. After a lapse of two days, in which his schedule
was no less crowded (he posted twenty-seven letters and cards on January 27),
he added two more pages but ended in the middle of a dialogue where what was
probably to be the major intrigue of the novel was beginning to take form. The
words of Swan Sonnenschein may still have been echoing in his ears, but his
enthusiasm for the manuscript had vanished.

From the day on which Shaw had first picked up the titleless novel until the
day he had put it down for the last time—about nine months—he had published,
among other things, twenty-one art reviews in the *World* and thirty-one literary
reviews in the *Pall Mall Gazette* as well as theater reviews and nearly a dozen
other contributions—some related to "Bloody Sunday." They required more
than the writing. The art columns necessitated tramping the galleries, and his
six *PMG* musical columns meant concertgoing. One of his book review columns
alone noticed, if not examined, twenty-two volumes of verse. He had also spoken at dozens of public meetings of political and radical groups, from the
Chiswick Liberal Club to the Peckham and Dulwich Radical Club, and from the
Bedford Debating Society, where the subject was contemporary fiction, to the
South Place Religious Society, where he debated with the Reverend Ford on the
subject "That the welfare of the community necessitates the transfer of the
land and existing capital of the country from private owners to the State."

His energies were being spread in so many directions that there was little
opportunity for the writing of fiction. When he had first begun writing novels,
he wrote whether or not he had anything to say; and being unemployed and
directionless, he had all day to do it. Now he had more work than time.

In February 1888, Robert Louis Stevenson, elated after reading a copy of
Cashel Byron's Profession sent to him by William Archer, hungered for more
Shavian fiction. In a letter to Mrs. Archer, Fanny Stevenson commented from
Saranac Lake, "Louis has been ill indeed with a complication of disorders, but
really seems to be over the worst. I wish he had another 'Shaw' to read. Nobody
writes amusing books now. There is nowhere gaiety. All is serious and more or
less dull. . . ."[10] In a second letter that month, one from husband to husband,
Stevenson added a postscript: "Tell Shaw to hurry up: I want another."[11] That
very month, however, was Shaw's first as an ex-novelist.

An Unfinished Novel begins the story of Dr. Kincaid, who arrives in the country town of Little Beltham after a London training. His aim is experience in general practice, to be achieved as assistant to Pelham Maddick, an apprenticeship-educated physician who needs a qualified diplomate on hand to sign medical certificates. It was not Shaw's first extended treatment of the medical profession, nor was it the last. Always interested in the exposure of the false masquerading as the true, he found medicine as susceptible to sham as the arts.

Shaw had known physician Kingston Barton almost since arriving in London. It was at Barton's flat a decade earlier that an arrogant young Shaw had quieted a party by offering to repeat the disputed atheist experiment attributed to Charles Bradlaugh of holding up his pocket watch and daring God to strike him dead in five minutes. The previous spring he had begun his abortive novel immediately after returning from Barton's, which suggests that something said at dinner, or about the emergency call which ended it abruptly, had precipitated the few pages Shaw had written that night. But his continuing interest in medicine may be traced, too, to the spring of 1881, which was almost his last. Although vaccinated and supposedly immune, he was felled by the smallpox epidemic then raging in London, and *Love Among the Artists*, his novel in progress, had to be abandoned temporarily. He survived, but his faith in orthodox medicine and its practitioners was badly shaken. Thousands of Londoners were stricken by the disease, overtaxing municipal medical facilities, and not far from Shaw's home there was set up a temporary Fulham Smallpox Hospital, which operated through the epidemic in spite of local protests and the restricting injunctions nearby apprehensive residents sought from the courts.

Shaw recovered elsewhere, remaining at home until he was able to travel in June to Leyton, then a country district in Essex on the borders of Epping Forest but soon to be swallowed up by East London as the country houses "were demolished and replaced by rows of little brick boxes inhabited by clerks in tall hats supporting families on fifteen shillings a week."[12] Practicing in Leyton was his "blasphemous Rabelaisian" uncle, Dr. Walter Gurly, an impressively bearded former ship's surgeon. It may have been amiable Uncle Walter who restored in some measure Shaw's perspective toward the medical profession. At Leyton, Shaw returned to his work on *Love Among the Artists*, wrote letters to publishers about his two completed novels, and fruitlessly answered newspaper advertisements for employment.

The earliest "big scene" exposing the hypocrisy and chicanery Shaw attributed to much of the medical profession appears to be a lengthy deathbed scene in *An Unsocial Socialist*, in which "sooner than betray his colleague's inefficiency, [the specialist] would have allowed him to decimate London." In his earliest play, *Widowers' Houses*, the leading male role is assigned to Harry Trench, who happens to be a doctor. However, in Shaw's abortive novel (begun after he had laid aside the first two acts of *Widowers' Houses* and abandoned before he picked up the play again), the hero is more than an individual assigned the profession of medicine in order to give him socially respectable employment—he appears instead to be an attempt at portraying a medical man as hero. Although Dr. Kincaid and Dr. Trench are nearly contemporaneous creations of Shaw, and both worked as medical students handling slum-area outpatients, Kincaid appears genuinely distressed at the state of the poor, while Trench is not concerned enough to let it affect his financial interests in slum housing.

It had been painfully apparent to Shaw through the 1880s that in his first five novels he had not found the prescription to interest either publisher or public. In the sixth, compromise is in evidence. All the ingredients for popular appeal seem to have already been compounded in the beginning of the novel he abandoned: the popular profession of medicine, a personable hero, a stage villain in Pelham Maddick, and two unsatisfactorily married women eager for the hero's attentions.

Mrs. Maddick, Kincaid notes on arrival, is young, freckled, and attractive, with an expression of "suppressed resentment and quick intelligence." Her husband (who "dressed at being a young, handsome, and dashing man, and had neither youth enough nor character enough nor money enough to be more than a passable counterfeit") is a failure both at home and in his consulting room, treating everyone but his wife with large doses of sham solicitude. To Kincaid, who must reside in the Maddick household, the stormy nature of their domestic relations is as ill concealed as the ravages of their three small children upon their shabby furnishings. Since Mrs. Maddick complains openly, Kincaid listens circumspectly and once explains to her (in the major Shavian social comment in the fragment) why he left London for the grubbing practice and dismal conditions which have helped to make her depressed:

> I was a bit disheartened by the frightful poverty in London. The surgical work is all very well; but the medical part of the business, as far as the out patients is [*sic*] concerned, is shocking. What they want—ninetynine in a hundred of them—is rest and sufficient food; but you might as well prescribe sable cloaks and diamond rings. It is really very poor practice to sit there telling women with from nothing a week upward to eighteen shillings that what their baby wants is nourishing food. Roughly speaking, nearly every case you get in a London hospital is complicated by drink, overwork, or starvation. Then there is a lot of white lead poisoning, housemaid's knee, sweep's cancer, and other things which neednt be. I want to study disease among people who have a fair chance—who are properly fed and clothed and housed. . . .

Readers of *Mrs Warren's Profession* (written five years later) will recall echoes of Kincaid in Mrs. Warren's justification of her choice of occupation.

It does not take long for Dr. Kincaid to become further impressed with Maddick's incompetence and sloth and with Mrs. Maddick's eyes and slender form. Neither does it take long for Mrs. Maddick to entangle Kincaid in domestic discussion and personal revelation. Not reticent herself, she reveals that she mistrusts her husband's habitual oversolicitousness toward certain young matrons of the town, and she regularly opens his mail. That some of the young matrons might be eager to accept services other than professional, Kincaid already knows, having attended Lady Laurie in Maddick's absence (and having accepted an invitation for Saturday lawn tennis). Lady Laurie, Kincaid had observed, was an attractive hypochondriac with a wealthy, aged husband and obviously lacked nothing but inhibitions. Having found the physician's bullying (after the indulgences of Maddick) "novel and delicious," she had lost no time in proposing that Kincaid should become her new personal physician.

Equally determined to test Kincaid's self-possession is Mrs. Maddick, who interests him because of the intensity and variety of her emotions—"her restless suspicion, her shyness, her audacity, her impulsive frankness, her insatiable curiosity, base jealousy and vulgar envy." Near the end of the novel fragment, she induces him to accompany her on an afternoon shopping excursion—a walk which afterward continues at her behest into the country, while they "criticized the scenery, sounded each other's tastes and accomplishments, and discussed Herbert Spencer, George Eliot, Browning, Turgenieff, Walt Whitman, socialism, spiritualism, and other subjects that would very greatly have amazed the Little Belthamites of earlier generations."

Kincaid, a good listener, allows Mrs. Maddick to be "happy in the full play of her egotism" as they walk. But abruptly after they have gone a considerable distance, she stops and begins to draw aside the transparent pretenses between them. And it is there that the manuscript abruptly ends.

Since the fragment trails off with the hero hungered after by two attractive, unsatisfactorily married women—a condition not entirely foreign to the author's personal experience—one may wonder whether Shaw's dilemma was that his earnest hero of twenty-five (originally twenty-eight) lacked the evasive wit and glibness of the thirty-one-year-old Shaw. Or perhaps the author lacked interest enough in his plot to develop the situation further and involve or extricate his hero. Busy with journalism and Fabianism, he apparently had little inclination to exploit further what was largely—in spite of his social criticism— one of the staple plot formulas and fashionable situations of popular English fiction.

There may be even another reason for the abandonment of opus 6—Edith Nesbit, authoress and wife of Shaw's Fabian associate Hubert Bland. The attractive Mrs. Bland (two years younger than Shaw) may have been the prototype for Mrs. Maddick. There are even a few traces of Hubert Bland in Pelham Maddick. Still, if Shaw intended the parallel, he covered his tracks well. Once he had written (in the preface to *Immaturity*): "I have used living models as freely as a painter does, and in much the same way: that is. I have sometimes made a fairly faithful portrait founded on intimate personal intercourse, and sometimes . . . developed what a passing glance suggested to my imagination." In *An Unfinished Novel* the former method may have been utilized.

The admirable Kincaid may be in part a fictionalization of James Kingston Barton, who had learned his trade at St. Bartholomew's Hospital and by the 1890s was "such a swell," according to Shaw, that he was taking few new patients. But Kincaid was also a self-portrait. Just as Shaw and Hubert Bland were professional associates through their Fabian activities and their journalistic work, so were the fictional Kincaid and Maddick professional associates. Both Maddick and Bland had dandified mannerisms in dress, the fashionable Bland disdaining the Bohemianism of Shaw and affecting frockcoat, tall hat, and monocle. Whereas Maddick appears to be indulging in petty and perhaps (the novel fragment is not extended enough to clarify this) innocent intrigues with local matrons he visits professionally, he is weak and ineffectual. Bland, however, had great surpluses of virility and maintained several women simultaneously, with three (including his legitimate wife) bearing him children. More successful in winning women than he was as a breadwinner, Bland obtained regular journalistic employment through the intervention of his friend Shaw. Mrs. Bland, well known as a minor poetess and novelist and as a writer of children's books, was a fellow Fabian and in a position to watch Shaw's reputation as Don Juan grow as rapidly as the other reputations he was acquiring. That she was soon attracted to him is indicated by a letter she wrote to a friend at the close of 1884. In spite of her careful laying of a false scent, her infatuation shows through:

The said Society is getting rather large now and includes some very nice people, of whom Mr Stapelton is the nicest and a certain G. B. Shaw the most interesting. G.B.S. has a fund of dry Irish humour that is simply irresistible. He is a very clever writer and speaker—is the grossest flatterer (of men, women and children impartially) I ever met, is horribly untrustworthy as he repeats everything he hears, and does not always stick to the truth, and is *very plain* . . . and yet is one of the most fascinating men I ever met. Everyone rather affects to despise him 'Oh its only Shaw.' That sort of thing you know, but everyone admires him all the same. Miss H— pretends to hate him, but my own impression is that she is head over heels in love with him.[13]

Depressed by her husband's numerous and open infidelities, Edith Nesbit Bland was extremely susceptible to Shaw's wit and charm. Making little attempt to disguise her sentiments, she even addressed several fervent poems to him—in which the evidence was later somewhat suppressed when financial need required their being sold for publication. By 1886 she was one of several women making demands on Shaw's time, although he, in his usual manner, tried to make light of the situation and cool the passion down into a harmless friendship. Still, Mrs. Bland—often on the spur of the moment—wanted Shaw's company on long and unreasonable expeditions. As St. John Ervine put it, "If suddenly she took it into her head that G.B.S., after a long and tiring meeting, should travel to Blackheath with her and walk about the roads in the vicinity of her home, this was the right and proper thing for him to do; and the fact that he missed the train to London and had to walk home, arriving there at 3.30 A.M., after a weary tramp lasting for 2½ hours, caused her no contrition. The number of times he missed the last train to London and had to walk the whole way back from Blackheath to Osnaburgh Street was extraordinary. . . ."[14]

Early in 1887—the year Shaw began *An Unfinished Novel*—Edith Nesbit was still asserting herself. After taking tea with her, Shaw once wrote in his diary, she "insisted on coming to Fitzroy Square," to which he and his mother had moved. "My mother was out," Shaw's entry records, "and she [Edith] went away after an unpleasant scene caused by my telling her that I wished her to go, as I was afraid that a visit to me alone would compromise her." (Kincaid, it should be noted, is also extremely rigorous in maintaining a diary—"a little journal which he kept as a record of his movements.")

Shaw's friendship with both Blands weathered the affair but might not have if the novel fragment had been pursued to completion. Perhaps Shaw recognized that the Blands—if no one else—might see through his characterization of the Maddicks, particularly realizing this after he had begun the last scene he attempted: the long walk and pregnant conversation into which Kincaid is led by the crafty Mrs. Maddick. Shaw's own explanation of his abandonment of the novel appears in the brief preface to it written in his ninetieth year. He found nothing, he indicated, but a conventional plot unsuited to his virtuoso manner. "It is not surprising," he wrote, "that I found nothing new for me to do in that direction, and abandoned my abortive attempt to return to it so soon and completely that I dropped it and forgot all about it when I had barely introduced the three leading characters in their three degrees of mental scope."

In spite of the brevity of the fragment, it is of great interest for its revelation of new facets of Shaw's personality and interests in 1887 and 1888. The profound and sympathetic treatment of the physician far antedates the sardonic, yet no less sympathetic, portraits of the general practitioners Schutzmacher and Blenkinsop in *The Doctor's Dilemma*. And the abbreviated characterizations of the vixenish Mrs. Maddick and the kittenish Lady Laurie reveal the increased Shavian knowledge of women since the innocent days in which the earlier novels were written.

Several felicitous touches brighten the abandoned novel. Maddick's more imaginative than industrious stableboy, with his system of fancied penalties for his master commensurate with the indignities he suffers, is the only clearly defined minor character but one who might be placed beside the deft pen portraits of minor characters in the later plays. And perhaps unique in Shaw is the all-too-brief account of the impact upon each other of Kincaid and the three Maddick children, the latter who, "playing at being the new doctor . . . had carried it to the length of pretending to go to sleep in his bed." Nevertheless, the musty odor of the least-appealing traits in Victorian fiction and drama are also present, and what the reader witnesses is Shaw's battle to break free from them. Considering the size of the fragment and the knowledge that correction and revision were denied it, it may be unfair to declare the battle lost. It had hardly been joined.

There is no likelihood that Shaw's unfinished novel will ever rank with the great aborted masterpieces of English fiction. Unlike Dickens's *Edwin Drood* and Stevenson's *Weir of Hermiston*, it shows no significant heightening or change in direction of the author's powers. In the preponderance of dialogue over narration, however, the novel moves (as did the earlier ones) in the direction of the play, with the author leaving the conversation-novel he anticipated in his six attempts at fiction to be brought to maturity by other hands in future decades. In 1888, G.B.S.'s enthusiasm for the novel was almost gone. Before it could revive, it had been diverted into a reawakened enthusiasm for playwriting. His contempt for novel writing thereafter would have a touch of bitterness to it, for he knew that although he was no Dickens, he had still been better than the drudges whose fiction he had reviewed in the 1880s. "What am I to do?" he would write in mock horror as a music critic in 1890 about listening to more mediocrities. "No: [I would] rather sweep a crossing—write novels. . . ."

As Shaw put it himself in his manuscript preface to the abandoned novel sixty-one years later, "It is not surprising that I found nothing new for me to do in that direction, and abandoned my abortive attempt to return to so soon and so completely that I dropped it . . . when I had barely introduced the three leading characters. . . . Let who will and can finish it to their taste if they can bear to give it another thought."

4 G.B.S., Pugilist and Playwright

To celebrate the occasion when, in early 1882, Pakenham Beatty, dilettante poet and gentleman pugilist, became a father, his friend and sparring partner, a lean red-bearded young Irishman with literary aspirations named Bernard Shaw, composed a commemorative ode. "Hail! many named son of Paquito," it began, mocking the fact that the infant, like royalty, had been given five Christian names, one of them Mazzini, after a parental political hero. By the fifth stanza, young Mazzini was warned of the unreliability of boxers, and the seventh stanza, like the others in the rapid measure of Swinburne's notorious "Dolores," urged the boy to gain pounds quickly in order to reach fighting weight and mentioned such boxing experts as Ned Donnelly and Sammy the Dutchman. Both men taught the manly art, and Donnelly was Beatty's own boxing "professor." He was also Shaw's.

Shaw's interest in the manly art had begun when he was a skinny, gangling boy in Dublin and prizefighting was an illegal hole-and-corner activity often broken up by unsympathetic policemen. A half century later his recollections of the ring were still furnishing Shaw with metaphors. To Frank Harris,[1] Shaw's picture of unwarranted panic was his memory "of a certain prize fighter who flourished when I was a boy. His skill and power were such that he was always victorious at his weight; but he was so nervous that they had to keep a mirror in the ring to show him his face between every round to disprove his piteous pleas that his features were obliterated and that they must throw up the sponge for him, as he would surely be killed if he went on." Memories of prizefighters would turn up in his writings, early and late.

Although the verses celebrating young Pakenham William Albert Hengist Mazzini Beatty remain unpublished,[2] they are a link to one of the happier episodes in Shaw's prentice years, his love affair with pugilism. Then in his mid-twenties, Shaw had trained with both Beatty and his ring mentor for the Queensberry amateur competitions. Possessing the leisure of the unemployed (except for his daily writing stint at a desk in the British Museum Reading Room), Shaw had accepted from Beatty as preliminary instruction a copy of Donnelly's book *Self-Defence*. With it was born his own interest in boxing and his fourth novel, *Cashel Byron's Profession* (1882), in which Donnelly becomes Ned Skene.

By 1899 Beatty's fortunes had declined, and Shaw, in effect, repaid his old sparring partner for the lessons with Ned Donnelly. "A friend of mine drank himself mad twice," he recalled, without identifying the hapless Beatty. "In my innocence I wanted him to become a teetotaller. Finally I discovered that the chief obstacle was his unfortunate wife. The house was so miserable, and her children so wretched, when he was abstaining, that the evil of his periodically drinking too much was less than the continuous evil of his not drinking at all." Shaw—by then the playwright of *Candida* and *The Devil's Disciple*—underwrote young Mazzini's schooling.

Prizefighting then, Shaw remembered, "was supposed to be dead. Few living men remembered the palmy days when Tom and Jerry went to Jackson's rooms (where Byron—not Cashel, but the poet—studied 'the noble art') to complete their education as Corinthians; when Cribb fought Molyneux and was to Tom Spring what Skene was to Cashel Byron; when Kemble engaged Dutch Sam to carry on the war with the O.P. rioters; when Sharples' portraits of leading bruisers were engraved on steel; when Bell's Life was a fashionable paper, and Pierce Egan's Boxiana a[n] expensive publishing enterprise. . . . The sport was supposed to have died of its own blackguardism by the second quarter of the century; but the connoisseur who approaches the subject without moral bias will, I think, agree with me that it must have lived by its blackguardism and died of its intolerable tediousness; for all prize-fighters are not Cashel Byrons, and in barren dreariness and futility no spectacle on earth can contend with that of two exhausted men trying for hours to tire one another out at fisticuffs for the sake of their backers. . . . In the eighties many apparently lost causes and dead enthusiasms unexpectedly revived: Imperialism, Patriotism, Religion, Socialism, and many other things, including prizefighting in an aggravated form, and on a scale of commercial profit and publicity which soon made its palmy days insignificant and ridiculous by contrast. . . ."[3]

Until the revival of prizefighting, relatively demure matches with boxing gloves, under the Marquess of Queensberry's rules, kept pugilism, in Shaw's words, "faintly alive." It was not popular "because the public, which cares only for the excitement of a strenuous fight, believed then that the boxing glove made sparring as harmless a contest of pure skill as a fencing match with buttoned foils. This delusion was supported by the limitation of the sparring match to boxing. In the prize ring under the old rules a combatant might trip, hold, or throw his antagonist; so that each round finished either with a knockdown blow, which, except when it is really a liedown blow, is much commoner in fiction than it was in the ring, or with a visible body-to-body struggle ending in a fall. In a sparring match all that happens is that a man with a watch in his hand cried out 'Time!' whereupon the two champions prosaically stop sparring and sit down for a minute's rest and refreshment. The unaccustomed and inexpert spectator in those days did not appreciate the severity of the exertion or the risk of getting hurt; he underrated them as ignorantly as he would have overrated the more dramatically obvious terrors of a prize-fight." As a result, Shaw realized, public interest in the sparrings for the Queensberry Championships every spring was confined to the few who had some critical knowledge of boxing, "and to the survivors of the generation for which the fight between Sayers and Heenan had been described in The Times as solemnly as the University Boat Race." What had happened was that pugilism had gone out of fashion "because the police had suppressed the only form of it which fascinated the public by its undissembled pugnacity." The spark that was needed to rehabilitate it "was the discovery that the old glove fight is a more trying and dangerous form of contest than the old knuckle fight. . . ."[4]

Shaw, who would watch the annual Oxford-Cambridge boat race religiously from a vantage point on William Morris's long back lawn at Hammersmith, which swept down to the Thames, found boxing more compelling—and more available—as a spectator sport. Besides, since he had become a participant, he knew the fine points from experience. The Amateur Boxing Championships in 1882 were held at St. James's Hall, Regent Street, where the feature contest of the nine-and-one-half-hour-long tournament had been the heavyweight final between Hubert Murray and H. T. Dearsley. Murray lost on points wasted in the first two rounds but came back so fiercely in the last round, according to *The Times* of April 17, that among the spectators brought cheering to their feet must have been the pugilistic novice Bernard Shaw. Classics don Gilbert Murray told me long ago that Shaw had once mentioned Sir Hubert to him, and it is possible that at least a little of that memorable match emerges in the hero of Shaw's novel, who has emigrated to Australia and returns, for the Murray brothers had themselves come from Australia. In print Shaw identified Cashel Byron as drawn from Jack Burke, whom he had seen only in an exhibition spar. Although only a lightweight, Burke had the reputation of being able to survive the marathon contests often fought in midcentury. Cashel Byron would fight one, and even as late as 1915 the heavyweight bout in Havana in which Jess Willard wrested the title from Jack Johnson would go twenty-six grueling rounds.

In 1883, a year after Shaw's introduction to the Queensberry competitions, the event was held at the Lillie Bridge Grounds. Both he and Beatty were entered in the middleweight division ("Exceeding 10 st., not exceeding 11 st. 4 lb.") and Shaw, with the recklessness of the beginner, also entered himself in the heavyweight division ("Any weight"). Neither he nor Beatty appears to have been selected for competition, but immersion in the boxing ambience had already led to Shaw's putting the experience in a novel. Young Cashel Byron would fall in love with a frail millionairess who is unaware of his profession, which she considers "anti-social and retrograde," until he flees from the police (since prizefighting was still illegal) at the conclusion of the great fight with the brutal William Paradise which Cashel had already planned as his last.

Shaw's diary[5] through the middle 1880s records a continuing but slackening interest in boxing. He was a regular purchaser of the penny *Sporting Times* and in March and April 1885 went with Beatty to several amateur boxing contests. The competition at the West London Club, Neumeyer Hall, he judged as a poor show, but he made no comment about the day he spent in St. James's Hall at the Amateur Boxing Association's events other than his sixpence investment in a program. A few days later he walked to Brompton to the annual Queensberry competitions, and on April 15—two days later—he spent the evening at Ned Donnelly's gymnasium to see more boxing. The diary notes not only purchases of additional penny sporting papers, such as *Sporting Set* and *Sportsman*, but mentions that Shaw sympathetically tipped Caseley, the loser at Donnelly's, a halfcrown.

The best that boxers could then do was to "spar for points" awarded by judges—"three gentlemanly members of the Stock Exchange, who would carefully note the said points on an examination paper and the ring side, awarding marks only for skill and elegance, and sternly discountenancing the claims of brute force. It may be that both the author of the rules and the 'judges' who administered them really believed all this. . . ."[6] The tipping—as close as boxers got to prizes—represented for Shaw a great deal of money. He had just begun to earn a little from journalism—a very little.

In May 1885 Shaw notes visiting Fabian colleagues Edith and Hubert Bland at Blackheath and putting on the gloves with Bland to have a friendly spar. In November he spent another evening with Beatty at Donnelly's and this time gave two shillings to the loser. The following April he was again at the Amateur Boxing Championships and chanced writing an article about them for the *Saturday Review*. It was not published.

Entries in his diary show Shaw busier and busier with reviewing, lecturing, politicking, and romancing, but in January 1887 there is again a reference to a boxing show at St. James's Hall, and in April he was to meet Beatty there for another competition and to go with Beatty to Donnelly's, where he notes that he gave Jem Hook a shilling but does not indicate whether Hook won or lost. (Boxing, in fact, was beginning to pall a bit when measured against newer interests, for that month he left a bout before it was over to visit his demanding mistress, Mrs. Jenny Patterson.)

In January 1888 Shaw would put together another prizefighting piece, this time for the *Star*, which was buying other journalism from him. Again it would not be published. Nor would the *Pall Mall Gazette*, for which he was also writing, take it. But he would not be denied when he had something he wanted to say, and in April, after attending a program at the Imperial Theatre consisting of "no less than thirty glove fights," he recorded his conclusions as to whether gloves had lessened the ferocity of competition, and had them published anonymously as from "a correspondent" in the previously uninterested *Pall Mall Gazette*. His ploy, given the paper's political sympathies, was to refer sarcastically to the London police commissioner, Sir Charles Warren, a villain to the Left after his suppression of the "Bloody Sunday" Trafalgar Square demonstration in November 1887. "Without any disparagement to the noble art of self-defence," he asked, "may one ask Sir Charles Warren whether glove-fights are legalized by such special incentives to ferocity as £10 cups and 'amateur championships' for the victors?"

At the Imperial, he noted, when "distinguished members of the prize ring" discussed fine points of the contests with "undistinguished members of the House of Lords," they observed that gloves had now become "as brutal as bare knuckles—an advance which the world owes to the researches of J. L. Sullivan." Wearing boxing gloves, "The light-weight champion 'knocked out' his first two opponents. Cardiff sent up two boxers of a new school, devoted solely to the study of banging hard enough to produce insensibility. The more terrible of this twain eventually succumbed to a talented Irishman, who knocked out the would-be knocker. The indignant Welshman thereupon endeavored to throw his opponent off the stage, for which the judges, with unwonted moral courage, disciplined him."

Shaw saw less moral courage when a bantam-weight boxer, after being stunned, "was knocked down four times before the referee interfered. . . . The audience seemed to enjoy nothing so much as the spectacle of the British boxer, after a lucky knock-down blow, eagerly waiting to pound his dazed and helpless opponent frantically about the jaws the moment he was technically on his feet after the prescribed ten seconds. The notion that the glove cannot hurt is confined to persons who have never seen or felt them used."

Shaw, who had used gloves as well as felt them, thought that "sloggers" who made boxing dull could be disqualified by the Boxing Association, but that the Association, by its verdicts, could also encourage "artistic sparring." The problem as he saw it was that six years of legal toleration of amateur boxing in Britain had only resulted in fisticuffs becoming "steadily more brutal, and of course more lucrative . . . , systematizing an evasion of the law against prize-fighting." He was not against boxing as honest commerce, but against hypocrisy. He was not against a hard fight, but against pandering to the brutal lower instincts of the crowd; and he would deal with both issues when, late in 1889, he got around the *Star*'s lack of interest in the ring by writing a "Corno di Bassetto" music column on the subject. His contribution for December 27 began innocently enough with mention of Christmas caroling and was entitled "Christmas in Broadstairs," where he had gone for the holidays. But on Christmas Eve, he wrote, en route to Broadstairs, he had made his way to Holborn Viaduct, where he found "a betting, loafing, rowdy crowd, with a large infusion of fighting men in it. The fighting men were much the most respectable of the company. They had quite an air of honest industry about them, being men without illusions, who will calculate your weight and earn your money by the sweat of their brow if the opportunity looks good enough—who are not courageous but fitfully hopeful, not fearful but anxious, fighting being to them not a romantic exploit but a trade venture."

The crowd had been waiting for the return of two pugilists from Bruges, where they had fought to a draw (the bout was illegal in England) in what was to be the last bare-fisted competition under the old London ring rules, which had been succeeded by the Queensberry code. And Frank Slavin (who had fought Jem Smith) played the piano, Shaw observed, a veritable "Orpheus of the ring." Shaw had his column.

In the train, Corno di Bassetto added,

> I read some indignant articles on the unfairness of the Bruges prizefight, evidently written by men who do not know that the proceedings which caused Mr Slavin to demand with noble indignation whether the occupants of Mr Smith's corner were Englishmen, are in every respect typical of the prize ring, and were as familiar in every detail to our grandfathers as Handel's Messiah is to me. Of course the cornermen were English; and I am bound to say that they seem to have earned their money faithfully, which is more than can be said for the mere betting men—real gentlemen, bent on getting money anyhow except by working for it.
>
> I have no illusions about pugilism or its professors. I advocate the placing of the laborer in such a position that a position in the ring will not be worth his acceptance, instead of, as it now is, a glorious and lucrative alternative (for a while) to drudgery and contempt. . . .

One could forgive Shaw for wondering why he had to bootleg a boxing column into his musical criticism, for his boxing novel itself had briefly caught on. Not entirely a misfire despite its rejections by all the established London publishers, *Cashel Byron's Profession* had been printed as padding in a socialist magazine in 1886 and then, from the magazine's plates, in awkwardly oversized book form. The thousand copies sold out, and the book was even pirated across the Atlantic. It remained alive thereafter, always to Shaw's professed surprise. "As long as I kept sending my novels to the publishers," he claimed, "they were as safe from publicity as they would have been in the fire. . . . But when I flung them aside as failures, they almost instantly began to show signs of life."

One of those evidences of life was the interest on the part of professional pugilists in playing Cashel Byron on the stage—an opportunity for ex-champions to milk their ring publicity. (Jack Burke and his wife would tour in vaudeville.) Competing versions of *Cashel Byron* turned up at New York theaters, one of them starring "Gentleman Jim" Corbett, who had been relieved of his heavyweight title by Bob Fitzsimmons in 1897 and failed to come back against James J. Jeffries in 1903.

According to one review, Corbett "had a dramatic go at Bernard Shaw last night and knocked Shaw out in three rounds." According to another, "The prize-fighter takes all the sting out of Shaw's cynicism." Obviously Shaw had to protect his English dramatic rights as well as his theatrical reputation, and he quickly constructed his own adaptation to head off American importations. Using Elizabethan blank verse, which he claimed was "childishly easy and expeditious," he burlesqued his own novel, retitling the new work, after the footman who also loved the lady, *The Admirable Bashville*.

"So cruel are all callings," claimed the verse Cashel, defending his occupation. Yet his gloved hand, he reminds the audience, "That many a two days bruise hath ruthless given," neither murdered animals for sport, nor kept men behind bars, nor robbed the poor. Behind the levity, the farce—like the novel—had the serious theme Shaw dramatized more seriously in the similarly titled *Mrs Warren's Profession* (1893) as well as in *Major Barbara* (1905), which Shaw once thought of calling, after its munitions potentate, "Andrew Undershaft's Profession." As he declared in 1901 in "A Note on Modern Prizefighting," "The word prostitute should either not be used at all, or applied impartially to all persons who do things for money that they would not do if they had any other assured means of livelihood." Yet the tradition of regulated violence at the heart of pugilism, so alien to Shaw in every other walk of life, magnetized him. His Ned Skene even talks of boxing as art and as science. Benny Green, in *Shaw's Champions*,[7] quickly dismisses the paradox by hypothesizing that "prizefighting, so far from being a contradiction in [Shaw's] life, was a highly promising if unexpected area in which to demonstrate the viability of the life force, the 'march onward and upward,' the triumph of mind over matter, the mystical belief in a benign biological force which was pushing ignoble Man towards Godhead despite himself." Shaw himself declared in his nineties that professional boxing "attracted me first on its economic side by the comedy of the contrast between the visionary prizefighter as romantic hero and the matter-of-fact trader in fistcuffs at certain weights and prices and odds." As for its amateur side, he explained, "There are . . . no sports which bring out the difference of character more dramatically than boxing, wrestling and fencing." Yet, whether staged for money or participated in as sport, it could not have escaped Shaw that boxing at bottom was unleashed aggression in the guise of drama.

Was the attraction what Shaw identified as the "protagonist spectacle" of a glove fight? Was it the macho image generated by the boxer? Cashel Byron's millionairess, Lydia Carew, is as transfixed by his Greek-god physique as is the acquisitive Epifania Ognisanti de Parerga of *The Millionairess* (1935), more than a half century later, by her husband-to-be Alastair Fitzfassenden. "I saw him win an amateur heavyweight championship," she confides. "He has a solar plexus punch that no other boxer can withstand." Besides, she says, "He stripped well, unlike many handsome men. I am not insusceptible to sex appeal, very far from it." But Fitzfassenden is not a success between the sheets. "All his ardor," sighs Epifania with disappointment, "was in his fists."

It is even possible that Shaw remembered, in Fitzfassenden's solar plexus punch so admired by his wife, as well as in his name, Bob Fitzsimmons, who had so felled Corbett. From ringside Mrs. Fitzsimmons had shouted, "Hit him in the slats, Bob!" The story made the papers; Shaw may have borrowed from it.

For years Shaw the playwright maintained only a peripheral interest in the affairs of professional or gentleman pugilists, but he could draw on the ring for metaphor when the occasion arose. After a bicycle crash with Bertrand Russell in 1895, in which he was hurt more seriously than he cared to confess, he wrote to Pakenham Beatty that he "got up within the prescribed ten seconds, but had subsequently to admit knock-out. . . ."[8] His continuing presence at ringside is unrecorded; however, in the third act of *Man and Superman* (1901–02), Mendoza, the brigand chieftain who waylays John Tanner's automobile in the Sierra Nevada, boasts to Tanner's chauffeur, "I come from a famous family of fighters; and . . . you would have as much chance against me as a perambulator against your motor car." Like his feisty namesake a Jew, Daniel Mendoza had been the great English prizefighter of the early nineteenth century. No punches are thrown in the scene, but there is a brief mill at the close of Shaw's next play, the one-act farce *How He Lied to Her Husband* (1904). Henry Apjohn, the youngest member of the *ménage à trois* which constitutes the cast, boasts, "Like all poets I have a passion for pugilism." But when eluding the rage of the jealous Teddy Bompas, he "*suddenly executes the feat known to pugilists as slipping,*" Apjohn falls backward over a stool and raises a lump on his head. Only the intervention of the adored Aurora Bompas leaves the fight a draw.

Shaw made an early talkie film of the farce in 1930, when he was seventy-four. As observer, he did not interfere with the director until the fight scene. "He was so disgusted with the laborious way in which I rose to my feet," Robert Harris, who played the lover, recalled, "that he jumped onto the set, threw himself down, and jumped up like a bouncing deer. Extraordinary performance, at his age. Made me ashamed of myself." Vera Lennox, who played the lady, remembered Shaw's peeling off his coat, "more or less slinging it at somebody. 'This is the way you go at it! You've got to—!' The old boy himself! Shaw was pounding out at Teddy Gwenn, and Teddy Gwenn was coming back with a wallop! Cecil [Lewis, the director] and I were having hysterics, laughing at them."

According to Shaw's secretary, Blanche Patch, who had visited the set with Shaw, Edmund Gwenn not only came back at Shaw but knocked him down. "You see," said Shaw, getting to his feet, "it's easy."[9]

When Shaw wrote *Overruled* (1912), another domestic farce, his quarrelsome quartet indulged in boxing talk but no illustrative action: the aggressive talk was a metaphor for English belligerence on a larger scale:

> JUNO. I tell you flatly if you say I did anything wrong you will have to fight me. In fact I think we ought to fight anyhow. I dont particularly want to; but I feel that England expects us to.
> GREGORY. I wont fight. If you beat me my wife would share my humiliation. If I beat you, she would sympathize with you and loathe me for my brutality.
> MRS LUNN. Not to mention that as we are human beings and not reindeer or barndoor fowl, if two men presumed to fight for us we couldnt decently ever speak to either of them again.

GREGORY. Besides, neither of us could beat the other, as we neither of us know how to fight. We should only blacken each other's eyes and make fools of ourselves.

JUNO. I dont admit that. Every Englishman can use his fists.

GREGORY. Youre an Englishman. Can you use yours?

JUNO. I presume so: I never tried.

MRS JUNO. You never told me you couldnt fight, Tops. I thought you were an accomplished boxer.

JUNO. My precious: I never gave you any ground for such a belief.

MRS JUNO. You always talked as if it were a matter of course. You spoke with the greatest contempt of men who didnt kick other men downstairs.

JUNO. Well, I cant kick Mr Lunn downstairs. We're on the ground floor.

Earlier, in 1905, the boxing talk had already become just talk. In the Salvation Army shelter scene of *Major Barbara*, the East End bully Bill Walker is confronted by the threat of the unseen Todger Fairmile, the Balls Pond boxer who has given up the National Sporting Club—"worth nigh a hundred a year to him"—for the consolation of religion. "He'll convert your head into a mashed potato," Bill is warned. But no on-stage action develops. Only in the 1938 film version does Shaw write Fairmile physically into the script,[10] to squash Bill Walker. Todger's big speech updates the play into the 1930s by referring to Welsh heavyweight Tommy Farr, who would give Joe Louis one of the great fights of his career. To a bystander's remark that the Salvation Army was easier than fighting, Fairmile responds with some vintage Shaw:

"No, my friend, it's not easier; but it's ever so much happier. And who told you that I have given up fighting? I was born a fighter; and, please God, I'll die a fighter. But the ring was too small for a champion like me. It was no satisfaction to me to knock out some poor fellow, or to get his shoulders down on the mat for a purse of money. It was too easy; and there was no future in it for either of us, though we were both facing eternity. One day I gave an exhibition spar for the benefit of charity. Our General was there; and I was introduced to her. She said I was a wonderful young man; and she asked me was I saved. "No" says I "but I can go fifteen rounds with Tommy Farr if youll put up the money." "Of course you can," she says. "God built you big enough for a trifle like that. But will you go, not fifteen rounds, but eternity, with the devil for no money at all? He is the champion the Army has to fight. Have you pluck enough for that?" I tried hard to make light of it; but it stuck; and a week after I took the count for the first time and joined up. And now I fight the devil all the time; and I'll say for him that he fights fairer and harder than some champions I have tackled. But God is against him. And in that sign we shall conquer. And now shall we have another hymn?"

By then, however, Shaw had long since renewed his interest in the squared circle. Ned Donnelly's gymnasium at 18 Panton Street, Haymarket, had vanished, and the art of fisticuffs was now big business and high drama. For that burgeoning audience, nearly twenty years before Todger Fairmile was fleshed out on the screen, Shaw had written "The Great Fight, by the author of *Cashel Byron's Profession*" for the *Nation* (December 13, 1919).

Perhaps because Arnold Bennett had agreed to report the Georges Carpentier-Joseph Beckett European heavyweight championship fight for the *New Statesman*, Shaw had been lured back to the ring. But whatever the reason, his interest rewakened and persisted, and he saw other contests and even reviewed the Carpentier-Dempsey and Dempsey-Tunney fights from the flickering black-and-white ringside of the Leicester Square Cinema.

Even in defeat, the stylish Carpentier became a hero figure for Shaw, who regularly referred to the Frenchman as a model of boxing élan, or at least did so until he met Jack Dempsey's conqueror, the sophisticated, almost scholarly James Joseph Eugene Tunney. As Benny Green puts it, "The prolonged exhibition spar between Gene Tunney and Bernard Shaw began in the late summer of 1928, when Tunney, having dispatched [Tom] Heeney and gone into sporting retirement, arrived in London. . . ." Among the forty dinner guests invited to meet him by Sir Harry Preston was G.B.S., but he was out of the country when Tunney arrived and sent his regrets in a note which was the opening round of a friendship which lasted into Shaw's last years.

Early in their acquaintance, the inevitable Cashel Byron intruded. Film producers saw Tunney as the screen's Corbett, and Shaw warned him of such "blind snatches at your publicity and mine by people who don't know the book. . . . There is not a single really likeable character in it: Cashel, though honest and super-competent professionally, is selfish and limited; the lady is a prig and a bluestocking. . . ." Then, one evening in 1929, Shaw recalled to Tunney, "I amused myself . . . by inventing quite an amusing boxing film for you; but it was a movie; and since then the advent of the talkies has upset everything. I could not produce genuine American dialogue. . . ." One might wish for a way to materialize that scenario.

In 1929 too, writer and ex-spy Robert Bruce Lockhart recalled seeing the elderly Shaw at an amateur boxing tournament (a fund-raising event for, of all things, day nurseries) at the Holborn Stadium. "Primo Carnera," Lockhart wrote in his diary for November 28, 1929, "was late in appearing, there being some fuss about his kit. Apparently, at the Stadium boxers must appear in full kit and not in drawers only. He boxed three amateurs. There was some good amateur boxing. George Bernard Shaw and Lady Lavery were there. G.B.S. was asked by Anne [Lady Islington] to give the prizes away. He refused and, as he left, someone hissed." The circumstances are obscure, but it was very likely Shaw's last appearance at an amateur boxing event.

But Shaw had not left boxing behind. The aged retired amateur and Tunney, the young retired professional, would meet when the logistics of their careers and holidays intersected and otherwise would exchange letters until the summer of 1948, when Shaw, at ninety-two, wrote Tunney about then-champion Joe Louis and closed, "I hold you in affectionate remembrance. I am damnably old and ought to be dead." The process of life imitating art had become complete, for Tunney was the boxer become gentleman, Cashel Byron come to life.

5 Bernard Shaw, Actor

"You're always acting," Charlotte Shaw complained regularly to her famous husband (his role: G.B.S., his synthesis of Shakespeare and Voltaire). It was Shaw's most successful and sustained characterization (witness its long run), yet it was not the only role he acted in his long lifetime. To a small degree his acting at one time had been of the on-stage variety.

A little of Shaw's firsthand knowledge of acting came as a result of his friendship with one of the earliest English Ibsen enthusiasts, the dark, clever Eleanor Marx. It was in the early 1880s, while he was attending his free university, the British Museum Reading Room. Eleanor, youngest daughter of Karl Marx, had become interested in Shaw when he announced his socialist sympathies; but before the Shavian charm (still unripe then) could exercise its spell, she was drawn to the brilliant, unscrupulous Dr. Edward Aveling, atheist, Marxist, swindler, and seducer, who was to be the chief model for the artist Dubedat in *The Doctor's Dilemma* (1906).

Shaw's playing opposite Eleanor, he recalled, occurred on the first floor of a lodging house in Bloomsbury, "when Miss Lord's translation of A Doll's House appeared in the eighteen-eighties, and so excited some of my Socialist friends that they got up a private reading of it in which I was cast for the part of Krogstad. . . . I had made a morally original study of a marriage myself [in the unsuccessful 1880 novel *The Irrational Knot*], and made it, too, without any melodramatic forgeries, spinal diseases and suicides, though I had to confess to a study of dipsomania. At all events, I chattered and ate caramels in the back drawing-room (our green-room) whilst Eleanor Marx, as Nora, brought Helmer to book at the other side of the folding doors."[1] It was that event which led Eric Bentley to proclaim that the "history of the modern [English] drama begins with Shaw the actor."

Eleanor Marx had long wanted a stage career. Although her histrionic talents were modest, Shaw thought he could play Pygmalion to her Galatea and had written, only a few years earlier, an unsalable novel, *Love Among the Artists* (1881), in which a crusty expert in elocution successfully trains an attractive young woman to speak and move like a lady and finally to act. Eleanor and G.B.S. had even acted together once before the historic Ibsen performance, in a Socialist League benefit production of a "comedy drama" by Palgrave Simpson and Herman Merivale, *Alone*, on January 30, 1885, at Ladbroke Hall in Notting

PART II

PIANOFORTE SOLO ... " Wanderstunden." ... ... *Heller*

KATHLEEN INA

◁ "ALONE" ▷

An original Comedy-Drama in Three Acts

By PALGRAVE SIMPSON and HERMANN MERIVALE

COLONEL CHALLICE	EDWARD AVELING
STRATTON STRAWLESS	...G. B. SHAW
BERTIE CAMERON	... PHILIP SYDNEY
DR. MICKLETHWAITE	J. HUNTER WATTS
MAUDE TREVOR	MAY MORRIS
MRS. THORNTON	ELEANOR MARX AVELING

REVOLUTIONARY SONG " The March of the Workers."
To the tune of "John Brown." Words by WILLIAM MORRIS
The audience are requested to join in the singing in unison.

Programme for the Socialist League production of *Alone*,
Ladbroke Hall, 30th January, 1885

Programme for the Socialist League production of *Alone*, which included Shaw as "Stratton Strawless," Ladbroke Hall, 30 January 1885. (Berg Collection, New York Public Library)

Hill. She and her "husband" (without benefit of clergy or registrar), the stage-struck Aveling, had teamed in a Tom Taylor melodrama the previous December 15. In *Alone* they were joined by three other actors, one of them Shaw, who played "Stratton Strawless." A benefit for a needy socialist veteran, Adam Weiler, the program included a reading by William Morris and a closing song by Morris, "The March of the Workers" (to the tune of "John Brown"), in the singing of which the audience was asked to join.

Also in the cast was William Morris's daughter May, who as "Maude Trevor" succeeded mainly in her ambition to be as close to Shaw as she could be, as often as possible, and with whom Shaw was—cautiously—in love. "I have not rehearsed a play with Miss Morris," Shaw explained to a mutual friend, "without some damage to my self possession. I do not love her—I have too much sense for such follies; but I hate and envy the detestable villain who plays her lover with all my soul. . . . Imagine learning live emotion—live thought—from dead matter—linen rag and printer's ink."[2]

The revelation that lines in a play script could move actors as well as audiences was a new one for Shaw, who had been struggling through the beginnings of his first play—*Widowers' Houses*—with William Archer, a collaboration which would end in futility with the play unfinished, for Shaw to complete seven years later. Since the production of *Alone* had been fun, Shaw continued to discuss theater (and other things) with Eleanor Marx on the many occasions he visited—usually when Aveling, whom he thoroughly disliked, was not home. On February 25, Shaw noted in his diary, "Mrs. Aveling asked me to call and have a chat. Went at five & stayed until 8 nearly. Aveling absent at Crystal Palace Concert. Urged her to go on the stage. Chatted about this, death, sex, & a lot of things."[3]

That May he discussed with Eleanor and Aveling the proposal to do *Nora*—as the Englished version of Ibsen's play was then called. A performance had just been attempted, so unsuccessfully that it might have finished Ibsen in England, by a student group at the School of Dramatic Art; even Archer, the Norwegian's chief missionary in London, felt that the production had proved Ibsen to belong to the *"theâtre impossible."*[4] Now the Avelings thought something had to be done to "make people understand our Ibsen." Thus in June Eleanor had written to Shaw to urge him to acquire May Morris as the other actress necessary for the performance—and, one may assume from her language, to promote Shaw's restrained courtship of May. "She was here yesterday," Eleanor wrote, "looking as sweet & as beautiful as the flower she is called after. It was like a breath of fresh air to look at her. . . ."

Shaw had apparently resisted the idea of playing Krogstad, the blackmailer, but Eleanor persisted.

> It is not in the least necessary that you should be sane to do that. Au contraire. The madder the better. . . . I wish some really *great* actors would try Ibsen. The more I study the greater I think him. How odd it is that people complain that his plays "have no end" but just leave you where you were, that he gives no *solution* to the problem he has set you! As if in life things "ended" off either comfortably or uncomfortably. We play through our little dramas, & comedies, & tragedies, & farces & then begin it all over again. If we *could* find solutions to the problems of our lives things would be easier in this weary world.[5]

The *Doll's House* production had taken place at the Aveling house on Great Russell Street, near the British Museum, on January 15, 1886. Eleanor and

Aveling played Nora and Helmer; Shaw played Krogstad; and May was Nora's confidant, Mrs. Linde. For the most part Shaw's few ventures on the stage would continue to be in amateur theatricals, as they were often included in the soirees of William Morris's Socialist League. In 1887 Morris sought out Shaw's talents for a larger audience, writing to May on September 21, "Shaw has consented to act in the 'Interlude.'" The "Interlude" was *The Tables Turned, or Nupkins Awakened*, a topical dramatic entertainment written by Morris and performed at the Farrington Road offices of the Socialist League—the top floor of a warehouse—on October 15 for the benefit of the *Commonweal*, the league's organ. The principal characters were Sir Peter Edlin, Lord Tennyson, and the Archbishop of Canterbury. Sir Peter, Shaw thought, "owed the compliment to his activity at that time in sending Socialists to prison on charges of 'obstruction,' which was always proved by getting a policeman to swear that if any passer-by or vehicle had wished to pass over the particular spot in a thoroughfare on which the speaker or his audience happened to be standing, their presence would have obstructed him. The contention, which was regarded as quite sensible and unanswerable by the newspapers of the day, was put into a nutshell in the course of Sir Peter's summing-up in the play. 'In fact, gentlemen, it is a matter of grave doubt whether we are not all of us continually committing this offense from our cradles to our graves.' This speech, which the real Sir Peter of course never made, though he certainly would have done so had he wit enough to see the absurdity of solemnly sending a man to prison for two months because another man could not walk through him—especially when it would have been so easy to lock him up for three on some respectable pretext—will probably keep Sir Peter's memory green when all his actual judicial utterances are forgotten."

At the last moment, Shaw begged off, although he was loyally present at the performance. Morris had wanted him to play the obstructionist defendant, but the part went by default to Halliday Sparling.[6] "It was a roaring farce, and a great success," Shaw recalled, adding that the applause was terrific when Morris entered in the garb of the archbishop. Unfortunately, the highly successful first night was witnessed by only one dramatic critic—Shaw's friend Archer, there on a busman's holiday.[7]

Less than a year earlier, Shaw had taken a holiday from the unpaid Fabian lecture platform to appear on another kind of platform in his first really public—but perhaps least known—stage performance. His name on the playbill provides the sole reason for the farce's claim to a vestige of literary immortality. This affair, fortunately only a single matinee performance, was a lark for Shaw, who good-naturedly turned actor for his friend Edward Rose, a mediocre actor and not nearly so good a playwright. (Of his thirty-five plays, many of them adaptations of novels, only *The Prisoner of Zenda*, in 1896, would be a hit, and Shaw as drama critic in the 1890s even panned a play by Rose, *Under the Red Robe*, a dramatization of a Stanley Weyman novel. Shaw preferred the novel.)

Odd: To Say the Least of It required a reading at Rose's house in Bedford Park, and a run-through at Toole's Theatre. For the performance on November 6, 1886, at the Novelty Theatre, Shaw remained home that morning preparing his role, "Chubb Dumbleton," and then went off to borrow a hat from Archer, hire a wig (at two shillings, sixpence) and purchase wig paste (sixpence). The acting venture would cost him even more. His diary notes that he tipped the dressing room lady a shilling. Acting would never be the road to riches for Shaw.

NOVELTY THEATRE

Great Queen Street, Lincoln's Inn Fields

Directors:

MESSRS. J. & H. NATHAN

On the 6th November, 1886
will be performed a Farcical Comedy
in three Acts, entitled

**ODD:
TO SAY THE LEAST OF IT!**

BY EDWARD ROSE

CHARACTERS

Fite

MR. CHARLES MYERS

Bodkin

MR. EDWARD ROSE

The Rev. Ambrose Bodkin

MR. C. P. COLNAGHI

Merewether Smalls

MR. HAROLD STAFFORD

Chubb Dumbleton

MR. G. BERNARD SHAW

Announcement of the production of *Odd: To Say the Least of It*, by Edward Rose, at the Novelty Theatre, 6 November 1886, with Shaw as "Chubb Dumbleton." (Humanities Research Center, University of Texas at Austin)

Early in 1888 he would appear on the boards again, but this time under the pseudonym of "I. Roscius Garrick" in a sketch by his poet friend Dolly Radford, *The Appointment.* A reading of the play took place at Morris's Kelmscott House, where at supper on February 12, after the reading, Shaw noted in his diary, "an Irishman named Yeats talked about Socialism a good deal." The talk was apparently interesting, for Shaw missed the last train back home, and he and Yeats walked back together. On February 25 the performance at 13 Farringdon Road—a benefit for the Socialist League Strike Committee—was held, and amateur photographer Shaw played a photographer, opposite May Morris, who used her own name. He was scheduled to play the role again on April 14, but his diary reads, "No. Go and see the performance." The program still listed "I. Roscius Garrick," but it was someone else.

Shaw's diary notes no further stab at acting until the afternoon of February 14, 1894, when he appeared in the copyright performance of actress Janet Achurch's *Mrs Daintry's Daughter* at Ladbrooke Hall in Notting Hill. Although Miss Achurch completed her play after Shaw had written *Mrs Warren's Profession*, the idea for it had come from her, and she had urged it on Shaw even though her own play had parallels in plot and could be hurt by the competition. As it was, *Mrs Warren's Profession* was banned by the Lord Chamberlain's Office as immoral and would not be seen formally for years, but the action did *Mrs Daintry's Daughter* little good. Its only production was the script-in-hand one in which Shaw loyally read three roles and then took the Underground back to a Fabian committee meeting and to work on an article for Frank Harris's *Fortnightly Review*.

Shaw next appeared on stage identified as "Cashel Byron" in a copyright performance of his own *The Devil's Disciple* on April 17, 1897. The theater, officially the Bijou but more popularly known as Victoria Hall, was opened early for a Saturday twelve o'clock curtain. Although copyright performances usually meant little more than going through the motions and reading the lines, an official program was printed, announcing that "Cashel Byron" appeared in the role of the Reverend Anthony Anderson. Cashel, the boxer hero of Shaw's jejune novel *Cashel Byron's Profession* (1882), was G. B. S. When the novel was dramatized a few years later as *The Admirable Bashville* (1901), Shaw, who produced the farce for the Stage Society, created a mild sensation when the Policeman (actually the young C. Aubrey Smith) appeared made up as the auburn-bearded G. B. S. The playwright was satirizing himself from the sidelines.

Shaw appeared in only one other copyright performance of record, and that in a play not his own. It was on January 28, 1908, at the Savoy Theatre, London, in Harley Granville Barker's political drama *Waste*. Shaw—the play's intellectual godfather—also may have had something to do with preparing the playbill, for it advertised him extravagantly as "late of the Theatre Royal, Dublin."[8] That year may have been his busiest as an actor, although his next (and probably last) real acting chore is a matter of some dispute. Archibald Henderson records that "in an emergency" Shaw played Joseph Wollaston, the beadle to the borough council, in his own play *Getting Married.* In at least two of the surviving photographs of the play Shaw appears in his beadle's costume, one opposite Fanny Brough, who played Mrs. George Collins, the mayoress. In Mander and Mitchenson's *Theatrical Companion to Shaw* (1955), however, his role is described as stand-in for the absent Albert Sims at photo call, where the beadle's physical presence was needed to complete the scene. At any rate, the

Shaw as the Beadle in *Fanny's First Play*.

photograph of the 1908 scene also survives, with G. B. S. looking like a Gilbert and Sullivan Lord Admiral in his beadle's uniform.

Although Shaw's recorded acting stints ended there, he continued to coach actors in interpreting his roles as if he had spent all his mature years on the stage instead of writing for it. As he wrote to Ellen Terry early in their long epistolary relationship, "Come, I will teach you the part without your opening the book once. I will get a tandem bicycle; and we shall ride along over the celestial plains, I dinning the part into your head until you pick it up as one picks up a tune by ear. That is how all parts should be taught and learnt: in my ideal company there shall not be an actress who can read. I once learnt a part (and actually played it too)—learnt it from the book. What galley slavery it was."[9] But the experience helped shape Shaw as a director of his own plays.

Lewis Casson, who as a young actor appeared in the cast of *John Bull's Other Island* (1904) in its first season at the Court Theatre, admired the "mastery" of Shaw's rehearsal methods. Sir Lewis commented, "I had no idea then how very little experience of direction he actually had. . . . He could not, at that time,

Shaw rehearsing Lillah McCarthy and Granville Barker in *Androcles and the Lion.*

have directed more than three or four productions, almost all for private performances. How did he manage it? First, I suppose, because good actors at once
recognize and respect a good actor (even if they dislike him, an impossibility in
this case), and Shaw was a mighty good actor. Whether he could have carried a
characterization through a whole evening, I don't know, but in giving a vivid
half-minute sketch of a character as a demonstration, I know few better. . . . In
later years, when it was wanted, Shaw could and did coach his actors. His combined technical training in music and public speaking enabled him always to
analyze how effects were got, and to pass on the knowledge of *how* as well as
why."[10]

From Shakespeare to Cibber to Coward, Osborne, and Pinter, playwrights,
both major and minor, have often been professional actors, the duality usually
being evident in the heightened stage sense of their dramas. However, Shaw's
minuscule career as an actor—a little-known aspect of a many-sided man of the
theater—belongs more to theatrical curiosa than to theater history. When Fred
Terry of the Royal Theatrical Fund wrote to him in 1932 about acting in a benefit performance, Shaw returned a copy of the script with, "Good Lord, my dear
Fred Terry, no no no no no no no no No. I know my place too well; and it is not,
alas! on the stage."[11]

6   Exploiting Art: Shaw in the Picture Galleries and the Picture Galleries in Shaw's Plays

In the days of Shaw's boyhood, when English painting was still suffering from the blight of the sentimental academic subject picture and Ireland lagged culturally at least a generation behind, the young Shaw could have been guaranteed a surfeit of such "story" paintings in Dublin. When he left for London at twenty, in 1876, the art which English galleries found profitable, despite the inroads of Pre-Raphaelitism, was much the same. An index of the situation was the fate of Whistler's "Mother"—the *Arrangement in Grey and Black, No. 1*, which had been exhibited in London in 1874 and, being unsold and unsalable, was immured most of the following eighteen months in pawn, until the government of France purchased it for the Luxembourg Museum, for living painters the "vestibule to the Louvre."

The later years of that portrait's purgatory were Shaw's years as an art critic in London. It was an unanticipated career. His friend William Archer, who was dramatic critic of the *World* in 1885, had found himself suddenly compelled to double as art critic. He invited Shaw to accompany him. London galleries and studios had long been familiar places. Shaw had already written two unpublished novels in which art played a major role—*Immaturity* and *Love Among the Artists*—in which the artists of some worth had been influenced by Pre-Raphaelitism and Whistler, while the Philistine painters believed in society portraits, anecdotal pictures, and making money. Wandering the galleries and offering comments as he went was not work to Shaw, who was surprised when Archer sent him a check for £1.6.8.—half the fee. Shaw returned it; Archer sent it back; Shaw then "re-returned" it on December 14, 1885, claiming that he had been under no "external compulsion" to go, while Archer had been under the orders of his editor, Edmund Yates.

"As it is," Shaw explained, "I have the advantage of seeing the galleries for nothing without the drudgery of writing the articles. I do not like to lose the record of the art life, and yet going to a gallery by myself bores me so much that I let the [Royal] Academy itself slip last year, and should have done so this year but for your bearing me thither. . . ."[1] Archer solved the problem. He persuaded Yates, pointing out that Shaw had done the work, to name his friend as art critic, a post Shaw held, often concurrently with half a dozen other responsibilities, from February 1886 until January 1890. One of the more short-lived of the parallel posts was that of arts critic for Annie Besant's socialist organ *Our Corner*, in which several of his stillborn novels were being resurrected in serial form as padding; by no coincidence, the first time Shaw produced an "Art Corner" column about art (rather than music or theater) was for the February 1886 issue. If he were doing the gallery beat for Yates, there was no reason why he could not provide a sampling for Mrs. Besant, who would permit him to propagandize more freely.

The better his uncommercial novels had become, the more they had turned away the conventional-minded professional readers at the publishing houses; but as a critic, he boasted, "I came to the top irresistibly, whilst contemporary well-schooled literary beginners, brought up in artless British homes, could make no such mark." As a result, he felt, his weekly columns "on all the fine arts in succession"—since he went on from art to music and theater—remained readable. He had a critical strategy, he claimed:

> I was capable of looking at a picture then, and, if it displeased me, immediately considering whether the figures formed a pyramid, so that, if they did not, I could prove the picture defective because the composition was wrong. And if I saw a picture of a man foreshortened at me in such a way that I could see nothing but the soles of his feet and his eyes looking out between his toes, I marveled at it and almost revered the painter, though veneration was at no time one of my strong points. . . . I can only thank my stars that my sense of what was real in works of art somehow did survive my burst of interest in irrelevant critical conventions and the pretensions of this or that technical method to be absolute.
>
> When I was more among pictures than I am at present, certain reforms in painting which I desired were advocated by the Impressionist party, and resisted by the Academic party. Until those reforms had been effectually wrought I fought for the Impressionists—backed up men who could not draw a nose differently from an elbow against Leighton and Bouguereau—did everything I could to make the public conscious of the ugly unreality of studio-lit landscape and the inanity of second-hand classicism. . . .
>
> I am always electioneering. . . . I make every notable performance an example of the want of them, knowing that in the long run these defects will seem as ridiculous as Monet has already made Bouguereau's backgrounds, or Ibsen the "poetical justice" of Tom Taylor. Never in my life have I penned an impartial criticism; and I hope I never may. As long as I have a want, I am necessarily partial to the fulfilment of that want, with a view to which I must strive with all my wit to infect everyone else with it.[2]

Shaw's refusal to take the commercial perspective quickly made him a target for dealers—not for bribes but for special flatteries. At his first appearance at an advance "Press View"—he was twenty-nine and unknown—a dealer described to him "rapturously" the extraordinary qualities of what were to the novice critic "half a dozen respectable but quite ordinary sketches in watercolor by an unknown painter." He listened and then said, "How can you talk such nonsense to me? You know better." As a result Shaw was confidentially escorted to a private room in which the dealer kept "a few real treasures by old masters: mostly primitives."

The dealer's chief rival had a more subtle method. He invited Shaw to see the latest work by a well-known painter and then pretended disgust with the popular taste in art which the work represented. "Oh!" he said, "you've come to see this. Here it is. Pish! It is what you people like; and we have to provide it for you. Now here," he suggested, pointing to an inconspicuously hung picture, "is a picture to my taste worth ten of it. But it means nothing to you: you wouldn't know the painter's name if I told it to you. Look at his handling! Look at that sky. But you gentlemen of the Press pass it by without a glance."

Of course, thought Shaw, some of the people from the press would want to prove their connoisseurship and would fall for the ploy by discovering the neglected genius, but he "had not the heart to spoil the old man's comedy by telling him so." Still, his refusal to be gulled meant that he had passed the test, and the tricks of the trade were not further employed on him but were directed instead at newsmen employed by editors "who were ignorant of art and impatient of the convention that obliged their papers to notice it. They sent their worst and wordiest reporters to the galleries, the theatre and the opera, reserving their best for political meetings and the criminal courts."[3] For Shaw the experience helped complete his education.

One of his earliest campaigns as a critic was fought in a war that had already ended. Pre-Raphaelite painting had already made an impact upon contemporary art and had itself either faded into commercialism or been transmuted into new conventions. Still, Shaw (to the end a follower of Ruskin) regularly praised Dante Gabriel Rossetti, who had died in 1882; but he tempered his appreciation of Rossetti's later work by noting that although he had dazzled with his "wealth of color [and] poetic conception,. . .our eyes are now used to the sun; and . . . Rossetti's want of thoroughness as a draughtsman, and the extent to which his favorite types of beauty at last began to reappear as mere . . . conventions, with impossible lips and mechanically designed eyebrows, came as something of a shock upon many who had previously fancied him almost flawless."[4] He also continued to admire the earlier art of Rossetti's confreres Millais, Hunt, and Burne-Jones, all of whom had long since done their best work. The sheer labor they evidenced, of which Ruskin would have approved, led Shaw—ever the social critic—into observing that intended didacticism often had an improving effect, if not the one which the artist may have intended. The Holman Hunt works he approved of in one of his earliest "In the Picture-Galleries" columns were,

> elaborated beyond the point at which elaboration ceases to be improvement in the eyes of the normal Londoner; but even he must admit the apparent solidity, the convincing power, and the vital glow of these pictures in comparison with the works which artists like M. Bouguereau manage to finish so highly in half as many months as Mr. Holman Hunt would spend years. The difference in the result is a tremendous practical rebuke to the doctrine of art for art's sake. Mr. Holman Hunt, the catalogue tells us (it is a mine of instruction and amusement, that catalogue), painted *The Hireling Shepherd* "in rebuke of the sectarian vanities and vital negligences of the nation." The seriousness of the painter's aim probably did not bring a single Sandemanian into the fold of the Established Church, or induce one woman of fashion to give up tight-lacing (the most familiar form of "vital negligence"); but it is the secret of the perseverance and conscientiousness which has made this small picture one of the most extraordinary units of a collection that does not contain one square inch of commonplace handiwork.

Spencer Stanhope, he wrote in the *World* in 1886, "has imitated Mr Burne-Jones quite long enough. If he would imitate Hogarth for a season or two, and then look out of the window and imitate Nature, we might gain some adequate return from his praiseworthy industry." Conscientious industry was not enough, nor imitation of Burne-Jones, although Edward Burne-Jones remained to Shaw the giant of his art-critic decade, with "the power to change the character of an entire exhibition by contributing or withholding his work." It was not that he was more technically gifted, Shaw thought, but that he had more imagination, while others who displayed similar wares in Bond Street were "venal, ambitious, time-serving and vulgar." The "least sincere pictures" he observed in one show were by Burne-Jones's son, Philip, "who seems to have abandoned any designs he may have entertained of doing serious work as a painter." (Similarly, as we shall see, Shaw did not let his awe of Robert Browning's poetry cloud over his doubts about young "Pen" Browning's skills with a brush.) Of the Pre-Raphaelite Brotherhood (P.R.B.) survivors he found least to admire in John Millais, who was making more money and producing less art than ever before. His *Forlorn*, Shaw thought, reviewing an 1888 exhibition, "ought surely to have been called *Abandoned*. She is an arrant pot-boiler as ever was painted: her upper lip dripping vermillion, and her ill-made flaunting theatrical red sleeves, are intolerable to contemplate."

Whistler, once a P.R.B. crony, years later was still on the outside, as uncommercial as ever; and if only as rebel and wit, he was bound to receive Shavian support. However, Shaw was not merely playing critical politics, for he even felt, from his own visual experience, that Whistler's artistic perceptions were easily validated. Writing in his "Art Corner" in March 1886, he observed, "That our foggy atmosphere often produces poetic landscapes in the midst of bricks and mortar will hardly be denied by anyone who has watched the network of bare twigs lacing the mist in Lincoln's-Inn-Fields." Yet Shaw praised Whistler's art while warning imitators against it, and when he felt that Whistler was showing work not up to his abilities, as in the cleverly mounted Dowdeswell show of Venice etchings in 1886, he hoped—with some skepticism—for more formidable future results:

> Mr. Whistler's Notes, Harmonies, and Nocturnes are arranged in brown and gold, in a brown and gold room, beneath a brown and gold velarium, in charge of a brown and gold porter. It cannot be said of Mr. Whistler, as of Mr. Sparkler's ideal mistress,* that he has no nonsense about him. He has the public about him; and he not only humours their nonsense, but keeps it in countenance by a dash of nonsensical eccentricity on his own part, and by not standing too stiffly on his dignity as an artist, which is saved finally by the fact that his "Notes" are well framed, well hung, well lighted, suitably set forth, and exquisitely right so far as they go, except a failure or two which he unblushingly amuses himself by exhibiting as gravely as he might his very masterpieces. The "Chelsea Fish Shop," the Hoxton street scene, the Dutch seaside sketch (No. 47), are a few out of many examples of accurate and methodical note-taking, which is just the reverse of what the rasher spectators suppose them to be. As Mr. Whistler presumably takes notes with a view to subsequent pictures, it is to be hoped that something will soon come of them.

To Shaw, Whistler was a great artist, but his genius did not give him license to thrust anything with his butterfly mark before the public. His portrait of Lady Colin Campbell, Shaw wrote sharply in the *World* (December 8, 1886), "being unfinished, has no business in the gallery." Admiring a John Singer Sargent work, he nevertheless refused to ignore what he felt was halfhearted effort displayed elsewhere. "Mr Sargent," he wrote (*World*, May 8, 1889), "who has put the Academy off with a couple of amusing slapdash caricatures of Mr Henschel

---

*Edmund Sparkler appears in Dickens's *Little Dorrit*.

and Mr Henry Irving, has given the New Gallery his *Lady Macbeth*, a superb portrait of Miss Ellen Terry, more like she, except in rare inspired moments, is like herself."

Shaw was never to be satisfied, as literary critic, art critic, music critic or theater critic, with the work of an artist who was performing at less than his potential. As he put it in a music column in 1890, "A criticism written without personal feeling is not worth reading. It is the capacity for making good or bad art a personal matter that makes a man a critic. The artist who accounts for my disparagement by alleging personal animosity on my part is quite right: when people do less than their best, and do that less at once badly and selfcomplacently, I hate them, loathe them, detest them, long to tear them limb from limb. . . ."

Finding himself once, in the *World*, speaking "contemptuously" of the "elderly school," he confessed as much and then went on to observe that it was "not a time to be just to it. Its principle of giving a precise pictorial account of what it knew to be before it, led it to paint a great deal that it did not see, and to omit a great deal that it did see. It is now getting a tremendous lesson from the men [of the impressionist school] who are trying to paint no more and no less than they see; and I am more disposed to help to rub that lesson in than to make untimely excuses for people who for many years outraged my taste for nature until I positively hated the sight of an ordinary picture." As a result, although he could not reconcile himself "to the occasional prevalence of a ghastly lilac-coloured fog," still, "looking at the more elderly British wall-ornaments," he found it hard "to admit that such airless, lightless, sunless crudities, coloured in the taste of a third-rate toymaker, and full of absurd shadows put in *a priori* as a matter of applied physics, could ever have seemed satisfactory pictures."

Shaw's concern, he wrote later in the *Sanity of Art* (1908), was that when "Whistler and his party" forced the dealers and art societies to exhibit their work, and by doing so, to accustom the public to tolerate, if not appreciate, what at first appeared to be absurdities, "the door was necessarily opened to real absurdities. Artists of doubtful or incomplete vocation find it difficult to draw or paint well; but it is easy for them to smudge paper or canvas so as to suggest a picture just as the stains on an old ceiling or the dark spots in a glowing coal-fire do. Plenty of rubbish of this kind was exhibited, and tolerated at the time when people could not see the difference between any daub in which there were aniline shadows and a landscape by Monet. Not that they thought the daub as good as the Monet: they thought the Monet as ridiculous as the daub; but they were afraid to say so. . . ."

Among the early impressionists, Claude Monet was a particular hero of Shaw's picture-gallery period, and he regularly attempted to separate the daubers from such new masters. "Impressionism, or the misfortune of having indefinite impressions, which can happily be cured by attentive observation and a suitable pair of spectacles," he wrote (*World*, April 28, 1886), "is responsible for Mr Sydney Starr's nebulous *St John's Wood*." The British gallerygoer, he cautioned, would find such pictures very different from the usual Bond Street fare and very uneven in quality, but "nobody with more than half an eye will need more than a glance . . . to convince him that Monet, his apparently extravagant violets and poppy reds notwithstanding, is one of the most vividly faithful landscapists living." Still, Shaw responded coolly to innovation which seemed to him not fraudulent but lacking range, much as he criticized Whistler for working on a small scale. "As to the 'New English Art' reformers," he wrote, "they are, for the most part, honest as well as adroit; but so far they lack the constructive imagination to make pictures out of their studies." He had his doubts as to where the newness would lead:

> These gentlemen are painting shortsightedly in more senses than one. The trick of drawing and colouring badly as if you did it on purpose is easily acquired; and the market will be swamped with "new English art", and the public tired of it, in a year or two. Then there will be a vain lamenting over lost ground to recover bad habits to correct, and association with unsaleability to be lived down. The "new" fashion may be capital fun for Mr. Whistler, Mr. Sargent, and a few others who can swim on any tide; but for the feebler folk it means at best a short life and a merry one.

"As to my line in criticism," Shaw wrote his first biographer, Archibald Henderson (July 15, 1905),

> the only controversial question up in my time was raised by the Impressionists, of whom, in England, Whistler was the chief. People accustomed to see the "good north light" of a St. John's Wood studio represented at exhibitions as sunlight in the open air were naturally amazed by the pictures of Monet. I backed up the Impressionists strongly; refused to call Whistler "Jimmy" instead of Mr. Whistler; boomed the Dutch school vigorously and tried to persuade the public that James*Maris was a great painter; stood up for Van Uhde not only in defence of his pictures of Christ surrounded by people in tall hats and frock coats, but also of his excellent painting of light in a dry crisp diffused way then quite unfashionable; and, on the whole, picked out my men and supported movements with fairly good judgment as far as subsequent events enable one to say. And of course I did not fall into the Philistine trap & talk "greenery yallery" nonsense about Burne Jones & the pre-Raphaelite school.

The artistic direction which Shaw saw as most fruitful was one to which he had been converted first by Ruskin and then by William Morris, who had put his theories of decorative art to use well beyond the fresco and the frame. There was important art needed in the world, Shaw was certain, that not only did not require brushes and an easel but could be effected by craftsmen who were more useful and more accomplished with other tools than the conventional ones:

> It has been for a long time past evident that first step towards making our picture-galleries endurable is to get rid of the pictures—the detestable pictures—the silly British pictures, the vicious foreign pictures, the venal popular pictures, the pigheaded academic pictures, signboards all of them of the wasted talent and perverted ambition of men who might have been passably useful as architects, engineers, potters, cabinet-makers, smiths, or bookbinders. But there comes an end to all things; and perhaps the beginning of the end of the easel-picture despotism is the appearance in the New Gallery of the handicraftsman with his pots and pans, textiles and fictiles, and things in general that have some other use than to hang on a nail and collect bacteria. Here, for instance, is Mr. Cobden Sanderson, a gentleman of artistic instincts. Does Mr. Cobden Sanderson paint wooden portraits of his female relatives, and label them Juliet or Ophelia, according to the colour of their hair? No: he binds books, and makes them pleasant to look at, pleasant to handle, pleasant to open and shut, pleasant to possess, and as much of a delight as the outside of a book can be. Among the books he has bound are illuminated manuscripts written by William Morris. . . . The smaller unbound pages in the same case show better what Mr. Morris can do with his valuable time in his serious moments,

---

*Shaw's slip of the pen for Dutch landscape painter Jacob Maris (1837–99).

when he is not diverting himself with wall-decoration, epic story-telling, revolutionary journalism and oratory, fishing and other frivolities of genius. From his
factory he sends specimens of the familiar wall-papers and carpets; but the
highest point in a decorative manufacture is reached in his "arras" tapestries,
and in a magical piece of stained glass. . . .

What Shaw was then preaching with missionary zeal has now become a fact
of the art marketplace. One would not expect him to be anything less than
Shavian in his art columns, and they do not disappoint, as several extracts have
already shown. In a May 1886 "Art Corner" he noted a new piece of commercial
art by Millais, *Ruddier Than the Cherry*, "representing a ragged flower girl in
whose cheeks rosiness is complicated by sunburn, and who is likely to prove
more interesting to the dealers than to knowers of pictures." In the *World* in
1887 he reported that William Stott of Oldham "exhibits a nymph; and she,
basking in the sun on a couch formed by her own red hair, exhibits herself freely
and not gracefully. The red hair is ill painted." In another "Art Corner"—in
perhaps his strongest condemnation of establishment art—he brought up the
"painful subject" that "During the past month Art has suffered an usually severe blow at the hands of the Royal Academy by the opening of the [Academy's]
annual exhibition at Burlington House." And in the *World* he noted that Harry
Quilter (*The Times*'s critic, who was equally mediocre as an artist) was "pro-
gressing in his studies as a landscape painter." Unafraid of other critics, he was
equally unintimidated by the galleries which disapproved of his honesty. When
he had condemned the annual photography show in Pall Mall for its gold medals
"stuck on the most fraudulent examples of retouching or picture-faking," his
"public spirit," he confessed (*World*, October 9, 1889), cost him, all told, "a capital sum of thirty shillings, through the cutting off of my invitations to the press
views. I now perforce pay at the turnstile, and buy my catalogue like any ordinary unit of the mob; but when I look around and see the reformation I have
wrought, I bear my chastening stoically, and even laugh a little in my sleeve."

As season followed season, Shaw continued to turn out his weekly columns on
art, at the same time writing book reviews for the *Pall Mall Gazette*, music reviews for the *Dramatic Review*, and political and economic journalism for myriad radical publications in London. By early 1889, his music columns, now
written for the *Star* under the playful *nom de plume* of "Corno di Bassetto,"
were undermining his loyalties to the galleries. Winding down his columns on
art for the *World*, he wrote in the issue of October 23, 1889, "I cannot guarantee
my very favourable impression of the Hanover Gallery as I only saw it by gas-
light. That was the fault of Sarasate, who played the Ancient Mariner with me.
He fixed me with his violin on my way to Bond Street, and though, like the
wedding guest, I tried my best, I could not choose but hear." The concert hall
had won out.

To Archibald Henderson he explained (July 15, 1905) that once he took to
music criticism, he began to examine whether the "very hard work of plodding
through all the picture exhibitions" was worth continuing. Counting his
printed paragraphs, for which he received fivepence a line, he discovered that he
had been earning less than forty pounds a year for columns he felt were worth
two hundred. Edmund Yates professed to be as staggered by the revelation as
Shaw had been and proposed that Lady Colin Campbell, who wrote a "Woman's
Walks" column, share the duties, with Shaw taking the major shows at a higher
fee plus a £52 annual retainer. Instead Shaw used the opportunity to relinquish

the entire responsibility. He claimed that he was too busy, and it was true, although he always found time for what he wanted to do. He was delivering lectures two or three times a week for such organizations as the West London Social and Political Reform Association, the Plumstead Radical Club, the Finsbury Radical Club, the Fabian Society, the Socialist League, the Upper Chelsea Institute, the Chiswick Liberal Club, and the South Place Religious Society. And he was already trying his hand at playwriting, beginning and then discarding or putting aside a number of experiments for the stage.

Yet Shaw's final withdrawal as art critic (he had needed the income and hung on) did not occur until 1890. First he applied unsuccessfully to become art critic for a new journal about to begin publication that January, the *Speaker*. Then he signed on with Henry Labouchere's feisty *Truth* to write art criticism with his left hand while doing music columns elsewhere. When, however, Labouchere's editor, Horace Voules, insisted that Shaw admire the painting of Frederick Goodall, a Royal Academician whose work he thought mediocre, Shaw wrote a friend (May 16, 1890) that his "connection with the paper may not survive the language I have used in consequence." It was the end of G.B.S. the art critic in the sense of a regular commitment to a column. He did write an article on the next Academy show (April 1891) for the *Observer*, then as well as now a Sunday paper, but it appeared "with profuse interpolations" and unsigned on May 3, 1891. Shaw quickly resigned. The editor, not understanding art, had given it to the proprietor, who (Shaw wrote his friend Emery Walker on May 7, 1891) "proceeded to mutilate it, interpolate scraps of insufferable private view smalltalk, break it into paragraphs in the wrong places, season it with obvious little puffs of his private friends, and generally reduce its commercial value (not to speak of its artistic value) about 1800%. If you look at the article you will see at a glance the broken fragments of Shaw sticking ridiculously in the proprietary mud."

Despite his claim that he immediately gave up going to the picture galleries, his diaries in the 1890's are full of references to press views and private views, and as late as December 1893 he was still helping his successor on the *World*, Lady Colin Campbell, by writing notices for her while she was away from London. Even as late as March 13, 1897, one of his theater columns for the *Saturday Review* is titled with the names of two artists and a playwright: "Madox Brown, Watts, and Ibsen." Art was still a point of reference.

Although painting had palled for him, Shaw's on-the-job art education would prove to be useful for him as a working playwright in ways he could never have anticipated. The experience had also convinced him of the effectiveness of art as an instrument of culture, a subject he wrote about explicitly in the influential *The Sanity of Art* and in prefaces to *Misalliance* and *Back to Methuselah* and implicitly wherever he put his pen to paper. "We all grow stupid and mad," he concluded in the *Misalliance* preface, "to just the extent to which we have not been artistically educated." Earlier, in *The Sanity of Art*, still under the powerful influences of Ruskin and Morris, he had made as wide-ranging a claim for the importance of art in human life as he ever enunciated:

> The claim of art to our respect must stand or fall with the validity of its pretension to cultivate and refine our senses and faculties until seeing, hearing, feeling, smelling, and tasting become highly conscious and critical acts with us, protesting vehemently against ugliness, noise, discordant speech, frowsy clothing, and foul air, and taking keen interest and pleasure in beauty, in music, and in the open air, besides making us insist, as necessary for comfort and de-

cency, on clean, wholesome, handsome fabrics to wear, and utensils of fine material and elegant workmanship to handle. Further, art should refine our sense of character and conduct, of justice and sympathy, greatly heightening our self-knowledge, self-control, precision of action, and considerateness, and making us intolerant of baseness, cruelty, injustice, and intellectual superficiality or vulgarity. The worthy artist or craftsman is he who responds to this cultivation of the physical and moral senses by feeding them with pictures, musical compositions, pleasant houses and gardens, good clothes and fine implements, poems, fictions, essays, and dramas which call the heightened senses and ennobled faculties into pleasurable activity. The great artist is he who goes a step beyond the demand, and, by supplying works of a higher beauty and a higher interest than have yet been perceived, succeeds, after a brief struggle with its strangeness, in adding this fresh extension of sense to the heritage of the race. This is why we value art; this is why we feel that the iconoclast and the Puritan are attacking something made holier, by solid usefulness, than their own theories of purity. . . .

Shaw's early dramatic settings could not help but be influenced, even when he intended to use a scene ironically, by what English eyes were accustomed to encountering in art. One can visualize what Shaw himself saw, as he tramped through Bond Street and Burlington House and the art clubs and societies in the 1890's, in his earliest plays. In the final stage directions in *Candida* (1894), for example, young Marchbanks, spurned, turns to Candida and her husband for the last time, and "*She takes his face in her hands; and as he divines her intention and falls on his knees, she kisses his forehead.*" In his tableau Shaw was parodying the sentimental Victorian anecdote in painting, although his first audiences, aware only of the artistic genre, took it straight. (In *The Devil's Disciple*, the first act includes a reading of the will—an obvious grouping of people for a Royal Academy set piece, and in fact a painting of that name by David Wilkie was famous.) In the last act, the scene of Dick Dudgeon mounting the scaffold owes much, as Shaw freely confessed, to dramatizations of Dickens's *A Tale of Two Cities* but perhaps even more to Frederick Barnard's popular painting *Sydney Carton*. "*A Tale of Two Cities*," exhibited at the Royal Academy in 1882 and much reproduced.[5] "Mr. Fred Barnard's studies from Thackeray," Shaw once noted in the *World* (July 6, 1887), "are by no means so happy as his Dickens pictures."

When Vivie Warren, in *Mrs Warren's Profession*, draws aside the curtains of her window and proclaims, "What a beautiful night!" Shaw's stage directions add, "*The landscape is seen bathed in the radiance of the harvest moon rising over Blackdown.*" It may be no coincidence that Frederick Leighton's *Summer Moon*—which fits the description—was exhibited in London shortly before Shaw wrote the play. The New England Puritan interiors of *The Devil's Disciple* suggest Dutch genre painting, although no special subject can be pointed to. Rather, a Shaw letter to the actor Ian Robertson complains that classic actor Johnston Forbes-Robertson (Ian's distinguished brother) would become interested in the play only after asking "whether I could not alter the last act . . . so as to make it like a Delaroche picture."[6] Shaw sometimes conceived his plays in painterly images. Paul Delaroche had produced smoothly finished, sentimental depictions of historical scenes, engravings of which decorated thousands of English parlors. *The Devil's Disciple* had been written to expose the fraud rather than to perpetrate it. Yet Shaw's painterly images were not necessarily ironic. Putting the case for realistic theater in a *Saturday Review* column (July 17, 1897), he declared, "The most advanced audiences today, taught by Wagner

Frederick Barnard, *Sydney Carton, "A Tale of Two Cities,"* from *A Series of Character Sketches from Dickens*. (British Library, London)

and Ibsen (not to mention Ford Madox Brown), cannot stand the drop back into decoration after the moment of earnest life. They want realistic drama of complete brainy, passional texture all through, and will not have any pictorial stuff or roulade at all. . . . " He intended to provide the intellectual realism.

G.B.S. always did his homework before writing a scene, even researching American Civil War memoirs as preparation for a play in which war would play a part, *Arms and the Man*. He was thus quick to respond (April 23, 1894) to his critic friend William Archer, who reviewed the play unfavorably, "Do you think war is any less terrible & heroic in its reality—on its seamy side, as you would say—than it is in the visions of Raina & of the critics who know it from the engravings of Elizabeth Thompson's pictures in the Regent St. shop windows?" Elizabeth Thompson (Lady Butler) was famous for her obsessively detailed paintings of British feats of arms during the Napoleonic and Crimean wars: Shaw's play was at least in part a response to her sentimental pictures, one of which, *The Roll Call* (1874), was purchased by Queen Victoria. But there were certainly others Shaw had in mind, as well, as he suggests in the opening stage directions of the later *Man of Destiny* (1895), in which he describes Napoleon as having been *"trained in the artillery under the old regime. . . . Cannonading is his technical specialty . . . dignifying war with the noise and smoke of cannon, as depicted in all military portraits."* The romanticizers of war were only slightly less numerous than its casualties.

Lady Butler's best-known works received wide and continuing distribution in the form of engravings, as Shaw observed, and several of these suggest some of Captain Bluntschli's lines in *Arms and the Man*, in particular *Scotland Forever!* (1881), with its dramatic canvas of cavalrymen charging headlong at the viewer, flank to flank. Describing a cavalry charge to the wide-eyed Raina, Bluntschli cynically pictures it as "slinging a handful of peas against a window pane" and then notes that one can tell the young horsemen "by their wildness and slashing. The old ones come bunched up under the number one guard: they know that they are mere projectiles. . . . Their wounds are mostly broken knees, from the horses cannoning together." But Raina's beloved, the blustering Major Saranoff, out of "sheer ignorance of war," according to Bluntschli, charges "like an operatic tenor," and one can see the operatic—or romantic—idealization of cavalry charges in the colorful, crowded canvases of Lady Butler. One can even wonder, since *Arms and the Man* is set in Bulgaria, during a real war with Serbia which occured there in the 1880s what Shaw might have remembered from "some melodramic Servian incidents by M. Joanowits," now forgotten, which he saw at McLean's Gallery and noted in his "Art Corner" in May 1886.

Sometimes in Shavian drama a painting seems displayed perfunctorily, as in Dr. Paramore's reception room in *The Philanderer* (written in 1893), where a framed reproduction of Rembrandt's *The Anatomy Lesson* is hanging on the wall above a cabinet containing "anatomical preparations." It is the obvious work for the location. But later in the scene Leonard Charteris *"strolls across to the cabinet, and pretends to study the Rembrandt . . . so as to be as far out of Julia's reach as possible."* As the dialogue develops, he is *"still contemplating Rembrandt."* The picture has no more than its obvious relationship to a physician's office, but it is there to provide the philanderer of the play with something innocuous upon which to temporarily fix his attention. Seldom is a work of art put into a Shaw play for only such mechanical purposes.

Candida was a much more complex response to art. Shaw called it his "modern Pre-Raphaelite play" and intended it on one of its many levels as an analogue to medieval religious painting. Even its curious subtitle, "A Mystery," suggests medieval associations. In the sitting room of the comfortable London parsonage in which the play is set, a single picture is seen on the wall, described in Shaw's opening stage directions as *"a large autotype of the chief figure in Titian's Assumption of the Virgin"* (the upper half, showing Mary ascending into the clouds). In the original manuscript Shaw had described, instead, a reproduction of Raphael's *Sistine Madonna* ("a large photograph of the Madonna di San Sisto")[7] over the mantel, but he substituted the Titian afterward, possibly because there was in it no distracting babe in arms. But *Candida*, he wanted to make plain by a recognizable work of art, was an ironic Shavian mystery play about Madonna and Child, with the heroine of the title the Holy Mother. At Candida's first entrance, Shaw's stage directions comment, *"A wise-hearted observer, looking at her, would at once guess that whoever had placed the Assumption of the Virgin over her hearth did so because he fancied some spiritual resemblance between them, and yet would not suspect either her husband or herself of any such idea, or indeed of any concern with the art of Titian."* For Candida's philistine father, Burgess, it is "a high class fust rate of work of ort," but the reproduction is the gift of the eighteen-year-old Eugene Marchbanks, the sensitive and emotional young poet whom the Reverend James Morell and his wife have befriended. The resemblance he perceives will vanish through the play, and with it his idealism.

In letters to Ellen Terry, Shaw confided that Candida was "the Virgin Mother and nobody else" and that he had written "THE Mother Play." To Janet Achurch, for whom he had written it, he suggested that she make herself up for the role by recourse to examples in art, having been horrified by the idea that she would play his Madonna in frizzed, bleached-blond hair. "Send to a photograph shop," he urged, "for a picture of some Roman bust—say that of Julia, daughter of Augustus and wife of Agrippa, for the Uffizi in Florence—and take that as your model, or rather as your point of departure. You must part your hair in the middle, and be sweet, sensible, comely, dignified, and Madonna like. If you condescend to the vulgarity of being a pretty woman, much less a flashy one . . . you are lost."[8] What he wanted emphasized to desensationalize the situation was "dignity," and he found his guide to it, as he had found his initial inspiration, in Italy, having spent a few weeks in Florence in the autumn of 1894, where (as he wrote in his Preface to *Plays, Pleasant*) he occupied himself "with the religious art of the middle ages." He had hurried back from an earlier Italian visit to fulfil a music-criticism assignment in Birmingham and had discovered there that a "very remarkable collection of the works of our British 'pre-Raphaelite' painters were on view. I looked at these, and then went into Birmingham churches to see the windows of William Morris and Burne-Jones. . . . When my subsequent visit to Italy found me practising the playwright's craft, the time was ripe for a modern pre-Raphaelite play." That his 1927 recollection to Ashley Dukes was completely accurate can be seen in the letter he wrote to Florence Farr, then his mistress, from Birmingham (October 7, 1891), after seeing Rossetti's beatific, Italianate women. "This is to certify," he wrote effusively, "that you are my best and dearest love, the regenerator of my heart, the holiest joy of my soul, my treasure, my salvation, my rest, my reward . . . my secret glimpse of heaven, my angel of the Annunciation, not yet herself

Titian's *Assumption of the Virgin* [central figure, inset], Church of Santa Maria dei Frari, Venice.

awake, but rousing me from a long sleep with the beat of her unconscious wings, and shining upon me with her beautiful eyes that are still blind." The enraptured Eugene Marchbanks would not do better in Shaw's 1894 play.

Observing that his feminine lead was a composite of influences from art, Shaw suggested to Dukes that Titian's *Assumption of the Virgin* in the Accademia in Venice and Correggio's less famous Virgin in the dome of the cathedral at Parma had been "boiled down into cockney Candida."[9] By then he had forgotten the Madonnas of Raphael, Murillo, and others he had seen in Italy and the special effort he made in July 1894 to see the *Madonna* of Hans Holbein in Darmstadt; but no matter, the point was clear.

Ellen Terry had wanted to play Candida, but Shaw offered her as consolation prize a role for an even more mature woman. When Lady Cicely Waynflete in *Captain Brassbound's Conversion* failed at first to interest her, Shaw appealed: "I try to shew you fearing nobody and managing them all. . . . Here then is your portrait painted on a map of the world—and you prefer Sargent's Lady Macbeth!"[10] He persuaded, as he wrote, in images from art. But it took a half-dozen more years and a dearth of alternative roles before Ellen Terry played Lady Cicely.

Shaw's fascination with the Virgin figure failed to be satisfied by the completion of *Candida* or even by the creation of the more matronly and asexual (yet

The Assumption of the Virgin, full panel.

still attractively marriageable) Lady Cicely. Later he found a Virgin figure at the Reims cathedral that impressed him so much that he "intended some day to put [her, too] in a play."[11] But he did not, although he did not forget her, writing of Reims in the preface (1919) to *Heartbreak House* that "no actress could rival its Virgin in beauty." No play thereafter suggests what he might have done.*

---

*Even before Shaw's playwriting career began in earnest—and even before he had written the earliest of his jejune novels—he had toyed with a Passion play and had written several scenes of one in blank verse. The 1878 script suggests the setting and allegedly irreverent realism of John Millais's early and once-controversial Pre-Raphaelite painting of the Holy Family, *Christ in the House of His Parents* (1850), which remained well known in Shaw's early years in London.

John Millais, *Christ in the House of His Parents*, which was possibly in Shaw's mind when he wrote his unfinished youthful *Passion Play.*

The extent of artistic influence on Shaw's Napoleonic drama *The Man of Destiny* (written August–September 1895) seems considerable from the first page of the play, which observes how melodramatic military portraits give a spurious dignity to war. The short play depicts a very young Napoleon, a twenty-six year-old who had barely begun the dazzling military campaigns which were to establish his fame and power. Most artistic portrayals of Napoleon represent the later triumphs, after the young general had become *"l'Empereur."* However, Shaw reminds the reader in his first stage directions that these *"Napoleonic pictures of Delaroche and Meissonier"* were yet to be produced at the early point in the general's career which the play dramatizes. He was recalling such well-known paintings as Meissonier's *Napoleon in 1814* (1863) and *Campaign of France* (1864) and Delaroche's *Napoleon at Fontainebleau* (1845), *Napoleon Crossing the Alps* (1848), and *Napoleon at Saint Helena* (1852). All were exhibited in London shortly after they were first painted and in subsequent retrospective exhibitions, and three of them were owned by private British collectors in Shaw's time. They were also widely reproduced in England during the late 1880s, for Delaroche and Meissonier were highly esteemed artists during the nineteenth century, and Napoleon was a popular artistic subject. It is likely that Shaw had firsthand knowledge of such *"Napoleonic pictures."*

Of the period of Napoleon's life which Shaw depicts in *Man of Destiny*, few artistic works were accessible to him. One work exists, however, which may have touched off the very episode Shaw invents; although there is no evidence that Shaw saw it or a reproduction, he well might have. The opening stage directions read, *"The twelfth of May, 1796, in north Italy, at Tavazzano, on the road from Lodi to Milan. . . . Two days before, at Lodi, the Austrians tried to prevent the French from crossing the river by the narrow bridge there; but . . . Napoleon Bonaparte, who does not respect the rules of war, rushed the fireswept bridge, supported by a tremendous cannonade. . . ."* The Milanese Andrea Appiani's *Napoleon after the Battle of Lodi* (c.1797), commissioned by the victor himself

Appiani's *Napoleon after the Battle of Lodi* (original in the collection of the Earl of Rosebery; reproduction from National Galleries of Scotland).

and well known thereafter from engravings, shows that very Napoleon, unsheathed sword in hand and the gunfire-raked bridge at Lodi in the background. And did the attractive and allegorical young woman in the foreground who appears to be the Muse of History, inscribing the event for posterity on a golden plaque, provide the inspiration for the young woman who confronts Napoleon in the play? We can only guess.

The opening scene of *The Man of Destiny*, which reveals Napoleon, immersed in his work, seated at a table littered with writing materials and dishes, may itself have been partially inspired by a painting by the Parisian historical artist François Flameng. This untitled work, completed some time between 1875 and

1885, portrays a youthful, long-haired Napoleon who also works at a table cluttered with books and papers. His discarded boots lie in a heap on the floor, and his jacket hangs on a peg behind him, as in the play the young Napoleon's hat, sword, and riding whip are *"lying on the couch."* The similarities between Flameng's picture and Shaw's opening scene are striking, and it is no surprise to find that Shaw's diary for March 31, 1894—little more than a year before he began the play—notes the opening of a show of Flameng's "Napoleon pictures" at the Goupil Gallery. Shaw missed the opening, having to review a concert at the Crystal Palace, but it is clear from *The Man of Destiny* that he was at the Goupil later and remembered what he saw.

The Shavian play in which critics have begun to explore the impact of the visual arts is *Caesar and Cleopatra*, written in 1898. As he insisted to his German translator Siegfried Trebitsch, in sending him some crude sketches for the play:

> Barbarous as my drawings of the scenery are, a great deal depends on them. Even an ordinary modern play like Es Lebe das Leben, with drawingroom scenes throughout, depends a good deal on the author writing his dialogue with a clear plan of stage action in his head; but in a play like Caesar it is absolutely necessary: the staging is just as much a part of the play as the dialogue. It will not do to let a scenepainter & a sculptor loose on the play without a specification of the conditions with which their scenery must comply. Will you therefore tell the Neues manager that we will supply sketches. I will not inflict my own draughtsmanship on him; but I will engage a capable artist to make presentable pictures.[12]

Shaw was taking no chances. Ancient Egypt had tremendous appeal for a pre-cinematic, Bible-familiar public, and cheap color lithographs were a popular commodity. Society painter Edward Poynter (later President of the Royal Academy) even achieved his first successes with enormous scenes from the times of the pharaohs, with one crowded and carefully researched ten-foot panorama, *Israel in Egypt* (1867), being typical of the genre. There was no end to Victorian visual opportunities for exposure to pre-Cleopatra Egypt.

At least two paintings seem to have inspired specific Shavian scenes. Martin Meisel points to Luc Olivier Merson's 1879 painting *Répos en Egypte*, citing a Shaw letter to Hesketh Pearson in 1918 which establishes the source of the famous tableau.

> The Sphinx scene was suggested by a French painter of the Flight Into Egypt. I never can remember the painter's name, but the engraving, which I saw in a shop window when I was a boy, of the Virgin and child asleep in the lap of a colossal Sphinx staring over a desert, so intensely still that the smoke of Joseph's fire close by went straight up like a stick, remained in the rummage basket of my memory for thirty years before I took it out and exploited it on the stage.

The "relevance of the new god in the arms of the old" is implicit in the scene, whether or not the influence of the Merson painting is known, but the suggestive relevance is more than a matter of scenery, for knowledge of the artistic source of the scene opens up a new avenue of interpretation. Shaw places Caesar in the Sphinx's lap, the position occupied by Christ and the Virgin in the Merson painting. Thus, as Meisel suggests, Caesar "explicitly equates himself with his successor, the unborn Christ."[13] Likewise, the young and barely nubile Cleopatra is equated with the Virgin, already a familiar figure in Shaw.

The so-called "rug scene" in Act III of *Caesar and Cleopatra*, in which Cleopa-

Luc Olivier Merson's *Répos en Egypte* (Museum of Fine Arts, Boston. Bequest of George Golding Kennedy).

tra, wrapped in a rug, is delivered to Caesar, has also been traced to a painting. The incident itself is described in Plutarch's life of Caesar, but as George W. Whiting asserts, Jean-Léon Gérôme's painting *Cleopatre Apportée à Caesar dans un Tapis* (1866) may have influenced Shaw's rendering of the scene.[14] The picture focuses upon a more mature and nubile Cleopatra than Shaw's child-woman, standing amid the folds of the carpet from which she has just emerged and turning toward Caesar, who is seated at a table. An apprehensive Apollodorus (having just unwound the rug) kneels behind her, and several male Romans in the background look on curiously. Gérôme's Caesar is younger and less bald than Shaw's or history's; also, the details differ from Shaw's exterior conception of the scene. However, Gérôme's conception is one of its rare evocations in art, and Shaw declared in a letter to Trebitsch (December 15, 1898) that his handling of the incident would give considerable pause to the French painters who were so fond of her.

As with the rug episode, Shaw's apparent familiarity with Gérôme's work emanated not from exhibitions but from reproductions, for the artist often sold his paintings directly to an American patron with only the most brief opportunities for the canvases to be seen before shipment. But Gérôme had prudently married Marie Goupil, the daughter of an influential art dealer and publisher, and benefited enormously from the worldwide distribution of Goupil photogravures of his paintings, which although in black and white emphasized their wealth of archeological detail. Through Goupil and other reproductions, Shaw may have seen not only several Gérôme-depicted Caesars and Cleopatras but also Roman gladiator and martyr scenes which could have enriched his background information for *Androcles and the Lion* (1913). Unquestionably the most important source for the dramatization of the fable was the familiar Victorian Christmas pantomime; however, Gérôme had painted the popular and widely reproduced *The Gladiators* (1874) and *Ave Caesar, Morituri Te Salutant* (1859), both of which depicted, from the perspective of the Coliseum floor, gladiators looking up from the arena toward the audience. Perhaps more importantly, Gérôme had also painted, in muted colors, *The Christian Martyrs' Last Prayer* (1883), showing a noble lion moving slowly across the arena of the Circus Maximus toward a group of huddled, ragged Christians. It became one of

Gérôme, *Cleopatra apportée à Caesar dans un tapis*. From the lithograph.

Gérôme's best-known works in reproduction, communicating an electric tension even in black and white.

Gérôme's Caesar was not Shaw's. If Shaw borrowed Caesar's physical appearance from an artistic representation, it is most likely that he was influenced by one of the hundreds of busts of the great conqueror which exist in collections throughout Europe. The most probable sculptured model for Shaw's middle-aged, "rather thin and stringy," balding Caesar is a life-sized white marble head and neck of Caesar acquired in 1818 by the British Museum. There is no doubt that Shaw was familiar with this bust, for he was one of the museum's most frequent visitors. The marble head, considered to be contemporary with Caesar, was the most widely known Caesar bust in Shaw's time. T. Rice Holmes, in *Caesar's Conquest of Gaul*, describing it, observes,

Gérôme's *Christian Martyrs—The Last Prayer* (Walters Art Gallery, Baltimore).

> The face appears that of a man in late middle age. He has lived every day of his life; and he is beginning to weary of the strain; but every faculty retains its fullest vigor. . . . The man looks perfectly unscrupulous; or, if the phrase be apt to mislead, he looks as if no scruple could make him falter in pursuit of his aim; but his conduct is governed by principle. . . . He is kindly and tolerant, but to avoid greater ills he would shed blood without remorse.[15]

Holmes captures the essence of the bust eloquently and in so doing unintentionally describes Shaw's Caesar—which he may have known—as well. The parallels between the Shavian Caesar and the British Museum bust are striking, and Shaw's familiarity with the artistic prototype seems indisputable. Yet by the time he was ready to publish the play in *Three Plays for Puritans*, he had changed his mind about the authenticity of the bust and for an illustration in the book acquired a photograph of another reputed bust of Caesar from the Berlin Museum. However archeologically sound the decision was, literally it was a blunder, for the Berlin Caesar possessed a head of hair in which Shaw's hero might have taken sufficient pride to forsake his cosmetic wreath of laurel. Also included, perhaps to give value for money, was a portrait of General Burgoyne (representing *The Devil's Disciple*)[16] and—again illustrating *Caesar*, as he wrote young critic Golding Bright—was a "reproduction of an Italian photograph of the mosaic in St Marks representing the lighthouse of Alexandria."[17] A Latin inscription built into the thirteenth-century mosaic on the curved ceiling of the church identifies the conventional cylindrical, three-stage lighthouse with the legendary structure, but its usefulness was mainly that it was sufficiently ancient to satisfy Shaw's illustrative needs. It had not been in his mind when he conceived his third-act description of *"the famous lighthouse, a gigantic square tower of white marble diminishing in size storey by storey to the top, on which stands a cresset beacon."* His rare exercise into book illustration had had nothing to do with the way he actually exploited art in his plays.

In *Caesar and Cleopatra* itself were the opportunities for Shaw to illustrate the play from the art of his near contemporaries, for mid-Victorian painters loved Roman scenes, and Shaw good-naturedly satirizes his own Pre-Raphaelite sympathies. Apollodorus the Sicilian is a young purveyor of decorative art transplanted in time, *"handsome and debonair, dressed with deliberate*

Bust of Caesar acquired by the British Museum in 1818.

aestheticism in the most delicate purples and dove greys, with ornaments of
bronze, oxydized silver, and stones of jade and agate. His sword, designed as
carefully as a medieval cross, had a blued blade shewing through an openwork
scabbard of purple leather and filagree." He does not "keep a shop," he explains
to a sentinel as he arrives fortuitously with rugs for Cleopatra. "Mine is a
temple of the arts. I am a worshipper of beauty. My calling is to choose beautiful things for beautiful queens. My motto is Art for Art's sake." If Pre-
Raphaelitism had become Aestheticism and been weakened and debased as the
century came to a close, Shaw nevertheless defended its values against allegations of insanity and "degeneration" in *The Sanity of Art*; and Apollodorus is
sane indeed, and tough and brave although an admitted "votary of art." At the
close of the play, Shaw mocks the flabbiness of conventional English art and
England's willingness to expend some of its imperial wealth to compensate for
its flagging creativity. "I leave the art of Egypt in your charge," Caesar informs
Apollodorus. "Remember: Rome loves art and will encourage it ungrudgingly."
    "I understand, Caesar," says Apollodorus—and for Rome, read England—

The Lighthouse of Alexandria, detail from the XIII century mosaic, St. Mark's, Venice. Reproduced by Shaw when he published *Caesar and Cleopatra*.

"Rome will produce no art itself; but it will buy up and take away whatever the other nations produce."

"What!" exclaims the conqueror. "Rome produce no art! Is peace not an art? is war not an art? is government not an art? is civilization not an art? All these we give you in exchange for a few ornaments. You will have the best of the bargain."

Earlier, in *Mrs Warren's Profession*, Shaw had mildly satirized Aestheticism not with a work of art but with a weaker representative of the movement than the shrewd Apollodorus—the sensitive and naive architect Praed, who responds to Vivie Warren's description of her practical, masculine tastes, "I am an artist; and I can't believe it." Later Praed adds, unaware of what is happening around him, except that people are unhappy, "The Gospel of Art is the only one I can preach," and urges Vivie, as might a proper inheritor of Pre-Raphaelitism, to "come with me to Verona and on to Venice. You will cry with delight at living in such a beautiful world." The dialogue which follows will turn the invitation into an irony, but the setting is already remote from Praed's escapist Pre-Raphaelite dreams, for it is the cold, ultrabusinesslike Chancery Lane office of Vivie and her professional partner, *"with a plate-glass window, distempered walls, electric light, and a patent stove."*

Man and Superman (written 1901–02) owes at least one element both to popular nineteenth-century art and to a favorite and archetypal eighteenth-century image—that of the collector in his gallery or study surrounded by the acquisitions which reflect the personality he wanted to evoke. Thus Johann Zoffany painted his famous *Charles Townley in His Gallery* (1782) in the sanctum of Townley's house in Westminster, amid a clutter of the works of art—from paintings to portrait busts—which were to establish his client's neoclassical tastes. The canvas remained well known in Shaw's day.

Roebuck Ramsden's study, described in the opening scene of *Man and Superman*, might be another Zoffany. It contains, in addition to busts and portraits of famous contemporaries, *"autotypes of allegories by Mr. G. F. Watts ... and an impression of Dupont's engraving of Delaroche's Beaux Arts hemicycle, representing the great men of all ages."* (Shaw's two pages of notes labeled "Look up at Museum &c. for Superman" include, in the list, "Title of Delaroche's Beaux Arts painting. . . .")[18] Shaw's selection of the works he describes helps to establish both the atmosphere of the scene and Ramsden's personality. George Frederick Watts, the fashionable Victorian painter referred to in the description, painted portraits, classical scenes, and biblical settings in addition to his allegorical works, but it is significant that Shaw chose the latter category with which to decorate Ramsden's study. Watts's idealized representations fit into Ramsden's thinking, as when he and Octavius call each other "the soul of honor." Allegorical representations such as Watts's *Time, Death, and Judgment, Love and Death,* and *Hope* possess a very literal, uncomplicated quality, and they would appeal to the relatively unimaginative mind—to Ramsden's conservative point of view, for example, for he "believes in the fine arts with all the earnestness of a man who does not understand them," according to Shaw's description of him. The choice of the Beaux Arts hemicycle engraving is Shaw's commentary on the pompous Ramsden and on the cluttered atmosphere of his study, with its assemblage of "great men" (and one great woman—George Eliot's picture also graces the "gallery"). Paul Delaroche's *Hemicycle* (1837–41), so named because it occupies the semicircular frieze of the Palais de Beaux Arts ampitheater, depicts Appelles, enthroned within the portico of an Ionic temple, flanked by Ictinus and Phidias. Near them are five allegorical figures (reminiscent of Watts's allegories in Ramsden's study): Fame, Greek Art, Gothic Art, Roman Art, and Renaissance Art. At each side of this ideal group sit and stand seventy-five colossal figures of the great artists of the world, a complement to Ramsden's own miniature collection of Victorian celebrities. Ramsden's study, then, is in effect a "Hemicycle" in miniature.

Little if anything of Shaw's description of Ramsden's crowded study is perceptible to the stage audience, only the reader thus being "in" on Shaw's satirical treatment of the ultrarespectable, well-to-do Englishman of liberal persuasion whose views have not changed in a generation. But the studied clutter is itself Victorian, and the suggestion that change has passed Ramsden by is thus palpable to people in the furthermost seats.

To Max Beerbohm, in his critic's role, the play was "not a play at all" and had no flesh-and-blood characters. "In vain," Shaw wrote him on September 15, 1903, "do I give you a whole gallery of perfectly miraculous life studies. . . . They are reduced, for you, to the same barren Shavian formula by the fact that they are not Italian prima donnas. The chauffeur, the Irishman & his American son are positively labeled for you as Hogarthian life studies—in vain. . . ." Earlier, Shaw had written to actress Gertrude Knight (June 20, 1900) about the part of the militant Reverend Anthony Anderson in a production of *The Devil's*

Zoffany, *Charles Townley's Library*, Townley Hall Art Gallery, Burnley.

Disciple that he was worried about the casting. Anderson "must be a *very* good man." She was to tell her husband, Ian Robertson, who was directing the play, "to look up Hogarth's portrait of Captain Coram, and get me a man like that. . . ." Despite the bows to William Hogarth, whose art he admired unstintingly and seemed often to have at the back of his mind, and the denial to Beerbohm of any indebtedness to Verdi or Puccini, most of the stage images in *Man and Superman* come from music rather than art, Mozart rather than Hogarth. With the first dialogue of the play, its indebtedness to nineteenth-century art ends.

Although one can sometimes point to a direct precursor for a scene or character, the larger work of which it forms a part is usually the product of a myriad of subtle influences. In 1901 Max Beerbohm may have contributed to the critical

mass of inspiration for two plays when he exhibited among his caricatures at
Robert Ross's Carfax Gallery (in which Shaw held shares) a mock frontispiece
for a "second edition" of Shaw's *Three Plays for Puritans*. In it a girl of the
streets with "DRAMA" written on her hat is being summoned to redemption
by G.B.S. in Salvation Army uniform, with a pamphlet labeled "The Shaw Cry"
sticking out of his pocket. (The Salvation Army's periodical was the *War Cry*.)
Beerbohm's "Miss Tolty Drama" answers Shaw with "Garn! 'Ow should I earn
my livin'?" Shaw's Salvation Army play, *Major Barbara*, would emerge from

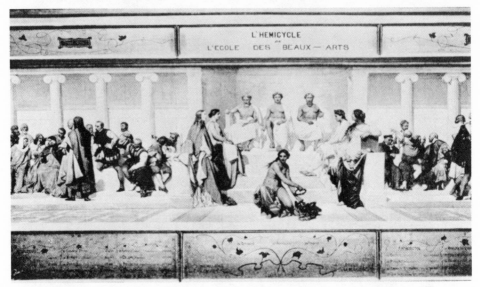

Delaroche, *Hemicycle in the Palais des Beaux Arts Ampitheatre*, Paris.

incubation in 1905, while in 1912 he would create his own Cockney guttersnipe
who needed redemption and began sentences with "Garn!"—Eliza Doolittle of
Pygmalion. Had Shaw seen it? "The Salvation caricature had come out of its
box," he wrote Beerbohm on December 17, 1901, "& was flaunting itself unashamed on the walls."

When Shaw came to *The Doctor's Dilemma* (1906), a number of artistic temp-
tations affected his dramaturgy. His scamp of a hero, who dies operatically with
an artist's credo on his lips, must evoke the tensions of ambiguity about his
supposed genius in order to leave the weight of guilt at his death unresolved. "I
believe in Michael Angelo, Velasquez, and Rembrandt," he declares, and "in the
might of design, the mystery of color, the redemption of all things by Beauty
everlasting, and the message of Art that has made these hands blessed. Amen.
Amen." But the chief believers in his genius—aside from his ultraloyal wife—
are a group of physicians who buy his work and bicker about his medical treatment. Shaw notes early in the play, as he works his spell upon his doctors, that
*"his artist's power of appealing to the imagination gains him credit for all sorts
of qualities and powers, whether he possesses them or not."* Based upon Aubrey
Beardsley, from whom he inherited his mortal disease, and Dante Gabriel Rossetti, from whom he acquired his unscrupulousness in mulcting patrons, Louis
Dubedat (his surname is suggestive of double-dealing) is seen sketching during

Hogarth's *Captain Coram*, whom Shaw suggested to the wife of actor Ian Robertson as a model for her husband's portrayal of Anthony Anderson in *The Devil's Disciple* ("only a few years younger and a few pounds stronger").

the play, although none of his drawings are seen by the audience.* But in the fifth act—an epilogue following Dubedat's death—Shaw succumbs to a self-defeating dramatic device. He portrays a posthumous show of the artist's work and displays the art itself.

---

*Another personality whose more vicious unscrupulousness went into Dubedat's character (including bigamy) was the common-law husband of Shaw's friend Eleanor Marx, Edward Aveling, a chemist and amateur playwright.

Max Beerbohm's caricature marking the 2nd edition of Shaw's *Three Plays for Puritans*, and suggesting the future *Major Barbara* (in the Salvation Army attire) and *Pygmalion* (in the "Garn!" of Miss Totty Drama). The Beinecke Rare Book and Manuscript Library, Yale University.

Stage directions for Act V note that the setting is *"one of the smaller Bond Street Picture Galleries. . . . the walls . . . are covered with Dubedat's works. Two screens, also covered with drawings, stand near the corners right and left of the entrance."* For the first production at the Court Theatre, Shaw borrowed representative contemporary drawings from the Carfax Gallery, compounding his failure to leave the problem of the artist's genius to audience imagination, for the gallery attendant asks the widow, "Have you seen the notices in Brush and Crayon and in the Easel?"

"Yes," says Jennifer Dubedat indignantly—"most disgraceful. They write quite patronizingly, as if they were Mr Dubedat's superiors. After all the cigars and sandwiches they had from us on press day, and all they drank. I really think it infamous that they should write like that." But the drawings on display are by Beardsley, William Rothenstein, Augustus John, Charles Ricketts, and Charles Shannon, creating not ambiguity but confusion. The ex-art critic in Shaw had pressed himself too convincingly upon the playwright. As Max Beerbohm (who doubled as artist himself) observed in the *Saturday Review* dramatic column he had inherited from Shaw,

> Dubedat seems to have caught, in his brief lifetime, the various styles of *all* the young lions of the Carfax Gallery. . . . We are asked to accept him as a soon-to-be-recognised master. Of course, it is not Mr. Shaw's fault that the proper proofs are not forthcoming. But it certainly is a fault in Mr. Shaw that he wished proper proofs to forthcome. He ought to have known that even if actual masterpieces by one unknown man could have been collected by the property-master, we should yet have wondered whether Dubedat was so remarkable after all. Masterpieces of painting must be left to an audience's imagination. And Mr. Shaw's infringement of so obvious a rule is the sign of a certain radical lack of sensitiveness in matters of art. Only by suggestion can these masterpieces be made real to us.[19]

Shaw might have countered that it was safer to portray artistic genius in the pages of a novel and that he might be given credit for his daring, but he never attempted such a characterization again on stage. His next several plays (but for *Androcles*) eschewed echoes of the arts altogether; however, in *Pygmalion* (1914)—also the subject of a Gérôme canvas—he returned to a less hazardous dramatic formula. As with Roebuck Ramsden's study in *Man and Superman*, the art in Henry Higgins's laboratory-study and in his mother's Chelsea drawing room help establish their personalities both to readers of the printed play and the theater audience. On the walls of the "laboratory" are engravings—"mostly Piranesis and mezzotint portraits." Giambattista Piranesi remains best-known for his architectural drawings and theatrical perspectives, and Higgins's interest in them suggests the mechanical nature of his mind. Visitors to Mrs. Higgins's at-home can expect a warmer personality:

> *Mrs. Higgins was brought up on Morris and Burne Jones; and her room, which is very unlike her son's room in Wimpole Street, is not crowded with furniture and little tables and nicknacks. In the middle of the room there is a big ottoman; and this, with the carpet, the Morris wall-papers, and the Morris chintz window curtains and brocade covers of the ottoman and its cushions, supply all the ornament, and are much too handsome to be hidden by odds and ends of useless things. A few good oil-paintings from the exhibitions in the Grosvenor Gallery thirty years ago (the Burne Jones, not the Whistler side of them) are on the walls. The only landscape is a Cecil Lawson on the scale of a Rubens. There is a portrait of Mrs. Higgins as she was when she defied the fashion in her youth in one of the beautiful Rossettian costumes which, when caricatured by people who did not understand, led to the absurdities of popular aestheticism in the eighteen-seventies.*

Again the once-advanced taste of the occupant is immediately apparent, although the Cecil Lawson landscape is a private Shavian tribute to a long-dead young friend. In 1879 an unemployed young Irishman, resident in London only three years, who spent his evenings at free public meetings or in wandering the

Cecil Lawson: a landscape possibly similar to that in Mrs. Higgins's drawing room in *Pygmalion*.

artists' sectors of Chelsea off the King's Road or the Embankment, wrote his first novel, titled ("with merciless fitness," Shaw confessed later) *Immaturity*. It was set partly in the gallerylike Richmond mansion of the wealthy art patron Halket Grosvenor, Shaw's transmutation of the Grosvenor Gallery and its proprietor, the patron of Aesthetic art Sir Coutts Lindsay. Ambitious and utterly unknown at twenty-three, Shaw first acquired his ideas of Aesthetic art—and no artistic movement was ever as social as the Aesthetic movement—from the one family associated with it whose Sunday evening at-homes he had the courage to attend, the Lawsons. He wrote, fifty years afterward:

> When I lived at Victoria Grove [in Fulham], the Lawsons: father, mother, Malcolm and two sisters, lived in one of the handsome old houses in Cheyne Walk, Chelsea. Cecil and another brother, being married, boarded out. Malcolm was a musician; and the sisters sang. One, a soprano, dark, quick, plump and bright, sang joyously. The other, a contralto, sang with heart-breaking intensity of expression, which she deepened by dressing esthetically, as it was called then, meaning in the Rossettian taste . . . so that when she sang . . . she produced a picture as well as a tone poem.

Only the landscape-artist brother is important in the novel: "Cecil, who had just acquired a position by the few masterpieces [of his] which remain to us, was very much 'in the movement' at the old Grosvenor Gallery, then new, and passing through the sensational vogue achieved by its revelations of Burne-Jones and Whistler."[20] The Cyril Scott of the novel was Cecil Lawson, who never recognized himself in print because Shaw failed to find a publisher for his fiction.

Lawson, who painted the crumbling, picturesque, pre-Embankment Thames, died at thirty, in 1882, only four years after his Grosvenor Gallery show had created such a demand for his few canvases that they brought great prices while still on the easel. Preparing an etching from another man's picture was for Whistler, who generally ignored other contemporaries' work, including that of his closest followers, the rarest kind of tribute; for a memorial volume, Whistler produced an etching from an unfinished composition by Lawson of a swan startled under Old Battersea Bridge. Giving the place of honor in the eminently sensible Mrs. Higgins's drawing room to an oversized Cecil Lawson canvas was Shaw's tribute to his old friend as well as a symbol of the good taste of the professor's tough-minded mother. "The Rossettian Mrs Higgins in her Burne Jones costume and Morrisian drawingroom" was Shaw's description to Feliks Topolski on a 1940 postcard, but again, although a general impression of her personality can be derived by the theater audience from her drawing room decor, the subtleties (she prudently purchased Burne-Jones but not the radical Whistler) are available only to the reader, through that extra dimension derived from Shaw's use of art.

Victorians were obsessed with the Pygmalion legend, not only in poetry (as with Shaw's master William Morris's "Pygmalion and the Image" in *The Earthly Paradise*) and in drama (as with W. S. Gilbert's *Pygmalion and Galatea*) but in art. It would have been impossible for Shaw to escape some of the emotionally prurient examples to which his coolly ironic comedy of manners seems an antidote, in particular Burne-Jones's four canvases, *Pygmalion and the Image* (1868), intended for an edition of his friend Morris's book. Shaw not only read Morris but was a regular at the Grosvenor Gallery in London when the gallery exhibited the group in 1879. More important, perhaps, he was in London when the Tate Gallery showed them again in 1911–12. Burne-Jones's treatments were typically mid-Victorian in their sexual repression. The second, with the pining sculptor adoring the virgin marble (or the virgin in the marble), was captioned *The Hand Refrains*. In the third, *The Godhead Fires*, the statue plasticizes into womanly flesh, while in the fourth, Pygmalion kneels before his nubile creation, a placid lady whose breasts he surveys with an apprehensive devotion while touching only her fingertips. The picture is titled *The Soul Attains*. Perhaps the lubricious fantasy lay in the unpainted but hardly unimagined (at least by the viewer) fifth panel, in which the hand attained. Shaw's unsentimental and antiromantic version would defy such daydreams.

With all the literary forbears available to him and suggested since by generations of scholars, he hardly needed the impetus of the Tate exhibition of 1911–12, with Burne-Jones's reminder of the legend in its most saccharine form. But it was there. And Shaw began his play on March 7, 1912.

The movement out of which came Lawson and Whistler and Burne-Jones also inspired a scene out of Shaw's next major play after *Pygmalion*, *Heartbreak House* (written in 1916–17), although it was many years later that he revealed his indebtedness. In his 1949 puppet play *Shakes versus Shav*, written when Shaw was ninety-three, "Shakespeare" taunts the puppet G.B.S., "Where is thy Hamlet? Couldst thou write King Lear?" Shav counters, "Aye, with his daughters all complete. Couldst thou have written Heartbreak House? Behold my Lear." And in Shaw's stage directions, *A transparency is suddenly lit up, shewing Captain Shotover seated, as in Millais' picture called North-West Passage, with a young woman of virginal beauty.* " The captain raises his hand and intones lines from Act II of *Heartbreak House*, and the young woman responds with lines of Ellie Dunn's, after which the captain warns, "Enough. Enough.

John Millais, *Pygmalion and the Image*, the four panels beginning with the thought striking the pensive Pygmalion through to the goddess's making the statue into flesh and the sculptor's first tentative caress.

Millais, *Northwest Passage*. Tate Gallery, London. (Shaw's Lear and Cordelia, Captain Shotover and Ellie)

Let the heart break in silence." The picture then vanishes, but the revelation is clear.

John Millais's 1874 painting parallels Shaw's scene in other respects than the two seated figures, for the setting is a room with a nautical flavor, as is Shotover's house, and visible are a log book, flags, maps, and telescopes. The young woman in *Northwest Passage* is more idealized than Shaw's Ellie, whom life's insecurities only too quickly cause to become hard; but her youth and beauty and affection for the old captain make the scene a dramatic representation of Millais's once-famous work. Pre-Raphaelite art and that of the Aesthetic movement which emerged from it clearly had a profound and continuing impact upon Shaw the playwright.

A brief and literally pre-Raphael reference in Shaw's long dramatic cycle *Back to Methuselah* (written 1918–20) suggests a more familiar use of art in Shaw. Savvy, in *The Gospel of the Brothers Barnabas*, the second play, is described as a *"vigorous sun-burnt young lady with hazel hair cut to the level of her neck, like an Italian youth in a Gozzoli picture."* Thus the fifteenth-century Italian master is utilized to provide a more precise image of Shaw's character. But later in the cycle, in the futuristic parable *As Far as Thought Can Reach*, the scorn of art ("pretty-pretty confectionery" and "vapid emptiness") by the inhabitants of the world of A.D. 31,920 is utilized to reflect the coldness and soullessness of an earth in which the physical body and its needs have been reduced to an ever-diminishing minimum, and the pleasures of the intellect take precedence, intimating a condition in which the body might eventually disappear altogether. People quickly outgrow an adolescence which is the only period of life in which the business of art is thought to be the creation of beauty. Only the reflection of "intensity of mind"—a superrealism—is important thereafter, and art is condemned as "dead" because only the creation of life (or pseudo-life, as in the inventor Pygmalion's stimulus-responding human substitutes) has practical value. The sculptor Arjillax reflects the prevailing point of view in retelling the "legend of a supernatural being called the Archangel Michael" who was

> a mighty sculptor and painter. He found in the centre of the world a temple . . . full of silly pictures of pretty children. . . . He began by painting on the ceiling the newly born in all their childish beauty. But when he had done this he was not satisfied, for the temple was no more impressive than it had been before. . . . So he painted all around these newly born a company of ancients, who were in those days called prophets and sybils, whose majesty was that of the mind alone at its intensest. And this painting was acknowledged through ages and ages to be the summit and masterpiece of art. Of course we cannot believe such a tale literally. It is only a legend. We do not believe in archangels; and the notion that thirty thousand years ago sculpture and painting existed, and had even reached the glorious perfection they have reached with us, is absurd. But what men cannot realize they can at least aspire to. They please themselves by pretending that it was realized in a golden age of the past. This splendid legend endured because it lived as a desire in the hearts of the greatest artists. The temple of Mediterranea never was built in the past, nor did Michael the Archangel exist. . . .

But Arjillax, having matured from abbreviated adolescence, "cannot pretend to be satisfied now with modelling pretty children," although the immature Ecrasia maintains with the steadfastness of youth, "Without art, the crudeness of reality would make the world unbearable." To her the She-Ancient suggests better wisdom. "Yes, child: art is the magic mirror you make to reflect your invisible dreams in visible pictures. You use a glass mirror to see your face: you use works of art to see your soul. But we who are older use neither glass mirrors nor works of art. We have a direct sense of life. When you gain that you will put aside your mirrors and statues, your toys and your dolls." Yet the art-starved Ancients are unhappy and bored, their lives long but bleak, their brave new world gained at great price.

The writing of *Back to Methuselah* exhausted Shaw. He saw no likelihood of another play. Yet in 1913, when he was touring what he referred to as "the Joan of Arc country," he had seen at Orleans a bust "of a helmeted young woman with a face that is unique in art [of the period] in point of being evidently not an ideal face but a portrait, and yet so uncommon as to be unlike any real woman one has ever seen." It was "yet stranger in its impressiveness and the spacing of its features than any ideal head, that it can be accounted for only as an image of a very singular woman; and no other such woman than Joan is discoverable."[21] The discovery was a slow-burning fuse, but from Orleans Shaw did write to Mrs. Patrick Campbell—his Eliza in Pygmalion—that he would do a Joan play "some day,"[22] and he described his proposed epilogue for it, complete to English soldier rewarded in heaven for the two sticks he tied together and gave Joan for a cross as she went to the stake. Ten years later he wrote the play which was preface to that epilogue.

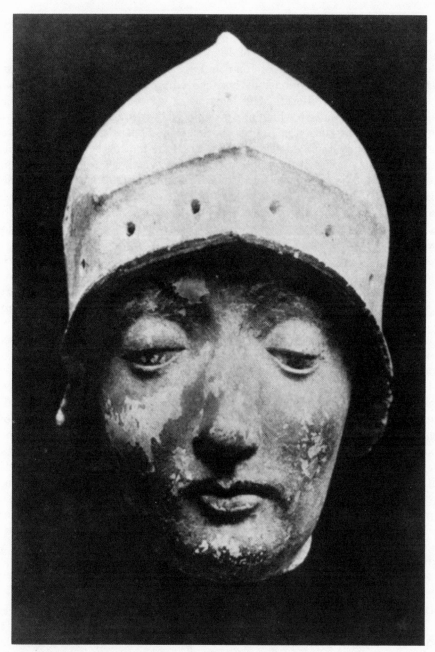

Head of Saint Joan. Musée Historique, Orléans.

The helmeted head, once in the Church of St. Maurice and attributed to the fifteenth century, is surmised to have been inspired by Joan. According to tradition, when Joan entered Orleans in triumph with the relieving force, a sculptor modeled the head of his statue of St. Maurice from Joan herself. When the church was demolished in 1850, the head of the statue was preserved. After Shaw saw it, he declared that although no proof existed, "those extraordinarily spaced eyes raised so powerfully the question 'If this woman be not Joan, who is she?' that I dispense with further evidence, and challenge those who disagree with me to prove a negative."[23] The eyes do cast a spell; one can imagine the woman beneath them as capable of Joan's visionary uniqueness.

Throughout France images of Joan on tapestry and canvas, in relief and statuary, in manuscript illuminations and contemporary woodcuts, and even on medals and coins, proliferate. Her legend has invited artistic representation, but most of the events in which she is depicted defy stage dramatization—the panoply of the coronation at Reims, the sieges and battles, Joan's capture and her burning. Shaw handled each of these on stage indirectly, but his indebtedness to the visual art of Joan's period is strong nevertheless. His description of the immature twenty-six-year-old Dauphin is memorable. The future Charles VII is "*a poor creature physically; and the current fashion of shaving closely and hiding carefully every scrap of hair under the head covering or head-dress . . . makes the worst of his appearance. He has little narrow eyes, near together, a long and pendulous nose that droops over his thick short upper lip, and the expression of a young dog accustomed to be kicked, yet incorrigible and irrepressible.*" That the Dauphin seems to have been imagined from the Jean Fouquet portrait on wood of Charles VII now in the Louvre is unquestionable, as Shaw's description is exact, from the Dauphin's glum expression to the shaven rim of skull which emerges from under a large and ugly hat. That Shaw knew Fouquet's work is clear indeed. In the epilogue to the play, Charles is discovered in bed reading—or rather looking at the pictures—in a Fouquet-illustrated Boccaccio.

How well Shaw researched his characters can be seen also from Dunois, the Bastard of Orleans, for the preface to the play refers to "Dunois' face, still on record at Chateaudun," probably in a painting or engraving encountered on a Shavian exploration of the "Joan of Arc country." But not all representations of Joan he knew were contemporary or came from Lorraine. In Scene V, for example, Shaw ingeniously bypassed Charles's coronation by beginning the action with Joan alone in the cathedral afterward, "kneeling in prayer . . . beautifully dressed, but still in male attire." The image was familiar, and at least two such representations were known to Shaw: an anonymous sculpture at Domremy and a Millais painting which antedated the *Northwest Passage* which had inspired a scene in *Heartbreak House*. Millais's *Joan of Arc*, painted in 1865, was exhibited that year at the Royal Academy and again in 1898.* And Shaw came upon the Domremy statue in 1913, when he traveled through the village "for the sake of Saint Joan of Arc."

It is even possible that one picture Shaw described in a column of art criticism in the *World* in 1886 lingered in his mind as an example of how not to portray St. Joan and resulted in the third scene of the play. The mediocre Pre-Raphaelite-influenced son of famous parents, Barrett ("Pen") Browning, had taken uneasily to the brush, and "G.B.S." noted in an "In the Picture-Galleries" column that Browning had "made a careful life-school study of a nude woman; brought it into startling relief against a background of vivid verdure; labelled it 'Joan of Arc and the Kingfisher.' . . . As the face of the model is turned away, and her

---

*Mention of Millais in this context recalls the words of Brigid Brophy's Voltaire figure, in his dialogue with Shaw, in her *The Adventures of God in His Search for the Black Girl* (London, 1973): "Your play is nothing but a succession of tableaux . . . whose producer was severely under the influence of the pre-Raphaelites."

figure no more than ordinarily expressive, the title and quotation assigned the picture in the catalogue may be dismissed as a humorous imposture." Whether or not Shaw remembered the picture, he dramatized the scene which had been identifiable in "Pen" Browning's work only by its caption.

At her trial, Shaw's heroine appears in a "page's black suit," a costume possibly suggested by *Le Depart de Vaucouleurs*, a painting by J. E. Lenepveu which became part of his Pantheon mural in Paris. Here Joan is short-haired and dressed in a page's short black smock, stockings, and short ankle boots. Similarly, in a book Shaw knew and referred to, artist Louis Maurice Boutet de Monvel's *Jeanne d'Arc* (1907), a too-prettified Joan is clothed in page's garb for her trial. Possibly Lenepveu lent his artistic imagination for yet another—but off-stage—scene, the priest John de Stogumber's hysterical but moving report of the burning. It, too, is in the Pantheon mural and has many of the details described by the unhappy Englishman. Like de Stogumber's description, it features English soldiers and clergymen and the French priest (Shaw's Ladvenu) who struggles to hold the cross high above the throng, while Joan, at the stake, looks imploringly up to heaven. But Lenepveu's martyr has no makeshift wooden cross in her bosom. Shaw knew of it from contemporary accounts of Joan's execution and needed no prompting from pictures to reproduce it himself, however much he otherwise adopted from art in giving flesh to the trial transcripts which were his primary source for the play.

Shaw's only wartime visit to France came four years after his exploration of Lorraine. He kept mentally busy on a dull stretch of road between Calais and Boulogne "on an evening stretch of the journey," he reported in a newspaper account in 1917, "by inventing a play on the Rodin theme of The Burgesses of Calais, which like the play about the Reims Virgin, I have never written down, and perhaps never will."[24] But he did, although it was not until 1934 that he consulted Froissart's *Chronicles* and brought the sculpture to life in a short play. Rodin's *Les Bourgeois de Calais* (1884–86) and Shaw's *The Six of Calais* depict an event which occurred in 1346–47, when, for eleven months, Calais was besieged by the English under Edward III. Edward agreed to lift the siege on the starving city if six hostages, wearing sackcloth and halters and carrying keys, would surrender themselves at his camp outside Calais. Rodin's work commemorates the bravery and selflessness—and misery—of the six burgesses who submitted themselves to Edward's humiliating conditions and immortalizes the wretched men, half-naked and wearing halters at the moment of their surrender. Shaw's play dramatizes the statue, but not with strict exactitude.[25]

Shaw's Eustache, like Rodin's (the sculpture's central figure), is the elderly leader of the group. When the burgesses first appear in the play, Eustache immediately kneels before King Edward. This same humble attitude is suggested by Eustache's bronze counterpart, for although he does not kneel, the sculpted figure stands with bowed head and shoulders, his haggard face reflecting both the humiliation of his surrender and his resignation to fate.

Shaw did not dramatize his characters directly from Rodin's sculpture, for neither their attitudes, names, nor physical descriptions match those of the Calais monument. In his preliminary individual studies of the figures, Rodin had identified the other figures as Pierre de Weissant (on Eustache's right), Jacques de Weissant, Eustache de St Pierre (central figure), Jean d'Aire (on Eustache's left), Jean de Fiennes, and Andrieu d'Andres (behind Jean d'Aire). He used only four of these supposedly historical names (the Froissart account lists only these

Rodin, *The Burghers of Calais*. Rodin Museum, Paris. (Shaw also knew the London cast.)

four names used by both Shaw and Rodin), replacing Jean de Fiennes and Andrieu d'Andres with Giles d'Oudebolle and Piers de Rosty. For the program of the first production in 1934 Shaw noted that Rodin had "contributed the character of Peter Hardmouth; but his manner of creation was that of a sculptor and not that of a playwright. Nothing remained for me to do but correct Froissart's follies and translate Rodin into words." For his published preface he added that Peter is "the only one without a grey or white beard," while Eustache is the only Rodin burgess *with* a beard. The differences are insignificant. Shaw was not playing Pygmalion and seeking to bring a statue directly to life, but perhaps no one else in drama brought so many artistic scenes to life on the stage as Bernard Shaw.*

---

*A low relief rather than a statue had been one of Shaw's earliest dramatic inspirations from art, but the play was never completed. In an art column in the *World* for April 24, 1889, Shaw had praised Burne-Jones's "skill as a domestic craftsman" as displayed upon "a golden 'cassone' or ark, with a picture in gesso of the Garden of the Hesperides. The ark is the most beautiful simple object in the exhibition." Before the year was out he had begun a play he tentatively titled "The Cassone," in which Eleanor asks Ashton to design a cassone for her. "Oh!" says Ashton, "one of those chests like an altar—an ark, in fact, to hold things." "It must be," Eleanor explains, "a beautifully formed box—noble and beautiful and Grecian, and gilt all over with pure gold. The panels must have pictures in gesso, in deep, rich, heartfelt colors. . . ." It would be, we discover, "a trap for a man's soul," but the play remains a tantalizing fragment.

In the 1930s Shaw would draft the beginning of a play about the Garden of the Hesperides, perhaps an echo of the cassone. Again only a fragment exists.

Memories of the art galleries refused to fade. Explaining to Ellen Terry her son Edward Gordon Craig's set-designing deficiencies (May 15, 1903), he observed that "Tedward" had a passion for moonlight and "rows of spears borrowed from Paolo Uccello, a certain Tintoretto picture in Venice, and the Surrender at Breda, by Velasquez. Now the first act of [Ibsen's] The Vikings should be a most lovely morning scene, all rosy mists, fresh air, virgin light and diamond dewdrops. . . . Instead of which, Signor Teduardo, not being able to manage full light and local color, turns the dawn into night. . . ." Writing in 1921 of poet and artist George Russell (*"AE"*), Shaw recalled first meeting him "before a lovely modern picture" in the National Gallery of Dublin. It was Shaw the art critic more than Shaw the memoirist describing the work in question. "The master who painted it," Shaw remembered, commenting on the blindness of the gallery's curators, "had suppressed his name, not in modesty, but because he found that he could get fully a hundred times as much for his work by adopting the name Correggio."[26]

A few years earlier, Shaw had described English Philistines as those who "imply that Frith's Derby Day and the Christmas chromolithographs of Santa Claus are the only art for healthy souls." But he had also moved in space and time from the Grosvenor Gallery of the early 1880s to the Grafton Gallery of Georgian London, where he had admired the Post-Impressionists. Cezanne and Matisse, he realized, "Being possessed, by nature and through practice, of a distinguished mastery of their art in its latest academic form [and] . . . finding themselves intolerably hampered by so much ready-made reach-me-down thoughtstuff . . . deliberately returned to primitive conditions so as to come in at the strait gate and begin at the beginning with all the knowledge of the men who begin at the end."[27] He was still willing to claim some expertise as a critic, writing a correspondent, on a printed postcard explaining why he didn't have time to answer letters, that a reproduction he had been sent suggested that the original was not, as the owner hoped, a Rembrandt. "It seems to me that if such a picture were by Rembrandt his hand would be unmistakable. The small reproduction does not suggest him in the least. The scale, the composition, and the background and properties place it within 40 years of 1800 either way. . . ."[28] It was forty years after Shaw had given up art criticism.

As his American expatriate protégé Molly Tompkins, for whom he had been playing Pygmalion, turned, in the early 1930s, from mediocre acting to uninspired but competent painting, Shaw even offered advice there, although he was less than a Leonardo. Despite his denials, he had never stopped being an art critic or drawing from the art critic experience. Her case as a painter, he told Molly (September 21, 1930), was "by no means hopeless," although her faults of execution were "frightful counter-qualities, not to say vices." He recommended hours of pen drawing, to acquire "elegance of line."

> But there is something deeper than this. Absence of drawing is mere slovenly want of conscience resulting in a low standard of draughtsmanship. But there is something positive the matter. When you deal with human subjects your taste is depraved, wicked, beastly. You should take in a French nudist magazine called *La Vie Integrale* and think seriously about the effect of clothes on the figure. If an Italian contadina (or a Venetian Rennaissance courtesan for that matter) heaps herself with heavy petticoats and skirts and never changes them, never airs or suns herself, she has only to be stripped to reveal herself as a most repulsive pile of flesh. To strip her is simply indecent; if you paint her you must paint her clothes, not the degraded lump they hide. Until you feel

this, and cannot bear to show the human figure except in its healthy natural beauty your nudes will always be disgusting. A fine natural figure always has delicious drawing in it: that is why people who cannot draw, but who have a sense of beauty, always want to get their hands on you. Think about it, Molly: cultivate your taste.[29]

By the 1930s, Shaw was no longer visiting galleries. He was too old to collect things and found problems in responding to the newest artistic fashions. To a dealer who invited him to a new show in 1932, he wrote that he was not a collector of art and was reluctant to disappoint a shopkeeper by walking out without buying anything.[30] Still, the old pictures retained their hold upon him. When Shaw was eighty, he was asked by William Morris's daughter May, then preparing a collected edition of her father's writings, to promote the project by contributing a memoir. A once-lovely girl whom the young G.B.S. had admired, May Morris had aged unhandsomely, yet Shaw built into his recollections a flattering vignette. "Among the many beautiful things in Morris's two beautiful houses," Shaw wrote in *William Morris as I Knew Him*," was a very beautiful daughter, then in the flower of her youth. You can see her in Burne-Jones's picture coming down the *Golden Stair*, the central figure. I was a bachelor then, and likely to remain so, for . . . I was so poor that I hardly could have supported Morris's daughter on Morris's scale for a week on my income for a year. . . . These material considerations only made the Morris paradise more celestial and my part in it quite irresponsible. For if I could not immediately marry the beautiful daughter I could all the more light-heartedly indulge my sense of her beauty."

Although *The Golden Stairs* now languishes in the basement of the Tate Gallery, to which it had been bequeathed by Lady Battersea (Constance Rothschild), the nine-foot by four-foot canvas had been the sensation of 1880, and reproductions of it had even been used during that decade and after by Floriline Hair Tonic and Epps Cocoa. May had been the central figure of thirteen beautiful maidens on Burne-Jones's winding staircase, all daughters of late-Victorian luminaries. To remember her that way showed remarkable tact and showed as well that it was not just for his plays that Shaw extracted metaphors from art.*

The rest is epilogue. To the end of his life Shaw found mental pictures for his dramatic concepts from his encounters with painting and sculpture. *In Good King Charles's Golden Days*, written when he was eighty-three, included— anachronistically by two generations—the court painter Geoffrey Kneller, as Shaw was unable to find a significant artist of Isaac Newton's own time to parallel the physicist. (He had wanted to use Hogarth.) Yet Kneller is more a debating opponent to Newton than portraitist, insisting—with the ample charms of a royal mistress to point to as microcosm of an Einsteinean curvilinear universe—that because space is curved, "the line of beauty is a curve. My hand will not draw a straight line." Another mistress, Barbara Villiers, Duchess of Cleveland, compares Kneller unfavorably with the recently dead Peter Lilly (or Lely), who had painted her portrait for King Charles, and thus provides the director with a lens through which to see her; but all the figures of the play were oft-painted, and the play can be visualized in one sense almost as a three-dimensional composite of seventeenth-century royal portraiture.

---

*At about the same time that Shaw conjured up his *Golden Stairs* image for May Morris, he was writing his screenplay of *Major Barbara*. For the great Salvation Army rally, the scene was to open with the enthusiastic singing of a hymn in progress. Shaw chose "Climbing Up the Golden Stairs."

Edward Burne-Jones, *The Golden Stairs*. Tate Gallery, London.

A comedy completed when Shaw was ninety, *Buoyant Billions* (1947), had been begun some years before, but the third act, the germinal one about which the others were integrated, found its shape when Shaw, visiting a neighbor, saw a print of Leonardo's *The Last Supper.*[31] He then conceived a "last supper" for a wealthy old man who had brought his guests together to solicit their advice on how to dispose of his money. When he wrote the scene, however, he had old Bill Buoyant invite his children instead and through his solicitor warn them of the difficult future which will await them when he dies and the Buoyant billions revert largely to the state via death duties and charitable bequests. But a picture had been its impetus. And in his last year, in *Shakes versus Shav*, he summoned up for the stage his recollection of the Millais painting that had inspired the *Lear*-like scene in *Heartbreak House*. To the end, the art of his own formative years remained a catalyst for his playwriting, and his encounters with the visual arts added an unique dimension to his plays.

The last side of Shaw's involvement with art exists off stage. From his earliest public years his striking features—first set off by red hair, jutting beard, and Mephistophelean eyebrows and later metamorphosed into white-maned, white-bearded Old Testament sage—captivated artists. His vanity teased by such interest, Shaw encouraged the practice, in some cases assuming that he was engaging in art partonage rather than self-indulgence. As a result, his flats at Adelphi Terrace and then Whitehall Court and his study at Ayot St. Lawrence were narcissistic art galleries, always including a number of Shavian portraits and busts.

More than most public figures outside politics, he was also the subject of caricaturists and cartoonists, worked over by such masters as "Ruth" in *Vanity Fair*, Partridge (Bernard Gould) in the *Sketch*, "Max" (Beerbohm) in myriad publications, and Low in the *New Statesman*. As early as the 1890s he was painted by Chelsea artist Bertha Newcombe as a platform spellbinder. It was, Shaw said as an old man, "the best vision of me at that period," and it may have been the artist's best work because she—a fellow Fabian—was in love with Shaw, and her rapture gave new impetus to her brush.

The best photographers of the day vied for the opportunity to take his portrait—not only Evans, Sarony, Coburn, and Elliott & Fry in Shaw's earlier years, but Karsh in the last years. Alvin Langdon Coburn's nude study of Shaw in the pose of Rodin's *Thinker* is the most striking and seemingly most narcissistic of all, but his subject explained that most portraits were only masks of one's reputation—in fact, disguises:

> The result is that we have hardly any portraits of men and women. We have no portraits of their legs and shoulders; only of their skirts and trousers and blouses and coats. Nobody knows what Dickens was like, or what Queen Victoria was like, though their wardrobes are on record. Many people fancy they know their faces; but they are deceived: we know only the fashion mask of the distinguished novelist and of the queen. And the mask defies the camera. When Mr Alvin Langdon Coburn wanted to exhibit a full-length photographic portrait of me, I secured a faithful representation up to the neck by the trite expedient of sitting to him one morning as I got out of my bath. The portrait was duly hung before a stupefied public as a first step towards the realization of Carlyle's antidote of political idolatry: a naked parliament. But though the body was my body, the face was the face of my reputation. So much so, in fact, that the critics concluded that Mr Coburn had faked his photograph and stuck my head on somebody else's shoulders. . . .[32]

The Rodin pose resulted from Shaw's interest in having the man he regarded as the "greatest sculptor of his epoch" do his bust. To Shaw, Rodin was akin to a "river god turned plasterer," and the three busts he accomplished—in bronze, plaster, and marble—would "outlive plays." A thousand years hence, he suggested, he would be certain of a place in the biographical dictionaries as "Shaw, Bernard: subject of a bust by Rodin: otherwise unknown."[33]

Few of the many portraits and busts Shaw commissioned or encouraged re-

Shaw in 1906 in the nude, striking the famous Rodin pose. Exhibited by photographer Alvin Langdon Coburn as *Le Penseur*. (Photo courtesy George Eastman House)

sulted from anything like modesty. The playwright was offering a friend a viable subject, enabling a young artist to make his mark with a picture likely to
attract notice or feeding his vanity by having a famous creative personality
paint or sculpt him. "A man's interest in the world," Shaw had a character in
Heartbreak House say, frankly, "is only the overflow from his interest in himself," and after Rodin he permitted, or abetted, busts of himself by Kathleen
Bruce (afterward Lady Scott), Jacob Epstein, Jo Davidson, and such fashionable Continental sculptors, in their time, as the Russian Prince Paul
Troubetskoy, the Yugoslav Sava Botzaris, and the Hungarian Sigmund de
Strobl, provoking H. G. Wells's remark that it was impossible to move in Eu-
rope without being confronted by an effigy of Shaw.

Only Epstein's bust resulted in a troublesome aftermath for the sitter. Shaw
had been an outspoken champion of the American expatriate's work in days
when the artistic establishment had attempted to shut the sculptor out. The
sitting had even been arranged because Shaw thought that Epstein could "benefit materially"[34] from it, and he praised the sculptor's primitivism and his rejection of classicism, admiring the way he "broke up the brassy surfaces of his
busts in his determination to make them flesh."[35] But the striking, prophetic
head was not sedate enough for Charlotte Shaw, who, G.B.S. wrote to Epstein,
"said that if that bust came into our house she would walk out of it."[36] Privately,
he defended his wife's tastelessness—while admitting that Epstein's "ata-
vism" was part of his appeal as a sculptor—by describing the work as "Neanderthal Shaw, not a XX century one."[37] Perhaps the most powerful image
inspired by Shaw's person, it was never to reside at a Shavian address.

Shavian portraits abound, ranging from the curious one by the third Earl of
Lytton in 1905, showing a robed G.B.S. on a golden throne, orb in one hand and
red skull cap on his head, like some mysterious pope, and the quizzical one by
John Collier strangely rejected by the Royal Academy Hanging Committee, to
more conventional pictures like the benign canvas by Dame Laura Knight, the
puckish drawings of Feliks Topolski, and the celebrity likeness by Augustus
John. Invited to Lady Gregory's home at Coole Park in 1915 specifically to do
Shaw's portrait, John produced three—actually six, Shaw suggested, but "as
he kept painting them on top of one another until our protests became over-
whelming, only three portraits have survived." One showed the subject with
eyes closed, apparently asleep, which he described to Mrs. Patrick Campbell as
"Shaw Listening to Someone Else Talking." He purchased the two more vigorous representations (the Queen Mother now owns the third), giving one to the
Fitzwilliam Museum and keeping the other at Ayot St. Lawrence, where he described the breezy, posterish picture as the "portrait of my great reputation."[38]

In one way or another, all the drawings, paintings, and busts he commissioned or inspired were portraits of his reputation. When Sir Harold Nicolson
traveled to Ayot the month after Shaw's death to assess the property's possibilities for the National Trust, he noted in his diary with amazement, "The pictures, apart from one of Samuel Butler and two of Stalin and one of Gandhi, are
exclusively of himself. Even the door-knocker is an image of himself."[39] (He was
wrong. There was also a large pastel portrait of Charlotte as a young woman.)
But Shaw would have seen nothing wrong in art as a celebration of self. As is
written in Ecclesiastes, a book he knew well, "Wherefore I perceive that there is
nothing better, than that a man should rejoice in his own works; for that is his
portion: for who shall bring him to see what shall be after him?"

7 G.B.S. Borrows from Sarah Grand: *The Heavenly Twins* and *You Never Can Tell*

"They call us the Heavenly Twins."
"What, signs of the Zodiac?" . . .
"No, signs of the times," said the Boy

G.B.S. seldom interrupted a theater review to tout a work of fiction; yet three times early in 1895 he went out of his way to praise Sarah Grand's three-volume novel *The Heavenly Twins* (1893).[1] That July he began writing *You Never Can Tell*, a play which suggests that he had not put the Victorian tri-decker out of his mind as one might have forgotten most mawkish and melo-dramatic contemporary fiction. The difference seems to have been that Sarah Grand (actually Mrs. Frances Elizabeth McFall) not only concocted preposter-rously plotted mixtures of Trollope and Mrs. Braddon but included what ap-peared to be heady doses of Ibsen. George Meredith had turned down the manuscript for Chapman and Hall, reporting that the young authoress "had ideas" but could not "drive a story." There was nothing of the New Realism in its structure or its style, but William Heinemann, the next to see it, was new in the business, and nervous about its frankness. He consulted his friend Sydney Pawling, a manager of the Mudie bookshop lending library chain and nephew of the founder, since Mudie's purchasing power (and its implicit censorship in re-fusing to exercise it) was still able to make or break a novel. Pawling more than approved of it; he even became a partner in the Heinemann firm—just in time to cash in on the tremendous success *The Heavenly Twins* was to have in the li-braries and bookstalls.

Shaw's remarks through 1894 and 1895 make it clear that he had not com-pletely given up reading forgettable three-volume novels when he was able to afford to give up fiction reviewing for the *Pall Mall Gazette* in 1888. One even gathers some insight into the characterization of the title figure of Shaw's *Candida* (written 1894) through Sarah Grand, for Burgess, Candida's father, in lines in the manuscript Shaw afterward canceled, tells Eugene Marchbanks that she is teaching a child to read, using *The Heavenly Twins* as text.[2] (Since the novel was considered one of the most liberated of its time, it suggests that a philistine interpretation of *Candida* was in Shaw's mind when he wrote the play.)* In any case, apparently having already read *The Heavenly Twins*, Shaw in a letter to young critic Golding Bright on November 19, 1894, put Madame Grand (already publicly known as an ardent feminist) in company with Ibsen, Whistler,[3] and Wagner as having "a touch of genius."[4] In January 1895 he again referred to her in that vein, this time publicly, in a theater column in the *Saturday Review*.[5] Reviewing Dorothy Leighton's *Thyrza Fleming*, he observed that it was "a courageous attempt at a counterblast to The Heavenly Twins." But, he concluded,

> The contest between Miss Leighton's talent and Sarah Grand's genius is an unequal one; and the play evades the challenged issue in a sufficiently ridiculous way. Sarah Grand's heroine married a gentleman with "a past"; discovered it on her wedding day; and promptly went home, treating him exactly as he would have been conventionally expected to treat her under like circumstances. To this Miss Leighton says, in effect: "Let me show you what a frightful mistake it is for a woman to take such a step." She accordingly creates a heroine who leaves her husband on their wedding day, and presently returns repentant to confess that she was wrong, the proof being that her husband is really a blameless gentleman with no past at all.

In a column in March, discussing the stage censorship by the Lord Chamberlain's Office, he wondered whether Grant Allen's notorious novel *The Woman Who Did* would have been licensed "if it had been a play, or whether The Heavenly Twins could have been written under the thumb of a Censor. . . ."[6] Again in May, in discussing works which were serious criticisms of life, he soberly equated "The Heavenly Twins and Ibsen's plays," and in the next year, a month after he completed *You Never Can Tell*, he devoted part of a theater column meant to review a revival of *The School for Scandal* to noting—via Madame Grand—the shift in sexual attitudes since Sheridan's time:

> But now see what has happened. A terrible, gifted person, a woman speaking for women, Madame Sarah Grand to wit, has arisen to insist that if the morality of her sex can do without safety-valves, so can the morality of "the stronger sex," and to demand that the man shall come to the woman exactly as moral as he insists that she shall come to him. And, of course, not a soul dares deny that claim. On the other hand, the fact that there is an obvious alternative way out of the difficulty does not escape those to whom Madame Grand's position is a *reductio ad absurdum* of our whole moral system; and accordingly we have Mrs Kendal asking every night at the Garrick why Man—meaning Woman—should be so much more moral than God. As for me, it is not my business as a dramatic critic to pursue the controversy: it concerns me only as the explanation of how Lady Teazle's position is changed by the arrival of audiences who read edition after edition of The Heavenly Twins. . . .[7]

In 1897, still before *You Never Can Tell* was either published or performed, he was back with yet another *Saturday Review* column[8] on *The Heavenly Twins*, this time while theoretically reviewing a romantic melodrama, *Nelson's Enchantress*:

---

*Candida Morell opts for a life of continued but rather dull domestic bliss with her minister-husband, rather than accept the romantic but unrealistic invitation of eighteen-year-old Eugene Marchbanks to run off with him to a garret, and inspire his poetic effusions. The decision is made for her own sake as well as the young poet's, which could suggest Shaw's definition of *Philistine* in *The Quintessence of Ibsenism* (1891) as the kind of person "who comfortably accept[s] marriage as a matter of course, never dreaming of calling it an 'institution,' much less a holy and beautiful one." Candida would have found no idealist picture of marriage in *The Heavenly Twins*.

In order to realize what a terrible person the New Woman is, it is necessary to compare Nelson's Enchantress with that ruthlessly orthodox book, The Heavenly Twins. It is true that Madame Sarah Grand, though a New Woman, will connive at no triflings with "purity" in its sense of monogamy. But mark the consequence. She will tolerate no Emma Harts; but she will tolerate no Nelsons either. She says, in effect, "Granted, gentlemen, that we are to come to you untouched and unspotted, to whom, pray, are we to bring our purity? To what the streets have left of your purity, perhaps? No, thank you: if we are to be certified pure, you shall be so certified too: wholesome husbands are as important to us as wholesome wives are to you." We all remember the frantic fury of the men, their savage denunciations of Madame Sarah Grand, and the instant and huge success of her book. There was only one possible defence against it; and that was to deny boldly that there was anything unwholesome in the incontinences of men—nay, to appeal to the popular instinct in defence of the virility, the good-heartedness, and the lovable humanity of Tom Jones. Alas for male hypocrisy! No sooner has the expected popular response come that another New Woman promptly assumes that what is lovable in Tom Jones is lovable in Sophia Western also, and presents us with an ultra-sympathetic Enchantress heroine who is an arrant libertine. The dilemma is a pretty one. For my part, I am a man; and Madame Grand's solution fills me with dismay. What I should like, of course, would be the maintenance of two distinct classes of women, the one polyandrous and disreputable and the other monogamous and reputable. I could then have my fill of polygamy among the polyandrous ones with the certainty that I could hand them over to the police if they annoyed me after I had become tired of them, at which date I could marry one of the monogamous ones and live happily ever afterwards. But if a woman were to say such a thing as this about men I should be shocked; and of late years it has begun to dawn on me that perhaps when men say it (or worse still, act on it without confessing to it) women may be disgusted. Now it is a very serious thing for Man to be an object of disgust to Woman, on whom from his cradle to his grave he is as dependent as a child on its nurse. I would cheerfully accept the unpopularity of Guy Fawkes if the only alternative were to be generally suspected by women of nasty ideas about them: consequently I am forced to reconsider my position. If I must choose between accepting for myself the asceticism which I have hitherto light-heartedly demanded from all respectable women, and extending my full respect and tolerance to women who live as freely as Nelson's Enchantress, why then—but space presses, and this is not dramatic criticism. To business! . . .

Shaw's real dramatic business was playwriting, and there he turned again to Sarah Grand, this time on the first page of his new play, titling it, in ironic reversal, "The Terrestrial Twins." Somewhere in the writing, however, he scratched the punning title out,[9] rightly guessing that it would narrowly restrict the play, in which, like Sarah Grand's novel, the twins themselves are not the protagonists. In *You Never Can Tell* the philandering hero (made by Shaw, antiromantically, an unsuccessful dentist) is asked scornfully by the woman with whom he is smitten, "What gifts were you born with, pray?"—and his answer is "Lightness of heart." The play, a romantic comedy of ideas, treats the grave themes of Sarah Grand with such lightness of heart that its apparent relationships to *The Heavenly Twins* have gone unnoticed. Shaw's plot places the formidable Mrs. Clandon, not merely an "emancipated" woman but a prolific writer on related subjects, in England for the first time since she left her husband eighteen years before. No household is complete without her works, collectively titled *Twentieth Century Treatises* and described by her twins as

DOLLY. Twentieth Century Cooking.
PHILIP. Twentieth Century Creeds.
DOLLY. Twentieth Century Clothing.

PHILIP. Twentieth Century Conduct.
DOLLY. Twentieth Century Children.
PHILIP. Twentieth Century Parents.
DOLLY. Cloth limp, half a dollar.
PHILIP. Or mounted on linen, for hard family use, two dollars. . . .[10]

During the long separation from her husband (about whom her children have been told nothing), Mrs. Clandon, her impregnably rational elder daughter Gloria, and her high-spirited twins Dorothea ("Dolly") and Philip have lived on the island of Madeira. The entire action of the play takes place at a seaside resort in Devon, amid entanglements caused by love, by the larking of the twins (especially after they discover who their real father is), and by mistaken identity. A believer in "advanced" women and in a libertarian upbringing for children (including female children), Shaw nevertheless found ironic fun in the issues he dramatized in *You Never Can Tell*—parent-child relationships, the equality of women in society, and the power of the sex instinct. Mrs. Grand took these far more seriously, using her twins (where not treated gravely themselves) for comic relief.

Except for the appearance of the boy-and-girl teenage twins, a bad marriage which results in an early separation (Malta is involved here, rather than Madeira), and a trio of women with Mrs. Clandon's frankness, one of them the estranged wife, there is little resemblance between Mrs. Grand's novel and Shaw's play other than a thematic one. Still, it seems likely that *You Never Can Tell*, if it had happened at all, would have taken some different directions had it not been for his almost obsessive attraction to *The Heavenly Twins*. Mrs. Clandon, for example, is said (it is almost a cliché of Shaw criticism) to have been founded on Shaw's friend and feminist crusader Mrs. Annie Besant, but there are strong parallels to Sarah Grand and her characters. There is in the novel Mrs. Orton Beg, who—like Mrs. Clandon—writes and who admires Shelley and Mrs. Gaskell, in particular a passage from her *Ruth* which reads like a precursor to Shaw's own *Quintessence of Ibsenism* (published two years before *The Heavenly Twins*):

> The daily life into which people are born, and into which they are absorbed before they are aware, forms chains which only one in a hundred has moral strength enough to despise, and to break when the right time comes—when an inward necessity for independent action arises, which is superior to all outward conventionalities. (I, 41)

Her niece Evadne, a cousin to the Twins, appears to echo a tenet of the *Quintessence* even more emphatically.

> There is one word more I would say, although I do not wish to influence you, Mrs. Orton Beg began hesitatingly.
> You mean *submit*, Evadne answered, and shook her head. No, that word is of no use to me. Mine is *rebel*. It seems to me that those who dare to rebel in every age are they who make life possible for those whom temperament compels to submit. It is the rebels who extend the boundary of right little by little, narrowing the confines of wrong, and crowding it out of existence. (I, 115)

Afterward Evadne's disastrous marriage, apparently a combination of Mrs. Alving's in *Ghosts* with Nora Helmer's in *A Doll's House*, becomes the central action of the novel, despite the twins of its title. Lady Adeline, however, mother of the Twins, is the closest figure we have in the novel to the outspoken Mrs.

Clandon, and her long moralizing letters provide an equivalent to Mrs. Clandon's tracts on modern ethics. One example suffices:

> I have been thinking much of all you have told me about Evadne. She had already struck me as being a most interesting child and full of promise, and I do hope that now she is out of the schoolroom I shall see more of her. I know you will trust her to me—although I do think that in parts of her education you have been acting by the half-light of a past time, and following a method now out of date. I cannot agree, for instance, that it is either right or wise to keep a girl in ignorance of the laws of her own being, and of the state of the community in which she will have to pass her existence. While she is at an age to be influenced in the right way she should be fully instructed, by those she loves, and not left to obtain her knowledge of the world haphazard from anyone with whom accident may make her acquainted—people, perhaps, whose point of view may not only differ materially from her parents, but be extremely offensive to them. The first impression in these matters, you know, is all important, and my experience is that what you call "beautiful innocence," and what I consider *dangerous ignorance*, is not a safe state in which to begin the battle of life. In the matter of marriage especially an ignorant girl may be fatally deceived, and indeed I have known cases in which the man who was liked well enough as a companion, was found to be objectionable in an unendurable degree as soon as he became a husband.
>
> You will think I am tainted with new notions, and I do hope I am in so far as these notions are juster and better than the old ones. For, surely, the elder ages did not discover all that is wisdom; and certainly there is still room for 'nobler modes of life' and 'sweeter manners, purer laws.' If this were not allowed, moral progress must come to a standstill. So I say, 'instruct! instruct!' The knowledge must come sooner or later; let it come wholesomely. A girl must find out for herself if she is not taught, and she may, in these plain-spoken times, obtain a whole erroneous theory of life and morality from a newspaper report which she reads without intention in an idle moment while enjoying her afternoon tea. We are in a state of transition, we women, and the air is so full of ideas that it would be strange if an active mind did not catch some of them. . . . (I, 49-50)

The lines might have come out of one of Mrs. Clandon's treatises, which belong, says Shaw, not to 1896 but to "say 1860-1880," for she is, in Shaw's stage directions, *"a veteran of the Old Guard of the Women's Rights movement which had for its Bible John Stuart Mill's treatise on The Subjection of Women."* (679) But while her long residence in Madeira has kept them from encountering Ibsen, Sarah Grand's emancipated women possess nevertheless a post-*Doll's House* disdain for their traditional roles.

Mrs. Clandon's lively eighteen-year-old twins, Dorothea and Philip, are said on the basis of no known evidence to have been suggested by "a pair of very spritely real twins, Maurice and Bonté Amos, members of a distinguished legal family."[11] The idea, however, came clearly from Angelica and Theodore ("Diavolo"), the irrepressible twins of Sarah Grand's novel. "Not that there was ever much monotony in the neighborhood of the Heavenly Twins; they managed to introduce variety into everything. . . ." (I, 159) They have "a code of ethics which differed in some respects from that ordinarily respected in their state of life. They honoured their mother—they couldn't help it, as they said themselves, apologetically; but their father they looked upon as fair game for their amusement." (I,166) They have "vivid imaginations" and a "love of mischief," and their helpless mother worries

> that no one can manage them at all. They are everywhere. They know everything. They have already mastered every fact in natural history that can be

learnt upon the estate; and they will do almost anything, and are so unscrupulous that I fear sometimes they are going to take after some criminal ancestor
there may have been in the family, although I never heard of one, and go to the
bad altogether. Now what is to be done with such children? I hardly dare allow
myself to hope that they have good qualities enough to save them, and yet—
and yet they are lovable. . . . (I,167)

Like Shaw's twins, "Angelica was rapidly outstripping Diavolo, as was inevitable at that age. He was still a boy, but she was verging on womanhood, and
already had thoughts which did not appeal to him, and moods which he could
not comprehend. . . ." (II, 1) Later, Angelica "wished she was a child again playing pranks with Diavolo; and she also wished that she had never played pranks,
since it was so hard to break herself of the habit; yet she enjoyed them still, and
assured herself that she was only discontented now because she had absolutely
nobody left to torment." (III,31)

Eventually *both* twins mature, a development with which Shaw—who re-
stricts his action to a single day—has no concern. Diavolo becomes an officer in
the Guards, and Angelica, married, grows impatient with purposeless domes-
ticity and becomes a quiet power behind her staid husband's career in the manner of *Candida* (written a year after publication of *The Heavenly Twins*)
and—even more—Barrie's *What Every Woman Knows* (1908), as a letter from a
friend to their mother reports:

> Her devotion to her husband continues to be exemplary, and he has been
> good-natured enough to oblige her by delivering some of her speeches in Parlia-
> ment lately, with excellent effect. She read the one now in preparation aloud to
> us the last time I was at Ilverthorpe. It struck me as being extremely able, and
> eminent for refinement as well as for force. Mr. Kilroy himself was delighted
> with it, as indeed he is with all that she does now. He only interrupted her once.
> 'I should say the country is going to the dogs, there,' he suggested. 'Then, I am
> afraid your originality would provoke criticism,' Angelica answered. (III, 130)

It is only natural that Angelica should carry her mother's philosophy a step
further, in the process sounding more than a little like Shaw and the dramatic
instruments of his ideas. She refuses to be put by her husband on a pedestal,
"which is, I can assure you, an exceedingly cramped and uncomfortable position. There is no room to move on a pedestal." (II, 278) She refuses, despite her
undeniable physical attributes, to be "*an exquisite womanly creature!* No, thank
you! It isn't safe to be *an exquisite womanly creature* in this rotten world. The
most useful kind of heart for a woman is one hard enough to crack nuts with. No
one could wring it then." (II, 100) One is reminded of Shaw's strictures about
the womanly woman in the *Quintessence of Ibsenism.*

Shaw would have agreed, too, with Angelica that the "best pleasures of life
are in art, not in animalism" (II, 279), and with her claim, paralleled earlier in
the *Quintessence*, that woman's first duty is to herself.

> I should have been held to have done my duty if I had spent the rest of my life in
> dressing well, and saying the proper thing; no one would consider the waste of
> power which is involved in such an existence. You often hear it said of a girl that
> she should have been a boy, which being interpreted means that she has supe-
> rior abilities; but because she is a woman it is not thought necessary to give her
> a chance of making a career for herself. I hope to live, however, to see it allowed
> that a woman has no more right to bury her talents than a man has; in which
> days the man without brains will be taught to cook and clean, while the clever
> woman will be doing the work of the world well which is now being so shame-
> fully scamped. (II, 272)

Mrs. Clandon's elder daughter, Gloria, equally rejects duty, informing her father (who had insisted upon filial "duty, affection, respect, obedience"), "I obey nothing but my sense of what is right. I respect nothing that is not noble. That is my duty. As to affection, that is not within my control. I am not sure that I quite know what affection means." (730–31) This, like Angelica's retort, was strong stuff for its time, and Shaw, realizing that the theater was an even more conservative medium than fiction, was careful to bottle his own new wine in *You Never Can Tell* in the familiar container of fashionable comedy, complete with resort hotel (and comic waiter) and intriguing new stage set of a dentist's office in which the irascible father has a tooth extracted under gas. In three diffuse volumes, rather than the three concise acts to which stage comedy restricted Shaw, Sarah Grand had nearly a thousand pages in which to bury her heresies within a dozen sentimental plots and subplots.

Although the evidence is only internal and circumstantial, it suggests that Mrs. Grand may have learned from Ibsen (and perhaps even from Shaw) and that Shaw in turn borrowed from Mrs. Grand for some aspects of *You Never Can Tell*. Probably, too, he echoed her novel again in *Man and Superman* (1901–03). Ironic lines given to John Tanner–Don Juan about marriage sound much like these bold earlier observations of Evadne.

> "You glow and are glad from morning till night. You have a great yearning here," she clasped her hands to her breast. "You find a new delight in music, a new beauty in flowers; unaccountable joy in the warmth and brightness of the sun, and rapture not to be contained in the quiet moonlight. You despise yourself, and think your lover worthy of adoration. The consciousness of him never leaves you even in your sleep. He is your last thought at night, your first in the morning. Even when he is away from you, you do not feel separated from him as you do from other people, for a sense of his presence remains with you, and you flatter yourself that your spirits mingle when your bodies are apart. You think, too, that the source of all this ecstasy is holy because it is pleasurable; you imagine it will last for ever!"
>
> Edith stared at her. That Evadne should know the entrancement of love herself so exactly, and not reverence it as holy, amazed her. (I, 294)
>
> Saints should find a reward for sanctity in marriage; but the Church, with that curious want of foresight for which it is peculiar, induced the saints to put themselves away in barren celibacy so that their saintliness could not spread, while it encouraged sinners satiated with vice to transmit their misery-making propensities from generation to generation. I believe firmly that marriage, when those who marry are of such character as to make the contract *holy* matrimony, is a perfect state, fulfilling every law of our human nature, and making earth with all its drawbacks a heaven of happiness; but such marriages as we see contracted every day are simply a degradation of all the higher attributes which distinguish men from beasts. For there is no contract more carelessly made, more ridiculed, more lightly broken; no sacred subject that is oftener blasphemed; and nothing else in life affecting the dignity and welfare of man which is oftener attacked with vulgar ribaldry in public, or outraged in private by the secret conduct of it. No. You are not to blame, nor am I. It is not our fault that we form the junction of the old abuses and the new modes of thought. . . . (II, 130)

It is no wonder that Shaw found this outspoken but otherwise mawkish and overlong three-volume novel worthy of the genius of Wagner, Whistler, and Ibsen. The lightheartedness of *The Heavenly Twins* is invariably leaden, and its moralizing is usually sentimental and obtrusive, but it seems to have provided Shaw with some of what he needed to develop a comedy which went beyond the illusions of conventional love to show its biological and irrational truth, and went beyond the illusions of fast-fading Victorian parent-child relationships to show it unsentimentally and unsparingly. *The Heavenly Twins* is long forgotten and unread; perhaps as much of it as will ever live survives in the pages and performances of *You Never Can Tell.*

8 Shaw's Lady Cicely and Mary Kingsley

When Bernard Shaw in 1912 tried to account for the inability of his *Captain Brassbound's Conversion* (1899) to achieve a popular success, he took the strange position that its subject matter was too familiar to the theatergoing public. As an appendix to the first printing of the play he had attached notes which identified his confessed sources, notably the memoirs of his adventurer friend Robert Cunninghame Graham as related in *Mogreb-el-Acksa* (Morocco the Most Holy), which Shaw suggested had been "lifted into the second act."[1] That had explained Captain Brassbound but not the indefatigable Lady Cicely, a role he had written for Ellen Terry when she had complained after the birth of a son to Gordon Craig, "Now that I am a grandmother, nobody will ever write a play for me."[2]

The explanation for Shaw's reticence in the matter of Lady Cicely's prototype may have been that she was then still alive. (So was Cunninghame Graham, but he was a friend whom one thus had license to spoof.) Mary Kingsley's adventures had been in the newspapers in the middle 1890s, and in 1897 her *Travels in West Africa* was published. In 1899 her *West African Studies* appeared, and that year Shaw wrote *Captain Brassbound*, which at first he had intended to title, after the female lead, *The Witch of Atlas*—a Shelleyan suggestion as well as a reference to the Atlas range in northwest Africa.[3]

No witch, Mary Kingsley nevertheless prevailed in her African travels as if she were one, and Shaw pointed out in his 1912 program note that "the material" of his play "had been spread before the public for some years by the sharply contrasted travels of explorers like Stanley and Mary Kingsley, which shewed us, first, little troops of physically strong, violent, dangerous, domineering armed men shooting and bullying their way through risks and savage enmities partly conjured up by their fear-saturated imaginations, and partly promoted by their own terrified aggressions, and then, before we had recovered the breath their escapes had made us hold, a jolly, fearless, good tempered, sympathetic woman walking safely through all those terrors without a weapon or a threat, and finding more safety and civility than among the Apaches of Paris or the Hooligans of London."

The saving grace of the Lady Cicelys and the Miss Kingsleys—and here the term can be applied quite literally—is their respect for the best qualities in human nature and their ability to discover such qualities in every individual they encounter. "I am quite sure," Miss Kingsley observed with typical demure irony, "that the majority of Anglo-Saxons are good men and I am equally sure that the majority of Negroes are good men—possibly the percentage of perfect angels and calm, scientific minds in both races is less than might be desired but that we cannot help."[4] Lady Cicely confidently sees kind faces symbolizing kind hearts so often that she is—vainly—cautioned to "restrain your confidence in people's eyes and faces." But seeing the best in each man and announcing it publicly became a subtle form of coercion in encouraging even the unlikeliest to behave better than might otherwise have been expected.

Only privately had Shaw earlier indicated the depth of his indebtedness to a real-life prototype and, in the process, his admiration for her achievement; for the resourceful Mary Kingsley was a "born boss" of the type Shaw would dramatize in later plays, an instinctive manageress who prevailed in a man's world through wile, wit, and will. In July 1899 Shaw had finished *Captain Brassbound* and sent a copy to Ellen Terry. Her reaction was disappointing. "I believe it would never do for the stage," she wrote Shaw, dismissing the idea of her acting the Lady Cicely role. "I don't like the play one bit. Only *one* woman in it? How *ugly* it will look, and there will not be a penny in it."[5] Shaw responded on August 8 with a letter that was more a verbal lashing than his usual cajoling:

> Send to your library for two books of travel in Africa: one Miss Kingsley's (have you met her?) and the other H.M. Stanley's. Compare the brave woman, with her commonsense and good will, with the wild beast man, with his elephant-rifle, and his atmosphere of dread and murder. . . . Have you found in your own life and your own small affairs no better way, no more instructive heart wisdom, no warrant for trusting to the good side of people instead of terrorizing the bad side of them. I—poor idiot!—thought the distinction of Ellen Terry was that she had this heart wisdom, and managed her own little world. . . . I accordingly give you a play in which you stand in the very place where Imperialism is most believed to be necessary, on the border line where the European meets the fanatical African. . . . I try to shew these men gaining a sense of their own courage and resolution from continual contact with & defiance of their own fears. I try to shew you fearing nobody and managing them all as Daniel managed the lions, not by cunning—above all, not by even a momentary appeal to Cleopatra's stand-by, their passions, but by simple moral superiority.[6]

Like Shaw's heroine, Mary Kingsley was the exception to the Victorian rule, a lady brought up in the usual secluded fashion to manifest the diffidence and modesty, the tender-heartedness and self-abnegation of her sex and period, yet who confounded expectation by going exploring fearlessly where few white men trod, and doing so as a lady, in voluminous Victorian dress. According to Sir George Goldie, then director of the Royal Niger Company, Miss Kingsley "had the brain of a man and the heart of a woman,"[7] a summation that would fit Shaw's Lady Cicely Waynflete. When the death of her parents freed her at thirty from the conventional restraints of her sex and time, Mary Kingsley indulged the curiosity whetted by her reading books of science and travel in her father's library by a voyage to west Africa. An untrained amateur zoologist, she embarked with the aim of collecting fish and insect specimens for the British Museum, whose curator in the field was a family friend. Other friends expressed horror that she was going and, when she remained determined, showered her with advice, equipment, and medicines. Shaw may have seen a kindred spirit in her published reaction to some of the advice. She had been referred to the missionaries for firsthand information. "So to missionary literature I addressed myself with great ardour; alas! only to find that these good people wrote their reports not to tell you how the country they resided in was . . . but how necessary it was that their readers should subscribe more freely and not get any foolishness into their heads about obtaining an inadequate supply of souls for their money."

Shaw opens his play with a specimen missionary in his well-kept garden on the west coast of Morocco, a hearty Scot who has been at work in Africa for twenty-five years and for his pains has only one unlapsed convert, a derelict, alcoholic Englishman. But his lack of success among the natives fails to disturb him. "I hope I have done some good," he explains. "They come to me for medicine when they are ill; and they call me the Christian who is not a thief. That is something." It is to his door that Lady Cicely comes on her travels, dressed (in Shaw's stage directions) *"with cunning simplicity not as a businesslike, tailor made, gaitered tourist, but as if she lived at the next cottage and had dropped in for tea in blouse and flowered straw hat."* Mary Kingsley had gone on her African travels almost the way she later went on her widely popular lecture tours in England, in sweeping skirts and curious, old-fashioned hat. In her African kit she had made only one concession to the terrain, taking along an old pair of her brother's trousers, which she wore, when necessary, unseen under her "good thick skirt."

Like Lady Cicely, Miss Kingsley by choice traveled without another valuable article of masculine equipment—a husband. On her second voyage she had some difficulties with the colonial authorities, who had discovered that she was planning to explore the rapids of the Ogowe River, in the French Congo, in a native canoe. Uneasy about her crew of Igalwas, they observed that the only other woman who had visited the rapids, a French lady, had been accompanied by her husband. Mary Kingsley replied—she reported—that neither the Royal Geographical Society's checklist, in its *Hints to Travellers*, nor Messrs. Silver, in their elaborate lists of articles necessary for a traveler in tropical climates, "made mention of husbands."

Nevertheless, she invented one when circumstances made it practical, for explanations to natives were fruitless. "I have tried it," she recalled, "and it only leads to more questions still." The best reaction, she noted, was to say that she was searching for her husband and to "locate him away in the direction in which you wish to travel; this elicits help and sympathy." The important thing, Lady Cicely observes when planning an expedition, "is . . . that we should have as few men as possible, because men give such a lot of trouble travelling. And then, they must have good lungs and not be always catching cold. Above all, their clothes must be of good wearing material. Otherwise I shall be nursing and stitching and mending all the way; and it will be trouble enough, I assure you, to keep them washed and fed without that." On the subject of husbands in particular she insists, practically, "I have never been in love with any real person; and I never shall. How could I manage people if I had that mad little bit of self left in me? That's my secret."

Shaw's understanding (it may have been instinctive in Miss Kingsley) was that selflessness could exist, in advanced humans, in the form of complete selfishness. It is a concept which he explored in three successive plays—with Dick Dudgeon in *The Devil's Disciple*, Caesar in *Caesar and Cleopatra*, and Lady Cicely in *Brassbound*: his *Three Plays for Puritans*. Shaw described the quality as "originality" in his notes to *Caesar*:

> Originality gives a man an air of frankness, generosity and magnanimity by
> enabling him to estimate the value of truth, money, or success in any particular
> instance quite independently of convention and moral generalization. . . .
> Hence, in order to produce an impress of complete disinterestedness and mag-
> nanimity, he has only to act with entire selfishness. . . . Having virtue, he has
> no need of goodness. . . . The really interesting question is whether I am right
> in assuming that the way to produce an impression of greatness is by exhibit-
> ing a man, not as mortifying his nature by doing his duty. . . but as simply
> doing what he naturally wants to do.[8]

Mary Kingsley has such "originality," and Shaw, it seems clear from a reading of *Travels in West Africa*, admired more than Miss Kingsley's "commonsense and good will." The very first sentence of her book even quotes his
favorite author: "It was in 1893 that, for the first time in my life, I found myself
in possession of five or six months which were not heavily forestalled, and feeling like a boy with a new half-crown, I lay about in my mind, as Mr. Bunyan
would say, as to what to do with them." Thereafter her wit never falters. She
reads a French book of phrases in common use in Dahomey which begins with
"Help, I am drowning" and includes—exemplifying the white man's attitude
toward the African—"Get up, you lazy scamps!" She "fully expected to be
killed by the local nobility and gentry; they thought I was connected with the
World's Women's Temperance Association, and collecting shocking details for
subsequent magic-lantern lectures on the liquor traffic." And as a collector of
"beetles and fetishes" she blithely brought into the houses of horrified settlers
"abominations full of ants . . . or things emitting at unexpectedly short notice
vivid and awful stenches. . . ." Lady Cicely, according to her brother-in-law,
"from travelling in Africa, has acquired a habit of walking into other people's
houses and behaving as if she were in her own." As she explains, "I always go
everywhere. I know the people here won't touch me. They have such nice faces
and such pretty scenery."

But the seeming naivete masks a modern and methodical mind. Like Mary
Kingsley, who is befriended by old chiefs and young cannibals alike, because she
is uninhibitedly tolerant of their behavior among themselves, whether it be eating, marrying, or praying, Lady Cicely claims to be "only talking commonsense" when suggesting that customs are relative and that respect works
better than a revolver. "Why do people get killed by savages? Because instead
of being polite to them, and saying How dye do? like me, people aim pistols at
them. Ive been among savages—cannibals and all sorts. Everybody said theyd
kill me. But when I met them I said Howdyedo? and they were quite nice. The
kings always wanted to marry me." Later, when Brassbound warns her about a
particularly dangerous trip into the interior by saying, "You dont know what
youre doing," she answers with confidence. "Oh, dont I? Ive not crossed Africa
and stayed with six cannibal tribes for nothing. . . . Ive heard all that before
about the blacks; and I found them very nice people when they were properly
treated."

Lady Cicely's breezy indifference to Western shibboleths in Africa could be
taken as having only coincidental resemblance to Mary Kingsley's memoir if we
did not know that Shaw not only read it and admired it and even offered her as
exemplar to the prospective stage Lady Cicely but also that Miss Kingsley's
prose reads as if she were a lady G.B.S. In a *Times* review of her *West African
Studies*, published on February 4, 1899, just three months before Shaw began

his play, Mary Kingsley is also described in ways which anticipate Cicely Waynflete. "Respect for established institutions is not her strong point. . . . One feels
behind the whole thing a perfect intellectual honesty, a determination to give
the devil, or even the Colonial Office, his due, and . . . the shrewdest observation
and unfailing animal spirits." Just as Lady Cicely explains her handling of
black Africans, Miss Kingsley explains, in the reviewer's words, "Now, the African is not a European baby who can be taught to grow up into a European; he is
a man with a definite set of ideas, especially relating to justice. . . ."

Conversely, Miss Kingsley sounds in places as if she had read Shaw's *The
Quintessence of Ibsenism* (1891) in the years just before she escaped her domestic cage. "One by one," she writes, summing up the lessons of her African experience, "I took my old ideas derived from books and thoughts based on
imperfect knowledge and weighed them against the real life around me, and
found them either worthless or wanting." Supporting her point by an anecdote,
she told a story which would have been appropriate for the *Quintessence*:

> The difficulty of the [primitive] language is . . . far less than the whole set of
> difficulties with your own mind. Unless you can make it pliant enough to follow
> the African idea . . . you will not bag your game. I heard an account the other
> day—I have forgotten where—of a representative of her Majesty in Africa who
> went out for a day's antelope shooting. There were plenty of antelope about,
> and he stalked them with great care; but always, just before he got within shot
> of the game, they saw something and bolted. Knowing he and the boy behind
> him had been making no sound and could not have been seen, he stalked on, but
> always with the same result; until happening to look round, he saw the boy
> behind him was supporting the dignity of the Empire at large, and this repre-
> sentative of it in particular, by steadfastly holding aloft the consular flag. Well,
> if you go hunting the African idea with the flag of your own religion or opinions
> floating ostentatiously over you, you will similarly get a very poor bag.

Shaw's Lady Cicely, a compulsive nurse, gets her way in the play in part by
managing to use her healing resources in pursuit of her larger goals. She
emerges as unscathed as she does unmarried. Miss Kingsley in Africa protects
herself as well as bargains to get her way by poulticing ulcers and disinfecting
wounds; but after Shaw had written his play, Miss Kingsley's nursing propensi-
ties were called upon in the Boer War. Although she sympathized with the
plight of the Boers, her work was with her own people, in a hospital in South
Africa. Even there she was moved by the suffering of the enemy wounded as
they paid the price for defending their land. "They want their own country, their
very own," she wrote a friend in May 1900, and "it works out in all their delir-
ium—'ons Land, ons Land!' One of them held forth to me today, a sane one, how
he knew every hill's name, every bend of the river's name, every twist in the
road—his hills, roads, rivers, not England's, or Germany's, but 'ons Land.' It is
a rocky problem for the future."[9]

A few weeks later she was ill herself—with enteric fever. Soon she realized
that she was dying and asked the other nurses to leave her alone, explaining
that she wanted no one to see her in her weakness. Animals, she said, went away
to die alone, and she felt like them. "It was hard for us to do this," a colleague
recalled, "but we left the door ajar, and when we saw she was beyond knowledge
[we] went to her."[10] On June 6, 1900, she died, and at her own request she was
buried at sea. Six years later, when a too-elderly Ellen Terry, at the Royal Court
Theatre, finally played the role written for her, she could not remember her lines

and worked instead at being charming. No one by then remembered Mary
Kingsley well enough to connect anything in Miss Terry's mangled Lady Cicely
with the indomitable author of *Travels in West Africa*. Yet Lady Cicely may be
her monument.

9 Shaw's Mommsenite Caesar

To an interviewer, on April 30, 1898, Shaw confided that he was then in the middle of the first act of a new play in which he was going "to give Shakespeare a lead," a play about Caesar and Cleopatra. Asked whether he had been reading up on such historians of Rome as "Mommsen and people like that," Shaw lied: "Not a bit of it. History is only a dramatization of events. And if I start telling lies about Caesar, it's a hundred to one that they will be the same lies that other people have told about him. . . . Given Caesar and a certain set of circumstances, I know what would happen, and when I have finished the play you will find I have written history."

Because it was impossible to write history—or a history play—without some knowledge of history, Shaw eventually confessed his indebtednesses, but he did so as if he had leaned upon all the Roman chroniclers since Caesar's own day. The list appeared in the program for the traditional copyright performance (at the Theatre Royal, Newcastle-on-Tyne, March 15, 1899) as part of the description of the setting:

> PERIOD OF THE PLAY.—The end of the XXXIII Dynasty in Egypt. The winter of 706-7 in Rome. Christian computation, October 48 B.C. to March 47 B.C.
>
> THE ACTION takes place in Egypt, the first Act on the Syrian Border, the remaining four in Alexandria.
>
> THE PLAY follows history as closely as stage exigencies permit. Critics should consult Manetho and the Egyptian Monuments, Herodotus, Diodorus, Strabo (Book 17), Plutarch, Pomponius Mela, Pliny, Tacitus, Appian of Alexandria, and, perhaps, Ammianus Marcellinus.
>
> Ordinary spectators, if unfamiliar with the ancient tongues, may refer to Mommsen, Warde-Fowler, Mr. St. George Stock's Introduction to the 1898 Clarendon Press edition of Caesar's Gallic Wars, and Murray's Handbook for Egypt. Many of these authorities have consulted their imaginations, more or less. The author has done the same.[1]

Although G.B.S. may well have consulted all the works and monuments he listed (and more besides, for he often sought expert technical advice from his classicist friend, Oxford professor Gilbert Murray), only one was of importance in shaping Shaw's own conception of Caesar and his times: Theodor Mommsen's *Römische Geschichte* (5 volumes; Berlin, 1854–56). The first complete translation was by William P. Dickson, who based his text on Mommsen's fourth edition. His third edition (1894), based on Mommsen's augmented and revised eighth edition, was a new translation.[2] In its preface (I, ix) Dickson wrote that his versions of Mommsen's history had been "largely in use at Oxford for the last thirty years." Whether Gilbert Murray (and through him, Shaw) thus made its acquaintance is only conjectural. Shaw could hardly have escaped its immense reputation, and Oscar Wilde had already written challengingly in *The Decay of Lying* (1889): "It is a question whether we have ever seen the full expression of a personality, except on the imaginative plane of art. In action, we never have. Caesar, says Mommsen, was the complete and perfect man. . . ." What is more to the point is that if Shaw were going to go to Mommsen, he would have had to use the Dickson version, for it was the most complete and most readily available English rendering, and Shaw admitted to only a plodding proficiency in German, generally put to use only on trips to Bayreuth.

As Shaw did his research for the play, Mommsen was in the news. His eightieth birthday was celebrated on November 30, 1897, and *The Times* of London in its "Literature" supplement for December 4 hailed him as a "Jupiter of Literature . . . an incomparable writer and an exquisite writer." But Shaw had not needed *The Times* to introduce him to Mommsen. The "contrast between mere knighthood and military capacity which is the theme of Arms & the Man," he wrote his friend Golding Bright, "was elaborated years ago in Mommsen's History of Rome, one of the best known books in Europe. . . ." And earlier, also to Golding Bright, while he was still working on *Caesar and Cleopatra*, he wrote that his play was "now finished, except for the final revision and the arrangement of stage business. . . . It is in five acts, containing eight scenes, & involving considerable variety and splendor of mounting. It begins with the arrival of Caesar in Egypt in pursuit of Pompey after the battle of Pharsalia, & ends with his departure after his six months stay in Alexandria with Cleopatra. The whole episode was rejected by Froude as a mere romance; but Mommsen describes it in considerable detail. . . ." (May 2, 1900, and December 15, 1898)

It is now clear* that Shaw wrote his play with the volumes of Mommsen before him, as several pages of notes in Shaw's hand outlining the Caesar story from Mommsen survive, dated "Pitfold, Haslemere, Surrey," and from 1898. Furthermore, two leaves of the British Library manuscript of the play have verso notes, one to "Luxury. M. vol IV 513 &c" and the other to "M. 514, footnote." No historian represented the pro-Caesar side so effectively, Shaw understood, and he determined to use Mommsen's narrative of Caesar in Egypt as well as Mommsen's perspectives. Very likely Shaw assumed, too, that educated readers and playgoers would see contemporary analogues to the rise and fall of Imperial Rome, as Mommsen had intended.

Theodor Mommsen (1817–1903) had been torn from his first love—the collection of Latin inscriptions—by the revolutions of 1848. Liberal journalism occupied his time for several years, and the small share that had been his in the making of history provided him with fresh perspectives toward the writing of history. From 1854 to 1856 he published the opening volumes of his brilliantly narrated *History of Rome*, "interpreting the downfall of the Republic in vividly intelligible terms of nineteenth century political life."[3] Academic historians recoiled (and still do) from its personal involvement, frank partisanship for Cae-

---

*When this essay was published in its original form as "Shaw's Mommsenite Caesar" in *Anglo-German and American German Crosscurrents*, P. A. Shelley and A. O. Lewis, eds. (Chapel Hill: University of North Carolina Press, 1962), II, 257-72, Shaw's manuscript notes verifying his indebtedness to Mommsen were unknown, and the essay was based upon other internal and external evidence. The Pitfold notes were first published as appendix to Louis Crompton's *Shaw the Dramatist* (Lincoln: University of Nebraska Press, 1969) and are reprinted here as a tailpiece.

sar, modern phrasing, and lack of the scholarly paraphernalia of references and footnotes. Defending his approach, Mommsen wrote: "I wanted to bring down the ancients from the fantastic pedestal on which they appear, into the real world."[4] This was exactly the goal of Shaw, whose historically based characterizations, from Napoleon to Charles II, reflect this perspective. One critic has declared of Shaw's conception of Caesar that the Shavian aim was not to comfort us with the idea that the so-called great man is an ordinary chap like ourselves but to state a double paradox: "He *did* bring the hero off his pedestal, but only to demonstrate that the flesh-and-blood man was much more of a hero than the statue and the legend."[5]

Mommsen had defended his history by saying, "Those who have lived through historical events, as I have, begin to see that history is neither written nor made without love and hate."[6] When the historian died in 1903, he had long since abandoned plans to complete his Roman chronicle with the aid of more impeccable information. Instead, he had diverted his energies into more than a thousand specialized publications. The history had gone as far, however, as was necessary for Shaw's purposes, for it had not only encompassed the career of Julius Caesar but had a point of view the playwright could embrace. Later Shaw wrote as much to Hesketh Pearson.

> It is what Shakespeare called a history: that is, a chronicle play; and I took the chronicle without alteration from Mommsen. I read a lot of other stuff, from Plutarch, who hated Caesar, to Warde-Fowler; but I found that Mommsen had conceived Caesar as I wished to present him, and that he told the story of the visit to Egypt like a man who believed in it, which many historians dont. I stuck nearly as closely to him as Shakespeare did to Plutarch or Holinshed. I infer from Goethe's saying that the assassination of Caesar was the worst crime in history, that he also saw Caesar in the Mommsen-Shaw light.
> . . . When I wrote Caesar I was stumbling about on crutches with a necrosed bone in my foot. It had been brought on by an accident occurring at the moment when I was plunging into one of those breakdowns in middle-life which killed Schiller and very nearly killed Goethe . . . but I cannot see any mark of it on the play.[7]

Caesar's "unpoetical but strongly logical temperament," Mommsen had written, "was the temperament of Romans in general."[8] "At first glance," Gordon Couchman remarks in a revaluation of the historical and dramatic validity of Shaw's play, "this undramatic announcement would appear to be a kind of key to Shaw's choice of subject. There is not much doubt that in this 'strongly logical temperament' of the Romans and their most famous exemplar lay the secret of Caesar's appeal to the skeptical and rational being that was, to be sure, only *one* side, but a conspicuous side, of Shaw. If an unheroic hero was what Shaw wanted, here he was."[9] Reflected in Shaw's appended notes to the published text of the play is the temperament Mommsen attributed to Caesar. Elaborating on his own assertion that "Caesar is greater off the battlefield than on it,"[10] G.B.S. continued:

> I cannot cite all the stories about Caesar which seem to me to show that he was genuinely original; but let me at least point out that I have been careful to attribute nothing but originality to him. Originality gives a man an air of frankness, generosity, and magnanimity by enabling him to estimate the value of truth, money, or success in any particular instance quite independently of convention and moral generalization. . . . He knows that the real moment of success is not the moment apparent to the crowd. Hence, in order to produce an impression of complete disinterestedness and magnanimity, he has only to act with entire selfishness; and this is perhaps the only sense in which a man can be said to be *naturally* great.

In the famous "Better than Shakespear?" preface to *Three Plays for Puritans*, Shaw outlined the differences between the conventional (or—to him—Shakespearian) portrait of the great man and the new perspective as conceived by him through Mommsen (and also through Carlyle):

> When Shakespear... came to deal with Henry V and Julius Caesar, he did so according to his own essentially knightly conception of a great statesman-commander. But in the XIX century comes the German historian Mommsen, who also takes Caesar for his hero, and explains the immense difference in scope between the perfect knight Vercingetorix and his great conqueror Julius Caesar. In this country, Carlyle, with his vein of peasant inspiration, apprehended the sort of greatness that places the true hero of history so far beyond the mere *preux chevalier.* . . . This one ray of perception became Carlyle's whole stock-in-trade; and it sufficed to make a literary master of him. In due time, when Mommsen is an old man, and Carlyle dead, come I, and dramatize the by-this-time familiar distinction in Arms and the Man, with its comedic conflict between the knightly Bulgarian and the Mommsenite Swiss captain. Whereupon a great many playgoers who have not yet read Cervantes, much less Mommsen and Carlyle, raise a shriek of concern for their knightly ideal as if nobody had ever questioned its sufficiency since the middle ages. Let them thank me for educating them so far. And let them allow me to set forth Caesar in the same modern light, taking the platform from Shakespear. . . with no thought of pretending to express the Mommsenite view of Caesar any better than Shakespear expressed a view which was not even Plutarchian, and must, I fear, be referred to the tradition in stage conquerors established by Marlowe's Tamerlane as much as to the chivalrous conception of heroism dramatized in Henry V.[11]

"According to the facts before the public, " Mommsen had written, "Caesar was a dexterous party-leader and party-orator, of undeniable talents, but as notoriously of unwarlike and indeed of effeminate temperament" (V, 107). One must accept the term "effeminate" in its older sense, wherein this, too, is the playgoer's introduction to the Shavian Caesar, whether he is orating eloquently at the base of the sphinx, piously castigating the murderers of his archenemy Pompey with equal eloquence, or advising young Ptolemy hardheadedly, "Always take a throne when it is offered to you." It is also the Shavian Caesar who hates war, vengeance, and capital punishment, and it is again the Shavian Caesar who is fastidious about his baldness and who offers the passionate Cleopatra a "brisk and fresh, strong and young" Mark Antony in "exchange" for his "cold," "lean," "old"—and seemingly unwilling—self. The playwright carefully ignores the conception and subsequent birth of Cleopatra's (and Caesar's) son Caesarion and breathes no hint, at Caesar's fifth-act departure from Egypt, of the queen's future visit to Rome. Mommsen, significantly, also suppressed Caesarion.

"But as a statesman as well as a general," Mommsen wrote, "Caesar was a peculiarly daring player, who, confiding in himself and despising his opponents, gave them always great and sometimes extravagant odds" (V, 128). Throughout Shaw's play Caesar seeems deliberately to court disaster, particularly illustrating Mommsen's interpretation of the Roman's tactics at the close of the fourth act. In his presence the wily young queen is accused of plotting Caesar's murder. Although she denies it, he knows it is true; yet Caesar's attitude toward all violent solutions remains, wearily, that "to the end of history, murder shall breed murder, always in the name of right and honor and peace, until the gods are tired of blood and create a race that can understand." When Rufio warns his commander to stop preaching—that the enemy is at the gates—Caesar agrees that "as dogs we are like to perish now in the streets." Still, he does nothing to halt the enemy, keeping at bay only his despairing companions. Proudly he pontificates: "He who has never hoped can never despair. Caesar, in good or bad fortune, looks his fate in the face." When the news soon breaks that Mithridates of Pergamos has arrived in his relief, Caesar immediately plans (on a napkin, with a finger dipped in wine) a pincers movement to trap the Egyptian army. Still reflecting the Mommsenite nature of the characterization, Shaw's Caesar offers his most extravagant odds as he embarks for Rome, his Egyptian adventure over. Warned by Rufio not to leave him—"Caesar's shield"—behind, Caesar answers: "It matters not . . . I have always disliked the idea of dying. I had rather be killed."

Shaw's later Caesar can be seen in Mommsen's summation of him as mystical realist.

> Prudently as he laid his plans and considered all possibilities, the feeling was never absent from his breast that in all things fortune, that is to say accident, must bestow success; and with this may be connected the circumstance that he so often played a desperate game with destiny, and in particular again and again hazarded his person with daring indifference. As indeed occasionally men of predominant sagacity betake themselves to a pure game of hazard, so there was in Caesar's rationalism a point at which it came in some measure into contact with mysticism (V, 308).

In his Caesar, Shaw presents an amalgam of the Mommsenite mystic with the Mommsenite orator. The historian had written: "With justice men commend Caesar the orator for his masculine eloquence, which, scorning all the arts of the advocate, like a clear flame at once enlightened and warmed. With justice men admire in Caesar the author the inimitable simplicity of the composition, the unique purity and beauty of the language" (V, 309). G.B.S., while at work on the play, had been closing out his career as a drama critic. In his *Saturday Review* columns he struck a blow at bardolatry by pointing out that Shakespeare's Julius Caesar says "nothing worthy, or even nearly worthy" of the historical Caesar: "There is not a single sentence uttered by Shakespeare's Julius Caesar that is, I will not say worthy of him, but even worthy of an average Tammany boss."[12] If Goethe, Shaw added, had treated the subject, "his conception of it would have been as superior to Shakespear's as St. John's Gospel is to the Police News. . . ."[13] In Caesar's famous and eloquent apostrophe to the Sphinx, and in later episodes in which he fatalistically expects—and prophesies—treachery and death, Mommsen's "clear flame" flares in the lines Shaw gives his Caesar. Nowhere else in Shavian drama—excepting perhaps in the persons of Saint Joan and Father Keegan[14]—are the mystical and the eloquent and the rational more carefully joined in a hero's words.

H. G. Wells was at variance with his friend Shaw on many things, including Julius Caesar. In his *Outline History of the World*, Wells describes Caesar as an "elderly sensualist or sentimentalist . . . rather than the master ruler of men" and concludes that "his vulgar scheming for the tawdriest mockeries of personal worship is a silly and shameful record; it is incompatible with the idea that he was a wise and wonderful statesman, setting the world to rights."[15] St. John Ervine, who sided with Shaw, remarked that he was not enough of a historian to say whether Wells or Shaw was right, although he acknowledged that Shaw had Mommsen on his side. It seemed to Ervine irrelevant whether Shaw's Mommsenite Roman was the Caesar of history: "What does matter is that the Caesar of this remarkable play is Shaw's conception of a great man. . . . He drew the picture of a genius as he conceived a genius to be, and for purpose of convenience, called it a portrait of Julius Caesar. . . . We shall fail in understanding if we do not perceive the fact that in this play we have G.B.S.'s conception of greatness rather than a faithful portrait of an historical character."[16] Paraphrasing Ervine, one may say that the convenience suiting Shaw's purpose was Mommsen's *History of Rome*—which was for the playwright as much a handbook as a history. Most critics today perceive in the play's hero some Shavian self-portraiture, but Mommsen would have recognized his own Caesar. John Mason Brown, reviewing a production of the play, even added that although Shaw's admiring portrait of Caesar would not have been recognized by Suetonius or Plutarch—neither of whom liked Caesar:

> the man who wrote *The Gallic War* would have recognized this Shavian Julius—with gratitude and relief. The clemency and statesmanship, the largeness of mind and spirit, which for the sake of the record he had been careful to establish as his, are qualities that shine in Shaw's Caesar. Caesar's self-love could not have been greater than Shaw's almost romantic infatuation with the benevolent despot he depicted.
>
> But there was a difference—an immeasurable difference. Where Plutarch was dignified, Suetonius scurrilous, Caesar determinedly official, and Shakespeare rhetorically athletic, Shaw was Shavian. This in itself represented a complete abandonment of the orthodox ways of writing not only history* but historical plays. It meant that, more than upsetting an apple-cart, Shaw had brought about a one-man revolution in the theatre and in literature.[17]

A comparison of passages, however, demonstrates the pre-Shavian origin of the revolution ascribed to Shaw by Brown. According to Mommsen, Caesar, being "in urgent pecuniary embarrassment, landed in Alexandria with the two amalgamated legions accompanying him to the number of 3200 men and 800 Celtic and German cavalry, took up his quarters in the royal palace, and proceeded to collect the necessary sums of money and to regulate the Egyptian succession, without allowing himself to be disturbed by the saucy remark of Pothinus that Caesar should not for such petty matters neglect his own so important affairs" (V, 274). Complete to the saucy remark, the incident appears in *Caesar and Cleopatra*:

> POTHINUS [bitterly]: Is it possible that Caesar, the conqueror of the world, has time to occupy himself with such a trifle as our taxes?
> CAESAR: My friend, taxes are the chief business of a conqueror of the world.

According to Gordon Couchman, "Caesar's debts, as estimated by Mommsen and others . . . Shaw conveniently ignores."[18] However, Mommsen may be noted as having described Caesar as arriving in "urgent pecuniary embarrassment" and G.B.S. has Caesar declare unequivocally, "Now, Pothinus, to business. I am badly in want of money." Shaw even uses Mommsen's exact figures when talking about the money owed to Rome by Egypt. The translator of the English edition of 1894 had interpreted the historian's reckoning of the Egyptian sestertius in terms of the contemporary value of silver as one hundred sesterces to the English pound (I, x), valuing the entire debt in the account of the squabble as £400,000. Shaw's figure, at which Pothinus gasps, is forty million sesterces—exactly the same reckoning. His note on the verso of a manuscript page referring to "M." confirms the source: "100 sesterces = £1."

One scene out of Mommsen was cut—one, Shaw wrote his German translator, Siegfried Trebitsch, in 1903, in which Caesar received four ambassadors and "humbugged them all." Meant to display Caesar's skeptical pragmatism, it dramatizes an audience in which the Syrian, Nabatean, and Rhodian envoys

---

*Mommsen undoubtedly deserved this accolade, rather than Shaw.

describe what support their states will furnish Rome. Britannus, in character, naively accepts the expressions of loyalty. Caesar, ever practical, wants to know how many men and how many galleys can be expected, and he wants precise figures. The Cretan ambassador reports the presence of enemies among his people, and again Caesar is impatient with "a mere handful" as an answer."How many in the handful?" he wants to know.

Mommsen had mentioned a Roman order to the Syrians, Nabateans, Cretans, and Rhodians "to send troops and ships in all haste to Egypt" to help relieve the siege. He also identified the components of the "motley army" that Mithridates of Pergamos led from Syria to assist Caesar: "Ityraeans of the prince of Libanus, the Bedouins of Jamblichus, son of Sampsicheramus, the Jews under the minister Antipater, and the contingents generally of the petty chiefs and communities of Cilicia and Syria." When Caesar asks the Syrian, in the deleted scene, about the constituents of his army, the response is very close to Mommsen's description. But the scene did not survive beyond the copyright performance in 1899. The play was too long.

An interesting but perhaps inadvertent debt to Mommsen is found in Shaw's exceedingly youthful Cleopatra. The playwright preferred to draw the portrait of a deceptively kittenish girl who under Caesar's tutelage flowered into a queen—the mentor-and-disciple theme which recurs throughout the Shavian canon. But nowhere in Roman or later chronicles exists an excuse for the Shavian sixteen as Cleopatra's age at the time of Caesar's arrival in Egypt. Mommsen, however, recorded the young queen's accession to the throne to become joint ruler with her brother as having taken place in May of the Roman year 703, when she was sixteen and Ptolemaeus Dionysus ten, adding further that "soon the brother or rather his guardian Pothinus had driven the sister from the kingdom. . . " (I,272). On the same page (but placed with events of three years later) is recorded Caesar's entry into Egypt and recall of Cleopatra. Perhaps—by accident or design—Shaw misread Mommsen here, for the only direct reference to Cleopatra's age on that page is in relation to the year of her coronation, not to the year of her return from exile. Shaw's emphasis on her youth—whatever its basis—"was more than a puritanic evasion. It was a Shavian device by means of which superstitions could be mocked and Caesar, the conqueror, humanized by being seen through the irreverent eyes of a child."[19]

One such irreverence in Shaw's play is Cleopatra's mocking of the aging Caesar's baldness. The conqueror was fifty-four at the time of the Egyptian venture. "He carefully covered the baldness," Mommsen remarks, "which he keenly felt, with the laurel chaplet that he wore in public in his later years, and he would doubtless have surrendered some of his victories, if he could thereby have brought back his youthful locks. But, however much even when monarch he enjoyed the society of women, he only amused himself with them, and allowed them no manner of influence over him; even his much censured relation to queen Cleopatra was only contrived to mask a weak point in his political position" (V, 307). Eagerly seizing upon Mommsen's version of history, Shaw shows Caesar embarrassed by Cleopatra's discovery of his reason for wearing the laurel wreath. The faithful (and fictitious) Britannus comes to Caesar's rescue by insisting that the laurel's purpose was not really cosmetic: "Peace, Egyptian: they are the bays of the conqueror."

Mommsen's theory that Caesar's dalliance with Egyptian (and other) women, including the unspecified relationship with Cleopatra, was performed strictly for strategic purposes is carefully upheld by Shaw in his account of the conqueror's relations with the young queen. Pothinus accuses Cleopatra of being infatuated with Caesar, an allegation which she denies. Caesar, she declares, has made her wise, not foolish. He has shown her kindness rather than love. "But," asks the prime minister, "how can you be sure that he does not love you as men love women?" Begging the question, Shaw has Cleopatra answer: "Because I cannot make him jealous. I have tried." The question whether she loves him is also begged rather than answered: "Can one love a God?" This, to Shaw, apparently seemed no contradiction of Mommsen's account of an amorous yet scrupulous Caesar, who enjoyed Cleopatra's attentions as much as he had in the past enjoyed the attentions of other attractive women. While the victorious Roman army encamped at Alexandria, the German historian recorded, "the beautiful and clever Cleopatra was not sparing of her charms in general and least of all towards her judge. Caesar also appeared among all his victories to value most those won over beautiful women" (V, 276). Although Plutarch explicitly details the fact that the amorous adventure with Cleopatra had concrete issue— "a son . . . whom the Egyptians call Caesarion"[20] —Mommsen ignores the event in his account, leaving Shaw free to choose again among the majority with Plutarch or the minority (where Mommsen is often a minority of one) with the German. Shaw even closes his drama with a farewell scene between Caesar and Cleopatra that offers little hint of any relationship between the two other than that of mentor and disciple. Caesar, in fact, not only does not notice Cleopatra at the quay where his ship is about to depart (although she is the most striking figure in the crowd, dressed coldly and tragically in black, in mourning for the assassinated Ftatateeta), he does not even miss her. When she asks him what part she has in the leave-taking, the omission dawns on Caesar: "Ah I knew there was something." His farewell kiss is upon her forehead.

In another event of the Roman occupation, Shaw's play follows a similar evaluation and rejection of sources inconsistent with his (and Mommsen's) idealistic portrayal of Caesar, and again his freedom in using other sources seems to stem from Mommsen's silence on the subject.[21] Although details differ, from the account in *The Civil Wars*, attributed to Caesar himself, through the histories of Plutarch, Appian, and the moderns, it is recorded that Pothinus is put to death by Caesar's order for plotting against Roman rule. Only Mommsen is silent about the death of the crafty prime minister. Since the incident was dramatically necessary to Shaw's conception, the playwright accepted the fact of Pothinus's death. However, as Mommsen (always his chief authority) had omitted the incident entirely—perhaps because it reflected adversely on his conception of a forgiving and merciful Caesar—Shaw imaginatively preserved the spirit of the German historian, it seems, by providing the hero with vast resources of indignation on hearing of the slaying from the loyal Rufio. "Assassinated!" cries Shaw's Caesar, "our prisoner, our guest!" Assessing this scene, a critic observes, "This is poetry, but not, apparently, history."[22] Either as poetry or as history, it is Mommsenite.

One scene to the taste of both historian and playwright is found in most earlier chronicles as well: Caesar's horror at the murder of his enemy Pompey and the presentation to him, by Theodotus and his henchmen, of Pompey's severed head. Perhaps the most melodramatic account occurs in Mommsen, where "with deep agitation" Caesar turns away from the grisly sight (V, 273). In Shaw it becomes a signal for discussion of the inefficacy of vengeance and, by implication, capital punishment—a subject that had preoccupied him since his earliest trembling remarks at debating societies when he was in his early twenties.

Little need be said about Shaw's treatment of the actual siege of Caesar's forces: the attack on the lighthouse, the escape of Caesar, the presence of Cleopatra, the burning of the fleet in Alexandria harbor and the devastation of the great library, and the raising of the siege by Mithridates of Pergamos. The chronicles generally concur regarding the incidents, and Shaw—with few exceptions—deviates only in the addition of details necessary to the drama. No detail added or retained, however, was intended to make the hero more heroic. The type of hero of whom Tennyson's Arthur was the epitome, Shaw declared, was no longer a worthwhile theatrical commodity:

> It is no use now going on with heroes who are no longer really heroic to us. Besides, we want credible heroes. The old demand for the incredible, the impossible, the superhuman, which was supplied by bombast, inflation, and the piling of crimes on catastrophes and factitious raptures on artificial agonies, has fallen off; and the demand now is for heroes in whom we can recognize our own humanity, and who instead of walking, talking, eating, drinking, making love and fighting single combats in a monotonous ecstasy of continuous heroism, are heroic in the true fashion: that is, touching the summits only at rare moments, and finding the proper level of all occasions, condescending with humour and good sense to the prosaic ones as well as rising to the noble ones, instead of ridiculously persisting in rising to them all on the principle that a hero must always soar, in season and out of season.[23]

In developing his realist-hero in the person of Caesar, Shaw actually destroyed the traditional superman-hero only to build upon his still-warm grave a more restrained variety, but no less the superman. In addition to Mommsen, he may have recalled—as did his biographer Henderson—Nietzsche's criteria of the great man: "Not to be able to take seriously, for a long time, an enemy, or a misfortune, or even one's own misdeeds—is the characteristic of strong and full natures, abundantly endowed with plastic, formative, restorative, also obliterative force."[24]

A parallel to the Nietzschean attributes appears in the Mommsenite Caesar of Shaw's play: indeed, it is easy to recognize in the Shavian dramatization of Caesar's personality Mommsen's vigorous analysis of the Roman:

> A thorough realist, he never allowed the images of the past or venerable tradition to disturb him; for nothing was of value in politics but the living present and the law of reason, just as in his character of grammarian he set aside historical and antiquarian research and recognized nothing but on the one hand the *usus loquendi* and on the other hand the rule of symmetry. (V, 311)

Whatever Caesar undertook and achieved, Mommsen wrote,

> was pervaded and guided by the cool sobriety which constitutes the most marked peculiarity of his genius. To this he owed the power of living energetically in the present, undisturbed either by recollection or by expectation; to this he owed the capacity of acting at any moment with collected vigour, and . . . the many sided power with which he grasped and mastered whatever understanding can comprehend and will can compel; to this he owed the "marvellous serenity" which remained steadily with him through good and evil days; to this he owed the complete independence, which admitted of no control by favourite or by mistress, or even by friend. It resulted, moreover, from this clearness of judgment that Caesar never formed to himself illusions regarding the power of fate and the ability of man . . . (V, 307).

To the worshipful Mommsen, Caesar was "the entire and perfect man" (V, 313). "A born ruler," the historian wrote, "Caesar governed the minds of men as the winds drive the clouds, and compelled the most heterogeneous natures to place themselves at his service—the plain citizen and the rough subaltern. . ."

(V, 311). Mixing fact and fancy, Shaw attaches such heterogeneous natures to the conqueror's staff as Britannus and Rufio. The battle won, Caesar attempts to reward the Briton's loyalty by offering him his freedom. Rejecting it, Britannus answers: "Only as Caesar's slave have I found real freedom." Overhearing the exchange, the Egyptian captain Belzanor remarks: "This Roman knows how to make men serve him." One is reminded of Mommsen's observation concerning this quality in Caesar: "The ordinary man is destined for service, and has no objection to be an instrument, if he feels that a master guides him" (V, 197). Such a subordinate officer is Rufio. Caesar's appointment of him as his deputy in Egypt has a basis in Mommsen and other chronicles, but it is romanticized by the usually antiromantic Shaw—an extremity that may be credited to the playwright's desire to display a Caesar with audience appeal yet having withal the coldly logical aspect necessary to Shaw's conception of a hero's personality. According to Mommsen, "For this position of trust a man was purposely selected, whose birth made it impossible for him to abuse it—Rufio, an able soldier, but the son of a freedman" (V, 281). Making Caesar's beneficence merely a mask for his astuteness, Mommsen adds later that "the legions stationed in Egypt were not entrusted to a man belonging to the former government, but this command was, just like the posts of tax receivers, treated as a menial office" (V, 343). Shaw, in Act V of *Caesar and Cleopatra*, embellishes the matter-of-fact commentary.

> RUFIO [*incredulously*] I! I a governor! What are you dreaming of? Do you not know that I am only the son of a freedman?
> CAESAR [*affectionately*] Has not Caesar called you his son? [*Calling to the whole assembly*] Peace awhile there; and hear me.
> THE ROMAN SOLDIERS. Hear Caesar.
> CAESAR. Hear the service, quality, rank and name of the Roman governor. By service, Caesar's shield; by quality, Caesar's friend; by rank, a Roman soldier. [*The Roman soldiers give a triumphant shout*]. By name, Rufio. [*They shout again*].
> RUFIO [*kissing Caesar's hand*] Ay: I am Caesar's shield; but of what use shall I be when I am no longer on Caesar's arm? Well, no matter—[*He becomes husky, and turns away to recover himself*].

The true soldier of Caesar, Mommsen had written, "ought to be not merely capable, brave, and obedient, he ought to be all this willingly and spontaneously; it is the privilege of gifted natures alone [such as Caesar's] to induce the animated machine which they govern to a joyful service by means of example and hope, and especially by the consciousness of being turned to befitting use" (V, 196). Shaw's adapted Rufio and coined Britannus come from such a mold.

It is curious that for years German critics of Shaw's play did not recognize what should have been more obvious to them than to Englishmen. Julius Bab, the leading German interpreter of Shaw in Shaw's lifetime, even described the Shavian Caesar as "die Synthese von britischer Tatkraft und irischer Geistigkeit."[25] But buried in the theater columns of the *Nation* is a review of the 1913 London production by H. W. Massingham, who wrote that the playwright might have consulted many sources but had utilized only one.

> Mr. Shaw's study of Caesar is modelled with almost a copyist's exactitude on Mommsen, and that the whole of this fascinating episode of the siege of Alexandria, and of the campaign which relieved it, may be seen, with Mommsen's following picture of the soldier-statesman, in his famous fifth book. Indeed, there is so much detail, so much history, that the action of the drama is impeded so as to get it all in. Caesar's clemency, the rapid movements of his soldier's

mind, and the still quicker instincts of his statesmanship, his temperance in eating and drinking, his elegance of dress, even his small personal vanities (such as the wearing of a wreath to hide his baldness)—all these habits of mind and body, and the cold, unrevengeful temper and realistic character which governed them—appear in Mr. Shaw's workmanship. But why did the theme attract him? Obviously, I think, because of Mommsen's description of Caesar as standing aloof 'from all ideology and everything fanciful'. Here, therefore, was a conqueror after Mr. Shaw's heart. Humane, but no idealist. A reconstructor of society, without prejudice. An artist and an ascetic, or next-door to one. Playing with worlds and states as on a chessboard, but all for utility. In a word, a true Fabian hero. Mr. Shaw takes this idealized but historic and brilliantly plausible sketch of a great man, and rearranges it with much literalness, and under the limitations of time and place that this theme imposed on him. His play is an essay in dramatic history—good or bad—and possibly made unseemly in British eyes by the presence of jokes. These jokes are no more and no less anachronistic than Shakespeare's study of Elizabethan politics in *Troilus and Cressida*. But the history is there all the same.[26]

Of course there was more than Mommsen in Shaw's Caesar. The rug episode and other incidents had come from Roman sources, and Shaw's interest in Caesar's ideas about leadership, revenge, passion, and blind idealism were borrowed from nineteenth-century thinkers. But in execution, where a Mommsenite conception required a parting of the ways with Carlyle or Nietzsche or with the standard historians, Shaw followed Mommsen. In almost every case where he came to a point in the development of his play at which the majority of authorities (even some of his most revered ones) turned in one direction while Mommsen set out alone in the other, Shaw followed the author of the *Römische Geschichte*. The Shavian hero, Eric Bentley wrote in his study of nineteenth-century hero worship, "is without courage, which, for Carlyle and Nietzsche, was a prime virtue. . . . If Nietzsche's hero is beyond good and evil, Shaw's is beyond courage and cowardice."[27] Mommsen, too, had illustrated this facet of Caesar's character, probably again not imparting any significant new direction to Shaw. He happened to be an authority who had handily anticipated Shaw's own developing thought; thus it was natural that Shaw should borrow Mommsen's facts as well as his philosophical perspectives toward them.

Without impugning the play, we may yet consider it unreliable as history. G.B.S.'s Caesar is no more than Shakespeare's Caesar the Caesar of history. And if Mommsen's work no longer bulks large with historians of Rome,[28] it is certain to be remembered at least as long as *Caesar and Cleopatra* is performed and read, for the German inscription collector turned historian played Plutarch to the author of one of the great historical dramas of the modern English stage.

Shaw's notes on Mommsen's
History of Rome for *Caesar and Cleopatra* (1898)

Line of Ptolemy Lagides ended on death of Pt. Sotor II
Sulla installed Lathyrus, or Alexander II, killed in his capital in a few days in a tumult.
Alex made a will bequeathing Egypt to Rome.
The Romans grabbed Alex's money in Tyre, but did not take Egypt, allowing Lathyrus's bastards

    Auletes (the Flute Blower), the new Dionysos)   to take { Egypt
    Ptolemy the Cyprian   Cyprus   81.

Explanation—Auletes paid rent for non-disturbance; and the post of governor of Egypt made the holder too powerful.
    Yet there was a Roman party in Alex[dria] because the royal guard deposed ministers & even kings & besieged the king in his palace when it wanted more pay.

Ptolemy, CI's uncle, was a miser & would not bribe the Romans. His treasure was 7000 talents (£1,700,000). In 58 Cyprus was annexed by Marcus Cato (armyless) & Pt poisoned himself. Cl was then 6.

Auletes in 59 purchased his recognition as K. of E. by decree of the Roman people for 6000 tal. (£1,460,000). The Egyptians could not stand the consequent taxation & the loss of Cyprus (see above) & chased him out of the country. He appealed to the Romans to be reinstated. They agreed that he had a claim on them, but could not agree who to send, as the job was a desirable one, with lots of pickings.

At last the Triumvirate, at the Conference of Luca, got a promise of an extra 10,000 tal (£2,400,000) from Auletes (total 16,000 tal or £3,860,000) & ordered the governor of Syria, Aulus Gabinius, to go ahead.

Meanwhile the Alexandrians had crowned Archelaus & Berenice. Gabinius got through the desert between Gaza & Pelusium through the cavalry leadership of Mark Antony. The Alexandrians were defeated, Archelaus killed, Auletes restored & Berenice beheaded. It was impossible to extract the ransom from the people; so the Romans left a garrison of Romans & Celtic & German cavalry, who took the place of the old guard & behaved in the same praetorian manner. Later on they intermarry with the Egyptians, & also runaway Italian slaves & criminals & old soldiers of Pompey. This is the stage in which Caesar finds them. Technically, they are the Roman army of occupation.

Caesar comes to Egypt to catch Pompey, but, finding him dead, has nothing to do there & is expected to go on at once to Africa to deal with Juba of Numidia.

Being in want of money, he lands in Alexandria with 2 amalgamated legions (3200 men & 800 Celtic & German cavalry), takes up his quarters in the palace & collects taxes & settles the Egyptian succession. (Pothinus sarcastic.)

Lets Egyptians down easy for 10 million denarii (£400,000).

Invites Cl. & P. D. to submit to arbitration. P. D. already in palace. Cl. comes thither. He makes them marry & gives them Egypt, agreeably to the will of Auletes (their father). He gives Cyprus to Arsinoe & Ptol. junior, cancelling the annexation by Cato in 58.

—Order of Events—

Caesar demands his £400,000, arrears of Aulete's debt.

Pothinus & P. D. send the treasures of the temples & the gold plate of the king to be melted at the mint, so as to make as big a scene as possible. Bare walls & wooden cups.

Pothinus and P. D. plot to attack Caesar with the Roman army of occupation under the command of Achillas. Meanwhile a good deal of sporadic assassination of the Caesarians goes on.

Caesar, detained by the N. W. winds, orders up reinforcements from Asia, & goes in meanwhile for revelry. Suddenly Achillas appears in Alexandria with the army of occupation, and the citizens make common cause with him. Arsinoe and Ganymedes head the insurrection. Caesar siezes the king & Pothinus, fortifies himself in the palace & theatre adjoining, burns his fleet which is in the harbor in front of the theatre & occupies the Pharos (island with lighthouse commanding harbor) with boats. He sends for troop and ships to the Syrians, Nabataeans, Cretans, Rhodians.

Street fighting daily. Caesar is cut off from Marea, the fresh water lake behind the town. He digs wells on the beach & finds drinkable water.

He releases P. D. to propitiate the insurrectionists.

Alexandrians try to introduce fireships into the east harbor & fail.

        "   equip a squadron to intercept the towing in by Caesar's ships of a legion from Asia Minor, but are beaten by the Rhodian mariners.

The citizens capture the Pharos & keep continually sea-fighting Caesar in the roadstead. Caesar forced to recover the Pharos at all costs.

He attacks by boats from the harbor & ships from the roadstead. He carries the Pharos & section A of the mole, & builds the wall C. While his troops are crowded near the wall a division of Egyptians rush the part of A nearest the lighthouse,

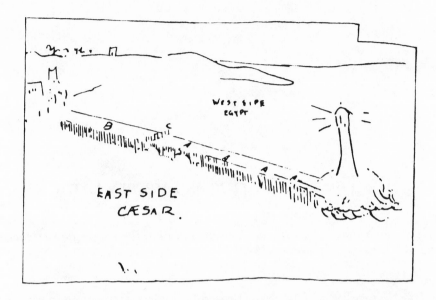

charge the Romans & sailors at the wall C, and drive them into the sea. Some are taken on board by Caesar's ships; but 400 soldiers & more sailors are drowned. Caesar has to swim for it twice—once on jumping off the pier & once when his overcrowded ship founders. The Pharos, and sections of the mole remain in his hands.

The relief by Mithridates followed.

—Relief by Mithridates—

Motley army from Syria—Ityraeans of the prince of the Libanus

    Bedouins of Jamblichus, son of Sampsiceramus

    Jews under the minister Antipater

    contingents from Cilicia & Syria under petty chiefs mostly robbers

Mithridates occupies Pelusium on the day of his arrival.

Takes the great road towards Memphis to cross the Nile above the Delta, getting support thereby from the Jewish peasants.

The Egyptians send an army commanded by P. D. to prevent M. from crossing. They meet beyond Memphis at "Jew's Camp" between Onion & Heliopolis. Mithridates outmanoeuvres them & crosses at Memphis.

Caesar, on hearing of the approaching relief, ships part of his troops to the end of Lake Marea (west of Alex[a]) & marches round the lake & up the Nile to meet Mit., advancing up the river. Junction affected without molestation.

Battle of the Nile

Caesar marches into the Delta, crosses a deep canal cut by the Egyptians, overthrows their vanguard & storms their camp. Egyptians swept into the Nile by an attack from 3 sides at once. P. D.'s overladen boat sinks; & he is drowned.

Caesar immediately makes straight for the Egypt quarter of Alex at the head of his cavalry. They receive him in mourning, with the images of their gods in their hands. His troops, in the Roman quarter, go wild with enthusiasm.

He lectures them (431 M[ommsen]) grants settled Jews equal rights with Greeks, & replaces army of occupation nominally under king of Egypt by Roman garrison under Rufio, who, as a freedman's son, is not well born enough to make himself formidable.

Cleopatra & Ptol the younger get the throne subject to Rome; Arsinoe is carried off to Italy lest she should become a pretext for dynastic insurrections; and Cyprus is added to Cilicia (a Roman province).

10   The Social Critic as Literary Critic

"For art's sake alone" I would not face the toil of writing a single sentence.—
Preface to *Man and Superman* (1903)

In a writing career seldom characterized by understatement Bernard Shaw remained remarkably modest about his contributions to nondramatic criticism.[1] However little known, his literary criticism stimulated by the printed page rather than by plays and performances furnishes uniquely Shavian insights into other writers and writing and provides the added bonus of reflecting Shaw's own creative methods and motives.

Literary criticism was at first more a job for Shaw than a joy. Most of it was done anonymously, when, in his late twenties and early thirties, he was a book reviewer for the *Pall Mall Gazette*. Later an enterprising editor would offer him as many guineas for a single piece under the already famous by-line as he had collected for many months' work in the defunct *Gazette*; and it would be for a book that really interested him.

As a body of criticism, whether produced originally for the *New Statesman* or the *Evening Standard*, as a preface to a publication of his own, or as an introduction to a new edition of someone else's work, Shaw's criticism remains remarkably consistent, especially once we pass that early period when he reviewed books less because he had something he wanted to say about them, or was interested in using them as platform for saying something cogent, but because he would be paid for the job. Yet even in that early phase, when he had improved his fortunes to the point that he had replaced writing unsalable novels with steady but unguaranteed journalism and no longer existed on his mother's earnings, he not only wrote honest reviews but often evidenced the direction his later criticism would consistently take.

Shaw's first serious literary criticism even antedated the *Gazette* stint—a response to a lecture on "Caliban upon Setebos" delivered to the Browning Society on April 25, 1884, and printed in the society's *Papers*.

> Shakspere, being a dramatic poet, has never labelled any work of his dramatic;
> Browning, being essentially undramatic, has called this Caliban poem a dramatic monologue. Now, there is a difference between the faculty of the dramatic
> poet and that of the epic or descriptive poet, and they are often strangely divided. The epic poet has a theory of the motives and feelings of his characters,

and he describes his theory. The dramatic poet, whether he has a theory or not, instinctively puts the character before you acting and speaking as it would do in actual life. The merely epic and descriptive poet cannot do this. Milton had not the dramatic faculty very strongly; Shakspere had. If you compare Browning and Shakspere, you will find the difference coming out strongly. Browning makes Caliban minutely describe his own feelings and analyze his own thoughts. A creature in the brutish condition of Caliban would not be able to do anything of the sort; and here you have an initial absurdity,—an essentially undramatic condition, which shows you at once that what you are reading is no dramatic monologue at all. Shakspere's method is very simple. His Caliban does not reason about God; but he is terrified by a thunderstorm.

This was the dramatic critic and playwright in Shaw, struggling for birth, as much as the literary critic to be. And as would always be the case, there was for his audience, however much he offended their predilections—and these were Browning idolators—the redeeming Shavian wit. "Browning's Caliban," he concluded to the Browningites, "is a savage, with the introspective powers of a Hamlet, and the theology of an evangelical Churchman. I must confess that I cannot conceive an evangelical Churchman possessing the introspective powers of a Hamlet." In a parenthesis following, the transcript noted, "Great laughter."[2]

A later Browning Society rejoinder again revealed the embryo playwright, as Shaw in 1886 (according to the *Abstracts* for June 5, for which he wrote his own transcript) declared that it was absurd to contend that Browning's poetry possessed only the metrical quality forced upon it by the enthusiastic reciter. "If the purely rhythmic element were subtracted from the work of some of most admired versifiers—Mr. Swinburne, for example," Shaw contended, "the poverty of the residue would astonish many readers who have a very inadequate idea of how much more goes to the making of a great poet besides ability to mark time. The prose of very great dramatic writers sometimes, at the crises of their narratives, acquires a rhythmic majesty and energy to which actual versification could add nothing." In his own plays Shaw would later prove his point.

In the early 1880s Shaw had become friendly with William Archer, a young man already successful in London journalism and with whom Shaw abortively collaborated on a play he later turned on his own into *Widowers' Houses*. Through Archer he also acquired literary employment, by the end of 1885 having begun reviewing art in the *World* and books in the *Pall Mall Gazette*. Archer had passed on several of his assignments, and in unauthorized but effective fashion Shaw quickly proved his ability to the editors. He got the jobs.

Between 1885 and 1888, while he was switching from art critic to music critic, Shaw continued producing anonymous reviews for the *Gazette*, 107 of them reaching print, along with occasional other writings ranging from musical and dramatic criticism to letters, notes, reports, and spoofs, some contributed under transparently pseudonymous by-lines. But few of the books he was assigned were worth the time he spent reviewing them—*"Verona," and other Poems*, by L. Ormiston Chant, a handbook on physiognomy, a biography of a minor Scottish painter, an excruciatingly bad novel by F. Marion Crawford, the memoirs of a forgotten physician. Others, meanwhile, two of them also young Irishmen, wrote reviews of the major writers. George Moore was reviewing Huysmans and Zola, and an even younger man named Oscar Wilde was being assigned Turgenev, Tolstoy, Dostoevsky, George Sand, William Morris, and Walter Pater. Shaw chafed quietly as long as the income seemed essential; then in September 1888, he wrote in frustration to the literary editor asking for something significant "as relief to the slow murder of the cursed parcels of rubbish with which you blast my prime. Surely it must be dawning on editors at last that any sort of live copy is better than the mechanical literary stuff poured out on ordinary novels and minor poetry. Why condemn me to read things that I can't review—that no artistic conscience could long survive the reviewing of!" And he went on to suggest that the *Gazette* might just as well review "boots, hats, dogcarts and so on" rather than the latest claptrap novel by Miss Braddon. "There ought to be legislation against this sort of thing—on the lines of the Factory Acts." Thus when Shaw had prepared a lecture the year before for one of the many literary, debating, and reading groups in which he was active, his theme was truth in fiction, a subject about which he railed in angry-young-critic fashion, he could speak from the painful experience of having read too much of their work, about the "earnest and able young writers [who], when they commit themselves to the maintenance of a wife and family, or to the habits of fashionable society, or to both at once, degenerate first into elegant triflers, and finally into incurable hacks, absolutely without consciences."

By the end of 1888, although he was finished as a regular book critic, he was just at the beginning of real literary criticism. Still, he had already made the most of his few opportunities, doing missionary work for a nonliterary effort by Samuel Butler, *Luck or Cunning?*, and for Thomas Tyler's thesis that Mary Fitton was the Dark Lady in Shakespeare's *Sonnets*. He had also reviewed bad novels by Wilkie Collins and George Moore—yet at least these were substantial writers. And where he could, even in a notice of a minor title, he would use the occasion for a pronouncement about a major figure, praising Anthony Trollope, for example, in a long paragraph in a review in which Trollope's name need not have been produced. "Society has not yet forgiven that excellent novelist," Shaw wrote, "for having worked so many hours a day, like a carpenter or tailor, instead of going periodically mad with inspiration and hewing Barchester Towers at one frenzied stroke out of chaos, that being notoriously the only genuine artistic method. Yet if we except the giants of the craft, he is entitled to rank among English writers as the first sincerely naturalistic novelist of our day. He delivered us from the marvels, senseless accidents, and cat's cradle plots of old romance."

Later, in a self-interview he published to promote one of his own plays, when asked to reveal a bit of the plot, Shaw teased that he was a dramatic poet, not a plotmonger. He was consistent in maintaining that a plot was the least important part of a story. Wilkie Collins, he had written in the *Gazette* in 1886, "shackled and crippled his genius" through "procrustean scaffolds" called plots. "The proper framework for a book is its own natural skeleton: if it be born without one, then let it perish as a shapeless abortion." Often, as here, Shakespeare was Shaw's negative example, his plots allegedly deforming his plays; and later in an essay on Dickens, Shaw withheld the admiration he felt for the later novels from the incomplete last work, *The Mystery of Edwin Drood*, in which he saw the baleful, plot-focused influence of Dickens's friend Collins. "Novels," Shaw insisted as early as the 1886 review, "are like other works of art: uninteresting just so far as they are machine made."

Late in 1889 Shaw began what he intended to be a long essay, "From Dickens to Ibsen." His intention was to be outrageous enough to be readable as criticism yet to make the points about the utilitarian element in art which he had espoused in his reviews. "A novel or play has two aspects," he wrote, "the documentary and the artistic. . . . The greatest work is not so much the greatest artistic feat as the greatest lesson, revelation, illuminant. . . ." He saw a need for discrimination between the two critical approaches—the artistic analysis, "a fine art in itself," and the "documentary criticism" ranging from "mere news to pure philosophy." Oversimplifying for purposes of his article, he went on to explain that "Dickens's documents belong to the struggle of Men for social equality; Ibsen's, to the struggle of Woman for individual liberty. I regard atheism as the first condition of true religion; I abhor the British family as an institution which degrades women . . . and I make no distinction whatever between the economic position of a gentleman of property and that of a thief. . . . My interpretation of two great writers may be interesting . . . to many who deplore my views as sincerely as I deplore theirs. . . ."

The critical article fortunately remained unfinished. It was immature beyond irreverence, and Shaw must have sensed it. Two years later he would write *The Quintessence of Ibsenism*. It would seem a generation removed from the juvenilities of the abandoned polemic.[3]

Criticizing the revered Shakespeare, even more than the beloved Dickens, was a sacrilege likely to place a bumptious young critic in jeopardy, but Shaw was maturing his own ideas about the role of a critic. It did not follow, he held, that the right to criticize Shakespeare involved "the power of writing better plays." An artist had to be criticized on other terms, among those his ability to reach and sustain his personal peak. "A man's work," he maintained as early as the 1887 lecture, "should be for his best audience, even if it be an ideal audience." It was an easy preachment for a young critic, who learned as he earned his bread among theater audiences that even the greatest writers had to find audiences with potboilers who could not be reached by masterpieces. In part Shaw the critic was exhibiting the critic's need for a certain kind of fulfillment he described well in a musical review in 1891—"that although the satisfaction of seeing a simple thing consummately well done is most joyful and soothing after a long and worrying course of complex things imperfectly done, the simple success must not therefore be placed above the complex half success." But a critic, he wrote at about the same time, was a missionary and elucidator, not a judge and executioner. He did not have the power of life or death over a work of art: "Though the east wind seems to kill the consumptive patient, he dies, not of the wind, but of phthisis. On the strong-lunged man it blows in vain."

For Shaw, there was no form of writing in which literary criticism could not assert itself. In his early letters we find such comments as that to critic Clement Shorter (January 9, 1891): "I was inexpressibly shocked by your disparagement of Olive Schreiner's volume in the *Star*. You ought to walk to South Africa and back with peas in your shoes by way of penance. What were you dreaming of? The book is a treasure." The book was not the classic *Story of an African Farm*, but Shaw was eager to push the causes, and career, of the young writer. And while his prefaces could be expected to include some literary criticism, where applicable, he also included such comments, where dramatically useful, in his plays. One play, *The Dark Lady of the Sonnnets* (1910), was an act of literary criticism itself, and in *Misalliance* (also 1910) the ebullient, self-educated underwear shopkeeper and library benefactor John Tarleton ends almost every speech he has in the play with a hortatory "Read Chesterton. . . . Read Mill. Read Jefferson . . . read Shelley: read Mrs Browning. . . . I'm for the Par-

liament of Man, the federation of the world. Read Tennyson." To an intruder in
the household he objects, "Judging from your conversational style, I should
think you must spend at least a shilling a week on romantic literature." Earlier—as "Corno di Bassetto" and as "G.B.S."—his music reviews and theater
reviews were full of literary criticism in which his major thesis (musical or dramatic as well as literary) is that public taste cannot be forcibly made sophisticated and that the popular arts, or the higher arts reduced to manageability by
the masses, inevitably improve the level of popular art and have a missionary
value often worth championing rather than attacking. Among other places,
Shaw made the point in an 1893 music review:

> Such conversions are always going on. The African heathen "embrace" the
> Christian religion by singing a Te Deum instead of dancing a war-dance after
> "wetting their spears" in the blood of the tribe next door; the English heathen
> (a much more numerous body) take to reading the Bible when it is edited for
> them by Miss Marie Corelli; the masses, sceptical as to Scott and Dumas, are
> converted to an appreciation of romantic literature by Mr Rider Haggard;
> Shakespear and Goethe become world-famous on the strength of "acting ver-
> sions" that must have set them fairly spinning in their graves; and there is a
> general appearance of tempering the wind to the shorn lamb, which turns out,
> on closer examination, to be really effected by building a badly ventilated sub-
> urban villa round the silly animal, and telling him that the frowsy warmth he
> begins to feel is that of the sunbeam playing on Parnassus, or the peace of mind
> that passeth all understanding, according to circumstances. When I was
> young, I was like all immature critics: I used to throw stones at the windows of
> the villa, and thrust in my head and bawl at the lamb that he was a fool, and
> that villa builders—honest people enough, according to their lights—were
> swindlers and hypocrites, and nincompoops and sixth-raters. But the lamb got
> on better with them than with me; and at last it struck me that he was happier
> and more civilized in his villa than shivering in the keen Parnassian winds that
> delighted my hardier bones; so that now I have become quite fond of him, and
> love to lead him out when the weather is exceptionally mild . . . and talk to him
> a bit without letting him see too plainly what a deplorable mutton-head he is.

A critic had a corollary duty as well, as Shaw observed after viewing an elabo-
rately and expensively mounted Christmas pantomime in 1890: "What struck
me most was the extraordinary profusion of artistic talent wasted through
mere poverty of purpose." In the 1887 lecture he could not comprehend the
"metaphysics" of "art for art's sake," for he was convinced that "a man can be
the better or [the] worse morally for going to the theatre or reading a book."
Because Art was not "outside the sphere of morals," he insisted that "a work of
fiction should have a purpose." Yet if the purpose were today's, or tomorrow's,
rather than yesterday's, he recognized that there would be consumer resistance. The novelist, he was aware, could set out to write on a different plan than
the mere reproduction of convenient bundles of personified virtues and vices.
His hero or heroine could be "simply the most highly evolved person in the
book; and if his actions be only dictated by sufficiently developed intelligence,
self-control, and, above all, foresight, they will appear a series of crimes, and he
an unfeeling scoundrel to the less evolved characters, and to the average reader,
whilst yet his superiority will be mysteriously evident throughout." It was a
theory he had tried out in his novels with conspicuous lack of success, for he had
conceived of several of his leading characters as "improved types of humanity."
Yet in a number of his best plays—*Caesar* and *Barbara* and *Joan*, for example—
Shaw's title figures are embodiments of his ideas about the possibilities of the
race. In his last years his views remained unchanged, and in a 1944 "Post-

script" to his *Back to Methuselah* preface to mark its publication in the Oxford World's Classics series he defined a world classic as a work which would "try to solve, or at least to formulate, the riddles of creation." But these might take the form of heresies, which he realized would inevitably be resisted; thus he saw high purpose and high art as the difficult twin concomitants of greatness in literature: "Heretical teaching must be made irresistibly attractive by fine art if the heretics are not to starve or burn." Still, he insisted that useful purpose was not necessarily high purpose. As he wrote to his French translator Augustin Hamon (January 9, 1907), "Social questions are too sectional, too topical, too temporal, to move a man to the mighty effort which is needed to produce great poetry. Prison reform may nerve Charles Reade to produce an effective and businesslike prose melodrama; but it could never produce *Hamlet, Faust*, or *Peer Gynt. . . .*"

Or *The Way of All Flesh*, he might have added, for Samuel Butler's novel to Shaw not only had a mighty purpose but had succeeded in it: "Butler forged his jests into a weapon which smashed the nineteenth century." There were never enough Butlers.

In Shaw's *Pall Mall Gazette* days the nineteenth century was still very much alive. "The most dangerous public house in London," he punned in 1887, "is kept by a gentleman named Mudie." Mudie's and Smith's bookstalls and lending libraries still retained their stranglehold on what the English reader read, for their bulk orders—or their withdrawal—meant the difference between profit and loss on most books and had resulted in a publishers' self-censorship which had emotionally and intellectually emasculated fiction. In a letter to the *Gazette* the same year Shaw, describing himself as "a sufferer from that strange brain disease which drives its victims to write long stories that are not true, and to delight in them more than in any other literature," suggested realistically that cheap editions by publishers would do more to break the power of the circulating libraries than impassioned declamations against their monopoly. Referring to their kind of book and its readership Shaw had noted in an anonymous *Gazette* review the year before, "We always have with us men and women who, born after their due time, clamour to have the clock put back, and would, if they might have their way, reinstate flogging, duelling, confiscation of the property of wives, and a dozen other barbarisms which the rest of us have outgrown." It meant, too, Shaw observed at about the same time, that writers could—and often had to—purvey a "No Man's Land of luxuries for which there is nothing to pay, of poignant griefs that do not hurt, thrilling joys that do not satisfy, virtuous aspirations that do not ennoble, and fierce crusades that leave evil none the weaker, but rather the more prosperous for the advertisement." It meant, too, that even the most courageous writers sometimes had to work at titillation while being less than direct and less than candid, Shaw paradoxically attacking one of George Moore's weaker novels, *A Mere Accident*, not for using a rape as his central incident and evading the crucial scene by having the victim insensible at the moment but because the incident—so far as it is described—"is described for its own sake. . . . The objection, in fact, to Mr. Moore is not that he is realistic, but that he is a romancer who, in order that he might take liberties, persuades himself that he is a pathologist."[4]

Pseudopathology was often licensed by Mudie's when Zolaesque honesty would land a publisher (as happened with Henry Vizetelly) not on Mudie's shelves but in prison. Searching for the success formula of one of the few popular novelists for whom he retained some grudging admiration, Shaw saw a half-voyeuristic, half-critical view of society which made the clever Ouida[5] both pander and perceptive critic. (She wrote of the pleasure-loving society about which people love to read and which "breeds monsters," in "half-reasoned but real" terms which imaginatively combined mock sociology and spurious sex.) The suggestive qualities of books by women novelists had long been an accepted fact of Victorian literary life, as a *Punch* cartoon in 1867 had indicated. A man, shopping for a novel at the counter of a bookshop, inspects one volume he has opened and announces through his muttonchop whiskers, "Ah! very Clever, I dare say. But I see it's written by a Lady, and *I* want a book that my *Daughters* may read. Give me Something else!" For the social criticism in fiction Shaw was willing to forgive much, but when he found insufficiently redeeming social content he was unwilling to forgive either the sensuality or the artificiality, noting in the *Gazette* that in some of the works of Ouida and her disciple Marie Corelli there was not only "an almost rancourous insistence on the corruption of society" but an artificiality of background ("drop scenery, in short") and "a partial view of character, resulting from a keen insight into the erotic impulses without sufficient observation or study of the rest of life."

Shaw consistently railed against the imposition of a gratuitous erotic interest into literature on the excuse that the public wanted it, pointing to the then-contemporary examples of Wells's *Time Machine* and Bellamy's *Looking Backward*, futuristic fictions sapped in intellectual power by the infusion of amorous sentimentality. "The pleasures of the senses I can sympathize with and share," he declared, "but the substitution of sensuous ecstasy for intellectual activity and honesty is the very devil . . . for all institutions have in the long run to live by the nature of things, and not by childish pretendings."

In a Fabian lecture in 1889 he even inserted a criticism of Bellamy's novel from another standpoint—that *Looking Backward* defeated itself by a middle-class limitation in vision.

> Mr Bellamy is so little able to conceive what the overthrow of the middle class means, that his fictitious perfect State is a thoroughly businesslike commercial Utopia in which every man is what a respectable Bostonian is today, and every young woman a realization of the ideal young lady heroine of the late Anthony Trollope. Like a true middle class man, Mr Bellamy believes that middle class piety, middle class family institutions, middle class morals are valid for all classes and for all time—that middle class standards of right and wrong are set up in heaven as our standards of length are set up in Trafalgar Square and at Greenwich observatory.

On the other hand, he noted in a Fabian lecture in 1920, "Socialism and the Labor Party," middle-class values were exactly the perspective a much earlier novel needed to assure its success and its significance.

> The middle class began to have a very high opinion of itself somewhere about the 17th century. There is a book which occupies in relation to the middle classes the same position that Karl Marx's Kapital does to the modern Socialist proletariat; that book is called Robinson Crusoe. I dare say that many of you have read Robinson Crusoe with the sense of reading a romance about a man who was wrecked and lived on a desert island, and you probably read it very young. But if you will reflect you will recall that almost on every second page of that book there was a certain amount of moralizing about the advantages of the middle station of life. It really was the preaching of the advantages and benefits and happinesses of the middle station of life which nerved Defoe to make the effort of writing Robinson Crusoe.

The social matrix of a work was integral to Shaw, not a peg on which a writer was free to hang his novel or play. Shaw did not feel he had to agree with an author's point of view: nevertheless, it had to be psychologically valid. Inevitably there would be some overlap, as one can see in his critique for the *Star* (June 27, 1893) of the book publication of George Moore's play *The Strike at Arlingford*. One of Shaw's more entertaining vehicles for criticism, self-criticism, and self-promotion was the fictitious interview, in which an invented reporter encountered G.B.S. eating a vegetarian meal in his shambles of a flat, taking the air in his cinnamon-colored Jaeger suit, or in some other allegedly stereotypical situation. For the Moore critique the *"Star* interviewer" interrupted Shaw's siesta in Regent's Park to glean from him the understanding that Moore's economic motive was sound but his psychology shaky. The hero was a weakling.

> "Well, the weak point of the play to me is the assumption throughout it all that Socialism is to a middle-class man exactly what keeping a turnpike was to old Mr. Weller in *Pickwick*—the last resource of a soured and desperate wretch. John Reid, jilted by Lady Ann, takes to Socialism as being just a degree more suicidal than taking to drink. He is supposed to have renounced everything that makes life worth living in exchanging the position of a private secretary for that of a great labor leader. Now no man could possibly become a great labor leader with such ideas in his head. . . . No: a labor leader may be far from an ideally virtuous republican: he may be an aristocrat, even an autocrat; he may laugh at the credulity and curse the folly of the mobs who cheer him; he may exhaust all the arts of the actor and the hypocrite in cajoling them, coaxing them, bullying them, stoking their enthusiasm up or down as may be necessary; he may be a bouncing liar and as great a blackguard as Napoleon; he may be utterly incapable of the attractively decent straightness and simplicity of private life that distinguishes such men as Burns and Mann; but he must be an able man with all his will and his ambition enlisted on the labor side, and with a daimonic power of throwing himself into a labor conflict and fighting to win with all his might. Now the hero of *The Strike at Arlingford* is above all things a failure. That is the note of him from beginning to end. And yet Moore asks me to believe for the sake of his play that this fellow is a great labor leader. Well, of course, I cannot: I know too much about it."

Shaw had always been, he confessed ironically in 1900, a Puritan in his attitude toward art. "I am as fond of fine music and a handsome building as Milton was, or Cromwell, or Bunyan; but if I found that they were becoming the instruments of a systematic idolatry of sensuousness, I would hold it good statesmanship to blow every cathedral in the world to pieces with dynamite, organ and all, without the least heed to the screams of the art critics and cultured voluptuaries." Still, he found value even in sheer pruriency, which, in the 1920s, he said he liked "when it was well done. It has never occurred to me to try to prevent anyone else reading it. You must let people eat what agrees with them, even if it seems to you to be garbage." But there was a higher utility for literary obscenity, or what passes for obscenity at different periods. Sending his rewrite of Frank Harris's *Bernard Shaw* (1931) for publication after Harris's death, Shaw included his views on the utility of *Lady Chatterley's Lover* (1928), then sufficiently notorious as to be denied entry into the U.K. by Customs agents. "If I had a marriageable daughter," Shaw quoted himself, "what could I give her to read to prepare her? Dickens? Thackeray? George Eliot? Walter Scott? Trollope? or even any of the clever modern women who take such a fiendish delight in writing very able novels that leave you hopeless and miserable? They would teach her a lot about life and society and human nature. But they would leave her absolutely in the dark as to marriage. . . . She would learn something from Lady Chatterley. I shouldn't let her engage herself if I could help it until she had read that book. Lawrence had delicacy enough to tell the best, and brutality enough to rub in the worst. *Lady Chatterley['s Lover]* should be on the shelves of every college for budding girls. They should be forced to read it on pain of being refused a marriage license. But it is not as readable as *Ivanhoe* or *A Tale of Two Cities*!!!"

Shaw was well aware that works of his own at various times had been castigated and even censored on grounds of obscenity of subject or language, and that he had been railed at himself from pulpits and editorial pages for so seemingly harmless a word as *bloody* when first used in a popular play (in *Pygmalion*). "The nation's morals," he wrote after an earlier censorship problem, "are like its teeth: the more decayed they are the more it hurts to touch them." It was the writer's task, he declared, to instruct as well as to outrage. In his preface to Hall Caine's *The White Prophet* (1909), he noted the writer's impact upon public opinion: "When our governing class loses the power of remembering yesterday and foreseeing tomorrow, and spends today in talking manifold folly, it is time for the man of letters to take the instruction of public opinion out of its hands." Public opinion, he noted, would be instructed by any popular work, good or bad, intentionally or unintentionally. As he put it in the preface to *Three Plays for Puritans*, "The worst of it is that since man's intellectual consciousness of himself is derived from the descriptions of him in books, a persistent misrepresentation of humanity in literature gets finally accepted and acted upon." One of the misrepresentations, Shaw thought, resulted from the extremes by which the sexual side of humanity was exposed—or censored. Seeing a "classic quality" in James Joyce, although self-confessedly too prudish to use some of Joyce's words, he thought nonetheless that there should be no limit to "blackguardly language. . . . It depends on what people will stand." The important thing to him about the controversial texture of Joyce's work was that his exposure of seaminess in Dublin had a moral value.[6] "You cannot carry out moral sanitation, any more than physical sanitation, without indecent exposures. . . . If a man holds up a mirror to your nature and shows you that it needs washing—not whitewashing—it is no use breaking the mirror. Go for soap and water." There had always been an economic moral in sex for Shaw, as had been apparent as early as his condemnation of an exploiting society in *Mrs Warren's Profession*; and in the 1920s he added that there would never be "a healthily sexed literature until you have a healthily sexed people; and that is impossible under Capitalism, which imposes commercial conditions on marriage as on everything else." Ideally, he thought, fiction should deal with healthy people in circumstances which are—for the imagined period—normal, while the abnormal and the morbid side of life belonged to the newspapers. But he understood that this was an impossibility as long as the reaction to nineteenth-century censorship and hypocrisy had to run its course. "I doubt if there is a single excess in modern fiction that cannot be traced to a suppression in the reign of Queen Victoria. It is just because Mr. James Joyce was brought up on the reticences of the heroes and heroines of Sir Walter Scott that he is so embarrassingly communicative as to the indiscretions of his own heroes and heroines."

Although Shaw refused to subscribe to the first edition of *Ulysses*, writing the publisher, Sylvia Beach, that no Irishman would pay one hundred and fifty francs for a book, and his explanation to her, based on his having read parts of the novel in serial form, has often been ascribed as negative, he nevertheless used such phrases about it as "truthful," "hideously real," and "literary genius," and in several thoughtful paragraphs in the autobiographical preface to the first printing of *Immaturity* (1930) referred to Joyce's Dublin as described "with a fidelity so ruthless that the book is hardly bearable." His first mention of Joyce in what could be called literary criticism had occurred even earlier, when he gave one of his rare lectures on literature, this one at the Little Theatre in Dublin in 1918.[7] An account of it survives in the diary of Joseph Holloway, an Abbey Theatre devotee and passionate Irish nationalist whose references to Shaw were almost always hostile:

> Saturday, October 26. . . . I went down to hear Shaw's discourse on "Literature in Ireland" at the little theatre. . . . His discourse was quite Shavian in his findings, and he kept nagging all the while he spoke; he afterwards said he knew he was nagging, but once set going he could not stop. Only those who don't succeed in art or literature make good critics was his opinion; therefore, he was no critic. He didn't read critically. It was only when they went to Paris Irishmen could write, and then he spoke of George Moore's and Joyce's works and their indecencies. He also said that Synge got his local colour in Paris, and that there is nothing Irish about The Playboy. The central idea is that the worship of crime is universal; in fact, the Irish people don't understand it. Then he went on to say that the Irish should be conscripted out of their own country so that they would learn to know what Ireland was really like. He also said they could never get anything until they ceased to have a grievance. Nobody liked people with a grievance; they were generally bores. The men who didn't leave Ireland wouldn't write like Synge. The plays that were written by Irishmen who never travelled were generally those that lacked poetic outlook and were sordid and abusive in character. . . . Shaw is always stimulating and entertaining and never dull. He mixed all he said with a very nimble wit, and his words came ever ready to his lips. He speaks excellently well always, and his delivery is clear and telling!

While Shaw will never be celebrated for his Joyce criticism or his appreciation of Irish writers in general, he remains one of the better commentators on Dickens, who, along with Bunyan, Butler, and (yes!) Shakespeare, was one of his major English literary heroes. But to Shaw there was a lesser and a greater Dickens, the former being the portrayer of great comic characters before he developed a social conscience. He made the point in a 1906 letter to G.K. Chesterton and elaborated on it in memorable prefaces to new editions of *Great Expectations* (1937) and *Hard Times* (1912). One paragraph to Chesterton sums it up:

> I find that Dickens is at his greatest after the social awakening which produced Hard Times. Little Dorrit is an enormous work. The change is partly the disillusion produced by the unveiling of capitalist civilization, but partly also Dickens's discovery of the gulf between himself as a man of genius and the public. That he did not realize this early is shown by the fact that he found out his wife before he married her as much too small for the job, and yet plumbed the difference so inadequately that he married her thinking he could go through with it. When the situation became intolerable, he must have faced the fact that there was something more than "incompatibilities" between him and the average man and woman. Little Dorrit is written, like all the later books,

frankly and somewhat sadly, *de haut en bas*. In them Dickens recognizes that quite everyday men are as grotesque as Bunsby. Sparkler, one of the most extravagant of all his gargoyles, is an untouched photograph almost. Wegg and Riderhood are sinister and terrifying because they are simply real, which Squeers and Sikes are not.

Shaw also had a theory for Chesterton to explain what both saw as a shift in tone between the two parts of *David Copperfield*. It is a convincing hypothesis.

> There is a curious contrast between Dickens's sentimental indiscretions concerning his marriage and his sorrows and quarrels, and his impenetrable reserve about himself as displayed in his published correspondence. He writes to his family about waiters, about hotels, about screeching tumblers of hot brandy and water, and about the seasick man in the next berth, but never one really intimate word, never a real confession of his soul. David Copperfield is a failure as an autobiography because when he comes to deal with the grown-up David, you find that he has not the slightest intention of telling you the truth—or indeed anything—about himself. Even the child David is more remarkable for the reserves than for the revelations: he falls back on fiction at every turn. Clennam and Pip are the real autobiographies.

For the text of *Great Expectations*, to which Shaw furnished his famous preface, he supplied as well the original, and perhaps more artistic, ending to the novel, which Dickens had discarded in favor of the false sentimentality Victorian readers craved. Shaw understood that both conclusions were wistful and that both provided the hero with some consolation, but in this first restoration of the original ending in a modern edition of the novel Shaw wanted readers to see not only how the story might have turned out for Pip and Estella but how ending a novel was a problem Dickens regularly had to face in the context of popular taste. In *Dombey and Son*, Shaw observed, Dickens had been planning an ending which would include the "degeneration and ruin" of Walter Gay, but instead Walter unexpectedly returns to marry Florence Dombey, providing "a manufactured ending to save a painful one." Similarly, he saw Mr. Pickwick turn from butt to hero of *Pickwick Papers* as Dickens studied reader reaction to the serial parts; and he found that *Martin Chuzzlewit* "begins as a study in selfishness and ends nowhere." Even in *Our Mutual Friend*, one of the peaks in the canon to Shaw, the dustman Boffin's apparent corruption by wealth[8] is only a benevolent pretense to satisfy middle-class morality. The happy endings, including the one in the intense and bitter *Our Mutual Friend*, are in Shaw's view "consolations" which become "unnecessary and even irritating" as, under Dickens's own tutelage, "our minds grow stronger and sterner."

"Trollope and Thackeray could see Chesney Wold," Shaw wrote of *Hard Times*; "but Dickens could see through it." It is the writer in maturity who, to Shaw, capsulized for Victorian fiction the preachments of Carlyle, Marx, Ruskin, and Morris "that it is not our disorder but our order that is horrible." Thus while never losing sight of the compromises which Dickens, even in his later, greater novels felt forced to make, Shaw emphasized the social critic and revolutionary that had emerged from Dickens's dissection of his world and his conversion during the 1850s to a sense of "social sin." "Marx knew he was a revolutionist," Shaw wrote, "whilst Dickens had not the faintest suspicion of that part of his calling. . . . Little Dorrit is a more seditious book than Das Kapital. All over Europe men and women are in prison for pamphlets and speeches which are to Little Dorrit as red pepper to dynamite." But Dickens would not have understood, whatever his sense of social outrage. He was hardly a systematic thinker, and as J. B. Priestley put it, while Shaw wanted to abolish the poor and replace them with sensible people, Dickens only wanted to make the poor happy. Shaw's embrace of Dickens as humorist and satirist was genuine, but his vision of the novelist would have embarrassed Dickens. In the words of George Ford, in *Dickens and His Readers* (1965), "his hug is hugely affectionate but so powerful that the object of his affections is squeezed out of shape."

Even in viewing the nineteenth-century romantic poets Shaw used a moral perspective. Shelley, he thought, had first been seen as a moral monster, but by the end of the century critics were attempting to find in him a latter-day sanctity by stressing the beauty of his lyrics and shunting aside his major poetic statements as indiscretions. The approach was one Shaw found repellent, emphasizing that Shelley's longer poems, like his political and philosophical writings, were serious and carefully thought out in their moral position, something Shaw found seldom to be so with English poets, up to and including the contemporary great name, Tennyson. If Shelley was a sinner, he declared, "he was a hardened sinner, and a deliberate one." Surprisingly, Shaw managed, in a convincing tour de force of critical imagination, to also find a radical social critic in Keats, in whom he saw more than a writer of lovely lyrics. "It often happens," he observed, "that a prophet-poet begins as a literary poet, the prophet instinctively training himself by literary exercises for his future work." But Keats, Shaw regretted, did not live long enough to effect the transition, although he "achieved the very curious feat of writing one poem of which it may be said that if Karl Marx can be imagined as writing a poem instead of a treatise on Capital, he would have written Isabella."[9] Few indictments of capitalistic exploitation of, and profiteering upon, human misery seemed to him more forcible than several stanzas of Keats beginning

> With her two brothers this fair lady dwelt
>   Enrichèd from ancestral merchandise;
> And for them many a weary hand did swelt
>   In torchèd mines and noisy factories. . . .

"Nothing could be more literary than the wording," Shaw wrote. "But it contains all the Factory Commission Reports that Marx read, and that Keats did not read because they were not yet written in his time. And so Keats is among the prophets with Shelley, and, had he lived, would no doubt have come down from Hyperions and Endymions to tin tacks as a very full-blooded modern revolutionist."

On rare occasions Shaw searched almost in vain for a moral focus in a writer he intended to praise, writing a centenary piece on Poe partly because he had accepted a commission to do it and partly because he genuinely enjoyed Poe as a lyric poet. There were only two writers then in the American pantheon, he thought, Poe and Whitman. (He would add Twain later, but the novelist was still alive.) At a time when even the best other American writers were philistines, Poe to Shaw was a natural aristocrat, a writer of "exquisitely refined" poetry that was magical in its beauty. But Poe was also great because he was in his writings (and here Shaw found his theme) "independent of sex, of patriotism, of fighting, of sentimentality, snobbery, gluttony, and all the rest of the vulgar stock-in-trade of his profession. This is what gives him his superb distinction."

With some strain Shaw had found a negative approach to explain his affection for Poe. It was what Poe did *not* resort to in subject matter that justified him. Elsewhere Shaw would continue to maintain that "the main thing in determining the artistic quality of a book is not the opinions it propagates, but the fact that the writer has opinions. . . . I cannot be a belletrist. No doubt I must recognize, as even the Ancient Mariner did, that I must tell my story entertainingly if I am to hold the wedding guest spellbound in spite of the siren sounds of the loud bassoon. . . . But a true original style is never achieved for its own sake. . . ."

Writing that aspired to the name of literature, Shaw insisted, and would insist to the end, "is not a keyhole for people with starved affections to peep through at the banquets of the body." Poe, to his credit, he said, did not seek that end. "Life cannot give you what he gives you except through fine art."[10] What the highest literary art should provide Shaw had explained in 1895, in a condemnatory review of Max Nordau's *Degeneration*—a book which, paradoxically, attacked the art-for-art's-sake school with which Shaw found little sympathy. Shaw's point of view never changed, no matter what he wrote, over the remaining fifty-five years of his life.

> The claim of art to our respect must stand or fall with the validity of its pretension to cultivate and refine our senses and faculties until seeing, hearing, feeling, smelling, and tasting become highly conscious and critical acts with us, protesting vehemently against ugliness, noise, discordant speech, frowzy clothing, and re-breathed air, and taking keen interest and pleasure in beauty, in music, and in nature, besides making us insist, as necessary for comfort and decency, on clean, wholesome, handsome fabrics to wear, and utensils of fine material and elegant workmanship to handle. Further, art should refine our sense of character and conduct, of justice and sympathy, greatly heightening our self-knowledge, self-control, precision of action, and considerateness, and making us intolerant of baseness, cruelty, injustice, and intellectual superficiality or vulgarity. The worthy artist or craftsman is he who serves the physical and moral senses by feeding them with pictures, musical compositions, pleasant houses and gardens, good clothes and fine implements, poems, fictions, essays, and dramas which call the heightened senses and ennobled faculties into pleasurable activity. The great artist is he who goes a step beyond the demand, and, by supplying works of a higher beauty and a higher interest than have yet been perceived, succeeds after a brief struggle with its strangeness, in adding this fresh extension of sense to the heritage of the race.

Although Shaw's artist-philosopher could be a poet with a purpose, he was more likely a writer of prose, and at his highest very likely a playwright like Sophocles or Shakespeare or a polemicist with an inherent sense of drama on the order of Bunyan. Poetry to Shaw was often "prosaic fabric disguised as poetry by the arts of versification"; and no man knew better than Milton, he wrote in his essay on Keats, that "prose has a music of its own, and that many pensters write verses because their ears are not good enough to enable them to write readable prose." Blank verse in particular failed to earn his awe. It was "so childishly easy and expeditious" that it explained Shakespeare's "copious output" to him and inspired his parody of Elizabethan blank verse, the farce *The Admirable Bashville* (1902), poetasted from his jejune novel *Cashel Byron's Profession* (1882) in a week, he claimed, when a prose version would have taken him a month.

Having discovered early that the novel was not his forte but that he could write crisp dialogue, Shaw naturally saw the novel as a lesser form of the writer's art than the drama, attacking with delight Arnold Bennett's thesis in *The Author's Craft* (1914) that "a play is easier to write than a novel." (Bennett,

Shaw diplomatically did not mention, was a failed playwright.) One simplistic reason Bennett had given for his elevation of the novel over the play is "that a play is shorter than a novel," leaving Shaw to quote Pascal's statement, "Excuse the length of my letter. I had no time to write a short one." And Shaw followed up his barb by rewriting the "Lay on, Macduff" scene from *Macbeth* "as a chapter in a novel in the style of my friends Bennett and Galsworthy when they are too lazy to write plays." That sort of writing, Shaw concluded, he could produce "by the hundred thousand words on my head" or even "make a typewriter attachment that would do it." But in truth he denigrated no literary genre. "Fine art of any sort is either easy or impossible."

For Shaw the art of criticism, especially when it came to music and theater, was easy; but his purely literary criticism, once he no longer had to produce it, was irregular in appearance and often uninspired. At its best it was intellectually agile, complementary to the philosophical biases of his plays, and a joy to read. Pillaged from the prefaces, looted from the lectures, or extricated from his journalism, his major statements on writers and writing demonstrate that however strong was his commitment to literary art, it was that extra dimension of a criticism of society that, to him, gave life to literature. Having declared that for art's sake alone he would not have produced a single sentence, he remained impatient with writers who were mere virtuosos with words, literary fiddlers playing stylistic cadenzas. One needed something worth saying. "Effectiveness of assertion," he insisted further in the preface to *Man and Superman*, "is the Alpha and Omega of style. He who has nothing to assert has no style and can have none: he who has something to assert will go as far in power of style as its momentousness and his convictions will carry him. Disprove his assertion after the style is made, yet its style remains." It was the reason one read, and even criticized endlessly, "a magnificent, débris of artistic fossils, with the matter-of-fact credibility gone clean out of them, but the form still splendid."

11 The Royal Court Theatre and the Shavian Revolution

On Easter Monday, 1956, the Royal Court Theatre—a small, shabby playhouse belying its pretentious name—reopened under a new management, the English Stage Company. Actor-director George Devine (1910–66) was in charge, and the play was a promising new one, novelist Angus Wilson's *The Mulberry Bush*. Reaction from critics was lukewarm. The not-so-new Arthur Miller drama *The Crucible* was next, and the notices were respectful. The third play on the schedule opened on May 8, a work in a harsh, realistic vein by an unemployed twenty-six-year-old actor, John Osborne. *Look Back in Anger* brought to the hallowed old boards a new generation's iconoclasms; when the shock waves reached the press and public, it was clear that the event had changed the direction of British drama.[1]

After Osborne there were others—Wesker, Pinter, Arden, Simpson, Dennis, Jellicoe. The Royal Court was hospitable, too, to the puzzling and often forbidding new European drama—Ionesco, Brecht, Beckett, Frisch, Genet. Some productions lost money, others sold out their runs; and the influence of the Court again radiated throughout the theater world. Fifty-two years before *Look Back in Anger*, the twentieth century had come to English drama in the small (it seated only 614) playhouse adjoining Sloane Square station on the Metropolitan District Railway,[2] far from the West End hub of London theater. Then—as later—an actor-director and a combination of original English plays and imported offerings by new continental dramatists had made the Royal Court stage the battleground on which a decisive struggle for a new drama had been fought, and largely won.

It had all begun with no revolution in mind; but the six hesitantly introduced matinees of *Candida* yielded a small profit and induced the cautious John E. Vedrenne, then manager of the Court, to join the young actor-director of the Shaw performances, Harley Granville Barker, in a limited play-producing partnership. Vedrenne's quiet prudence had been shaken as early as the first matinee of *Candida*, on April 26, 1904, when the curtain came down on repeated shouts of "Author!" Vedrenne finally mounted the stage and began a speech. "Ladies and Gentlemen," he explained, "I am not Shaw, who is probably on the platform of the station next door." The theater emptied almost before Vedrenne had finished, with the audience leaving its seats and hurrying to Sloane Square station to try to catch a glimpse of Shaw.[3]

As for securing the theater, it was the prospect of Greek adaptations by Gilbert Murray rather than outrageous "New Drama" by Bernard Shaw which convinced the skeptical lessee of the theater, J. H. Leigh, to let the Court to Barker. Leigh, Barker wrote Murray, had been "bitten" by the idea of *The Hippolytus* of Euripides, and on October 18, 1904, a season of twenty-four matinee performances was begun with the production of *The Hippolytus* in Murray's translation, followed by plays by Shaw, Maurice Maeterlinck, and Laurence Housman (with Barker). Because all the performances were to be in the afternoon, actors could be induced to play in them at a small salary; it left them free to accept evening engagements in the West End. Still, the low overhead of an out-of-the-way theater and part-time players had to be balanced by the fact that the Court had severely narrowed its potential audience to people who had their afternoons free.

By the following February the management had decided to take a full lease of the Court and offer a repertory of evening as well as matinee performances. Vedrenne and Barker agreed to take £20 a week as salary—actually an advance on hoped-for box-office receipts—and to spend no more than £200 to mount a production. At first members of the stock company were to be paid £3 a week, a wage which could have appealed only to dedicated artists. And these performers were dedicated. They flowered under the repertory system and the Barker-Shaw discipline, which encouraged creativity and exploited the possibilities of even the smallest roles, developing into satisfying opportunities parts which would have been only afterthoughts under the star system. The scripts contributed, too, for the Shavian philosophy of dramaturgy and direction, transmitted to Barker, was that when actors are asked to learn their lines, they should have lines worth speaking.

From the start Shaw was heavily involved, and his plays, old and new, were the backbone of the repertory (with one sometimes rushed into revival to replace a foundering drama by another hand). Vedrenne—at thirty-seven, ten years older than Barker—handled the business side of the theater's affairs, worrying as much about the pence as he did about the pounds, convinced—and sometimes rightly so—that the management daily trod the edge of insolvency. Barker was responsible for the artistic side, but when a Shaw play was produced—as happened in 701 of the 988 performances from 1904 through 1907—G.B.S. was his own director, choosing and rehearsing the cast and advising on related production matters, from music and scene design to props and stage machinery. He even wrote his own program notes, although not under his signature, as when *Man and Superman* was first produced in 1905.

> Messrs. Vedrenne and Barker beg leave to explain that the acting version of *Man and Superman* now presented has been prepared solely by the author. None of the omissions by which he has brought the performance within the customary limits of time have been made or suggested by the managers. They do not regard a complete performance, occupying both afternoon and evening, as impossible or unacceptable. But as Mr. Bernard Shaw designed the play from the beginning so as to admit of the excision, for practical stage purposes, of the scene in which John Tanner's motor-car is stopped in Spain by brigands, of the philosophical episode of Don Juan in Hell, and of the disquisition on the

evolution of morality as a passion, they feel that they can present the rest of the play as a complete comedy in three acts without injury to the artistic integrity of the work, or violation of the author's wishes, which have been unconditionally complied with on all points.

Important for Shaw as playwright was the opportunity at the Court to direct his own plays, locating their weaknesses for rewriting and for emphasizing their strengths. A great deal occurred that was dramatically useful but which never got into Shaw's substantial stage directions in the printed play, for example, his description of stage-managing John Tanner's capitulation scene at the close of *Man and Superman*:

> At the Court we devised a sort of pantomime at the point where Tanner and Ann are left together for the great final scene. Ann was in the centre of the stage; and Tanner took walks which began as resolute attempts to leave the garden by the gate or the terrace, and ended by vacillation, renewals of the attempt more and more feeble, always getting nearer and nearer to Ann. Finally he goes to her as if she were a magnet and he a rather reluctant needle, and stops close to her with a sort of collapse as if his backbone had visibly given way. Barker did this extraordinarily well.[4]

For the popular Court production, Barker was made up for his John Tanner role as a young, auburn-bearded Bernard Shaw, establishing a tradition often followed since; it has been the custom that the aged mariner-prophet Captain Shotover (of *Heartbreak House*, in 1921) should suggest the older, white-whiskered G.B.S. Roughly between the first productions of the two plays, Shaw—already forty-eight at the opening of the first Court season—became and remained the idol of a generation of young intellectuals who were excited and challenged by his brand of irreverence and eloquence, vitality and unconventionality. After *Man and Superman* Shaw was so much in demand—as a lecturer as well as a playwright—that he wrote facetiously to his agent to say that his terms to take the platform would be "a million dollars for a tour, not including the salary of Paderewski at the piano."[5]

The first Shaw play to premiere at the Court had been his comedy of Irish and English manners, *John Bull's Other Island*, on November 1, 1904. It was to have played only the standard opening six matinees, but Beatrice Webb brought the Prime Minister, A. J. Balfour, to a performance. Afterward, newspapers reported that he was so delighted by it that he came a second time with one leader of the Opposition (Campbell-Bannerman) and a third with the other (Asquith). It assured the play's popular success. A command performance had to be staged when King Edward VII expressed a desire to see it, for the play by then had completed a second scheduled run. The request must have come as a shock to G.B.S., for Edward, as Prince of Wales, had seen *Arms and the Man* in its 1894 premiere at the Avenue Theatre. While the audience had exploded with laughter, he had greeted the farce with studied grimness. His uncle, the old Duke of Edinburgh, could be heard in the stalls muttering that Shaw "must be mad." "His Royal Highness," a more moderate statement from the palace afterward had announced, "regretted that the play should have shown so disrespectful an attitude toward the Army as was betrayed by the character of the chocolate-cream soldier."

Edward's Court Theatre visit put the seal of the Crown upon Shaw's reputation as England's leading playwright, especially when it was learned that—contrary to the previous royal experience—the King, sitting in the Royal Box in special furniture Vedrenne had rented for the occasion, had laughed so heartily that he had broken his chair. The special performance (on March 11, 1905) gained the producers nothing at the box office and even set them back the price of an expensive chair, but they carefully offered Shaw the standard royalty for it anyway. Shaw returned the check with a facetious note, pointing out that the performance was an "unauthorized" one and that if he accepted royalties he would be "compounding a felony." It was not the only time Shaw had declined payment, for when a triple bill which included his own potboiler *How He Lied to Her Husband* flopped in February 1905 (the other two plays were by Yeats and Schnitzler), Shaw wrote to Vedrenne that since his play had proved worthless, in spite of the management's doing its best for it, he would not aggravate its failure by accepting royalties, "which I hereby formally waive, forego and disclaim."

The Court would become the temple of high theater art, with a following of playgoers from the educated middle classes who spoke respectfully, and even enthusiastically, of the New Drama. And plays like Shaw's, or Galsworthy's *Silver Box*, Barker's own *The Voysey Inheritance*, and Hankin's *The Charity That Began at Home* were indeed new. The West End theaters, as A. E. Wilson put it, would go on presenting plays which were "regarded as representing popular taste, plays which claimed attention because they dealt with amusing intrigues among the best kind of people."[6] They were not high art, but they dealt with high society, with epigrammatic dialogue, with manners, settings, and fashions appropriate to that increasingly irrelevant world. At the Court, the playgoer was invited to see plays which, in their deliberate evocation of symbolic and other presentational (rather than representational) techniques, were unconventional as theater—as with Murray's Greek adaptations or translations of new works by Maeterlinck and Schnitzler. Or they were attracted by settings and issues related to their own everyday existence, in which people like themselves were concerned and recognizable characters were represented in probable situations explored with as much dramatic intensity, or as much wit, as works about the gallant and gaudy world. The result was not a flood of entries into the New Drama but a gradual expansion of audience and repertory into the traditional bastions of Shaftesbury Avenue and the Strand. The New Drama would become commercial and spill over sufficiently so that when Winston Churchill, then Home Secretary, went to see a new Galsworthy play, *Justice*, at the Duke of York's Theatre, its prison scene moved him to recommend reforms in the solitary confinement system.

After his Court success, Galsworthy would become "box office" in a steady fashion. The command performance, however, initiated a Shaw boom that the playwright—after enduring a decade of indifference from theater managers—could only view with scorn. "I do most certainly resent being bothered about productions," he wrote his agent. "These idiots leave me in peace for ten years and then rush for me because the King orders a performance at the Court Theatre. They will make just as great a mess of producing me as they did before of *not* producing me. Put them out. Order them off. Call the police, if necessary. [Arnold] Daly [who had made *Candida* the hit of the New York season in 1904] and Vedrenne-Barker can still have me at 10%: all others 25%."[7]

Relations between the Court's management and its playwright-almost-in-residence were not always that smooth, although Granville Barker was fast becoming as much surrogate son as disciple to Shaw. Shaw encouraged bigger-than-life acting, while Barker (according to his biographer, C. B. Purdom) sought the "expressive detail" of the early Tom Robertson school of realism. Barker gradually altered his understated approach to accommodate G.B.S., but not enough to keep Shaw from declaring that Barker's style was "as different from mine as Debussy's from Verdi." Possibly Shaw was present at the rehearsal of one of his plays when Barker entreated the cast, "Do remember, ladies and gentlemen, that this is Italian opera." Borrowing further from Shaw, Barker would lament, "But, my dear child, you deliver your lines as if you were the trombone, whereas you are really the oboe in this ensemble. Remember that, please. The oboe, *not* the trombone!"

Although he would often blarney actors and management into doing his will, Shaw could blaze with invective when he thought he saw bad acting or direction or inept choice of plays. When Louis Calvert played the formidable Undershaft (in *Major Barbara*) weakly, Shaw was furious and told him so, afterward remarking to Beatrice Webb (who confided it to her diary) that Calvert had "lost his nerve" over the role, that he "could not understand or remember his part and was aghast at what he considered its black immorality." The mere physical filling of a role never satisfied Shaw. After some quibbling over casting a part, he once insisted to Barker, "It is all very well to say there are others. . . . But if you want the higher Shaw drama you must take higher chances." Later, Shaw castigated the casting of Galsworthy's *The Silver Box*, telling Barker and Vedrenne that excellence of direction could not conceal flaws in personnel: "Get your cast right, and get them interested in themselves and in the occasion. . . . Get your cast wrong; and you wreck your play just to the extent to which your cast is wrong. . . . As it was, the stage business was as perfect as a quadrille; but the parts simply did not exist. . . ."

The *How He Lied* debacle had proved Shaw capable of self-criticism as well as criticism, and at least once afterward in the Court years, rather than condemn the acting or casting, he blamed his own writing. In 1906 Ellen Terry had finally succumbed to his entreaties that she play Lady Cecily in six matinees of *Captain Brassbound's Conversion*, a role Shaw had written for her seven years before. In her sixtieth year (and fiftieth as an actress), she was suddenly self-conscious and unsure of herself, disappointingly no longer up to roles which demanded a lightness of touch; and the presence of a great lady of the theater was not the draw the Court management had hoped.

But Shaw admired Ellen Terry too unreservedly to discredit her performance. "All our real successes," he explained to Vedrenne, "have been with modest and youthful casts"; yet lest this rationalization infer a criticism of Miss Terry, he suggested, evading reference to the Lady Cecily part, that the play was at fault: "For some reason, Drinkwater is not amusing in the first act, and Brassbound is not thrilling in the second." However even at rehearsals, he knew, Miss Terry had been nervously garbling her lines, impelling Vedrenne to ask Shaw concernedly whether she was speaking what Shaw had written. "No," G.B.S. said, covering for her, "but she's speaking them as I ought to have written them." Nevertheless, it was a lesson learned—although for years Shaw continued to insist, with Ellen Terry in mind, that the Lady Cecily role required "artistic faculty and personal attraction of a very rare order." For the first and only time, the Court had succumbed to that despoiler of the repertory principle, star casting.

One of the rare occasions when Shaw did not direct a Court production of his own work was a revival of *You Never Can Tell*, rehearsed by Barker while Shaw was holidaying across the Channel. When Shaw saw the play later in production, he found "a degree of infamy which took my breath away." Writing to Barker (July 19, 1906), he asked, "What was the name of the author of that play?" Yet he ended the letter warmly: "P.S. We can put you up here and give you a room to write in if you would like." When Barker chose plays for matinees which Shaw felt were poor theater, and below Court standards—and the box-office take reinforced the impression—Shaw, who wanted the Court to pay its way, talked openly of bankruptcy. But the Court had to take chances in order to try to develop new dramatists, even when six matinees of a thin double bill by novelist Maurice Hewlett took in only £13. Sometimes—when he felt the playwright showed promise (as with a young seaman named John Masefield and his grim, Elizabethanlike tragedy *The Campden Wonder*)—Shaw applauded the attempt, although the play was both a box-office and a critical catastrophe. But he complained that Barker had wrecked its chances by double-billing the tragedy to follow a vapid comedy, Cyril Harcourt's *The Reformer*. "*The Campden Wonder*," G.B.S. prophesied, "in its proper place in a proper bill, can force the public to reverse the press verdict."[8]

There would be no chance to reverse the verdict on Masefield's play, for the final months at the Court followed its production, with the management finding the enterprise continuing to be financially precarious (although it actually ended by turning a small profit). Vedrenne and Barker felt that the out-of-the-way location of the Royal Court was the chief factor influencing its shaky economics and dreamed of transferring operations to the more prestigious West End. Actually, the Court management had created a following where it was and needed only to cultivate and enlarge it through appropriate choice of a repertory. It had become the first successful attempt to establish a repertory theater in England, and the patrons of the Court were already, in Shaw's words, "not an audience but a congregation." Neither Vedrenne nor Barker, Shaw wrote them, understood "what has made the Court possible. I have given you a series of first-rate music-hall entertainments, thinly disguised as plays, but really offering the public a unique string of turns by comics and serio-comics of every popular type. . . . Make no error, V.D., that is the jam that has carried the propaganda pill down [and] consoled the house for the super drama." It was not unfortunate geography but erratic choice of plays, he thought, which now and then had brought them precariously close to red ink. "Why," he asked Vedrenne, "do you deliberately choose the worse play, the less popular play, the stale play. . . ?"[9] The allegations were somewhat unfair, but it was true that the Court's choices often furnished more mental than visual stimulus, and realistic earnestness was not a guarantee of good theater.

Remembering the later days of the Vedrenne-Barker management at the Court, when he was a young University of London science lecturer with playwriting aspirations, Ashley Dukes, in *The Scene is Changed* (1942), recalled the dominance of the intellectual and naturalistic side of the repertory over the more experimental efforts. The new works, each cautiously presented at afternoon performances on Tuesdays and Fridays and promoted to the evening bill if successful, attracted him. "The acting standard was high," he thought, "but commonplace in its naturalism. Barker's direction was sensitive, shrewd, faithful. . . . What naturalism had meant in the 'free theatres' of Europe in the 1890s, intellectualism had begun to mean to the Court Theatre group and its followers. . . . I had a special link . . . through membership in the Fabian Society . . . [where] it was generally agreed that the theatre was taking or should take the place of the church in social enlightenment; and no other serious function was assigned to it." Middle-class revolutionaries, Dukes felt, were indifferent to art, and to them the message was the medium. Still, in Shaw's case he recognized an exception—that if "lifelikeness was the rule on Barker's stage," the brilliance of a Shaw kept his play from "lifelike" staging. Besides, no other Court dramatist "had Shaw's entertainment value, which was the true foundation of the [intellectual theatre] movement. . . . Wilde could never have become a Court Theatre playwright . . . he had no social gospel."

The Vedrenne-Barker seasons at the Court ended in the glow of three concluding successes, revivals of Barker's (and Laurence Housman's) popular fantasy *Prunella*, Shaw's *Man and Superman*, and a final double bill of Shaw's *Man of Destiny* and the dream interlude from *Superman, Don Juan in Hell*, in its first performances. (The *Don Juan* was a brilliantly staged and acted production, the four-character play so sumptuously costumed by Charles Ricketts that Vedrenne worried that the clothing bill would cause him to conclude the three years at the Court in debt.) On July 7, a week after the season ended, a testimonial dinner attended by leading figures in the London theatrical world honored the Vedrenne-Barker management. It was the crown upon the Royal Court's efforts. Even the shadowy Vedrenne was there; Charles Ricketts quipped to Shaw afterward that he had gone to the dinner "to find out, incidentally, if Vedrenne really existed: like all men, I had viewed him as merely a smart impersonation of Barker's done with a wig and a pair of blue spectacles."[10]

Sweetness and light pervaded most of the evening, but Barker made an uncomplimentary remark about the impact of actor-managers on the drama in the presence of the expansively gracious actor-manager Beerbohm Tree, and Shaw, interrupting a display of witty pyrotechnics, lashed out at the press, "which from first to last has done what in it lay to crush the enterprise. . . . There you will find a chronicle of failure, a sulky protest against this new and troublesome sort of entertainment that calls for knowledge and thought instead of the usual cliches." The attack was too sweeping, for there were now at least an influential minority of drama critics sympathetic to change, such as Desmond MacCarthy, whose criticism (particularly of Shaw) remains one of the best bodies of analytical writing on the Edwardian drama.[11]

There was also, almost in spite of himself, *The Times*'s A. B. Walkley, who shuddered as the gusts of change buffeted him in his seat on the aisle and refused to admit that such Court offerings as *Man and Superman*—the published version of which G.B.S. had dedicated to him—were plays at all. (Admittedly, they were scintillating intellectual entertainments, but improperly called dramas.) Yet Walkley found himself praising Barker as a "born interpreter of [Shaw's] talent," writing of the ensemble playing of the Court company, including its Shaw performances: "There is no such all-round acting in London as is nowadays to be seen at the Court Theatre. . . . Where all are excellent it is needless to single out names." There was also Shaw's other faint-praising old journalistic friend from the 1880s, the *Tribune*'s William Archer, who doggedly considered Pinero a dramatic genius and Shaw—whom he vainly strove to convert to Pineroticism—"clever rather than convincing." Even so, Archer, while temperamentally at odds with the Court's general choice of plays, was temporarily won over by *John Bull's Other Island* ("One of the richest pieces of comedy of modern times"). Archer celebrated the Court's first year by publishing *A Record and a Commentary of the Vedrenne-Barker Season, 1904-1905* (London, 1906), the model for MacCarthy's later, more comprehensive account in 1907, *The Court Theatre*, which reviewed the plays and published the programs.

Of more importance to the Shavian revolution than Archer or Walkley was Beerbohm Tree's half brother, Max Beerbohm, who in his *Saturday Review* critic's chair (to which he had succeeded Shaw in 1898) wrote understandingly of the new dramatists of the Court. Max's reviews of the plays of Barker, Hankin, and Galsworthy must have encouraged even Vedrenne.[12] More significantly, Max's Royal Court reviews of G.B.S. demonstrated the progress of a skeptical intelligence toward awareness of Shaw's aims and methods. Before the Court seasons he had seen Shaw in less effective productions and had reviewed the unproduced plays from the published editions, often coming to the standard contemporary opinion that a Shaw play was little more than a tract set in type in something resembling play form. In print, *Man and Superman* had seemed to him a "peculiar article" and "not a play at all. It is 'as good as a play'—infinitely better. . . than any play I have ever read or seen enacted. But a play it is not." Shaw, he concluded, "Having no sense for life," had "necessarily, no sense for art" (September 23, 1903).

Then, on a cold November afternoon, in the drafty Royal Court, remote from his usual West End haunts, he sat through a matinee of *John Bull's Other Island* and experienced the first of what would be a series of revelations:

> In a warm theatre, within the regular radius for theatres, after nightfall—in fact with just those cheerful commercial circumstances which are withheld from them—these plays would soon take the town. . . .
> The critics . . . have raised their usual parrot-cry: "Not a play." This, being interpreted, means "Not a love-story, split neatly up into four brief acts. . . . Not much actually happens in the play. The greater part of the play is talk: and the talk is often not relevant to the action, but merely to the characters, and to things in general. Pray, why is this not to be called a play? Why should the modern "tightness" of technique* be regarded as a sacred and essential part of dramaturgy? And why should the passion of love be regarded as the one possible theme in dramaturgy? Between these two superstitions lies the main secret of the barrenness of modern English drama. The first of them wards away the majority of men of creative literary power. . . . The second prevents playwrights from taking themes which would both invigorate their work through novelty and bring the theatre into contact with life at large (November 23, 1904).

It was obvious, then, from the first review of a Court-produced Shaw play signed "Max" that the Shavian revolution had begun to succeed. That its success was assured was proved thirteen months later, when Beerbohm, fresh from viewing the Court production of *Man and Superman*, attended the opening of *Major Barbara*. Rather than merely surveying the performance, he reviewed his, and other reviewers', past critical positions regarding the Shavian drama— that G.B.S. could not draw flesh-and-blood characters, that his *dramatis personae* were only Shaws in trousers or petticoats, that his so-called plays were

---

*Apparently a reference to the "well-made" play of the Scribe-Sardou school ("Sardoodledom" to Shaw), popularly represented in England by the tightly plotted society melodramas of Pinero.

devoid of the substance of drama. Max saw the Court premiere of *Major Barbara* attacked in this fashion not only as a nonplay but, because of the Salvation Army setting of its second act and some attendant religious references in the dialogue, as a piece of arrogant and tasteless sacrilege. Walkley had even concluded sadly that it was useless to argue with Shaw "over these things. He will do them. All we can do is be sorry." (Actually, Shaw had the delighted cooperation of the Army, which lent uniforms and technical advice and welcomed Shaw's sympathetic disagreement with its philosophy as good advertising. Some Salvation Army officials even had a box for the opening, although the Army usually discouraged theater attendance as sinful.) The act in question, Max observed, included characters who "live with an intense vitality," was "as cunning a piece of craftsmanship as any conventional playwright could achieve," and had "a cumulative appeal to the emotions which no other living playwright has touched."

Yet Max wrote of those of his colleagues still fighting a rear guard action against the twentieth century: "With all these facts staring them in the face, they still maintain that Mr. Shaw is not a playwright." But Max, at least, had "climbed down." "That theory might have held water in the days before Mr. Shaw's plays were acted. Indeed," he confessed, "I was in the habit of propounding it myself. . . . This simply proved that I had not enough theatrical imagination to see the potentialities of a play when reading it in print. . . ." Still, he had to admit, the "old superstition" had lingered, and he felt the need to recant his earlier remarks that plays like *Man and Superman* were "quite unsuited to any stage." After he had seen it done at the Court, he had changed his mind; and the Court's *Major Barbara* reinforced his feeling that it was "both unjust and absurd" to deny that Shaw was a dramatist of the first importance "merely because he chooses, for the most part, to get the drama out of contrasted types of character and thought, without action, and without appeal to the emotions. . . . His technique is peculiar because his purpose is peculiar. . . ."

The Royal Court would make the new techniques, and the existence of serious purpose in the drama, less "peculiar," and Shaw's testimonial dinner blast at the critics who still wore blinders was not a rationalization of failure. New dramatists had ventured out onto the Court's stage; a new theater audience had been created and cultivated; and acting, production, and playwriting had left the nineteenth century and entered the twentieth. Many of the Royal Court company would have long and distinguished stage careers, with one at least (Sir Lewis Casson) continuing for sixty years after his debut at the Court. Continental playwrights such as Maeterlinck, Schnitzler, and Hauptmann were introduced to the English public; and classical Greek drama, through the example of the verse translations of Gilbert Murray, was proved viable for the modern stage. Some of the new English dramatists proved disappointing, and Shaw tried to lure other writers via the Court's hospitable example—Wells, Conrad, Chesterton, Kipling—to try playwriting. Still, there were successes. A novelist named John Galsworthy would afterward give as much time to the drama as to fiction. Laurence Housman would continue to write plays, and John Masefield would produce a long series of verse dramas.

Two writers who raised the greatest expectations failed to realize them. St. John Hankin was a suicide at thirty-nine, a few years after his promising work at the Court; and Granville Barker himself was prevented by a combination of circumstances from fulfilling the potential of his Court plays. His *The Voysey*

Inheritance, staged at the Court in November 1905, was called by Walkley *"triple extrait de Shaw"* because of its apparent spare emotional content and sardonic irony and its willingness to question the assumptions upon which the lives of its audiences were based. But Barker, who had great gifts in characterization, although he was not strong on theatrical construction, ran into trouble with the Lord Chamberlain's censorship in his next play, *Waste*. (A political drama, it was refused a license when the playwright declined to cut references to, among other things, an abortion.) Afterward he wrote only one other play which reached the stage, *The Madras House*, a dryly intellectual study of sexual attitudes in Edwardian England. After World War I he ceased regular play producing and wrote little but Shakespearian criticism.[13] Two later plays were never performed, and his theatrical reputation emerges from the shadows primarily with reference to the years at the Royal Court.

Although the commercial theater could seem to remain grandly aloof from the influences of the Court, distant as were Shaftesbury Avenue and the Strand both geographically and metaphorically, they were changing under pressure. For one thing, the Court performances had created intense West End interest in the previously untouchable Shaw. Other Court playwrights, such as John Galsworthy, could find stages for their later plays, while playwrights such as Maugham could add Royal Court honesty of dialogue and theme to the post-Wildean comedies of manners. There was fresh interest in previously unfashionable dramatists from abroad, even those who violated previously sacrosanct Edwardian reticences and taboos. Other theaters and playwrights could follow and could offer in commercial terms what had been achieved earlier only with frustrating difficulty.

That the Royal Court did not enrich its management was no clue to its success or failure. Describing one of his own plays which premiered at the Court, Shaw—more than a dozen years later—could look back with satisfaction at his role in the experiment:

> I did not cut these cerebral capers in mere inconsiderate exuberance. I did it because the worst convention of the criticism of the theatre current at that time was that intellectual seriousness is out of place on the stage; that the theatre is a place of shallow amusement; that people go there to be soothed after the enormous intellectual strain of a day in the city: in short, that a playwright is a person whose business it is to make unwholesome confectionery out of cheap emotions. My answer to this was to put all my intellectual goods in the shop window under the sign of Man and Superman. That part of my design succeeded. By good luck and acting, the comedy triumphed on the stage; and the book was a good deal discussed. Since then the sweet-shop view of the theatre has been out of countenance. . . . And the younger playwrights are not only taking their art seriously, but being taken seriously themselves. . . .[14]

In an appeal for a national theater soon afterward, Shaw pointed out that the Royal Court, which could take in only £160 when every seat was filled and which was a complete critical success, concluded with a deficit of £6,000. It was "the merest fleabite" to a commercial manager, but to Shaw it proved conclusively the need for an endowed theater. In the Court's case Shaw quietly bailed the proprietors out, but such ventures could not be repeated without guarantee funds. "It was by a quite uncommercial accident that I shared their aims and, having an independent income, could afford to let them make extraordinary sacrifices of their commercial opportunities by repeatedly withdrawing my plays at the height of their success to produce equally deserving ones with the certainty of changing a handsome nightly profit into a serious loss. . . . The public good was worth the cost a hundred times over; but the cost fell on us, and the benefit went to the nation."

That benefit continued. Not only did the Court experiment rejuvenate drama in England and prove the theatrical values of the repertory system, but by fiscally proving, as Shaw put it, "its own insufficiency as a substitute for a national theatre," it forced the campaign for one into being. Without the Court, the great theatrical complex on the South Bank would have had harder going in becoming a reality. Shaw's dreams for the London stage were every bit as ambitious. As he wrote Granville Barker from Bayreuth in 1908, under a postcard photograph of the grandiose Wagnerian opera house, "This is what I call a Court Theatre."

12   Four Fathers for Barbara

G.B.S. was seldom as specific about the real-life models for characters in his plays as he was for *Major Barbara* (1905). He would title it "Murray's Mother-in-Law," he teased Gilbert Murray, and he made it clear that not only was Murray's stuffy mother-in-law, Lady Rosalind Howard, Countess of Carlisle, the play's dowager Lady Britomart but that Murray himself—a young Australian-born professor of Greek—was the model for Adolphus Cusins. (To make Cusins's identification obvious, Shaw not only borrowed from Murray's own version of *The Bacchae* the lines Cusins quotes from Euripides but prefaced his indebtedness.) Major Barbara herself, it later became known, was modeled after Murray's wife, Lady Mary, and the vivacious young American actress Eleanor Robson. "I want to see if I can make a woman a saint," he had confided to her, and wooed her for the cast of the first production in the epistolary manner with which he usually had such success. "I can't connect Barbara with anyone but you," Shaw wrote, "and am half tempted to take the play right up into the skies at the end because there is a sort of desecration in your marrying even your poet."[1] But Miss Robson chose to continue her American tour with the sentimental and successful *Merely Mary Ann,* and G.B.S. reluctantly found someone else for the role. Later she became the bride of United States Steel magnate August Belmont. It was almost as if she had married Andrew Undershaft.

G.B.S. identified Undershaft, Barbara's father, with no immediate prototype, although he suggested—more seriously this time—that he thought the character so overshadowed the rest of the cast that the play might well be called *Andrew Undershaft's Profession.* The profession itself was crucial for Shaw, although he used it to symbolize all antisocial sources of wealth, for no profession endorsed by Mammon—not even Mrs. Warren's well-known one—had such potential for negative dramatic impact. Three imposing figures in the armaments industry apparently were in Shaw's mind, as well as at least one more prototype forgotten everywhere but at Ayot St. Lawrence, where one of Shaw's friends and neighbors soon would be Stage Society playwright Charles McEvoy. McEvoy's father had supported the Confederate side in the American Civil War and by the close of the war had established a factory in the South for the manufacture of torpedoes and high explosives.[2] The gentle, humane McEvoy, of benign appearance but barbarous occupation, must have appealed to Shaw's sense of dramatic paradox.

There was a different, more sardonic, kind of paradox Shaw then could turn to in Swedish arms maker and inventor of dynamite Alfred Nobel. More a sufferer from *Schuldkomplex* than Undershaft (whose industrial motto, "Unashamed," nevertheless implies a moral dilemma), he elected in his last years to "make war on war" by endowing an international peace prize, first awarded in 1901, five years after his death. A complex man, Nobel had his intellectual and humanitarian side, which resulted in his other annual awards; Shaw himself received the one for literature in 1926. Before the posthumous Nobel Prizes however, Alfred Nobel was known for his activities in international finance and for the armaments firm he had inherited from his father and built up to enormous size through his hardheadedness in selling weapons and patents, like Undershaft, to all comers regardless of politics. His own politics belied his business practices. An ardent Social Democrat, he was, to his liberal friends, "the gentle Bolshevik," but he earned millions by selling weapons to nations all over the world, many of which desired nothing more than to suppress any form of social democracy; and his motto "My home is where my work is, and my work is everywhere" would have pleased the motto-loving Undershaft.[3]

Nobel alone might explain the character of a dealer in death who can quote Plato and espouse humanitarian principles, but there was also another reputation available to Shaw. Munitions entrepreneur Sir Basil Zaharoff, a man of mystery to millions of Europeans, not only sold to all comers and even arranged, for his even vaster profit, the large lines of credit necessary (in both cases like Shaw's unashamed arms dealer), he came, like Undershaft, from origins resembling the most romantic Victorian cheap fiction. Barbara's father is an abandoned East End orphan of mysterious origins. The goateed Sir Basil (whose eventual name was almost certainly neither that of his mother nor father) was born in 1849, probably in the brothel quarter of Constantinople, but rumor had him originating all over Europe, one version even claiming that he was an orphan from the slums of Whitechapel. By the early 1900s he was notorious as the Prince of Blood and Steel (Undershaft is called the Prince of Darkness and claims to Barbara that the Salvation Army's motto might be his own—"Blood and Fire"). In the 1890s he had formed a munitions-making partnership with Sir Hiram Maxim of the famous machine gun, and soon merged with Vickers, manufacturers of naval cannon. In the wars of the period—Japan and China, Turkey and Greece, Britain and the Boers, Russia and Japan, Bulgaria and Serbia—Zaharoff and his agents were on the scene selling to both sides and often accused of having provoked the conflicts for the firm's advantage. Regularly, he put his political affiliations to use, via shares he controlled in firms in which many who owned stock were influential in English public life, the Admiralty and the Army. To the end of his life, although he became a Knight Commander of the Bath, he was a public figure of undiminished secretiveness and mystery, having influenced a venal press in his client countries so effectively that it is not surprising that hardly any of his extensive press dossier is even remotely accurate. This underside of his career helps explain Undershaft's outburst to his naive and nearly forgotten son Stephen—*"with a touch of brutality,"* Shaw notes in the preliminary stage directions:

> The government of your country! *I* am the government of your country: I, and Lazarus. Do you suppose that you and half a dozen amateurs like you, sitting in a row in that foolish gabble shop, can govern Undershaft and Lazarus? No my friend, you will do what pays us. You will make war when it suits us, and keep

peace when it doesn't. You will find out that trade requires certain measures when we have decided on those measures. When I want anything to keep my dividends up, you will discover that my want is a national need. When other people want something to keep my dividends down, you will call out the police and military. And in return you shall have the support and applause of my newspapers, and the delight of imagining that you are a great statesman. Government of your country! Be off with you, my boy, and play with your caucuses and leading articles and historic parties and great leaders and burning questions and the rest of your toys. *I* am going back to my counting-house to pay the piper and call the tune.

And then there was the portly and unprepossessing Fritz Krupp, inheritor of the Krupp munitions dynasty, which he ruled from 1887 to 1902, building the cannonmakers of Essen into a world industrial power that sold arms from Chile to China, under the firm's unofficial motto "*Wenn Deutschland blüht, blüht Krupp*" (When Germany flourishes, Krupp flourishes).[4] Undershaft, like all of his dynasty, has taken, on the instruction of his predecessor, the name of the firm's founder. As Lady Britomart tells the story,

> The Undershafts are descended from a foundling in the parish of St. Andrew Undershaft in the city. That was long ago, in the reign of James the First. Well, this foundling was adopted by an armorer and gun-maker. In the course of time the foundling suceeded to the business; and from some notion of gratitude, or some vow or something, he adopted another foundling, and left the business to him. And that foundling did the same.* Ever since that, the cannon business has always been left to an adopted foundling named Andrew Undershaft.

Through this aspect of his play, Shaw, with brilliant, almost miraculous, foreshadowing, prepared the way for life to follow art. Aided by special governmental decrees (even one from Hitler later, in 1943), the Krupps had followed the strictest rules of primogeniture, endowing the whole of family wealth and power upon the eldest son. Siblings, when necessary, were absorbed into the firm, but only as drab underlings. All the world knew in 1905, as Shaw wrote his play, that the Krupp dynasty lacked a male successor. After Fritz Krupp's death in 1902, the succession had fallen awkwardly (as there was no male heir) to his daughter Bertha, with a younger sister, Barbara, disinherited. In 1905 both were approaching marriageable age. Barbara, Shaw could not help having observed with a fine sense of irony, might have been named for the patron saint of armorers and artillerymen. Shaw, after all, wanted a saint for his play.

Barbara is substituted for Bertha. Deliberately? In the play there is a weak son in addition to the two sturdier sisters, who complains, "I have hardly ever opened a newspaper in my life without seeing our name in it. The Undershaft torpedo! The Undershaft quick-fires! The Undershaft ten-inch! The Undershaft disappearing rampart gun! The Undershaft submarine! And now the Undershaft aerial battleship!" So too the headlines about the Krupps and their products, although Shaw can have been nothing less than uncanny in his foreshadowing of several weapons still to be turned out at Krupp arsenals, one the secret U-1, already under way and under wraps at Kiel. Further, the discussion in Act III about the Undershaft nursing home, libraries, schools, insurance

---

*Lady Britomart tells her son Stephen that Undershaft considers his company one of two successful institutions in history in which the mode of continuing the leadership was by adoption. The Antonine emperors adopted their successors—a key to their success, according to Undershaft. The Undershaft solution is Shaw's commentary on the difficulty of bequeathing talent and drive (as well as money) to one's natural heirs.

and pension funds, and building societies bears a resemblance to Krupp paternalism in Essen. As a foreign visitor to the *Konzern* reported in the days of Fritz Krupp,

> Everywhere the name of Krupp appears: now on the picturesque marketplace, on the door of a mammoth department store, then on a bronze monument, now on the portals of a church . . . over a library, numerous schoolhouses, butcher shops, a sausage factory, shoemakers' shops and tailoring establishments, over playgrounds and cemeteries. . . . There is a German beer garden close to each park, and over each of them is written plainly, "Owned by Friedrich Krupp."[5]

Far more uncanny, however (for there were more modest English equivalents to this industrial paternalism known to Shaw), is the parallel between what is to happen to Barbara Undershaft—her eventual marriage to the professorial Adolphus Cusins and his thereupon preparing to become, even in name, the next Andrew Undershaft—and what *does* happen in 1906 to Barbara Krupp's sister, Bertha.* Cusins himself may have been named to suggest consanguinity, as Murray's father had married, in Australia, where it was legal—the law was changed in England only in 1907—his deceased wife's sister, furnishing Shaw the "orphan" option the play requires in Act III. In Shaw's original 1905 manuscript he had been "Dolly" Tankerville, which would have been uncanny enough, as the Undershaft factory town turns out implements of war. A last-minute change of name kept Shaw from anticipating the tank, invented and first used in 1916. In the play Cusins promises rather to become, in our 20/20 hindsight, something else seemingly out of a crystal ball. Handpicked for Barbara's sister as consort by the Kaiser was a scholarly, obscure diplomat, Gustav von Bohlen und Halbach. And as a dramatic conclusion to the nuptials *Seine Majestät* announced that "To ensure at least an appearance of continuity of the Essen dynasty" (*damit wenigstens eine äusserliche Fortführung der Essener Dynastie ermöglicht ist*), henceforth the bridegroom would take the name of Krupp and the right to pass it and the armaments empire that went along with it to his eldest son. The huge instrument giving legality to the procedure, with royal red wax seal seven inches in diameter, reaffirmed "the special position of the House of Krupp" (*die besondere Stellung des Hauses Krupp*), but, the Kaiser added (as might Andrew Undershaft himself), it was up to the bridegroom to prove himself "*ein wahrer Krupp*"—a real Krupp.[6] Had *Seine Majestät* taken the idea from Shaw? German newspapers (G.B.S. was popular there) had been full of reports of the play. If so, it may be the most amazing case of life utilizing art in our time. But in any case, the possibility that Shaw in the play was, among other things, satirizing Krupp dynastic problems cannot be overlooked.†

That Shaw knew what he was doing when he thought in terms of Krupp became obvious two years after *Major Barbara* was produced, when for a German edition of *The Perfect Wagnerite* G.B.S. added lines about the mythic Alberich of *The Rhinegold*. Each would-be Alberich in real life, Shaw wrote,

> discovers that to be a dull, greedy, narrow-minded money-grubber is not the way to make money on the modern scale; for though greed may suffice to turn tens into hundreds and even thousands, to turn thousands into hundreds of

---

*After whom her husband sentimentally named the big 420-mm cannon used in France in 1914.

†Shaw was also satirizing, like Wilde in *The Importance of Being Earnest*, the Victorian dramatic cliché of foundlings recovering their identities, fortunes, and finances.

thousands requires economic magnanimity and will to power as well as to pelf. And to turn hundreds of thousands into millions, Alberic must make himself an earthly Providence for masses of workmen, creating towns, and governing markets. . . . Consequently, though Alberic in 1850 many have been merely the vulgar Manchester factory-owner portrayed in Friedrich Engels's *Condition of the Working Classes*, in 1876 he was well on the way towards becoming Krupp of Essen, or Cadbury of Bournville, or Lever of Port Sunlight.

As the last line makes clear, even beyond the four dealers in death there were—at a farther remove—other likely "fathers" for Barbara, not dealers in cannon but in chocolate and soap. But there was also a dealer in the stuff of armaments—steel. Shaw's curious statement in 1900 that he thought that "Mammon can be developed into a socialist power, whereas Jehovah makes any such change of mind possible,"[7] sounds like an anticipation of the Undershaft philosophy (as well as the Alberich lines); and it has been suggested that indeed it is, and that Shaw had industrialist Andrew Carnegie in mind.[8] J.P. Morgan had just purchased Carnegie's factories for an estimated hundred million dollars in order to form U. S. Steel, and Carnegie's ventures in philanthropic uses of the staggering sum had led him to the writing of "The Gospel of Wealth," in which he wrote in Bunyanesque cadences* that his gospel "but echoes Christ's words. It calls upon the millionaire to sell all he hath and give it in the highest and best form to the poor by administering his estate himself for the good of his fellows, before he is called upon to lie down and rest upon the bosom of Mother Earth." Shaw's response, in a new prefatory note to a reissue of his pamphlet "Socialism for Millionaires" (1901) was that "a Millionaire Movement" had taken place, "culminating in the recent expression of opinion by Mr. Andrew Carnegie that no man should die rich." Only in this way, Shaw thought, could Mammon develop into a socialist power, when traditional inheritance formulas were eschewed. English editor and crusader W. T. Stead reported Carnegie's ideas as to how this could be done in a way that seems to foreshadow the Undershaft scheme of disinheriting one's children—the basic plot device of *Major Barbara*:

> Carnegie laid it down as a fundamental principle upon which the partnership should be conducted that when a partner dies his estate should be settled up within thirty days, and his interest in the business acquired by the remaining partners, and also that no son or child of any of them should have a share in the concern or a voice in its management. This policy has been rigidly observed down to the present. The consequence is that the partnership from time to time has been refreshed and invigorated by infusions of new blood, and the active managers have been young and energetic men.

Stead also provided a link with the Salvation Army aspect of Shaw's play, suggesting that there were passages in Carnegie's exhortations which might lead one to predict that the industrialist "might even become a strong supporter of the social scheme of the Salvation Army." But it was a hint Shaw did not need, for one of his earlier writings had even sketched out what seems the germ of the West Ham Shelter act (II) of the play, with its salvationists and the grudgingly saved:

---

*Which Shaw must have recalled when he wrote, in the preface to *Major Barbara*: "I do not call a Salvationist really saved until he is ready to lie down cheerfully on the scrap heap, having paid scot and lot and something over, and let his eternal life pass on to renew its youth in the battalions of the future."

The solitary rough is not brave. He is restless and shamefaced until he meets with other roughs to keep him in countenance. He especially dreads that strange social reformer, the Hallelujah lass. At first sight of her quaint bonnet, jersey, and upturned eyes, he rushes to the conclusion that chance has provided him with a rare lark. He hastens to the outskirts of her circle, and after a few inarticulate howls, attempts to disconcert her by profane and often obscene interjections. In vain. He may as easily disconcert a swallow in its flight. He presently hears himself alluded to as "that loving fellow creature," and he is stricken with an uncomfortable feeling akin to that which prompted Paul Pry's protest, "Don't call me a phoenix: I'm not used to it." But the Hallelujah lass is not done with him yet. In another minute she is praying, with infectious emotion, for "his dear, precious soul." This finishes him. He slinks away with a faint affectation of having no more time to waste on such effeminate sentimentality, and thenceforth never ventures within earshot of the Army except when strongly reinforced by evil company or ardent spirits. A battalion of Hallelujah lasses is worth staying a minute to study. . . . As long as they speak strenuously, they consider themselves but little about lack of matter, which forces them to repetitions which, it must be confessed, soon become too tedious for anyone but a habitual Salvationist to endure. . . .[9]

Also a wealthy industrialist, and even less related to armaments than Carnegie, was the Englishman George Cadbury, whose community-planning work Shaw knew well. Perivale St. Andrews, the utopian community built by Undershaft for the workers in his factories, seems based in part upon the model town movement which Cadbury championed and which pioneered the decentralization of industries about planned communities complete to company-sponsored schools and municipal services. Cadbury had been a poor boy and was a self-made man. A Quaker and a humanitarian who believed in providing people with jobs rather than charity, he was the inverse of Undershaft in choosing to enter the chocolate business (in which the company is still eminent) rather than heavy industry. By the turn of the century his community-planning ideas were attracting wide attention, but the Boer War had begun, and he turned his wealth and energies to campaigning for peace.

Shaw was also aware of the paternalistic factory towns of the north, such as Saltaire, begun in 1850 by Sir Titus Salt; and even closer to home was Jonathan Thomas Carr's housing estate, Bedford Park, at the Turnham Green Station of the Metropolitan Railway on the western edge of London. Begun as a speculation by Carr, it offered such attractive features as churches, shops, club, and tavern as well as a variety of house-and-garden designs within the frame of a single architectural style, Queen Anne Revival. As Shaw realized from his artistic and literary acquaintances who gravitated there, Bedford Park was a triumph of planning over monotony, an oasis with just enough of an Aesthetic atmosphere to make the middle-class mind uneasy.

Cadbury's real successor, however—the direct progenitor of Andrew Undershaft's planned community—was Shaw's friend Ebenezer Howard. A high-minded dreamer less practical than Cadbury yet less imaginative than Carr, Howard had nevertheless founded the Garden City movement in 1898 and counted Shaw among his earliest supporters. Shaw even gave the movement the benefit of some of his most benevolent satire in *John Bull's Other Island* (1904), the immensely popular comedy about Ireland and Anglo-Irish manners which he wrote just before beginning *Major Barbara:*

BROADBENT. Have you ever heard of Garden City?
TIM [*doubtfully*]. D'ye mane Heavn?

BROADBENT. Heaven! No: it's near Hitchin. If you can spare half an hour I'll go into it with you.

TIM. I tell you what. Gimme a prospectus. Lemmy take it home and reflect on it.

BROADBENT. You're quite right: I will. [*He gives him a copy of Ebenezer Howard's book, and several pamphlets*] You understand that the map of the city—the circular construction—is only a suggestion.

TIM. I'll make a careful note of that [*looking dazedly at the map*].

BROADBENT. What I say is, why not start a Garden City in Ireland?

TIM [*with enthusiasm*]. Thats just what was on the tip of my tongue to ask you. Why not? [*Defiantly*] Tell me why not.

BROADBENT. There are difficulties. I shall overcome them; but there are difficulties. . . .[10]

Town-planners such as Howard, and company-town planners on the order of his predecessor Cadbury almost certainly were in Shaw's mind when he completed *John Bull* and began his new play, in which Undershaft's pollution-free factory community of Perivale St. Andrews *"lies between two Middlesex hills, half climbing the northern one. It is an almost smokeless town in white walls, roofs of narrow green slates or red tiles, tall trees, domes, companiles, and slender chimney shafts, beautifully situated and beautiful in itself."* Surveying the Undershaft domain, Cusins remarks half in elation, half in disappointment, "Not a ray of hope. Everything perfect! wonderful! real! It only needs a cathedral to be a heavenly city instead of a hellish one." But as Cusins quickly learns, Perivale St. Andrews has, in addition to the libraries, schools, building funds, community ballrooms, and banqueting facilities, several churches prudently provided by Undershaft, one ironically a "William Morris Labor Church."* But the most important church of all to Undershaft's Utopia may be one physically not in Perivale St. Andrews at all. In East London is the Church of St. Andrew Undershaft, erected 1520–32. It is called Undershaft—after an earlier church on the same site—according to the chronicler and antiquary John Stow because in the early days of its existence "an high or long shaft, or Maypole, was set up there, in the midst of the street, before the south side of the said church."[11] As it rose higher than the steeple, the church on the corner of St. Mary Axe, Leadenhall Street, became known as St. Andrew Undershaft, distinguishing it from the numerous other London churches dedicated to the popular St. Andrew.†

On one occasion during the reign of the first Elizabeth, Stow records, a puritanical cleric named Sir Stephen (here one may usefully recall Undershaft's mediocrity of a son, of the same name) preached against the shaft as a profane source of happiness, accusing the inhabitants of the parish of St. Andrew Undershaft of sacrilegiously setting up for themselves an idol, the proof being

---

*On which is the motto around the dome, "NO MAN IS GOOD ENOUGH TO BE ANOTHER MAN'S MASTER." (There actually was a Labour Church Union at the turn of the century, founded in 1891 in Manchester by John Trevor, who attempted, as did Christian Socialism, to combine the social and religious rebellions against the Establishment into one movement. There was even a William Morris Labour Church in Leek, Staffordshire. By 1895 there were fourteen congregations in the Labour Church Union, but the concept never caught on in London and did not survive the 1914-18 war.)

†Undershaft has clearly meant to suggest particular relevance to his vale-situated company town through the St. Andrews part of its name. The first of Shaw's "Saint Barbara's" many forefathers may thus be a saint himself, the St. Andrew of the lost Gospel (alluded to by tradition), who gave the playwright his excuse to title part of his preface "The Gospel of St. Andrew Undershaft," and who had special significance to Shaw's audience as (with St. George) one of the two patron saints of Britain.

their addition to the name of the church—"under that shaft." Stow further writes, "I heard his sermon at Paul's cross, and I saw the effect that followed." What followed was that the parishioners, eager to assert their religious ortho-doxy, pulled down their beloved Maypole, hacked it into pieces, and put it to the pyre.[12] Blood and fire.

Shaw's play has been called his *Divine Comedy*[13]—in brief, because its perva-sive religious aspect includes three acts possibly divisible allegorically into Dante's Hell, Purgatory, and Paradise.* If the genealogy of Major Barbara's father ironically recalls the conflict at the great shaft of Cornhill between bleak, negative orthodoxy and the small-scale but positive juxtaposition of divine and materialistic happiness represented by the paradox of the Maypole and the Mass merging at St. Andrew Undershaft—a literal *Divine Comedy* in itself—it may be that Shaw intended it so. Certainly his christening of Barbara's father suggests, as does the entire density of allusion in the drama, that he had thor-oughly done his homework. Yet had Shaw's Undershaft solved the spiritual problem in his armaments-dependent Utopia? "Try your hand on my men," he confidently invites Barbara as they tour his "City of God": "Their souls are hungry because their bodies are full." And Barbara is ensnared by that temp-tation, as has been her husband to be. It is not without reason that Cusins ear-lier had labeled Undershaft "Mephistopheles-Machiavelli," for ironic Faustian overtones are not merely in the Satanic mills which nourish the heavenly city but permeate the play.

There was, one must also own, a real Stratford St. Andrew Rectory, a house in Suffolk rented by the Webbs where Shaw in 1896 spent a long summer holiday. The skein of association in creativity is labyrinthine—Barbara's Salvation Army assistant, Jenny Hill, for example, recalls the music hall comedienne of the same name Shaw may have remembered who sang (shades of East Ham!) "The City Waif" and who died at forty-six in 1896. That Shaw's capacious sub-conscious stored the Stratford St. Andrew location is apparent by its postal address of "near Saxmundham," for Andrew Undershaft in Act II is asked to match a gift to the Salvation Army by Lord Saxmundham, who had been Horace Bodger the distiller until his benefactions to restore a crumbling cathe-dral were recognized—a bit of history Shaw borrowed from the Guinness brew-ing family, as he took Bodger's "letters of fire across the sky" illuminated sign (in Barbara's agonized description) from the pioneering one for Dewar's Whisky.

Four fathers for Barbara? The four armorers are but a beginning, in a play inspired not only by people and events Shaw saw around him but by the *Repub-lic* of Plato, the *Bacchae* of Euripides, the *Pilgrim's Progress* of Bunyan, *The Prince* of Machiavelli, the *Marriage of Heaven and Hell* of Blake, the *Emperor and Galilean* of Ibsen, and the *Ring* of Wagner.† In visualizing so many threads drawn together, we not only achieve an insight into a remarkable creative process but through that insight realize a sense of the ramifications of a single dramatic personality. A character with such complex origins cannot be one

---

*In an irony which very likely escaped G.B.S. it is St. Bernard who, when Dante reaches the heav-enly zone, assumes the role of guide and reveals to the poet the final aim of man.

†Also, unless the echo is no more than that, the *Past and Present* of Carlyle, in which a "Plugson of Undershot" is the owner of a firm located in the parish of "St. Dolly Undershot." Julian Kaye, who notes this in *Bernard Shaw and the Nineteenth-Century Tradition*, suggests that the "Dolly" might have further echoed in Shaw via Adolphus ("Dolly") Cusins.

from whom we can extract simple answers. Although much can be learned about Shaw's intentions within various levels of meaning from Barbara's many forefathers—not only from the four dealers in death—*Major Barbara* resists simplification and remains the most complex of Shaw's plays. Decades after he wrote *Man and Superman*, with its structure of preface, play, mythic play within the play, appendix purportedly written by one of the characters, and aphoristic fireworks of an appendix to that appendix, Shaw boasted that he had put all of his intellectual goods in the shop window in that play.[14] He had put even more into *Major Barbara*, but not with such shop-window obtrusiveness. In the paradoxes of Barbara's many fathers is the intellectual center of Shaw's most profound work for the theatre.

A final, postplay irony brings together Saints Barbara and Andrew—for a World War II air raid blotted out the buildings on the opposite corner of Leadenhall Street and St. Mary Axe, leaving the Church of St. Andrew Undershaft relatively unscathed. The bomb very possibly was manufactured by Krupp.

13 Brogue-Shock: The Evolution of an Irish Patriot

In 1914 few Irishmen would have looked upon Bernard Shaw as one of them. He had been born there, it was true, and had lived the first twenty years of his life there, but he appeared to have expressed little sympathy with Irish causes and had written only one play about Ireland—a comedy remote from the spirit of resurgent Irish nationalism. Yet the two years which followed 1914 saw the evolution of a patriot who would come to the spirited defense of Ireland's rebel sons, admit the necessity—under certain conditions—of civil war, and have his previously resented and neglected plays applauded by standing-room houses in Dublin. Under the shock of events, Shaw very likely failed at first to comprehend what had happened to himself.

Under the cover of anonymity he had attacked the English presence in Ireland as early as the 1880s, writing unsigned verses in the London *Star* on January 23, 1888, which ridiculed A. J. Balfour, then Chief Secretary for Ireland. Balfour had condoned, if not ordered, arrests and searches of radical suspects, and Shaw explained the purpose in Gilbertian stanzas which began with "I am a statesman bold. . . ." Stripping a suspect and throwing him in an unheated cell, Balfour was made to say, was his "plan to make it hot / For the Irish patriot" and was "subtler far than bludgeoning and hanging him."

A few months later, in the *Star* for April 30, 1888, Shaw was less facetious but still anonymous, hitting at the successful persuasion of Pope Leo XIII by the British government to condemn the boycotting (named for Captain Boycott, a landlord's agent) of those who bought or leased property from which an Irish tenant had been evicted. The "liberties of Ireland," he declared in an unsigned leader, "have been sacrificed to a base Tory intrigue." But few knew that Shaw's hand was involved in the editorial, and few remembered in 1914 that he had written, under his own name, other comments sympathetic to the Irish cause, for his contention long had been that Ireland would have the best of both worlds through self-government within a British federation.

If it had not been apparent to Irishmen before 1914, it seemed then that Shaw was not on their side. After all, when war began in Europe, Shaw came out for Irish participation, even an "Irish Brigade." What had happened was that in November 1914, smarting under charges that he was pro-German (which followed his controversial *Common Sense About the War* pamphlet) but unwilling to declare himself pro-Asquith, Shaw had tried to explain his position on Ireland. Telegraphing to George Russell ("AE") in Dublin, he inquired what the best Irish publication would be to print a letter of his urging Irish support of France and decrying the "silly Pro-German slosh" by which some Irish papers were mischievously getting back at England. Russell suggested the *Freeman's Journal*, the organ of the Irish Nationalist Party, and within five days a letter from Shaw appeared there which denounced pro-Germanism as a betrayal of Ireland's "old comrades, the French, for the sake of Prussia." (Pointedly, Shaw excluded England.) An editor's note following the letter took the steam out of the declaration by insisting that all it revealed was Shaw's astonishing ignorance of the real state of things, that pro-German sentiment was puny and not indicative of the swelling pro-Allied mood in Ireland.[1] It had long been a cliché that Shaw did not know his Ireland.

Before his piece had appeared Shaw had received from County Kerry a letter from Mabel McConnell, a former secretary of his now married to a young Irish revolutionary, Desmond Fitzgerald. His *Common Sense* pamphlet was a fine piece of work, she began, but its main impact upon her was that it made her "wish more than ever that you would stop bothering about such a childish and vacuous people as the English and come right over here to work . . . as Roger Casement is doing to make Ireland a Nation before Europe." Since Sir Roger had been attempting to get Germany and her allies to recognize Ireland, this was a subject Shaw had to handle gingerly. He had been "on the point of mentioning" publicly, he answered, that Casement "was perfectly in order in exercising our inalienable right as a nation to consult any other nation as to our future or present or past relations; but I didn't know what his credentials were; and in this war emergency I did not want to start more hares than I could help." As for devoting himself to his native land, Shaw confessed skepticism that it would appreciate his services. "The place is too small for me. The earth and all the fullness thereof are good enough for me. . . . Ireland must have an ambassador in the great world; so I am better as I am. You may possibly remember also that I am an elderly gentleman of 58½, and that my bolt is shot."[2]

Refusing to accept Shaw's shrinking from Irish revolutionary responsibilities as final, Mrs. Fitzgerald insisted that the *Freeman* failed to represent the true feeling of the country, which was pro-German, that Sir Roger was a true Irish knight "of the old times," and that she fully intended to subvert Shaw's allegiance. In vain Shaw insisted that it was in Ireland's best interests not to become another Belgium for Germany, much less an invited one, and that Ireland would cut its own throat by succumbing in war to its hatred of England. "I want to rub your eyes for you and waken you up," he told her with friendly bluntness. "The day of small nations is past. . . . Only as a member of a great commonwealth is there any future for us. We are a wretched little clod, broken off a bigger clod, broken off the west end of Europe. . . ." Ireland had to be, he thought, "a very highly civilized people or nothing," and that meant making the most of its ties with larger countries and the language which put the Irish into communication with a fifth of the human race. If nationalism and freedom meant shrinking Ireland into "a little village community" with a language "that nobody in the world speaks," he wanted no part of it.[3] It was a view of Ireland consistent with Shaw's pronouncements over more than a decade, since *John Bull's Other Island* and its long preface.

Paradoxically, Shaw as an Irishman in England was equivalent to an enemy alien; his views about his native Ireland and about the war with Germany, in both cases excluding nationalistic fervor, made him an unrecognized symbol of sanity in a pair of islands dominated by extremists. With Mabel and Desmond Fitzgerald promoting pro-Germanism and Irish insurrection, Shaw again in early 1915 tried vainly to turn them toward moderation. In the meantime they were expelled from Kerry by the British authorities and removed eastward to Wicklow. The unhappy revolutionaries appealed to Shaw, who wrote back unsympathetically that he wondered what else the Fitzgeralds expected the authorities to do, when in the middle of an appalling war they made it obvious— and from a western Irish coastal town—that they sought England's defeat and Germany's victory: "Surely not to leave you in the western coastguard station with all its possibilities of signalling to your friend the enemy?" Most of Ireland, he insisted, knew that there was no choice but "to see the English and French through this fight with Prussia . . . I had much rather you rallied to my banner. . . ."[4]

People in London—if one judged by what appeared in the press—had a different idea as to what Shaw's banner really represented, although he claimed to have reconciled his obligations as British subject with his objectivity as an Irishman. An English writer demonstrated how indefensible this reasoning was by describing a cartoon which had appeared in January in the New York *Herald*. It represented "a burglar (with a *Kaiserlichen* moustache) standing over the body of his victim as it lay on a bed decorated at its head with the Belgian crown. And the 'caption' of the cartoon ran: 'Under the pillow of the victim was found a weapon to be used for defence, thus absolving the burglar from all blame.'" Shaw's claim to objectivity about the war on grounds that he was an Irishman and thus could have the outlook of an alien "only takes the words out of our mouth," concluded Harold Owen. "Of course he is: he would be an alien anywhere."[5]

During Easter 1915, Shaw was in Ireland, a guest for a fortnight of Sir Horace Plunkett, Home Ruler, agricultural reformer, and founder of the Irish cooperative movement. After that he went on to Coole to stay with Lady Gregory, where another guest, Augustus John, kept Shaw busy sitting for his portrait, painting six variations in eight days.[6] Shaw thought they were splendid, which indeed they were. One went on display that spring at the New English Art Club, and John was not concerned about press reaction which might confuse subject and execution.

G.B.S. and Charlotte returned from Ireland in mid-May on a ship crowded with survivors of the *Lusitania*, all of them fearful that the waters between the two islands were infested with U-boats. Although he had lost friends among those who had sailed on the *Lusitania*, including Sir Hugh Lane, Shaw lost a great many more at home by scoffing at the tears and outrage lavished on the nearly twelve hundred "innocent victims" when hundreds of thousands of equally innocent human beings, he said, were being sent to their deaths on the Western front and at Gallipoli, the only difference being that they had been misled into khaki.

An outgrowth of his visit to Lady Gregory was an ironic playlet on war recruiting in Ireland intended to help her financially hard-pressed Abbey Theatre. (The idea for the play may have come from Shaw's protesting the jailing of Sheehy Skeffington, an unorthodox Irish nationalist who had made an anti-recruiting speech.) War and threat of civil war had thinned theater audiences in Dublin, and Shaw saw in Lady Gregory's need an opportunity to aid her while encouraging Irish enlistments in the British Army through a play paradoxically calculated to appeal to Irishmen through its satire of Englishmen. On both counts Lady Gregory was the appropriate destination for the play, for she symbolized Irish loyalty through her son Robert, an officer in the Royal Flying Corps. Shaw had promised it for the fall, and the writing of *O'Flaherty, V.C.* went quickly enough that he could tell her to put it on the Abbey's schedule.

On October 30 "Wayfarer" in the *Nation* reported, "Mr. Shaw's new play for the Irish Theatre, called 'O'Flaherty, V.C.,' is an entirely fresh and delightful frolic." It was exactly that, but not to the authorities in Dublin Castle. "Incomprehensible as it may seem to an Englishman," said Shaw in a postwar preface, "Irish patriotism does not take the form of devotion to England and England's king." Unable to understand this, the War Office had attempted to encourage recruiting in Ireland by covering walls with placards urging "REMEMBER BELGIUM," discouraging the formation of Irish units, and refusing commissions to Roman Catholics who lived in Ireland. Shaw had subtitled his playlet "a recruiting pamphlet" and thought of it as a "recruiting poster in disguise." To stimulate an Irishman's loyalty to Ireland would only encourage him to stay on the native soil and die for it, he thought, while a better device to get him to want to leave Ireland was to "appeal to his discontent, his deadly boredom, his thwarted curiosity and desire for change and adventure. . . ." There was another, unmentionable, inducement to recruiting, Shaw added—the conviction that the "happy home of the idealist" was an uncommon thing. "No one will ever know how many men joined the army in 1914 and 1915 to escape from tyrants and taskmasters, termagants and shrews, none of whom are any the less irksome when they happen by ill-luck to be also our fathers, our mothers, our wives and our children."[7]

Private Dennis O'Flaherty, a winner of the Victoria Cross, has come home to his native village as part of a recruiting campaign which has taken him wearily about Ireland. He is nervous about meeting his formidable mother because he had led her to believe that he had been fighting in the German Army, her loyalties making it impossible for her to believe that an Irishman could do anything else but fight against the English. The presence of the English general (but Irish landowner) Sir Pearce Madigan notwithstanding, she flies at him in rage, for she had learned the truth when the news of his V.C. was released, even to his shaking hands with the King. His explanations leave her cold:

> "I didn't shake hands with him: he shook hands with me. Could I turn on the man in his own house, before his own wife, and his money in my pocket and in yours, and throw his civility back in his face?"

> "You would take the hand of a tyrant red with the blood of Ireland—"

O'Flaherty adroitly mollifies her by declaring that he joined the army that would pay her the largest allowance. Tessie, his girl friend, is more interested in his prospects for a pension and in a gold chain taken from a German prisoner, evidence to Dennis that the interest shown in him by both women is primarily mercenary. Furious with both of them, he threatens to marry a Frenchwoman and leave Ireland, where he had been "imposed on and kept in ignorance," for good. Knowing that his mother will refuse the offer, he even suggests that she go with him. "Ask me to die out of Ireland, is it?" she cries, "and the angels not find me when they come for me!" Rather, she hopes that the war—and thus her dependant's allowance—will last a long time. There is a row, and the two women, unwilling to quiet down, are pushed into Sir Pearce's country house and the door is shut on them, leaving O'Flaherty in peace to ruminate to the general:

> "What a discontented sort of an animal a man is, sir. Only a month ago, I was in
> the quiet of the country out at the front, with not a sound except the birds and
> the bellow of a cow in the distance as it might be, and the shrapnel making little
> clouds in the heavens, and the shells whistling, and maybe a yell or two when
> one of us was hit; and would you believe it, sir, I complained of the noise and
> wanted to have a peaceful hour at home. Well: them two has taught me a lesson.
> This morning, sir, when I was telling the boys here how I was longing to be back
> taking my part for king and country with the others, I was lying, as you well
> know, sir. Now I can go and say it with a clear conscience. Some likes war's
> alarums; and some like home life. I've tried both, sir; and I'm for war's alarums
> now. I always was a quiet lad by natural disposition."

The play was clearly too much politically for the timid English authorities in
Ireland, and Shaw must have realized it, although he hoped to evade censorship
through production out of the Lord Chamberlain's jurisdiction. Nothing else
could have been reasonably expected for a play in which the hero confesses that
he killed so many of the enemy "Because I was afeard that, if I didn't, they'd
kill me" and responds to the general's talk of the "sacred right for which we are
fighting" and to his echo of the newspaper view of the war by saying, "There's
not many newsboys crying the evening paper in the trenches. They do say, Sir
Pearce, that we shall never beat the Boshes until we make Horatio Bottomley
Lord Leftenant of England. Do you think that's true, sir?"

Sir Pearce's explosion that in England the King is Lord Lieutenant and that
the war is a simple question of patriotism only leads to O'Flaherty's, "And
what good has it ever done here in Ireland? . . . The Boshes I kilt was more
knowledgeable men than me; and what better am I now that I've kilt them?
What better is anybody? . . . No war is right; and all the holy water that Father
Quinlan ever blessed couldn't make one right."[8]

The paradox that one might get unsophisticated Irishmen to fight on England's side while suggesting that England, not Germany, was the enemy was
viewed without humor at Dublin Castle. Augustine Birrell, Secretary for Ireland, declared to Shaw, "I have read your play with interest, but it won't get a
single recruit unless you are thinking of joining up yourself. And as for my doing away with oaths [to the King], you might as well ask me to do away with the
Thirty-nine Articles or the 'not's' in the Ten Commandments. Do use a little
common sense."[9] Furthermore, the commanding general of the Dublin District
sent an intimidating letter to W. F. Bailey, a trustee of the Abbey Theatre, while
the play was already in rehearsal for a November 23 opening. While not sup-
pressing the play outright, the general made it impossible to stage it. "My recollection of the letter," St. John Ervine (then the manager) wrote, "was . . .
that, knowing the sort of man G.B.S. was, he wished to warn us that if there
were a riot in the theatre as a result of the production, the theatre's license
would instantly be cancelled." Since the Abbey existed from one night's box-office take to the next, summary closure would have meant ruin; and Ervine, seeking advice, found that Yeats was in London and Lady Gregory in America.
There was only Bailey, an excitable little man whose opinion was a foregone
conclusion. Timidly, Ervine took it.[10]

Shaw had offered the playlet free of royalty, but even so the Abbey proved
unable to benefit from it. Commiserating with him, Horace Plunkett wrote from
Dublin that he could understand why the play would be unsuitable, given "the

present state of feeling," for either side could use the occasion for a demonstration that would only provoke counterdemonstrations. When conscription ceased to trouble Ireland, Plunkett hoped, "all could laugh and learn" from Shaw's play.[11] Sarcastically, Shaw's sister Lucy, who had written to Ann Elder asking for a copy of the playlet, returned her reaction to G.B.S.'s secretary while misnaming it in the process:

> Thank you for *Michael O'Flaherty*: it is obviously a play that could not have been produced during the war. It can easily be made into a three-act play by additions that I shall humbly submit to the author when I see him, if I ever do again.
> Why does he not offer himself as Lord Lieutenant for Ireland, he would soon make it anything but the figure head it has always been. He could have Horace Plunkett as Chief Secretary and McNulty as Under Secretary, and between them they could soon finish off Ireland.[12]

No Irish patriot, Lucy nevertheless thought herself more of one than her brother. G.B.S.'s boyhood friend, Edward McNulty (then a minor Bank of Ireland official), and his closest Irish friend, Horace Plunkett (an Irish Commissioner), hardly represented nationalistic aspirations.

Just after the *O'Flaherty* "poster in disguise" was suppressed by the military in Dublin, Shaw paradoxically received an appeal from Lieutenant-Colonel Matthew Nathan, then Undersecretary at the Viceregal Lodge, Dublin, asking for help in counterbalancing the failure of official recruiting and War Loan propaganda in Ireland. Shaw pointed out that appeals to English patriotism were useless in Ireland. "I drafted a poster for him," Shaw recalled, "and told him to print it on green paper and stick it up all over Ireland with instructions to the Royal Irish Constabulary to see that it was not torn down. He replied that the R.I.C., being a picked Protestant force, would themselves tear it down. . . ."[13] There the matter rested, and the conscription question never ceased to trouble Ireland during the war, for although the British eventually passed a conscription bill which included Ireland, threats to enforce it there became increasingly empty, especially after the events of Easter 1916. Shaw's recruiting playlet remained unperformed, and his poster was never printed.

Early in 1916 there was new trouble in Ireland concerning Shaw. Extremists still considered him disloyal, while adherents to the Crown found his alleged pro-Germanism even more likely to render him untrustworthy than his Irish birth. The symbolic absurdity in his case occurred in March, when the offices of the Gaelic Press in Dublin were raided by the authorities, and the most heralded of the suspect matter seized was a copy of Shaw's *Three Plays for Puritans* (1900). The puzzled manager of the press, recalling the fuss over *O'Flaherty, V.C.*, wrote to Shaw, inquiring whether the book contained "seditious matter or matter likely to prejudice recruiting." Shaw—correctly—replied that he didn't think the raid was planned with the object of seizing his book, although some references might have been mistakenly thought to be contemporary. There was a reference in *The Devil's Disciple* to a "pigheaded lunatic like King George," but the action of the play was set in 1777, and the George was the Third rather than the Fifth.

That April Shaw returned to his vain entreaties to the Irish about remaining loyal and united, publishing a piece in *The New York Times* aimed at counteracting revolutionary and separatist rhetoric. The large Irish-American population was a source of financial and political support to the Nationalists, who, if successful, Shaw insisted, would make Ireland independent and—simultaneously—utterly insignificant—a "cabbage garden." (The Irish separatists might have answered that at least it would be their own cabbage garden.) "The cry that England's Difficulty is Ireland's Opportunity," Shaw wrote, "is raised in the old, senseless, spiteful way as a recommendation to stab England in the back when she is fighting someone else and to kick her when she is down, instead of in the intelligent and large-minded modern way which sees in England's difficulty the opportunity of shewing her what a friendly alliance with Ireland can do for her in return for the indispensable things it can do for Ireland." Appealing to reason yet unable to conclude without the touch of levity which often defused the trenchancy of his argument, Shaw observed that "even an Irish patriot must not be surprised at not having it all his own way. He must console himself by considering that, in the words of a deservedly celebrated Irish dramatic poet,

> Fate drives us all to find our chiefest good
> In what we can, and not in what we would.

The poet was Shaw, in Cashel Byron's lines from the 1901 farce *The Admirable Bashville*.

The war, Shaw insisted in a masterpiece of poor timing—it was April 9, 1916—was Ireland's as well as England's and was a "convincing demonstration of the futility of the notion that the Irish and English peoples are natural enemies. They are, on the contrary, natural allies."

A week later—Easter Monday—everything changed. At eleven o'clock in the morning a party of twenty Irish revolutionaries shot and killed an unarmed policeman at Dublin Castle who refused them admittance to the Cork Hill entrance to Upper Castle Yard. When the shots brought out the other half dozen unarmed men on duty at the castle, the Volunteers fled, assuming there were still more troops. There was never another chance to capture the seat of British rule, but the first shot in the revolt had been fired. The battle plan of the Irish Citizen Army had been to seize and hold the center of the city while—they hoped—their comrades all over Ireland would rise in rebellion; but in the end (a week later), they held only the General Post Office in what was then called Sackville Street.

Watching the activity near the post office on Tuesday had been Shaw's friend Francis Sheehy Skeffington, a colorful Dublin character addicted to humanitarian causes. With his beard, spectacles, umbrella, cloak, and knickerbocker suit with a "Votes for Women" badge on a lapel, he was clearly not a rebel, but he had a prison record, having served time in 1915 for making a speech against conscription of Irishmen in a war in which he saw no Irish interest served. His wife had appealed to Shaw, who wrote a strong letter published in the *Freeman's Journal* in Dublin (June 16, 1915). His protests, Shaw confessed, were "quite useless. The Opposition in the House of Commons will not oppose. The Press will not defend public liberties. England is thoroughly intimidated by Germany so far as her civilians are concerned. . . . Something can be done with a tyrannical Government. Nothing can be done with a terrified government and a cowed people. . . . I can fight stupidity; but nobody can fight cowardice."

Shaw had then supported Sheehy Skeffington more for his pacifism and antiwar stance than for his Irish militancy; but that evening in 1916 "Skeffy" addressed a meeting he had called on the need for cooperation to stop the looting of stores in the battle zone and was arrested and shot the next morning by a firing squad. Less than three weeks before, he had written to Shaw, enclosing a copy of a letter he had sent to several London newspapers warning the English of the gravity and explosiveness of the Irish situation. "I think it quite likely that none of them will publish it," he told Shaw, "so I am sending you a copy for your personal information, that you may understand how critical the position is here. It will require all the efforts of all men of goodwill to avert bloodshed in Ireland; and perhaps you, having the ear of the press, may be able to intervene effectively." In his innocence, "Skeffy" had no idea how difficult it was for Shaw to be heard in the press on unpopular sides of unpalatable subjects. Shaw, in fact, had just had to direct his appeal to reason to Irishmen in Ireland by way of *The New York Times* (although it was then picked up by a Dublin paper).

The indefensible execution of Sheehy Skeffington outraged even the English, and the officer who had ordered it was subsequently court-martialed and declared insane. The widow was offered an indemnity by the government, and Shaw pressed her to be sensible and accept it. She refused.

Meanwhile, James Stephens had published a bitter open letter to Shaw in the *New Age*, answering the piece in *The New York Times* (reprinted in the *Irish Times*) which had so quickly become obsolete. It was easy, profitable, and even safe for Shaw to market his opinions about Ireland, Stephens suggested; furthermore, Shaw was covertly pro-German, and by residence and feeling he was English, not Irish:

> Your home is there, your fame, your bank. Even—and I say it with neither malice nor regret—your heart is there, for where the treasure is there will the heart be also, But the fact that you have negotiated with England does not entitle you to speak for your nation, not even in these days when the Gombeen Man straddles the world. Ireland has not made peace with England. It is true she is committing racial and economic suicide for her "dear enemy," but she is too small, too poor, too inconsiderable in every dimension to make either war or peace, or to make anything but a pitiable clamour and, perhaps, like an angry kitten, scratch a little. It, of course, serves kittens right when they are chastised with a club as big as an oak tree. Is it not better to say that England has not made her peace with Ireland, although, long enough, Ireland has been howling and begging and scratching for that peace?
>
> If England has been your country, and if you had said of her, and in that tone, the things you have said (in America) about your own country, it would not have been safe for you in England. But it is only your own country that you so write about, and are witty about, and superior and finely careless about, and you are quite safe in doing it. Did you not know it?
>
> You did not send your national counsel directly to Ireland. You sent it to Ireland via America—the Trade Route.
>
> We can all on occasion advise each other, and I will advise you to make a compact with yourself, and save your soul, by resolving, that if you can say nothing good of your country you will not say anything evil of her. It is not a too heroic resolve, and with your intellectual activity it will not be expensive. Every Irishman feels bitterly at times that there is nothing he can do for his land, but, at the least, he can hold his tongue for her, and he can refuse to make any profit out of her national bewilderment.
>
> To all literary men words at last cease to be speech and become merchandise. This is beyond assistance, and need not be deplored, but every literary man might take a vow of silence on some subject; and I suggest that Ireland is a subject on which you should never again either write or speak, and if you can cease to think of her that will be so much gained also.

Stephens had hurriedly written and posted his letter on the Saturday before the Easter rising, sending it to London "because I doubted that the Dublin papers would print it if I sent it to them, and I knew that the Irish people who read the other papers had never heard of Shaw, except as a trade-mark under which very good Limerick bacon is sold, and that they would not be interested in the opinions of a person named Shaw on any subject not relevant to bacon. I struck out of my letter a good many harsh things which I said of him, and hoped he would reply to it in order that I could furnish these acidities to him in a second letter."[14] By the time Stephens's invective had been printed, it had become as obsolete as Shaw's earlier advice had been.

In the *New Statesman* for May 6 appeared what seemed to be a new G.B.S. "Neglected Morals of the Irish Rising," under Shaw's signature, spoke of men who had "died heroically for their principles in the burning ruins of the General Post Office in Sackville Street." "No wise man now uses the word Traitor at all," he added. "He who fights for the independence of his country may be an ignorant and disastrous fool, but he is not a traitor and will never be regarded as one by his fellow countrymen. All the slain men and women of the Sinn Fein Volunteers fought and died for their country as sincerely as any soldier in Flanders has fought or died for his."

Had he stopped there, Shaw's apparent conversion would have seemed quick and complete. Yet G.B.S. was still G.B.S., and his compulsive levity broke in to destroy the effect. One of his "neglected morals" was that one should not assume that every building destroyed by an enemy was an irreplaceable masterpiece of architecture. Thus the demolition of the "dull eighteenth-century pseudo-classic" post office was actually overdue, and what did matter was that the slums along the Liffey had not been demolished. The feeling for the Dublin poor was meant to be kind, but the paradox was lost on the unhappy Dubliners. Yet Shaw then added, "Let us grieve, not over the fragment of Dublin city that is knocked down, but over at least three-quarters of what has been preserved. How I wish I had been in command of the British artillery on that fatal field! How I should have improved my native city."

Whatever Shaw's good intentions, they were misplaced and mistimed. Although the ire of Dubliners was understandable, Shaw never realized that he had blundered. Events were moving too quickly. Soon there were other executions. Twelve leaders of the Rising had been shot by May 10, when a Shavian protest appeared in the *Daily News* pointing out that the executed Irishmen "will now take their place beside Emmet and the Manchester martyrs in Ireland, and beside the heroes of Poland and Serbia in Europe; and nothing in heaven or on earth can prevent it."

Defending the right of Irishmen to resort to arms to achieve the independence of their country, Shaw added, "I remain an Irishman, and am bound to contradict any implication that I can regard as a traitor any Irishman taken in a fight for Irish independence." Inevitably, he made his case with what had to be for an Englishman an unpalatable paradox—that the Irish were doing "only what Englishmen will do if it be their misfortune to be invaded and conquered by the Germans in the course of the present war." More executions, he warned, only created more martyrs and heroes.

As Stephens afterward recalled, he rushed a letter to the *New Age* to withdraw his tirade, for events had "proved that it was unmeaning and ridiculous," although they had showed what "electricity was already in the air." In a foreword to his hastily written book on the insurrection, he added, "Every statement I made about him was erroneous; for, afterwards, when it would have been politic to run for cover, he ran for the open, and he spoke there like the valiant thinker and great Irishman that he is." It was quite a turnaround for both men:

AN APOLOGY TO MR. SHAW

Sir,—

On the subject of my letter headed "To Mr. Shaw", which appeared in your issue of May 4, I trust you will print the following.

J.S.

TO MR. SHAW

Sir,—

I humbly and earnestly apologise to you for everything contained in my letter to THE NEW AGE. It was written at a time of national unrest, and contains an utter and gross misconception of your character. Your public utterance on the Irish insurrection has given the lie to everything I said in that letter, and I beg you to believe that I am deeply sorry for having written it.

—Your obedient servant,

James Stephens.[15]

Shaw's turnaround would take an even more dramatic direction. In the *Daily News* article he had noted, in a paradox calculated to make Englishmen squirm, that an Irishman was "as much in order morally in accepting assistance from the Germans in his struggle with England as England is in accepting the assistance of Russia in her struggle with Germany." It was an argument he would have to face again in short order, for Sir Roger Casement, landed in Ireland by German submarine to help foment rebellion, had been captured almost immediately on stepping ashore and was in the Tower of London awaiting a trial that was almost certain to end the way it had in the past for so many notorious occupants of the gray tower.

At least one of Shaw's arguments was effective. He had warned the authorities that they were "canonizing their prisoners," and as shock over the Rising gave way to anger against the government and admiration for the rebels, the government suddenly listened. Two days after Shaw's widely publicized letter to the *Daily News* appeared, there were two more executions, one of the victims being the leader of the Irish Citizen Army, James Connolly (G.B.S. later subscribed heavily to a fund raised for Connolly's widow and children, contributing more than a third of the amount collected). But after that, the remaining ninety-seven death sentences were commuted to prison terms; and before the middle of May, Asquith himself had hurried to Dublin to try to restore confidence and establish goodwill. But as one Irish historian had put it, "it was already too late. Ireland was quickly passing under the most dangerous of all tyrannies—the tyranny of the dead."[16]

On May 12, the Shaws had W. F. Bailey, the Irish Estates Commissioner and Abbey Theatre trustee, to lunch and invited the Webbs and Sydney Cockerell to meet him and listen to his tales of the Rising. Cockerell was thrilled to hear that there were only three or four miscalculations between what happened and a major rebellion that might have taken a hundred thousand troops to put down. Shaw was sick at heart.[17] However strongly Shaw had urged unity and cooperation with England upon his countrymen, his sympathies with the proponents of Irish freedom were never stronger than in the wake of the bungled Rising.

"I never felt so morose in my life," Shaw wrote Mrs. Campbell. "I cant write: nothing comes off but screeds for the papers, mostly about this blasted war. I am old and finished. . . ."[18]

Through the summer months which followed the Rising, Shaw pressed his scheme to defend Sir Roger Casement from a hanging that appeared to be inevitable not because he was a traitor but because he was an Irishman. As Shaw knew, however, he was both. On June 26, after having been in the Tower since his arrest, Casement had been taken to the Old Bailey for what would be the last trial in the aftermath of the Easter Rising. A battery of attorneys defended Casement—Serjeant A. M. Sullivan of the Irish Bar, together with two English lawyers and an American legal advisor—and to newsman Henry W. Nevinson, Shaw complained that just as men felt that to die decently one needed doctors at hand, so they felt the need for lawyers in order to be hanged in a Christian manner. In this mood, G.B.S., with Charlotte, attended a luncheon at the Webbs' to meet their neighbor Mrs. J. R. Green, widow of the historian, who was trying to raise money for Casement's legal defense and counted heavily on the Shaws. (So did Casement's cousin, Gertrude Bannister, a suburban London teacher, who had visited the Shaws at Adelphi Terrace and won G.B.S. over with her air of capability and good sense.) Even before Alice Green's invitation, Shaw had been holding meetings at Adelphi Terrace to develop a course of action with his friends, few of whom had much sympathy with what Casement had tried to do, and none of whom could stomach his pro-Germanism; but their reluctance had been in the process of being overcome, when a shattering rumor reached them. The prisoner's "black" diaries had been seized, and their contents indicated that Casement had been involved in homosexual activities unmentionable before the ladies in the room.

The Adelphi Terrace committee's first thought was that the rumors were cunning attempts to discredit Casement, at worst only cheap forgeries. But Massingham announced that he would use the influence of his *Nation* to find out the facts, and he went to Scotland Yard. When he came back, it was clear to the group that Casement was lost. He had been shown the diaries, Massingham said, and their purport was as bad as could be imagined. Furthermore, they appeared to be genuinely in Casement's hand. The committee fell apart. In London clubs and drawing rooms, whispered references to the "black diaries" were the summer's most delicious gossip.[19]

In this atmosphere Alice Green's luncheon was a painful occasion, although no one alluded to the scandal; in her diary, Beatrice Webb recorded her bitterness at what she considered Shaw's callous levity:

> G.B.S. as usual had his own plan. Casement was to defend his own case; he was to make a great oration of defiance which would "bring down the house." To this Mrs. Green retorted tearfully that the man was desperately ill; that he was quite incapable of handling a court full of lawyers; that the most he could do was the final speech after the verdict. "Then we had better get our suit of mourning," Shaw remarked with an almost gay laugh. "I will write him a speech which will thunder down the ages." "But his friends want to get him reprieved," indignantly replied the distracted woman friend.
> . . . Shaw wants to compel Casement and Casement's friends to "produce" the defense as a national dramatic event. "I know how to do it," was G.B.S.'s one contribution to the tragedy-laden dispute. . . . And yet the man is both kindly and tolerant, but his conceit is monstrous. . . .[20]

What Beatrice failed to understand was that no conventional defense could save Casement, and her reaction was to vent her private irritation at Shaw's "argumentative perversities" and apparent intellectual detachment. Shaw always had sensed the undercurrent of Beatrice's hostility, realizing that his long, affectionate comradeship with Sidney had much to do with it; but he carefully ignored the existence of any problem and managed to remain working partners with both Webbs, a relationship which would last all their long lives. At the moment, however, Beatrice was furious, for Shaw insisted for himself and Charlotte that they would not "waste our money on lawyers." He went back to Adelphi Terrace to write a thundering speech for Casement anyway and to prepare a legal defense which he could elect to use, all or part. Basically it claimed prisoner-of-war status for Casement, thus eliminating the capital crime of high treason without denying any of the incontrovertible facts. Then Shaw would have had Casement plead not guilty to the charge of high treason upon which the government nevertheless would insist, pointing out that the plea did not deny the facts stated by the Crown but denied instead that any guilt was attached to them. For that purpose Shaw provided a speech with all the thunder he had promised, "to be made from the dock, not, of course, necessarily in my words, but in whatever paraphrase came most naturally to the accused":

> It may seem to some of you gentlemen of the jury that if I ought not to be hanged for being a patriot, I ought to be hanged for being a fool. I will not plead that if men are to be hanged for errors of judgment in politics, we should have such a morality in England and Ireland that hardly one of us would be left to hang the other. . . . I am not trying to shirk the scaffold: it is the altar on which the Irish saints have been canonized for centuries. . . . Will you understand me when I say that those three days of splendid fighting against desperate odds in the streets of Dublin have given Ireland back her self-respect. We were beaten, indeed never had a dog's chance of victory; but you were also beaten in a no less rash and desperate enterprise in Gallipoli. Are you ashamed of it? . . . I hope I have spoken here today as you would desire to hear an Englishman speak in a German Court if your country shared the fate of mine. . . . Gentlemen, I have done my duty: now it is your turn.

Casement pored over Shaw's draft defense and discarded most of it, heavily annotating his copy. "My failure is my crime—not my attempt," he insisted in a margin, rejecting the idea of claiming prisoner-of-war status. It was "excellent in many respects," he noted. "Shaw's view is all right; but he does not understand one tenth of the issue the Crown had in view. They are *not* after me—except in so far as they have to keep up with public feeling. They are out to befoul Germany [by identifying Irish rebels as] . . . misled and deceived by Germany and me. . . ." For the same reason he found no hope in the proposed speech from the dock. The trial then went as expected. Sullivan pleaded Casement's cause with vigor, collapsing in the middle of his closing speech, in which he had pitted his defense on a fine point of law—that high treason could only be committed *inside* the King's realm, while the prisoner had adhered to the King's enemies *outside* the realm. The Lord Chief Justice, Lord Reading, rejected Sullivan's construction of the statute, informing the jury that "contriving to assist the enemy" was the issue. The jury then returned the inevitable verdict, whereupon the Lord Chief Justice put on the black cap and pronounced sentence of death by hanging. "Then, if you please," Shaw recalled, "the virtually dead man got up and made his speech. A couple of members of the jury were, I am told, good enough to say that if they heard it before the verdict they would have dissented. But that possibility, on which I had banked, had been averted by the best possible legal advice, and Casement was duly hanged. . . ."[21]

Before the sentence was carried out Shaw tried other devices, including the drafting of a petition to the Prime Minister seeking commutation, but early in

August, discussing it with Clement Shorter, he said that he did not sign it himself "because my name might have frightened off some of the more useful signatures."[22] His last flurry of activity in Casement's behalf involved trying to place a long appeal asking "Shall Roger Casement Hang?" in leading newspapers. It was rejected by *The Times* and the *Nation* and was finally published on July 22 in the *Manchester Guardian.*

Shaw had accepted the inevitability of the sentence curiously—again permitting his levity in the face of inescapable circumstances to appear more like insensitivity. In his *Guardian* piece he had declared, "There need be no hesitation to carry out the sentence if it should appear, on reflection, a sensible one. Indeed, with a view to extricating the discussion completely from the sentimental vein, I will go so far as to confess that there is a great deal to be said for hanging all public men at the age of fifty-two, though under such a regulation I should myself have perished eight years ago. Were it in force throughout Europe, the condition of the world at present would be much more prosperous." Whatever point Shaw was making about the leadership of the great European nations at war, the suggestion was facetious and the clowning untimely. But this time, at least, Irish interests were not the victim.

At the eleventh hour he published another appeal for commutation. By then it was too late for any attempt at irony which might be misinterpreted.[23] At Pentonville Prison, on the morning of August 3, Casement was hanged.

August 1916, however, saw the beginning in Ireland of a surprising Shavian apotheosis. When the Abbey had reopened in the aftermath of the aborted insurrection, its first three offerings were three Shaw plays: *Widowers' Houses, John Bull's Other Island,* and *Arms and the Man*; and for the September 25 opening night of *John Bull,* Shaw's satire on Anglo-Irish manners, the queue extended into the Marlborough Street pit entrance, with many unsuccessful ticket seekers turned away long before eight o'clock. In February the Abbey would stage *Man and Superman,* and in March it was producing *The Inca of Perusalem,* while *The Doctor's Dilemma* was scheduled for May. It was a Shaw festival of a magnitude unseen since 1904–07 repertory of the Vedrenne-Barker Royal Court Theatre in London, and undoubtedly Shaw's outspokenness on Irish matters had had much to do with it. "The repatriation" of G.B.S., J. M. Hone reported to the *New Statesman* from Dublin, was proceeding swiftly.

> There was a time when Mr. Shaw could not lecture in Dublin, even on the Poor Laws, without a section of his listeners rising to leave the house; but his action last spring, when as an opponent of Sinn Fein he explained Sinn Fein better than its exponents, seems to have led to a change; at all events, the Irish National Theatre is now in the midst of a peaceful Shaw season. . . . Nothing is more curious than to observe the difference between a typically Irish and typically English reception of one of Mr. Shaw's plays. It is not that the standard of intelligence of Abbey Theatre audiences is abnormally high. For there are certain well-known plays in the repertory of that theatre which invariably produce Irish laughter at precisely the wrong moments; only Mr. Shaw's plays are not among these, which is the more remarkable, since in London cackling so commonly greets his most profound lines. While in England Mr. Shaw has had to struggle against the reputation of being a mere farceur, in Ireland he is too exclusively regarded as a commentator on politics—a good commentator if his sayings fit in with the popular mood, a bad [one] if they do not.[24]

The Inca of Perusalem, then, was received "exactly as an Irish audience might have been expected to receive a topical play by Mr. Shaw—*i.e.,* in silence,

save for an occasional political cheer." And the cheers were not in appreciation
of the Shavian lampoon of German royalty, in the form of a stage Kaiser which
would have horrified the Lord Chamberlain because of an authenticity in mous-
taches and mannerisms forbidden in London; for those the audience waited for
that moment when the Inca contrasts his country with others which have not
kept the peace for forty years. Clearly, the Irish Nationalists felt, Shaw was
pointing to England.

While the Shavian box-office success continued, the Dublin diehards complained that it was at the cost of the native drama. Architect and theater buff
Joseph Holloway, a conservative influence at the Abbey, complained that Shaw
was the fetish of J. Augustus Keogh, St. John Ervine's successor as manager.
And "when I chanced to remark," he noted in his diary, " 'We have had far too
much of Shaw of late at the Abbey, and many are saying so to me,' " Keogh was
furious, becoming even more enraged when Holloway suggested that Irish
plays had failed to draw as well as Shaw's because they were poorly played, "as
the Irish acting did not take kindly to the English methods. . . . When I said
that the Gaiety or the Royal were the proper places for Shaw's plays and not the
Abbey, Keogh could have slain me on the spot." But Holloway's kind would
have padlocked the Abbey rather than play "English" plays by an Irishman,
and Keogh paid the price for his advocacy. While *The Doctor's Dilemma* played
that May, Keogh was sacked by the Abbey board of directors, and Holloway
gleefully wrote a friend that "a love of Shaw and a hatred for Irish drama and
Irish acting were, I am sure, the cause. Keogh from the first wanted to make it a
sort of Shaw playhouse, and not caring a tinker's curse for the traditions of the
little theatre. . . ."[25]

Although Keogh had become the whipping boy for the superpatriots, he had
had little to do with the choice of repertory, other than his fatal accident of reo-
pening the crisis-closed Abbey—as a private speculation, since he was not yet
paid by the Abbey—with Shaw's *Widowers' Houses*. As Lady Gregory had
written G.B.S. the previous August, Keogh, an unknown who had taken Ervine's place because there was no one else to be had, acquitted himself well not
only as director but in the Dickensian comic role of Lickcheese. "There was a
good audience and it went extremely well, every point taken up, and great applause on the slum question. So a brilliant thought struck me . . . our peasant
plays for the moment knocked on the head, to do an autumn season of G.B.S.—
our Irish Shakespeare. . . ." She had her ideas about which plays would fare
best—*John Bull's Other Island* ("written for us and never acted by us"), *The
Devil's Disciple, The Doctor's Dilemma*, and *Androcles and the Lion* ("if we
could borrow the lion—it is so delightful, and religious discussion should be
popular here").[26]

As far as G.B.S.'s new-won status in Ireland was concerned, the band of small
minds at the Abbey who had overruled Lady Gregory and deposed the hapless
Keogh made little difference. He was again *persona grata*, something his persistent paradoxes about Ireland now failed to shake. In the *Nation* early that
spring, for example, he noted in regard to the inability of Ulster and the rest of
Ireland to live in peace that "civil war is one of the privileges of a nation," as
was the possibility "that they would exterminate one another." "Mankind still
longs for that consummation; but it has never happened, and is too much to
hope for." He doubted that Ireland would lapse into civil war but added, as he
would not have a year earlier, "I do not deprecate that method; for if hatred,

calumny, and terror have so possessed men that they cannot live in peace as other nations do, they had better fight it out and get rid of their bad blood that way." That it would not happen, he thought, had been made clear by the restraint of Irishmen north and south when, at the Easter Rising, England "supplied a sensational bombardment and a Reign of Terror to impress the imagination of the world with the heroism of the patriots and the magnitude of their blow for independence. . . ."[27] Shaw had labeled his article "Brogue-Shock," a reference to the government's having been rattled by the noisy but "depopulated little island." He hardly realized the extent of his own, and very different, brogue shock.

On a visit to Ireland during the "Troubles," Shaw dined with Michael Collins at the home of their mutual friend Horace Plunkett in Kilteragh. Collins had, a week before, succeeded to the presidency of the Irish Free State on the death of Arthur Griffith. Five days later, on August 22, 1922, while inspecting military installations in his native county of Cork, he was ambushed, with his party, by "die-hard" irreconcilables, and killed. Shaw had written in his preface to *Man and Superman* that the true joy in life was "being used for a purpose recognized by yourself as a mighty one; the being thoroughly worn out before you are thrown on the scrap heap; the being a force of Nature instead of a feverish selfish little clod of ailments and grievances complaining that the world will not devote itself to making you happy." Now he wrote[28] in the same vein to Michael Collins's sister:

> Dear Miss Collins
>
> Dont let them make you miserable about it: how could a born soldier die better than at the victorious end of a good fight, falling to the shot of another Irishman—a damned fool, but all the same an Irishman who thought he was fighting for Ireland—"a Roman to a Roman"?
>
> I met Michael for the first and last time on Saturday last, and am very glad I did. I rejoice in his memory, and will not be so disloyal to it as to snivel over his valiant death.
>
> So tear up your mourning and hang up your brightest colors in his honor; and let us all praise God that he had not to die in a snuffy bed of a trumpery cough, weakened by age, and saddened by the disappointments that would have attended his work had he lived.
>
> Sincerely,
> Bernard Shaw

The brogue-shock had not worn off.

14 Shaw's *Lear*

SHAKES. Where is thy Hamlet? Couldst thou write King Lear?
SHAV. Aye, with his daughters all complete. Couldst thou have written
  Heartbreak House? Behold my Lear.
—Bernard Shaw in Shakes vs. Shav (1949)

In a musical review in 1893 "G.B.S." joked, "It is impossible to say what a man can do until he tries. I may before the end of this year write a tragedy on the subject of King Lear that will efface Shakespear's; but if I do it will be a surprise, not perhaps to myself, but to the public. It is certain that if I took the work in hand I should be able to turn out five acts about King Lear that would be, at least, grammatical, superficially coherent, and arranged in lines that would scan."[1] At the time Shaw had completed only one play, *Widowers' Houses*, and was working on a second, *The Philanderer*, one of his least successful efforts. The likelihood of a Shavian *Lear* was remote. A dozen years later, when he tried to interest classicist and translator of Euripides Gilbert Murray in "a great dramatic theme . . . —a Woman Lear with three sons—just the sort of Aeschylean subject in modern life you want,"[2] the idea was no longer a flippant aside.

Just before World War I Shaw found his own *Lear*—although he had not yet recognized it—via the circuitous route of the Moscow Art Theatre. At the close of one of its London performances of Chekhov, Shaw reportedly told a friend who sat next to him, "I feel as if I want to tear up all my plays and begin all over again."[3] But although he subtitled his next major play, *Heartbreak House* (written 1916-17), a fantasia in the Russian manner upon English themes, and echoes of *The Cherry Orchard* unquestionably reverberate through it, the play might be profitably viewed as a fantasia in the Shakespearian manner upon Shavian themes. In particular, *Heartbreak House* seems clearly to have been designed, at least in part, as Shaw's *Lear*. Earlier he had tauntingly titled part of a preface to his *Caesar and Cleopatra* (1898) "Better than Shakespear?"— suggesting a parallel with the Bard's *Antony and Cleopatra*; yet by presenting a kittenish young queen and an aging Caesar, rather than an aging but still sultry Cleopatra and a younger admirer, he had evaded any direct comparison. Like his Cleopatra play, Shaw's *Lear* was offered not in competition but as commentary.

G.B.S. waited until his nineties to point publicly to *Heartbreak House* as his *Lear*. Even then he did so guardedly through the disarming medium of a puppet play, perhaps to prevent the comparison from being taken as seriously as he inwardly still meant it to be, for in his lifetime the play's now very considerable reputation had never measured up to his expectations for it. "If the critics had the brains of a mad Tom," he grumbled, using a suggestive association with *Lear*, "they would realize it is my greatest play. But they don't. They all go following after the Maid of Orleans."[4]

Privately, Shaw had suggested the *Lear* connection almost as soon as he had completed the play. In mid-1917, actress Lillah McCarthy had asked him for details of the work, hoping to persuade him to let her produce it or at least acquire a starring part in it. Shaw put her off. It was wartime, he pointed out, and the play was unpleasant, unsuitable fare for war conditions. The hero was an old man of eighty-eight, and there were no young male roles (its implicit recognition of the wartime dearth of leading men). The women were either too young or too old—an ingenue and two sisters in their middle forties. The sisters, Shaw confided—"I don't find them much more popular than Goneril or Regan"—were the old man's daughters.[5] Disgusted with the dragged-out war and its effect on theater as well as much else, he confessed finally that his heart was not in a London production of a new play. And Miss McCarthy—creator of some of Shaw's greatest roles, beginning with her Ann Whitefield in *Man and Superman*—appeared neither then nor afterward in a performance of *Heartbreak House*.

Just after Shaw completed *Heartbreak House*, he was asked to contribute to a Fabian Society series of lectures on the future of the Labour Party, and Goneril and Regan were still on his mind. Thus in the unlikely context of his lecture at King's Hall, Covent Garden, "The Climate and Soil for Labour Culture," delivered on May 10, 1918, he raised what he called "the practical problem" of "how much leisure can the country afford. . . ." "King Lear's daughter Regan, a grasping, unimaginative, typical rich middle class Englishwoman," he noted, "was of [the] opinion that the simple life was good enough for her father, and asked him what more he needed. Lear's reply is very much to the point:

> Oh, reason not the need: our basest beggars
> Are in the poorest thing superfluous:
> Allow not nature more than nature needs,
> Man's life is cheap as beast's. Thou art a lady:
> If only to go warm were gorgeous,
> Why, nature needs not what thou gorgeous wear'st,
> Which scarcely keeps thee warm."

Meanwhile the typescript of *Heartbreak House*, for which those lines were clearly commentary, remained in the drawer of his desk. "There is something about the play that makes me extremely reluctant to let it go out of my hands," he insisted, and at first he would let no one read it, and only on a few occasions would he read from it to his friends, although in his later years he found great satisfaction in performing such dramatic readings—with all the histrionic stops pulled—scene by scene and act by act as his plays were being written. He was, as Miss McCarthy discovered, not even interested in having it produced, and when it was discussed, he talked of it as having been inspired by Chekhov. Yet later he would insist, as he told Hesketh Pearson, that old Captain Shotover was "a modernized King Lear." As for its meaning, Pearson reported Shaw's stock reply, "How should *I* know? I am only the author."[6] Lillah McCarthy felt she knew, having accepted Shaw's hints about his play. It had, she thought, something that she found nowhere else in Shaw, "a quality which only once before an English playwright has contrived to give to the drama he has written. The quality which *King Lear* has: spaciousness. In *Heartbreak House* there is no stage. It is life speaking from the stage of life, a voice crying in the wilderness."[7]

What was to have been his *Cherry Orchard* had been transformed almost *in utero*, by events as much as by Shaw, although the Chekhovian atmosphere remained. (Shaw, in fact, told his biographer Archibald Henderson that *Heartbreak House* "began with an atmosphere and does not contain a word that was foreseen before it was written.") Chekhov had the charm of novelty as well as a doom-ridden nostalgia. *King Lear* had fascinated Shaw far longer, although not until the years of the 1914-18 war had he been confronted with a sense of helplessness and futility such as he was convinced Shakespeare had dramatized: a house—and a world—in disorder. Although he had never had the opportunity to review a production, Shaw had consistently tucked into other commentaries his insistence that it was a "masterpiece" and that "no man will ever write a better tragedy than Lear." Yet he had objected to the "blasphemous despair,"[8] thinking particularly of Gloucester's dark lines, lines he quoted afterward in the preface to his next play, where, writing of Shakespeare's "religionless condition . . . of despair," Shaw added, "His towering King Lear would be only a melodrama were it not for its express admission that if there is nothing more to be said of the universe than Hamlet has to say, then 'as flies to wanton boys are we to the gods: they kill us for their sport.' "[9]

Earlier he had made a similar point in explaining to Lady Gregory, "To me the sole hope of human salvation lies in teaching Man to regard himself as an experiment in the realization of God, to regard his hands as God's hand, his brain as God's brain, his purpose as God's purpose. . . . You will find it all in Man and Superman, as you will find it all behind Blanco Posnet. Take it out of my play, and the play becomes nothing but the old cry of despair—Shakespear's 'As flies to wanton boys so we are to the gods: they kill us for their sport'—the most frightful blasphemy ever uttered, and the one from which it is my mission to deliver the world."[10]

Shaw's final version of *Heartbreak House* eliminated from the manuscript several striking clues to its *Lear* origins. At first Shaw had Captain Shotover declare, early in the play, about the ingratitude of daughters, "Do you expect me to keep up my interest in a thankless girl for nearly half a century merely because I was the innocent instrument by which she was let loose in this miserable world?" Later came a pointed reference to such a fool as appears in *Lear*. "Yes, plays the fool," says Shotover. "He could not do that if he was a fool." Later yet is another remark by the captain, excised in Shaw's final cut: "There is something to be said for cruelty to men and women: they may learn from it. . . ."[11]

Out of context the stricken lines may suggest little, yet in the context of what survives one can perceive how the *Lear* dimension was built into the play and then subdued to the essentials.

When Shaw had finished the play, he found that *Lear* would still not leave him. In 1918, when he received a "next-of-kin" telegram informing him that actor Robert Loraine, whom he regarded as a surrogate son, had been severely wounded over France while flying with the R.A.F., Shaw wrote him[12]—his apparent facetiousness concealing real concern—that the first thoughts that had come to his mind were lines from *Lear*:

> Hadst thou been Gossamer! Feathers! Air!
> So many fathoms down precipitating,
> Thoudst shiver like an egg, but thou dost breathe. . . .
>
>   (IV.vi.49-51)

"Even the fool in Lear," Shaw had emphasized, "is tragic," and Lear's tragicomic aspects were also bound to attract a playwright who had been writing as though he meant his line that every jest was an earnest in the womb of time. As Shaw put it, although Shakespeare had often juxtaposed passages of "downright circus buffoonery" with the "deepest tragedy," it was only in *Lear*, his "greatest tragedy," that "we find the alternation of tragic and funny dropped for an actual interweaving of the two; so that we have the tragic and the comic simultaneously, each heightening the other with a poignancy otherwise unattainable."[13] To Shaw "the wonderful storm trio in which the king, the fool, and the sham madman have their parts 'concerted,' . . . like the statue, the hero, and the comic valet in . . . *Don Giovanni*," was "the summit of Shakespeare's achievement as poet and playwright."[14] Few plays from the pre-twentieth-century repertoire, as Jan Kott has shown,[15] while insisting (like Shaw) on the play's essential pessimism and near nihilism, lend themselves so readily to interpretation as black comedy. Even the core of the play, Wilson Knight has claimed in a famous essay, "is an absurdity . . . an incongruity," characterized by that kind of "grimmest humour" which warns against "sentimentalizing" its "cosmic mockery."[16] *Heartbreak House* suggests that Shaw's reading of *Lear* is that if Shakespeare had not meant it that way, he should have.

Sir Cedric Hardwicke (who was in one of the first English casts of *Heartbreak House*) was probably echoing Shaw when he observed that Captain Shotover was meant to be "an up-to-date King Lear," yet although Shaw intended recognizable similarities—his remark to Lillah McCarthy makes this clear—he seems to have intended as well some meaningful differences. In both lie a measure of *Heartbreak House*'s significance, in what has been identified as its *Lear* dimension. Even the title of the play recalls Kent's "Break, heart, I prithee break" (V.iii.312), and in fragmentary fashion critics have long pointed to tantalizing hints of *Lear* in Shaw's text. As one notes, it is "apocalyptic. Captain Shotover is eighty-eight and mad. His two daughters have an aspect in which they are fiends. Boss Mangan, the business man driven to a frenzy by Heartbreak House, proposes [like Lear] to strip himself naked."[17] Hector curses the Shotover daughters, and himself, in words that recall both Othello and Lear. "Fool! Goat!" he says of himself in Act I, striking himself on the chest, and at the end of Act II, after the humiliation of Randall, he exclaims, "Poor wretch! Oh women! women! women! [*He lifts his fists in invocation to heaven*] Fall. Fall and crush." (The cry parallels, perhaps, Albany's similar gesture and invocation, "Fall and cease!" near the close of *Lear*.[18]) Even the air raid that brings the play to a violent conclusion seems a modern embodiment of the great storm in *Lear*. "These reverberations," J. I. M. Stewart observes, "are not insignificant. For *Heartbreak House* is the play in which Shaw confronts, for the first time in his imaginative writing, the small extent of his faith in man. What lies just beneath the play's surface is despair. It is thus in intention, or impulsion, radically different from almost all the rest of his work. . . ."[19]

Albany's words in *Lear* sound the note of *Heartbreak House*:

> If that the heavens do not their visible spirits
> Send quickly down to tame these vile offences
> It will come,
>
> Humanity must perforce prey on itself,
> Like monsters of the deep.

(IV.ii.46-50)

Hector, Shaw's Albany, in words as reminiscent of Don Juan (in *Man and Superman*) as of *Lear*, provides a twentieth-century echo:

> [*Fiercely*]. I tell you, one of two things must happen. Either out of that darkness some new creation will come to supplant us as we have supplanted the animals, or the heavens will fall in thunder and destroy us.

G.B.S.'s play, basically the characteristic later Shavian juxtaposition of theatrical and intellectual elements one can label *serious farce*, was intended, indeed, as apocalyptic farce. Contrary to the fate of most prophecy, the thunder from heaven came even before the play had been completed, and in fact offered Shaw, via a Zeppelin raid he observed from his country house, an appropriate conclusion at a time when an ending was eluding him. Although the bursting bombs have their counterpart in the last-act thudding of axes upon Chekhov's cherry trees and the ominous and premonitory breaking string is paralleled by the Beethovenlike drumming of distant aircraft engines, that the major characters in *Heartbreak House* are as much at home in a *Lear* framework as in Chekhov's overheated drawing rooms suggests that the blending of concepts occurred early in the play's development perhaps before the first words were written. He had been thinking about *Lear* for a long time, and Europe, like Lear's sundered kingdom, a newly pessimistic Shaw realized even before the first shots were fired, was in its self-destructive selfishness (the only sense of purpose which European nations seemed to evidence) heading toward catastrophe.

Heartbreak House's outlook, nevertheless, is also radically different from that of *Lear* and in some ways almost its inversion. "There is nothing real in the world," says Ellie, "but my father and Shakespeare," and her favorite reading is *Othello*, whose recital of his exploits to Desdemona seems to have its parallel in Ellie Dunn's naive acceptance of Hector Hushabye's tall tales of heroism. The unconscious irony of her pointing to Shakespeare's epitome of nature's nobleman and to that impractical, naive anachronism of an idealist, Mazzini Dunn, as all that are real in the world may mean something more. To Shaw, in the middle of a brutal, wasteful war, there was no longer room or reason for impractical nobility of Lear's (or Othello's) stamp, and the element of weary hope and faith that concludes *Lear* is twisted sardonically in *Heartbreak House*; Hesione Hushabye and Ellie Dunn hope that the air raid which had put such excitement into their aimless lives will be repeated. "I hope they'll come again tomorrow night," says Hesione, and Ellie eagerly adds (*radiant at the prospect*, Shaw notes), "Oh, I *hope* so." Yet a note of ambiguity echoes through these final lines in what might also be a longing for the destruction of additional representatives of negation—a pentecostal flame to purify the world.[20]

That this savoring of the violence of war has brought new interest—and, paradoxically, new hope—into jaded lives is ironic and indicative not only of Shaw's
war-bred despair but, through contrast with Lear's daughters and especially
the scorned Cordelia, his reaction to it. To recall her and her relationship with
Lear, Shaw had earlier portrayed Shotover dozing on the shoulder of Ellie, to
whom he had declared himself mystically joined. (In the 1949 *Shakes vs. Shav*,
after Shakes asks, "Where is thy Hamlet? Couldst thou write King Lear?" and
Shav replies "Aye, with his daughters all complete. Couldst thou have written
Heartbreak House? Behold my Lear," the dramatist's stage directions read, *"A
transparency is suddenly lit up, shewing Captain Shotover seated, as in Millais'
picture called North-West Passage, with a young woman of virginal beauty."*[21]
And Shotover and Ellie speak, arialike, several passages from Shaw's play.) Ellie suggests Cordelia in other ways as well, for she is also "fresh, loving, dower-
less, heartbroken, and strong-minded," while Shaw's "old daughter-troubled
man has his Goneril and Regan [in] Hesione and Ariadne [who] are modern embodiments of the wicked sisters' sexuality and worldliness."[22] The three daughters in *Heartbreak House* (for Ellie is "adopted") live and thrive in their open
cynicism and their absorption in self-interest, while *Lear* closes with the three
daughters defeated or dead. At the same point in each play, mad old Shotover is
strangely satisfied (as war apparently begins) that all is for the better, while
Lear finds, contrastingly, his personal world crumbling still further as tranquil-
ity is apparently restored.

The paradox and the horror are, by comparison with *Lear*, "civilized" reactions. While Lear recovers his sanity only long enough to cry out when Cordelia
dies (largely as a result of his own irresponsibility),

> Why should a dog, a horse, a rat, have life,
> And thou no breath at all?
>
> (V.iii.307-308)

no one finds it necessary to ask why a bomb should drop without warning onto
the grounds of Heartbreak House, killing two people. (Only a few lines earlier an
unexplained order to black out the lights had been the only clue that there is a
war in progress or that one is imminent.) On the grounds of their opportunistic
morals and uselessness to the human race the two who die might be denied pity,
but Shaw rejects conventional poetic justice as he rejects questioning destiny's
selectivity.[23] Meaning lies less in who has died and more in the fact of death, as
Hector emphasizes in scolding the incurable idealist Mazzini Dunn for his concern about one of the victims: "Are you immortal that you need pity him? Our
turn next." The words recall us to the problem of finding meaning for existence
in an irrational world, the dilemmas of both *Lear* and *Heartbreak House*.

As absurd and irrational as are some of the rambling lines of the doting,
dreaming octogenarian Shotover, he shares with the quixotic Hector the words
of wisdom Shaw has written into his play. Lear, on the other hand, although he
reaches a condition of understanding, is given little wisdom of thought or act.
The aged Lear early in the play becomes a king more in memory than in fact,
while Shaw's half-mad Shotover, at eighty-eight, is a sea captain only in memory. He is nevertheless, a critic notes, "a King Lear without the tragedy (though
certainly with hints of pathos) and still, in spite of his calculated senile absent-
mindedness, in full command of his kingdom and his daughters. He is a prophet
thundering in navigational terms."[24] A "very foolish fond old man, / Fourscore

and upward," Lear is what Shotover describes as the "drifting skipper"—the irresponsible captain who runs his ship onto the rocks because he has trusted his navigation to Providence rather than to himself. In search of a life free at last from responsibility, his mind weakened by his years, Lear relinquishes his kingdom and his power to the selfish daughters who have flattered him with love they do not feel and have promised him the ease and the continued glory they do not intend to furnish. Shaw's ancient steadfastly remains the intellectual force and financial mainstay in the house of his daughter—legally still his own house. Although his mind sometimes drifts and wanders, his sense of purpose is too sharply focused to permit him to abdicate any of his failing (but still formidable) powers.

Shotover understands his daughters, too, whereas Lear does not. The old skipper's heart is not easily broken. Six years, he insists, is the normal span of filial affection; thus he has learned not to "make distinctions between one fellowcreature and another." Yet his children, although as sharp-tongued and cynical as Lear's, reverse Goneril's and Regan's unkindness and are indulgent to a fault. Lear expects total and permanent affection and is disillusioned when hypocrisy and deceit are what he receives instead. In short, while one realizes that heartbreak is "the end of happiness and the beginning of peace," the other, having raged helplessly against the storm, hopes, at best, to conclude his days in a state of happiness that is only freedom from anxiety. "Come, let's away to prison," he comforts his fellow captive, Cordelia:

> We two alone will sing like birds i'th'cage.
> . . . so we'll live,
> And pray and sing, and tell old tales, and laugh
> At gilded butterflies, and hear poor rogues
> Talk of court news; and we'll talk with them too—
> Who loses and who wins; who's in, who's out—
> And take upon's the mystery of things,
> As if we were God's spies. . . .   (V.iii.8-17)

Happiness, which Lear craves as the fulfillment of his old age, is the very thing Shotover most fears—the "accursed happiness . . . that comes as life goes, the happiness of yielding and dreaming instead of resisting and doing, the sweetness of the fruit that is going rotten." A sense of purpose—of using one's self up in finding and fulfilling that purpose—is the Shotover antidote to happiness. Thus he longs in his old age for the tests and trials of youth and is given by Shaw a grateful apostrophe to the sea storms that compelled him to savor his vigor. "I was ten times happier on the bridge in the typhoon, or frozen into Arctic ice for months in darkness, than you or they have ever been," he tells Ellie. "At your age I looked for hardship, danger, horror, and death, that I might feel the life in me more intensely. I did not let the fear of death govern my life; and my reward was, I had my life." (It is an ironic commentary upon the times that to do the same, Ellie and Hesione must summon back the bombs. It is all they have.) Shotover's nostalgic savoring of the typhoon is in obvious contrast to Lear's noble, yet pathetic, defiance of the storm:

> Blow, winds and crack your cheeks!
> . . . Rumble thy bellyful! Spit, fire; spout, rain!
> . . . I tax not you, you elements, with unkindness;
> . . . You owe me no subscription. Then let fall
> Your horrible pleasure. Here I stand your slave,
> A poor, infirm, weak, and despised old man.   (III.ii.1-19)

Weary, helpless, and insignificant, Lear no more wants to be a slave to the elements than he had wanted to be a slave to responsibility. He had divided his kingdom only in order "to shake all cares and business" and enable him to "Unburthened crawl toward death." Shotover is aware of the hazards of so yielding to one's years. "Old men are dangerous," he warns; "it doesn't matter to them what is going to happen to the world."

"Age . . . has its blindness and decay," writes a modern director of a highly regarded *Lear*. "However true sight comes from an acuteness of living that can transform the world."[25] The insight can be used to contrast Lear and Shotover, but the larger meaning of such a contrast must be Shaw's commentary upon those bleak lines of Gloucester so equally applicable to Lear: "The lot of the man who sees life truly and thinks about it romantically is Despair." That Lear's weakness is the strength of Shotover, G.B.S. knew from his own transient wartime bout with giant despair; and the heart of his indictment of Shakespeare is the Bard's "putative despair. . . . Lacking hope, and knowledge, Shakespeare and his characters lack will."[26] As opposed to Lear's "despair made stage-sublime," Shotover is a Bunyanesque hero. It is easy to recognize his ancestry—and his antithesis to Lear—in Shaw's insistence that "All that you miss in Shakespeare you find in Bunyan, to whom the true heroic came quite obviously and naturally. The world was to him a more terrible place than it was to Shakespeare; but he saw through it a path at the end of which a man might look not only forward to the Celestial City, but back on his life and say:— 'Tho' with great difficulty I am not hither, yet now I do not repent me of all the trouble I have been at to arrive where I am. My sword I give to him that shall succeed me in my pilgrimage, and my courage and skill to him that can get them.' "[27] It would not be too much to suggest that, his encomiums for the play's music and poetry notwithstanding, Shaw privately thought of *Lear* what he had written of *Othello*: "Tested by the brain, it is ridiculous: tested by the ear, it is sublime."[28]

Other themes may be organic to both plays: the increasing inhumanity that increasing civilization seems paradoxically to bring (our cruelties merely becoming more sophisticated), the dominating drive of the female of the species, the inevitable humiliation and defeat of the idealist and the dreamer, and the misleading appearances we mistake for reality, dramatized through symbolic unclothing in both plays. It is also possible, but not very fruitful, to find thematic reasons for seeing equivalents not only to Lear and his daughters, but to the Fool, to Cornwall, Edmund, Gloucester, and others in Shaw's play.[29] Yet the crucial fact is one of clear and intended reverberation. Although "the rack of this tough world" on which *Lear* is stretched is only technologically different from the world of *Heartbreak House*, Shaw's equivalent is less despairing—by its close even prophetic and almost hopeful. Still, for his wartime plunge into pessimism he had inevitably turned to the most bleak piece of theater he knew, *Lear*.

15 The Genesis of *Joan*

"**I** shall be remembered when men have forgotten where Rouen stood," Shaw's St. Joan contends. Half a millennium after Joan, Rouen still stands, but Joan's memory is the reason the world remembers Rouen. On the Place du Vieux-Marché, once the marketplace, now stands a tall, chic stream-lined stone cross, and on a wall of the uncompromisingly modern Church of Jeanne d'Arc nearby is André Malraux's ringing invocation to the saint—"*O Jeanne, Sans Sepulcre et Sans Portrait, Toi Qui Savait Que le Tombeau des Heros Est le Coeur des Vivants. . . .*" (O Joan, Unburied and Unpictured,* Who Knows that the Tomb of Heroes is in the Hearts of the Living)—cast in monumental letters. For a few francs, tourists can place a small white electronic device to the ear and listen to a purplish recorded oration on the life and death of Joan of Arc, who was incinerated there in 1431: "She could have been anyone's daughter . . . the girl next door."

Joan, a young farm girl who lived only her final two years out of the pastoral innocence of Domrémy, has already been the subject of more than three thousand books, ranging from pious schoolbook homilies to a contemporary "medieval" rock opera, *The Survival of Saint Joan* (1971), which identifies her as the bastard half sister of the Dauphin, saved from the stake by the substitution of someone else, only to have a love affair with a lonely farmer and to die in obscure sanctity, ironically burned by religious penitents by mistake. There has even been a science-fiction Maid, in the *Joan of Arc Replay* (1978), a French novel in which the Galactic scholar Celsar meets and marries a Joan of Arc analogue on the planet Noldaz, which is repeating late-medieval Earth history. With no succeeding work can we say, with Shaw's Executioner, "You have heard the last of her."

Of works about Joan there appears no end, and in our skeptical age the irreverent perspectives predominate. In an English medical journal, *The Practitioner*, F. E. Kenyon has theorized that Joan's visions may have been brought on by "gastroenteritis—upset stomach resulting from her imprisonment in her debilitated state" and perhaps even by food poisoning, something she complains about even in Shaw's play. Georgia endocrinologist Robert Greenblatt blames "testicular feminization" (causing "genetic males" to "look and think like females") for Joan's behavior. Another Englishman, Michael Harrison, has

---

*That there may be a sculpted head of Joan surviving in Orléans, and contemporary with her, is discussed in the "Picture Galleries" chapter, p. 87–88.

claimed in a study of medieval witchcraft that Joan was "certainly a witch" and "met her ritual death at Rouen," which to him was "obviously a holy place of the old [primitive] faith." Another contemporary scholar, Jean Benedetti, has hypothesized that Joan performed the role of the Maid in a white witch cult, seeing no inconsistency between the old religion with its white magic and Christianity with its own magic rituals. (Her "voices," according to this theory, were counsels of superior members of the cult.)

Show business has multiplied modern Joans. A Russian film, *The Debut* (1971), freely intercuts the progress of a movie version of Joan of Arc with the tangled life of its star. A pop opera *Joan* (1972) by Al Carmines, the unusual musical minister of the Judson Memorial Church in New York, takes place in Greenwich Village and features a lesbian, radicalized, bomb-throwing Joan in nun's habit and sneakers. A 1974 musical comedy, *Goodtime Charley* ("Charley" is the Dauphin, Charles VII), fails to mention most of Joan's ordeals, including the final one, and has her escorted off into the wings by English soldiers. And a robust novel published the same year by the Australian writer Thomas Keneally, *Blood Red, Sister Rose*, uses anachronistic language (Shaw did the same, but with more success) to suggest Joan's earthy reality, with Jean de Metz exhorting her early in the novel to prove her bona fides: "He still thinks you're a cowboy, Jehanne. Show him your tits." St. Joan is show business, and not only in the Joan of Arc wax museum in Rouen.

Versions of Joan's martyrdom have come a long way from Shakespeare's unlovely harridan (in *Henry VI*), Schiller's romantic heroine, and Mark Twain's sentimental idealist, and have even come a long way from Bertolt Brecht's tough-minded Chicago Salvation Army lass in *Saint Joan of the Stockyards* (1926), who is a parody of Shaw's Major Barbara as well as his Joan, and from Jules Feiffer's farce *Knock Knock* (1976), which appears to combine *Saint Joan* and *The Odd Couple* and includes zany variations on Shaw's lines. But Shaw's play seems to survive all predecessors and successors.

Aside from Quicherat's transcripts of her trial and rehabilitation hearings and Michelet's romantic history, which rekindled her fire in mid-nineteenth-century France, the most famous work about Joan remains Shaw's *Saint Joan*, written nearly five hundred years after her death but only a few years after the Papal declaration of her sainthood. Her canonization in 1920, however, was hardly the springboard for Shaw's writing his play; he often let works simmer in his mind for considerable periods before composing them. Yet a story about Joan which Shaw himself endorsed and which has gone into all the major biographies suggests a deceptively simple origin for the play. Sir Sydney Cockerell, it goes, the curator of the Fitzwilliam Museum at Cambridge and a good friend of the Shaws, after reading T. Douglas Murray's turn-of-the-century English translation of Quicherat, became convinced that he saw a play for Shaw there. Early in 1923 he passed the book on to G.B.S., who demonstrated no serious interest; however, Charlotte then worked on her husband with great wiliness, leaving books about the Maid of Orleans in places where Shaw was likely to pick them up. Eventually he came to Charlotte, who had watched him scan the planted texts, and announced that he had found a subject for a new play. It would be about Joan of Arc. "Really," said Mrs. Shaw, according to this story, "what a good idea!"

Although Shaw undoubtedly utilized Quicherat's transcripts in the 1902 Murray translation and did receive a copy of the book from his friend Cockerell as well as less-than-subtle suggestions from Charlotte, the play had a more complicated gestation. Shaw had been reading about and pondering Joan for years, becoming more and more convinced that no artist in any medium had done her justice. One of his first theatrical experiences had been Tom Taylor's melodramatic *Jeanne Darc (Called the Maid): a Chronicle Play in Five Acts* (1871), which structurally has some parallels to *Saint Joan*—possibly a result of Shaw's long memory. In 1885 he reviewed, with no enthusiasm, an operatic piece entitled *Joan of Arc at the Stake* (Arthur Honegger would later use the same title for an oratorio), and he dismissed a symphonic poem named after her as "decidedly stale." The work was Berlin composer Moritz Moskowski's *Johanna d'Arc*, a programmatic symphony on the Lizst order based upon Schiller's *Maid of Orleans*. "The first movement," Shaw noted in *Dramatic Review* (May 23, 1885), "describes Joan's pastoral life. 'Her exalted mission is revealed to her in a vision.' . . . Its effect was not entirely celestial. . . . The Andante is superscribed 'Inner Consciousness—Former Memories.' . . .'' It was, Shaw concluded, "never absolutely dull." The next year, as an art critic for the *World*, he wrote unsympathetically of a canvas by Robert Browning's son Barrett ("Pen"), who "made a careful life-school study of a nude woman; brought it into startling relief against a background of vivid verdure, labeled it 'Joan of Arc and the Kingfisher.' . . . As the face of the model is turned away, and her figure no more than ordinarily expressive, the title and quotation assigned the picture in the catalogue may be dismissed as a humorous imposture." But Shaw may have remembered, for his own play has a kingfisher scene.

As "Corno di Bassetto" he complained in 1890 of a Sarah Bernhardt performance of a Gounod *Joan*: "We all know her way of pretending to act when there is no part for her—how sweetly she intones her lines and poses like a saint. This is what she does in Joan. There is no acting because there is no play. . . ." The interest was in the actress, not the heroine. Ten years later, in his "Notes" to the published text of *Caesar and Cleopatra*, Shaw's awareness of Joan, like that of most Englishmen, remained one of skepticism about her soundness of mind and disbelief in her saintliness, for he referred to her in company with Admiral Horatio Nelson and King Charles XII of Sweden as "half-witted geniuses, enjoying the worship accorded by all races to certain forms of insanity." But his interest in Joan was only beginning, for as he worked on *Caesar* he also was writing a long critical essay, *The Perfect Wagnerite* (1898), in which Joan seems anticipated in a work in which she is not even mentioned. In a section entitled "Siegfried as Protestant," Shaw—talking in terms of late-medieval Christianity—refers to a "wave of thought" which impelled the strong in will "to affirm that every man's private judgment was a more trustworthy interpreter of God and revelation than the Church." The idea leads him, in what is both analysis and prediction, to a striking conclusion:

> The most inevitable dramatic conception, then, of the nineteenth century is that of a perfectly naive hero upsetting religion, law and order in all directions, and establishing in their place the unfettered action of Humanity doing exactly what it likes, and producing order instead of confusion thereby because it likes to do what is necessary for the good of the race. This conception was certain at last to reach some great artist, and be embodied by him in a masterpiece.

Here Shaw appears to be foreshadowing his own *Saint Joan* (although he was actually referring to Wagner's *Ring* cycle); but his interest in Joan was to develop still further, often—as here—without an apparent relationship to the Maid herself.

It remained difficult to avoid the Maid. French art was full of renditions of statuesque and less-than-believable Joans, such as Ingres's Second Empire canvas. Even the great Tschaikowsky had stumbled when doing a less-than-successful operatic version of her story. In England, where audiences still influenced by patriotic hostility made the commercial future of a play about her hazardous, Tom Taylor's mid-Victorian drama at the St. James's Theatre had been booed roundly. But one suspects that Shaw must have seen the page-one reference to Joan in the *Times*'s literary supplement (then called "Literature") on December 8, 1900. The now-forgotten Louis N. Parker, the "Notes of the Day" column reported, was said to be at work on a Joan play. "We wonder how Mr. Parker will treat the final scene in the story. . . . One difficulty in representing Joan of Arc on the stage is the impossibility of introducing the element of poetic justice. A play in which an immaculate heroine is disgraced and burnt is not likely to appeal to a British audience. We doubt that they will ever like to see on the stage more than a glimpse of Joan's story, such as Shakespeare gives us. The French seem to have scarcely attempted any literary treatment of Jeanne—their most conspicuous effort being the scandalous production of Voltaire."

Did the challenge lodge in Shaw's subconscious? Five years later he wrote to actress Eleanor Robson, for whom he had created *Major Barbara*, that he had heard that Edmond Rostand (of *Cyrano de Bergerac* fame) was writing a play for her. "Is it Joan of Arc? For this be all his sins forgiven him!" At that point, he told her some forty-four years later, when he was ninety-three, he had "already read everything on the subject I could lay hands on, both in English and French." And he had told her about the Barbara role (July 4, 1905) that he wanted "to see whether I can make a woman a saint."

Major Barbara would ask Undershaft, "Do you think I can be happy in this vulgar silly dress? I! who have worn the uniform." The words could have been Joan's. What had happened between 1900 and 1905? In 1902 the first English translation of Quicherat appeared in London. Had Shaw read the trial transcripts nearly twenty years before the Cockerell episode? Something clearly happened to reshape Shaw's view of Joan during the years immediately after his irreverent dismissal of her as half-witted genius.

In 1907 he went to see the famed Adeline Genée dance a Joan of Arc ballet at the Empire and to see American actress Julia Marlowe in Percy Mackaye's play *Jeanne d'Arc*. Neither was satisfactory. Also in 1907 he and Charlotte took a motoring tour of Rheims, Crecy, Amiens, and Rouen—the sector of France associated with Joan—and the tone of Shaw's references to the Maid thereafter continued to reflect a shift in view and building of interest. In 1908, in his preface to *Getting Married*, he spoke of Joan as one of those unique humans endowed with the "exceptional sanity" to be in the right "when we are in the wrong," and in the 1911 preface to *The Doctor's Dilemma* he observed that "even the vilest and stupidest action teaches us something about vileness and stupidity, and may accidentally teach us a good deal more: for instance . . . there can be no question that the burning of St Joan of Arc must have been a most instructive and interesting experiment to a good observer. . . ." At that point Joan had been beatified but not yet canonized. Shaw ignored that technicality; he had already canonized her. In 1915 she would reappear in the preface to his fable-play *Androcles and the Lion.*

In 1913, still a decade before he began his play, Shaw had again visited what he called "the Joan of Arc country," writing from Orléans to actress Mrs. Patrick Campbell that he would do a Joan play "some day" and describing his proposed epilogue for it, complete to English soldier rewarded in heaven for the two sticks he tied together and gave Joan for a cross as she went to the stake.

> I shall do a Joan play some day, beginning with the sweeping up of the cinders and orange peel after her martyrdom, and going on with Joan's arrival in heaven. I should have God about to damn the English for their share in her betrayal and Joan producing an end of burnt stick in arrest of Judgment. What's that? Is it one of the faggots?" asks God. "No," says Joan. "It's what is left of the two sticks a common English soldier tied together and gave me as I went to the stake; for they wouldn't even give me a crucifix; and you cannot damn the common people of England, represented by the soldier because a poor cowardly riff raff of barons and bishops were too futile to resist the devil."
>
> That soldier is the only redeeming figure in the whole business.* English literature must be saved (by an Irishman, as usual) from the disgrace of having nothing to show concerning Joan except the piffling libel in Henry VI, which reminds me that one of my scenes will be Voltaire and Shakespear running down bye streets in heaven to avoid meeting Joan. . . .

Shaw's prophecy to Stella Campbell was dated September 8. Six weeks later, when he was back in London, critic Edward Garnett's play *The Trial of Jeanne d'Arc* was performed at the Ethical Church, Bayswater, long hospitable to "fringe" drama. The venue was an acknowledgment of the play's limited theatrical appeal, but the fault, it would have been clear to Shaw, did not lie in the subject.

A year after Shaw's visit to Orléans World War I began and then swept through the St. Joan country. Patriotism reached obscene extremities in the warring countries, and Shaw in 1915, writing an epilogue for the published text of *Androcles and the Lion*, attacked clergy who served Mars in the name of Jesus and who encouraged anti-German excesses. The more grotesque aspects of English clerical behavior would be satirized in the person of the priest de Stogumber in *Saint Joan.* Soon wartime trials which made Joan's seem a triumph of fairness quickened Shavian interest in Joan, if one can judge from references to two such trials in Shaw's preface to the play. In 1915 a captured English nurse, Edith Cavell, was put on trial in Belgium by the Germans for aiding troops left behind after withdrawal to escape the enemy. The evidence in her case was a confession elicited from her after nine weeks' solitary confinement. She was condemned to death. "Well might Edith [Cavell] have wished that she could bring the Middle Ages back," Shaw wrote later in the preface to *Saint Joan*, "and have fifty civilians, learned in the law . . . to support two

---

*In Shaw's epilogue the ruffian soldier, by then in hell, is given an annual holiday in heaven (to him like "a wet Sunday"), a reward which he finds surprising for an impulsive act that had had no moral meaning to him. Borrowing from himself, Shaw may have first conceived the soldier's gesture—and reward—in a 1907 short story, "Aerial Football," in which the slatternly Mrs. Hairns confronts, just outside the heavenly gates, a horse ("Chipper") she and her husband had maltreated. "I brought her up [to Heaven]," says the horse to St. Peter, "because she once got out and walked on a hot Sunday when I was dragging her up a hill with her husband, three of his friends, their wives, eight children, a baby, and three dozen of beer." "Fancy you remembering!" said Mrs. Hairns. "Did I really?" "It was so unlike you, if I may say so," said Chipper, "that I have never forgotten it."

skilled judges in trying her case according to the Catholic law. . . and to argue it out with her at sitting after sitting for many weeks. The modern military Inquisition was not so squeamish. It shot her out of hand. . . ." Her countrymen, Shaw added, saw this as a good opportunity for condemning the intolerance of the enemy and put up a statue to her near Trafalgar Square. On the pedestal they put up only the second sentence of the two which constituted her last words as she awaited execution: "This would I say, standing as I do before God and eternity: I realize now that patriotism is not enough. I must have no hatred or bitterness for anyone." The English, Shaw noted, were "moral cowards," for they "took particular care not to inscribe on the pedestal 'Patriotism is not enough,' for which omission, and the lie it implies, they will need Edith's intercession when they are themselves brought to judgement. . . ." Bowing to Shaw's rebuke, the authorities added Edith Cavell's plea for humanity— "Patriotism is not enough"—to her statue. But her trial and death, and the perversion of patriotism Shaw rebuked, seem to have added to the pressures which resulted in a play centered on another trial.

In 1916, Irish patriot Sir Roger Casement had been captured smuggling weapons into Ireland from a German submarine. He was taken to the Tower of London and then tried for treason.* Although the outcome was never in doubt, Shaw had an idea he broached to Sir Roger's supporters: "I will write him a speech that will thunder down the ages." But the speech Shaw had in mind was for delivery after the sentence of execution was handed down, to turn the sordid end of a traitor into a national dramatic event. "I am not trying to shirk the scaffold," he wanted Sir Roger to claim, "it is the altar on which the Irish saints have been canonized for centuries." Casement discarded Shaw's defense scheme, was duly sentenced to be hanged, and then made what was essentially Shaw's closing speech anyway. The final gesture was of little theatrical effect. Sir Roger went to his expected end, yet Shaw had accomplished some writing that he did not yet know would lead to another and even more dramatic post-sentence speech from the dock—that of Joan of Arc. Events seemed to be leading inexorably toward *Saint Joan*.

At least one person thought he recalled Shaw confiding that he was already at work on such a play during the war years. According to Miles Malleson (then a young actor-playwright), he met Shaw on a London street and was invited to Shaw's flat at Adelphi Terrace to talk. "Then he went on to say that he was writing a play about St. Joan. . . . He described his play, walking up and down the room with long strides. . . ." Supporting evidence is lacking. Still, Shaw in 1916 had written a little story which suggests an answer to speculation about what Joan was like as a child. It was "The Emperor and the Little Girl," a tale written for the *Vestiare Marie-José,* a Belgian war charity for children, about a French (or Flemish) girl lost amid the trenches during a shelling, who comes upon Kaiser Wilhelm, inadvertently abandoned in the dark as his troops take cover. Naive yet shrewd, and irreverent about authority, the child is the Kaiser's intellectual match in their brief exchange; but another shell explodes nearby, obliterating the child and rendering her a disembodied voice chattering on to the bewildered and bespattered Kaiser, who is left alive and alone while she has been "set free by the shell" from the pain and privation of existence,

---

*For additional details of the trial, see Chapter 13.

much in the manner in which the lively Joan of Shaw's epilogue is freed from the body by her burning.

Soon afterward Shaw wrote a potboiler for his actress-friend Lillah Mc-Carthy, a "bravura" playlet which took its cues from events in Russia in 1917. On the surface it was about a grand duchess who is reported to have eloped with a young officer but turns out to have joined the revolution. The setting is a thinly disguised East European monarchy where the government, beset by dissension, has faltered into chaos, while the imperial general is too baffled about what to do to be able to do anything at all. Suddenly he is confronted by the once-unworldly duchess, Annajanska, who he does not know has joined the burgeoning revolution, convinced that the corrupt court must be replaced by a regime more worthy of popular support. When she is arrested as one whose activities run counter to the national interest and is accused of political blasphemy, she insists, confidently, "All great truths begin as blasphemies." Furthermore, she points out, she is on the side of the "energetic and capable minority" which must govern when people cannot govern themselves.

General Strammfest yearns for a hero who can provide, and embody, the necessary leadership. "I have won no victories," he explains helplessly, and "they will not rally to my call." "Suppose I find you a man and a soldier?" Annajanska offers, and to his shock she throws aside her cloak and reveals herself in resplendent military attire, ready to lead the forces of the future into battle.

In some ways this less-than-half-serious melodrama was another embryonic suggestion of a later play in which a misleadingly innocent young woman in love with war and soldier's uniforms, although accused of blasphemy and afterward arrested, confidently assumes command and leads her disorganized nation to victory. *Saint Joan* continued to evolve, apparently subconsciously, under pressure of war. First called *Annajanska, the Wild Grand Duchess*, the play was retitled by Shaw afterward, taking advantage of events, as "Annajanska, the Bolshevik Empress." But whatever its title, Shaw was inching closer to *Saint Joan*.

Another story about the play suggests the last weeks of 1919—several months before Joan's canonization in May 1920—as the point of inception. Dame Sybil Thorndike and her husband, Sir Lewis Casson, had been producing a series of matinees of *The Trojan Women* and *Medea* at the Holborn Empire in London, where a revival of *Candida* was in rehearsal. Shaw remained one afternoon to see *The Trojan Women*, afterward—so Dame Sybil's account goes—turning to his wife while walking down Holborn to declare, "I am going home to write *Saint Joan*." According to the same story Charlotte had been urging him without success for four years to write the play and had assembled all the pertinent historical materials for him; thus it was with surprise that she asked him what had made him change his mind. He implied that it was having seen Sybil Thorndike: "I have found at last someone who can play St. Joan." Unfortunately, Dame Sybil told the story somewhat differently another time, pointing to a 1922 revival of Shelley's poetic melodrama of murder and lust, *The Cenci*. "You see, Shaw had seen me in *The Cenci*. Now in *The Cenci* there is this wonderful trial scene, and he went back to his wife Charlotte and said, 'I'll write the play now; I've found the woman who can play it.'"

Also involved in the genesis of *Joan* was a book which seemed to have nothing whatever to do with her story. Shaw had met Lawrence of Arabia in the spring of 1922 and had borrowed from him an early version of *Seven Pillars of Wisdom*, Lawrence's epic of his own adventures. To Lawrence he wrote, later that year, "perhaps I shall put you into a play, if my playwriting days are not over." Shaw could not have realized then how soon he was going to put Lawrence in a play, or write any play at all, for at sixty-six he felt written-out, barren of new inspiration.

Ex-colonel Lawrence became a close friend—almost a surrogate son—and soon not only offered the Shaws the unpublished chronicle of his desert campaigns to read (and later to edit for him) but took the Shaws' name on joining the Army as a private in March, 1923. Thus as G.B.S. began researching and drafting his stage chronicle of a military commander even more unorthodox than Lawrence, he had at his elbow Lawrence's *Seven Pillars of Wisdom*, in many striking ways the chronicle of a modern Joan. The coincidence may have been of vital importance to the shaping of Shaw's saint.

Much of the picture of the Maid formed by her contemporaries startlingly fits Lawrence: Joan's shortness of stature, her eating and drinking sparingly, her avoidance of physical contact and her generally asexual behavior, her combination of the laconic with the lighthearted, her "superior, irresistible, and infectious bravery." Even her delight in beautiful horses and armor and the rich raiment she wore, which offended church authorities, can be visualized in the contemporary terms of Lawrence's fascination with the flowing dress and ornaments of an Arab sheik—which scandalized other English officers—and (in the days G.B.S. knew him) his infatuation with his mechanical steed, a Brough motorcycle, which Lawrence named as would a medieval knight his charger.

In many cases, except for the personal pronoun, it would be difficult to separate the personalities of these two figures, medieval and modern, with their immense appetites for glory, their abilities to put people in their pockets, their knack for unconventional strategy unconventionally set forth. "She lectured, talked down and overruled the plans of generals, leading troops to victory on plans of her own," Shaw wrote in his preface to the play. "She had an unbounded and quite unconcealed contempt for official opinion, judgement, and authority, and for War Office tactics and strategy. . . . There were only two opinions about her. One was that she was miraculous: the other that she was unbearable."

By December 1922 Shaw could write to a Catholic priest he knew, Father Joseph Leonard, that he was thinking of writing a play about St. Joan and needed some questions answered. It was clear from his letters that he had already done a lot of homework, including a close study of the trial and rehabilitation transcripts. As he would do in his play and preface, he described Joan to Father Leonard as the first nationalist in Europe as well as first Protestant, and he posed the dilemma of the Dauphin (by then the King) in recognizing that he owed his throne to a convicted witch, a situation which would come up early in the epilogue to the play. Thus, although Shaw did not suggest that as much as a word of *Saint Joan* was actually written at the time of Charlotte's alleged domestic scheme to get him to write it, a great deal of it was in Shaw's mind before the first date on the first known draft of the play, written in his idiosyncratic Pitman shorthand. When Joan had found her time, she could spring from Shaw's head fully armed, like Pallas Athene from the brow of Zeus. Only such gestation as this can explain the composition of a masterpiece in what seems an inspirationally brief span. Begun on April 29, 1923, the long play was recorded as completed on August 24. Its writing had taken less than four months, much of it while on holiday in Ireland, some of it "in rapidly moving trains between King's Cross and Hatfield" as Shaw commuted between his London flat and Ayot St. Lawrence.

"As I wrote," Shaw explained to Theatre Guild director Lawrence Langner some years later, "she guided my hand, and the words came tumbling out at such a speed that my pen rushed across the paper and I could barely write fast enough to put them down." But although the writing might have been measured in weeks, the act of creation had stretched over at least as many years.

Whatever the sources of his inspiration, the play had popular success written all over it, and Shaw had not had a box-office triumph since *Pygmalion*, nearly ten years earlier, on the eve of the war of 1914–18. The war had embittered his soul, and *Heartbreak House* and *Back to Methuselah*, the major works to come out of the war years, left little room for hope about humanity. But however tragic, the new play suggested an upswing. A species which could bring forth a being such as Joan, whatever her fate, was not altogether lost.

The Theatre Guild, offered the play by Shaw after its noble and money-losing effort in staging his *Methuselah* cycle, was galvanized into action and began rehearsing *Joan* in November 1923. Remembering its unhappy experience with the lengthy *Methuselah*, the Guild early in its planning decided to write to Shaw, urging him to make some deletions and appealing to his humanity as well as his desire for a good box office by observing that many potential theatergoers dwelt in the suburbs and would miss the last train home. Shaw cabled laconically:

> THE OLD STORY BEGIN AT EIGHT OR RUN LATER TRAINS AWAIT FINAL REVISION OF PLAY.

After the final dress rehearsal the Guild cabled Shaw again, entreating him to cut the play.

> JOAN OPENS FRIDAY EVENING. CONSENSUS OF OPINION AT FIRST DRESS REHEARSAL FATAL DROP OF INTEREST DURING TENT SCENE AND BEGINNING TRIAL SCENE. WERE YOU HERE SURE YOU WOULD AGREE WITH US. WE WILL NOT DROP ONE LINE WITHOUT YOUR CONSENT BUT FOR GOOD OF PLAY AND TURNING POSSIBLE FINANCIAL LOSS INTO ASSURED ARTISTIC FINANCIAL SUCCESS STRONGLY URGE YOUR CABLING CONSENT OUR EXPENSE FOLLOWING OMISSIONS. . . .

Shaw's silence on the matter was total, and the uncut play, ably directed by Philip Moeller, had its first performance on December 28, 1923, at the Garrick Theatre in New York. The public liked the play better than did the critics, whose notices were mixed, and Langner sent a personal cable, entreating Shaw to heed critical comment about the play's length:

> ONE CRITIC COMPARING YOU WITH SHAKESPEARE SAYS THAT JOAN CANNOT BE SUCCESSFULLY GIVEN UNTIL AFTER YOUR DEATH BECAUSE IT CAN THEN BE CUT. SPLENDID OPPORTUNITY TO PROVE AGAIN THAT YOU ARE GREATER THAN SHAKESPEARE BY CABLING THE GUILD TO USE ITS DISCRETION IN MAKING SOME OMISSIONS OF UNESSENTIALS. GUILD HAS DONE SPLENDID WORK. SURE YOU WOULD AGREE IF YOU WERE HERE.

Shaw refused, and when Winifred Lenihan, the Joan of the production, was pressed to send a cable asking him to "agree to some omissions" in order to keep the play running, he cabled her:

THE GUILD IS SENDING ME TELEGRAMS IN YOUR NAME. PAY NO
ATTENTION TO THEM.

Then he sent the Guild a long essay in which he set out his ideas about the
play, which he encouraged them to offer to the press in his own defense. The
Guild did not, but Shaw afterward frugally incorporated the essence of the essay into his preface to the published play. The key issue in the proposed article
was addressed to the apparent villains, the critics. He was not in the "popular
entertainment business," he insisted, where the play is tailored to the audience's attention span and to the needs of critics to rush back to newspaper offices and feed clamoring compositors. What was more important was that he
was "intensely interested, and to some extent conscience stricken, by the great
historical case of Joan of Arc. I know that many others share that interest . . .
and that they would eagerly take some trouble to have it made clear to them
how it all happened. I conceive such a demonstration to be an act of justice for
which the spirit of Joan, yet incarnate among us, is still calling." His play was
not for "connoisseurs of the police and divorce drama" or devotees of the "lilies
and languors and roses and raptures of the cinema" but for another breed of
playgoer whose neglected needs had brought the Theatre Guild itself into existence. When it came to entertainment, Shaw declared, people had to learn their
places just as they did elsewhere, for when a man went to church and disliked
the service or the doctrine, he did not ask to have it altered to his taste. Instead,
he went elsewhere. So with his play:

> However, even at the risk of a comprehensive insult to the general public of
> New York, I must add that the limitation of the audience to serious, intelligent,
> and cultivated Americans means that *Saint Joan* must be regarded for the
> present as an Exceptional Play for Exceptional People. It has cost a good deal
> to produce it for them, and is costing a good deal to keep the opportunity open.
> This will not matter if they seize the opportunity promptly with a sense that if
> they do not, they will miss it, and discourage the Guild from future public-spir-
> ited enterprises of this class. The solvency of a play depends not only on the
> number of persons who pay to witness it, but on the length of time over which
> their attendances are spread. Even a million enthusiasts will not help if they
> arrive at the rate of ten per week. *Saint Joan*'s present prosperity cannot in the
> nature of things last many months. . . .

Despite the critics, the play was successful enough to be moved to the larger
Empire Theatre to accommodate the crowds, and it ran for 214 performances,
by which time it had also opened at the New Theatre, London, where Joan was
played by Sybil Thorndike. There it would run for 244 performances and result
in that most unlikely of English events, a Shavian apotheosis. A. B. Walkley,
who had worked with Shaw on the London *Star* in the 1880s and to whom Shaw
had dedicated *Man and Superman* (Walkley nevertheless condemned it), had
long been drama critic of the prestigious *Times*; when *Saint Joan* was announced for production, he had written an extraordinarily sour article which
The Times had the bad taste to publish. Although he had not read the play and
could not have seen it, Walkley protested at length that the subject was far too
solemn and serious to be tampered with by an irreverent jokester. When the
play opened, he found himself writing reluctantly that in Shaw's hands the
story of Joan "remains a lovely thing, lovely in simplicity, lovely in faith."

Being Shavian, the play could not be severe tragedy, and the fantasy, farce,
and faith of the epilogue—prophesied ten years earlier in that postcard to Mrs.
Campbell—very likely came first in order of conception. Even the opening "No

eggs?'' scene surprises—certainly one of the most unexpected openings ever written for a play which from the beginning has the inexorability of tragedy. Supporting characters are drawn in a range of wit from sharp satire to sheer farce, and even those given lofty eloquence often have wry lines which rescue them from pomposity. Joan herself, despite a "heart high and humble," is pert, proud, and impatient—and inevitably lonely and lost until she determines to follow her voices to the end.

A bleak and noble masterpiece, despite its satiric texture, *Saint Joan* sealed Shaw's renown; its author remained almost alone in refusing to concede that it was his greatest play.

In Sweden even the Nobel Prize Committee could no longer look away. Its resident expert, writer Per Hallström, had in the past dismissed Shaw as a writer of prefaces and his genius as essentially perverse. Even *Joan* had "too little dramatic content," and thus Shaw was declared unacceptable again in 1924 and 1925. Then Hallström saw a production of the play and informed the Swedish Academy, "The character of Saint Joan on the stage appears as both gripping and vivid and even if the real Saint Joan was a different figure, Shaw has created a great one." Grudgingly, he revised his objections, suggesting that "For better or worse Shaw's works have played an important role in our time and will probably retain their historic significance . . . in addition to which his non-dramatic works are amongst the best of their kind." Shaw had first been turned down in 1911 and then again in 1912, 1921, 1924, and 1925. He was awarded the prize for literature in 1926.

To the consternation of the grantors, Shaw wrote "to discriminate between the award and the prize. For the award I have nothing but my best thanks. But after the most careful consideration I cannot persuade myself to accept the money. My readers and audiences provide me with more than sufficient money for my needs; and as to my renown it is greater than is good for my spiritual health. Under these circumstances the money is a lifebelt thrown to a swimmer who has already reached the shore in safety." But there was a compromise. At Shaw's request an Anglo-Swedish Literary Foundation was funded with the prize money, "to encourage intercourse and understanding in literature and art between Sweden and the British Isles."

Although he had written forty plays and would write fourteen more before his death, after 1924 Shaw remained, as far as the world was concerned, the author of *Saint Joan*. Yet he would disclaim about Joan, "I have done nothing but arrange her for the stage. There really *was* such a woman. She did and said all these things. Make your offering at her altar, not mine."

Criticism over the years has tended to focus on the historical validity of Shaw's *Joan* as much as on the play's theatrical values, for an event that has happened but rarely in art has apparently occurred with respect to *Saint Joan*. Shaw's Maid has become the popular image of Joan of Arc, who is no longer the Joan of history or hagiology but the Joan of Shaw's *Saint Joan*, much as the *Henry V* of Shakespeare has eclipsed the Henry V of history. *Joan* is thus one of those rare works of imagination which reshape forever our concept of a historical figure.

Literature at its most triumphant can achieve such effects, just as it can raise to near actuality in the popular mind a character who is entirely the product of the novelist or playwright. But Joan, too, has been interpreted according to the winds of political and social change. She has become a precursor of, or spokesman for, concepts which would have baffled the historical Joan even more than the ideas of nationalism and Protestantism Shaw sees being played about her person by individuals who themselves are more articulate than they would be in real life in order that they may understand themselves sufficiently to enable the audience to understand. The critics of Shaw's *Joan* have been Protestant, Catholic, and freethinking; they have been capitalist and Marxist; they have represented nations and languages in which Joan has been presented in translations which the nuances of interpretation have been in themselves a kind of criticism.

Critics, historians, and the sentimental recorded message in the Place du Vieux-Marché notwithstanding, Shaw's Joan is the Joan of the popular consciousness. Eager for evidences of divinity beyond ourselves, we have been ushered in his play into communion with, at the least, a touch of the nobility to which it is given some human beings to rise. Ironically, this sense was absent, but for a rare few, at the time of her execution. No one—certainly not the Dauphin for whose throne she fought—interceded in her behalf. Apathy greeted her long heresy trial and death at the stake, and only a handful venerated her memory. Nor did she become an object of worship or the subject of legend. How could people not have been satisfied by the fairness of her trial and the compassion of her judges? Even Shaw's Joan admits as much. Prelates with impeccable reputations and substantial academic credentials, they were headed by Pierre Cauchon, Bishop of Beauvais and a former Rector of the University of Paris, a man, according to contemporary accounts, "animated by an immense fervor of most singular charity," a characterization borne out by the painstaking length of the trial (for which he was admonished) and his opposition to routine torture of Joan.

Only when the Dauphin, twenty years later, became King Charles VII was the case reopened, not because anyone acknowledged the sanctity of her life or her death but because Charles found it embarrassing that his tottering Valois dynasty had been rescued by a girl who was at best a heretic and at worst a witch. Out of political expediency, Joan had to be posthumously exculpated, and because French help was being solicited for yet another crusade, the Church grudgingly cooperated in arranging to confess its earlier errors. In 1455, when Pope Calixtus III authorized the rehabilitation tribunal, the results were predictable. The dead—and expendable—Cauchon replaced Joan as villain.

Succeeding generations found Joan more or less interesting as cynicism and faith succeeded each other in the swing of history; but it was only in the century of Shaw's birth that she became a focus for French patriotism. First the shrewd Napoleon erected a monument to her in Orléans and restored the annual feast of May 8 in her honor. Then followed the publication of the exhumed accounts of her trial and rehabilitation as well as Michelet's melodramatic retelling in his *History of France*. But it was an event which occurred when Shaw was a teenager in Dublin that made Joan suddenly the necessary heroine of her country: the national disaster of the defeat by Prussia in 1870 and the amputation from France of Joan's home province of Lorraine. Over the years that followed, sentiment and desire for vengeance combined; what emerged, ironically, was pressure to canonize not the saint and martyr but the daughter of France.

For G.B.S. it would not have been enough to depict Joan as the sentimental heroine of a melodrama arrayed against a stageful of stock villains. Neither the militant nor the martyr in Joan was as important to him as her embodying the possibilities of the race. A species that could beget Joans could have greater aspirations for itself than getting and spending. It could, in fact, aspire to the acceptance of its Joans as part of the natural order of things. Thus, for Shaw, the Maid is not only Catholic saint and martyr but Shavian saint and martyr, a combination of practical mystic, heretical saint, and inspired genius. For this reason Shaw had to make the conflict irreconcilable in the sense of Sophocles' *Antigone*. To make Joan's greatness of soul credible, he had to make her adversaries credible, which meant that Shaw—with more courage than the Vatican itself—had to rehabilitate Cauchon and his clerical colleagues, much as Joan herself had had to be rehabilitated nearly five centuries earlier. Joan as the superior being (in the Inquisitor's words) "Crushed between those mighty forces, the Church and the Law," is the personification of the tragic heroine, but to Shaw it was not sufficient for his theme. Tragedy was not enough; thus the epilogue moves from satire to litany and transforms the play from a tragedy of inevitability to the embodiment of the paradox that as much as humankind fears—and often kills—its saints and its heroes out of a sense of its own unworthiness to live among them, it would remain unready for them until the very qualities it feared became the general condition of man.

When Shaw was nearly ninety and had decided that he would leave his modest, unpretentious house to the National Trust, he began to concern himself with its lack of attractiveness to visitors and commissioned a sculptress neighbor, Clare Winsten, to do a bronze, larger-than-life Joan to stand on a hillock in his garden. Clearly, the heroine of his play had continued to mean as much to him as she did when he was "arranging her for the stage."

Upon Shaw's death, his ashes and Charlotte's were strewn among the flower beds at the base of the bronze Joan, carrying out a provision in his will. Nearly eighteen years later, on the night of April 3, 1968, the statue of a young girl in flowing dress, rather than sword and shining armor, her hand shading her forehead in order to enable her to better peer westward into the future, was stolen from Ayot St. Lawrence by vandals and destroyed. The world, it was clear, was not yet ready to receive its saints.

16 "The Unknown Soldier":
Shaw's Unwritten Play

"**A**nd now tell me," Joan of Arc asks in the epilogue to Shaw's play: "shall I rise from the dead, and come back to you a living woman?" The idea causes consternation in the living, and its potential seems to have remained in Shaw's mind over the years, reappearing in its most provocative form in a play he never wrote.

Several nations after the 1914–18 war established Unknown Soldier monuments to memorialize the unidentified dead. The British erected a tomb in Westminster Abbey, where the body of the Unknown Warrior was laid to rest on November 12, 1920, having been brought from France the previous day and kept overnight at Victoria Station. High dignity had marked the procession from the station to the Abbey, and the King and the Royal Princes as well as the Archbishop of Canterbury and representatives of the military services filed into the venerable house of worship at midday to do final honors to the unidentifiable body.

The dread concept would eventually stimulate artists and writers, then still numbed by the carnage; William Gerhardie—a war veteran himself—wrote in his second novel, *The Polyglots* (1925), "Throughout the countries which had participated in the war there is still a tendency among many bereaved ones to assuage themselves by the thought that their dead had fallen for something noble and worthwhile. . . . Mischievous delusion! Their dead are victims—neither more nor less—of the folly of adults who having blundered the world into a ludicrous war, now build memorials—to square it all up. If I were the Unknown Soldier, my ghost would refuse to lie down under the heavy piece of marble; I would arise, I would say to them: keep your blasted memorial and learn sense! Christ died 1918 years back and you're as incredibly foolish as ever you were." Shaw told him that the paragraph was the best thing in the book.[1] Although it may have been the initial stimulus for an abortive Shavian scenario, Shaw may have also remembered reading in *The Times* of London, in the last months of the war, a report emanating from Germany that the shade of at least one great hero from the recent Imperial past was being invoked in case the Almighty proved unequal to the task. "German people," the *Reichsbote* exhorted, "go into your church and pray that your Kaiser may be given strength to wake our Bismarck from the dead, and bring back this Hercules to purge Germany's

Augean stables, slay the Hydra of dissension and save his people from faint-heartedness, treachery and ruin."[2]

The sources of creativity are mysterious and complex, and it is possible that these, and more, were in Shaw's mind, at least subconsciously, when the evidences of his scenario surfaced in 1928. Cecil Lewis, a Royal Flying Corps veteran, had produced a play entitled *The Unknown Warrior* in 1928 and invited G.B.S. to the opening at the Arts Theatre Club. Shaw responded with a provocative postcard on which he suggested how he would deal with the subject. "In *my* Unknown Warrior," he wrote, "a desperate necessity arises in a future frightful war to consult a survivor of 1914–18. Not one can be found. The Dean [of Westminster Abbey], the Prime Minister, & The Foreign Secretary resolve to raise the U.W. from the dead by black magic at night. They find Christ seated on his tomb. He offers to raise the U.W. for them, and does so. The U.W. asks what they want *in German*."[3]

The idea apparently teased Shaw. What began perhaps in fun became more elaborate in Shaw's retellings. When attending a League of Nations sitting in Geneva in the autumn of the same year, he spoke with reporters about the French tomb of the Unknown Soldier at the Arc de Triomphe, and the dramatic possibilities of the theme. However now forgotten, the news then traveled quickly. In Chicago, Ashton Stevens, the dramatic critic of the *Herald-Examiner*, told his readers that he was scooping the Theatre Guild, then producer of Shaw's American premieres, "because a friend of a very good friend of mine recently found Mr. Shaw in a very talkative and confiding mood at Geneva." Allowance must be made for the thirdhand nature of the information, yet the details are striking and the paradoxes Shavian:

> The place is London and the time just 1,000 years hence. Peace has reigned for more than nine centuries, the profession of arms is as obsolete as the profession of astrology. And the population, despite Science's many inventions and nostrums for birth-control, has increased so that, literally, standing room on the tight little isle is at a premium.
>
> What can England do to relieve herself of this stifling burden of over-population in which, as Mark Twain would have said, there is no room enough to swing a cat? Great and grave men go into council and one of them, something of a historian of ancient Britain, recalls the happy days when there were wars to keep the death rate in tune with the birth rate.
>
> "We must have a war," say the great men of the council.
>
> But how? Not in the memory of living man nor in the tradition of his family is it quite clear how wars are made—for 800 years now Englishmen have died only of old age or by accident, or by over-crowding, or by boredom. Apart from a few mistakes by the medical profession, no man has died at his brother's hand. Then one of the council recalls [that] in Westminster Abbey there is a grave of England's Unknown Soldier. So, in solemn procession, these great men visit the tomb as thousands of years earlier the Greeks visited the oracle.
>
> Headed by the Archbishop of Canterbury, they file down the historical aisles of the Abbey and come to the tomb of the Unknown Soldier. But the Archbishop is annoyed because standing by the tomb is an ill-dressed under-nourished man who does not make way for them.
>
> "Who are you and what are you doing here?" the Archbishop questions querulously.
>
> "I am," the man answered, "Jesus Christ and I am here to help you. If you say so I will raise the dead from his grave so that you can question him."
>
> "By all means do so, and pardon me if I spoke too hastily," answers the Archbishop, a polite man at heart.

So the Saviour raises the Soldier from his grave and the great men start to question him on how to make war. But England's Unknown Soldier does not understand their language and tells them so in a tongue that, according to an eminent philologist present, is ancient German.[4]

Reports of Shaw's intended play surfaced elsewhere, from the New York *World* to the London *Daily Telegraph*. One version reduced the futurism element drastically but offered other details.

Time: a hundred years hence.
Place: England.

In the intervening hundred years all civilization has been shot to pieces—commerce, art, caste, politics, religion, have crashed in the debacle which Shaw had previously hinted at in *Heartbreak House*. Not only in England but everywhere.

The English Cabinet call their inevitable meeting to find some desperate play that might straighten things out. The human race is on its last legs. Humanity has entangled itself so fatally in the meshes of its own devices that there is seemingly no way out. In England, however, there is one last thing left—the respect and veneration for the Unknown Soldier.

This amounts almost to a cult. The cabinet figures say that if they can revive faith in something they may be able to pull England out of this swamp. Faith in something, anything, may possibly save them. One inspired official is moved to the theory that if Christ could be induced to come back to earth He might again work with humanity through the still fervent emotion surrounding the unknown hero.

Christ does come back again (the mechanics of this accomplishment is still vague in my mind, as it may be in the mind of Mr. Shaw). When the Saviour arrives He is asked by the Cabinet if He would be willing to work another miracle. He replies that He will. They beg Him to raise the Unknown Soldier from the dead in the hope that here they may find the one last symbol that England may adopt, follow and worship. Christ descends into the tomb and, in a brief and touching scene, the Unknown Soldier arises from the dead. When he appears he makes a speech—a rather long speech, not one word of which can be understood by the waiting populace.

It seems to be a meaningless jumble of words—strange guttural words—until some scholar realizes that he is speaking an almost forgotten language, and out of the resources of his erudite memory manages to piece it together with astonishing results.

The Unknown Soldier was a German.[5]

Shaw was furious about the newspaper report, which apparently tipped his hand. "I am not writing that play or anything like it," he insisted. "The account . . . is not accurate, but it is cleverly put together, and will do as well as the original. The ill-dressed, ill-nourished Christ is a senseless addition. In my version Christ was a perfect gentleman who apologized to the Dean, not of course the Archbishop of Canterbury, for his 'intrusion.' " Perhaps the most important words in his disclaimer were "the original" and "my version," for they suggested that Shaw had nurtured a rather elaborate scenario which he identified as his own.[6] The denial that there was anything to it stuck for a time. Still, the belief that Shaw was working on an Unknown Soldier play was not quite dead, for an interviewer in mid-1930 resurrected the story (as it appeared in the Chicago version and was reprinted in the *World*). Shaw insisted that he had often thrown out suggestions "for fun," but in this case the suggestion had not only been taken seriously but repeated with "sentimental additions and transmogrifications." Again he disowned it.

Fear of another and greater world war became intense in the early 1930s, especially after the rise of Hitler to power in 1933. Antiwar plays were already a staple of London theater, with Robert Sherriff's realistic yet sentimental *Journey's End* the most successful and Sean O'Casey's surrealistic *The Silver Tassie* the most notable and least successful. Even Shaw, whose bitterness about the 1914 war had led to the nonrealistic *Heartbreak House* and the prophetic *Back to Methuselah*, had returned in *Too True to Be Good*, his Malvern Festival play of 1931, to forecasting a rain of bombs from the skies and the destruction of cities. But after turning to other subjects on completing *The Millionairess* in the spring of 1934, he seems to have begun thinking again about an antiwar play that would rip away the sentimental facade which he had only lightly satirized in *Arms and the Man* forty years before, when he was a stripling of thirty-eight. Was it again only a joke?

To American playwright Paul Green he confided in 1935 that he was thinking of a new play,

> ". . . the biggest thing I have attempted, one in which all the facilities of the theatre will be called on to their fullest. It's only an idea yet, an idea I've been thinking about. It has to do with this childish fanaticism about war—specifically with the Unknown Soldier." He stopped and gazed before him, his hands shoved deep in his pockets and that light, almost inaudible, whistle sounding through his lips again.
>
> "Yes, sir—" and I waited.
>
> "I've thought of using the combination of mysticism and science in this play, making use even of an actual miracle. There's to be a big scene when all the people are gathered on a certain night around the Unknown Soldier's tomb where the sacred and mysterious light is burning. Through some proper device and in the proper mood, this Unknown Soldier will rise from the grave. I've only thought about it in dim outlines. To the horror of those assembled, he proves to be not a soldier of their own country but one of the enemy who has been buried and honored by mistake."
>
> He snapped his fingers and whirled around, and stood with his back to the fire. "I'm only considering it, you see. I haven't thought it out clearly."[7]

In autumn 1935, after the Festival at Malvern, Mary Anderson de Navarro, an actress at the turn of the century and an old friend of the Shaws, was invited by them to tea. At first the talk was full of the usual pleasant trivialities exchanged when old friends meet, but Shaw apparently remembered that when the 1914 war began, Mary Anderson came out of retirement to act. He turned to her, she recalled, with a "mischievous look" and made her an offer:

> I am going to give you the plot of a play. You can do whatever you like with it. Here it is. The world has had no wars for centuries, and has entirely forgotten how to fight. Suddenly a war-cloud bursts, the English are in despair and do not know what to do; they have utterly lost the art of fighting. It is proposed that the Cabinet go to Westminster Abbey to pray for light at the tomb of the Unknown Warrior. Arriving at the sacred edifice they find the Lord seated upon the tomb. They pray to him to raise the dead warrior; the miracle is performed. The warrior, after his centuries in the tomb, rises! The ministers implore him to tell them how to fight; the warrior does not understand; he speaks to them in German—he *is* a German.

Shaw was still working the idea out in his head. Mary Anderson took it as pure Shavian fantasy, meant to enliven the tea table, but a Greek friend she had brought with her took it "in all earnestness" and asked, "How does it end?"

"That," said Shaw, turning to Mary Anderson, "depends on you. You can finish it as you like."[8] It was as if he had impulsively invented the idea to tease her.

Miss Anderson took the story as mere impishness, and in truth Shaw rarely discussed his plays until he was ready to read a draft to friends. In this case, however, he may have been trying to talk through a problem that had kept him from writing anything down.

Something much like the story Shaw had told to Paul Green and Mary Anderson was also told to Cedric Hardwicke, who had not only played the prophetic gentleman-burglar Aubrey Bagot in *Too True to Be Good* but had been one of the young English officers who at a makeshift chapel at St. Pol had stood guard over the plain wooden boxes of unidentified dead from which the choice of Unknown Soldier was made. Again central to the play was the paradox that when the coffin was opened, the Unknown Soldier would be discovered to be a German. It was, Hardwicke thought a generation later, one of Shaw's "more mischievous moments."[9] But one is not mischievous so insistently if the subject is only a long-running joke. Shaw had sketched in either the first or the last act of what might have been a drama as powerful as *Saint Joan*. There Shaw had turned his play from a witty yet gripping historical chronicle to—in its final scene—a flight of inspired and moving fantasy, as Joan materializes, newly canonized, only to be rejected by a world ready to reverence her but still unready for her purity and zeal. That had been a dozen years before. Now something about the new theme—or situation—had embedded itself in Shaw's subconscious; but although he had moved long before from Ibsenite realism to greater and more elaborate use of fantasy and extravagance, he was apparently at a creative impasse. "You should never tell anyone your ideas for plays," Charlotte Shaw had warned Sean O'Casey in 1931.[10] Had her husband followed that advice, we would know very little indeed about *The Unknown Soldier*. Not a line of it appears to have been set down.

17 The Playwright and the Pirate: Bernard Shaw and Frank Harris

In his dozens of bantering yet benevolent letters to Frank Harris over more than thirty years, Shaw regularly inserted references to Harris as "buccaneer" and "ruffian," and the old pirate objected. But, reduced to living off nostalgia for the good years past and begging letters that deflated the pride in the old buccaneering sails, Harris protested too much. The mostly well-earned reputation that had helped to do him in was, in his last decades, his only negotiable currency.

In one letter Harris reminded Shaw that both had emerged on the London intellectual scene almost at the same time, in the early 1880s, as journalists and reformers, and had achieved fame on the same journal, Harris as editor-proprietor of the *Saturday Review* and "G.B.S." (as he signed his columns) as its highly visible—and quotable—theater critic. Yet Harris, for once, had been deliberately modest, perhaps a gesture aimed at drawing Shaw's support for one of the pirate's dubious propositions at a time when Shaw was world-famous and Harris was down and out.

In truth Shaw had sought for years after his emigration from Ireland (at twenty, in 1876) to find a measure of literary success but did not see his first play produced, and that unsuccessfully, until he was thirty-six. He was nearly forty when he joined Harris's paper. Harris, on the other hand, was a boy immigrant from Ireland who became an American citizen and then returned to the Old World to make his fortune. By 1885, when he and Shaw were both twenty-nine, Harris was the upstart young editor of the London *Evening News*. Shaw, who had been an unemployed writer of unsalable novels, in 1885 had finally acquired the opportunity to write anonymous reviews of third-rate books for the *Pall Mall Gazette* and equally poorly paid notices for the *Dramatic Review*. Two years later Shaw was still writing reviews of third-rate books and was also tramping the galleries for unsigned art columns in the *World*. Meanwhile Harris, already a pompous, commanding figure in London, had married a widow of forty-eight with wealth and social position, was editor of the *Fortnightly Review*, and contemplated standing for Parliament.

Later, when Shaw's play royalties were pouring in, and Harris, grasping in his old age for something to publish, sent his old friend a questionnaire, Shaw answered, "You want to know what it feels like to be a rich man. Well, you should know; for if you are not a millionaire at this moment, you have been one for an afternoon, or for a week, or if rumor be true, for perhaps a year when you married a lady in Park Lane and spent all your money consorting with Randolph Churchill. . . ." Shaw was applying salt to an old wound, for in almost every way it had been downhill for Harris after that, and a precipitous ascent for Shaw as critic, playwright, and social philosopher; yet at one point their careers had converged. In the mid-1890s Harris had taken over the moribund *Saturday Review*, hired clever but largely unknown writers such as H. G. Wells, Arnold Bennett, Robert Cunninghame Graham, John Runciman, and D. S. MacColl to write for him, and turned out a weekly that was the most lively in London. For his drama critic Harris wooed away from the *World* a music critic who had begun in yet another paper under the pseudonym of "Corno di Bassetto." Then writing as "G.B.S.," Shaw had achieved his aim of making even Philistine stockbrokers who cared nothing about the arts read his column.

Harris had gone after Shaw even earlier. When editor of the *Fortnightly*, he had wanted some of Shaw's energetic prose in his own paper and had proposed an article in a letter now lost. In a letter dated November 7, 1891, to his critic friend William Archer, Shaw began, "I have just had a letter from Frank Harris asking me to put my oar into the discussion on criticism. I have refused on the ground that I have said all that need be said in the appendix to the Quintessence [of Ibsenism]." Then he went on at gossipy length on the very subject about which Harris had asked him, addressed two envelopes, and put his "no" to Harris in Archer's envelope and mailed his Archer letter instead to Harris.

The puzzled Harris returned it four days later with the comment, "I will confess to a sense of mystification upon reading the enclosed letter of yours, which none the less has afforded me much amusement. I tried to look on it as the eccentricity of a clever writer, but failed to comprehend its drift. . . . I felt as Alice may have felt in Wonderland."

"Horror on horror's head!" Shaw wrote to Archer when he discovered the blunder; at the bottom of the letter which Harris had returned, he added the postscript, "Has anything more unspeakably awful ever happened than my sending this to Harris & his letter to you?" Still, Harris wanted Shaw in the *Fortnightly* and persisted in suggesting ideas until one appealed.

What won Shaw was an invitation to contribute to a series, "What Mr. Gladstone Ought to Do." In the *Fortnightly* for February 1893 Shaw had little advice for the Prime Minister: "What on earth can Mr. Gladstone do with such opinions as his, except precipitate the inevitable smash?"

"The Religion of the Pianoforte," perhaps Shaw's finest musical essay, was written for Harris for the February 1894 issue, and another political piece followed later in the year. The first commission in 1893 even resulted in his first meeting with Harris, at the offices of the *Fortnightly*. He would not meet Harris again until December 1894, by which time the editor had moved to the proprietorship of the *Saturday Review*, where the wooing of G.B.S. would begin in earnest.

The inventive Harris later reminisced that he had invited Shaw by letter to write a weekly theater article. Shaw replied in "a letter somewhat after this fashion," Harris later wrote, in pure Harrisian:

> How the Dickens you knew that my thoughts had been turning to the theatre of late and that I'd willingly occupy myself with it exclusively for some time to come, I can't imagine. But you've hit the clout, as the Elizabethans used to say,

and, if you can afford to pay me regularly, I'm your man so long as the job suits me and I suit the job. What can you afford to give?

According to Harris, his answer was "equally prompt and the the point:"

I can afford to give you so much a week, more, I believe, than you are now getting.* If that appeals to you, start in at once; bring me your first article by next Wednesday and we'll have a final pow-wow.

In reality the business seems to have been settled at the meeting on December 4, after which Shaw gave appropriate notice to the *World* that his musical column would cease. "I return to town tomorrow afternoon," Shaw wrote Archer from Folkestone on December 28, "to take up the duties, fairly forced on me by Harris, of dramatic critic to the Saturday Review. . . . It is questionable whether it is quite decent for a dramatic author to be also a dramatic critic; but my extreme reluctance to make myself dependent for my bread and butter on the acceptance of my plays by managers tempts me to hold to the position that my real profession is that by which I can earn my bread in security. Anyhow, I am prepared to do anything which will enable me to keep my plays for twenty years with perfect tranquillity if it takes that time to educate the public into wanting them."

Harris, then, was the right person at the right time, for after six years as music critic Shaw was eager for a change and happy to make more money in the process. The only part of the operation Shaw disliked was the Monday lunch which Harris held for the staff and contributors at the Café Royal. He struggled impatiently through several months of them with the sense that they wasted his time and degenerated quickly into "brag and bawdry." Then, early in May 1895, in the midst of the Wilde trials (Oscar had come only once to the lunches, with young Lord Alfred Douglas in tow), Shaw reviewed a mediocre play by R. C. Carton, *The Home Secretary*. In the review were passages scoffing at the attempts to make a bogey of anarchism. Harris—thinking of his market—cut the offending lines, leaving only Shaw's remark that the "stuff" about "abysses of revolution opening at the feet of society" was a "mischievous kind of absurdity." It kept Shaw's point intact but gave him the excuse that the meetings provided—at least in his case—no meeting of minds. He never went again.

Although the Café Royal lunches themselves soon faded as a Harris institution, the weekly he had rejuvenated remained animated, and the years through 1898 were the apex of his reputation as editor. He had an eye for writing talent and an ear for lively controversy. A predilection for libel suits and for bad investments, however, would force Harris to look for ready cash, and his only asset was the *Saturday.*

At just the point Harris was preparing to sell, Shaw would leave, but not as a deserter. As drama critic for the *Saturday* he had become the most feared and most respected, as well as the most entertaining, columnist in London; but a foot infection and subsequent surgery would keep him from the theaters. It was his opportunity to resign and to turn more of his energies to playwriting, but he could hardly have done more as a critic. As he explained not entirely facetiously, in a valedictory column when he turned over his assignment to Max Beerbohm:

---

*In actuality, £6 a week, nearly a pound more than he had been paid as music critic for the *World*, and an opportunity, besides, to influence London theater in other ways than as a playwright.

> For ten years past, with an unprecedented pertinacity and obstination, I have
> been dinning into the public head that I am an extraordinarily witty, brilliant,
> and clever man. That is now part of the public opinion of England; and no
> power in heaven or on earth will ever change it. I may dodder and dote; I may
> potboil and platitudinize; I may become the butt and chopping-block of all the
> bright, original spirits of the rising generation; but my reputation shall not suf-
> fer: it is built up fast and solid, like Shakespear's, on an impregnable basis of
> dogmatic reiteration.

Shaw had taken his leave of Harris just in time. By 1900 Harris was clutching
at any opportunity to retrieve his fortunes. Once he had lost the *Saturday*, he
would edit a series of journalistic disasters, beginning with the *Candid Friend*,
each a greater money loser than its predecessor. It was rumored that Harris
recouped his losses and sustained his high living by quietly blackmailing other
high-living Londoners with the threat of exposure in his seldom-successful
magazines, which became increasingly ridden with scandal. One libel suit which
resulted when, as proprietor of *Modern Society*, his last English venture, he
published something he should only have threatened to publish even put him in
jail. He had lost his wife, who was jealous of his affairs with younger women
even before they happened—and they did happen, again and again. He was publishing his own fiction, some of it, such as *Montes the Matador and Other
Stories*, not bad for its time, but few critics noticed, and few readers bought any
copies. A career as a playwright would end after one significant play—significant primarily because Harris had purchased the scenario from Oscar Wilde at
a time when Wilde would have sold anything for a few pounds; and indeed Oscar
sold *Mr and Mrs Daventry* to several would-be dramatists, each transaction
conferring exclusivity to the purchaser.

Shaw, meanwhile (having married an Irish millionairess in 1898), was arriving
as the leading playwright in the language and one of his era's major public personalities. Harris was hurtling headlong in the other direction. Never quite respectable, he had been tolerated—even courted—as an amiable vulgarian when
he was a rising star. His booming voice and four-letter language, his inability to
look like anything other than an Albanian highwayman even when dressed in
tails, and his gluttinous gormandizing and insatiable womanizing quickly made
him a pariah in the circles where his income had been found. As his opportunities as editor and writer dwindled during the Edwardian years, he took on a
paranoid air.

The *Candid Friend* had appeared on May 1, 1901, with society photographs,
gossip, political and theatrical articles—and advertising. Shaw even contributed an article, "All About Myself," to an early issue. Even practical advice to
ladies on coiffures and costume, competitions, and prizes failed to pick up circu-
lation, and Harris then added exposé articles. After Countess Cowley sued for
libel when Harris claimed in print that she had demonstrated "contemptible
snobbery" by retaining her title after her divorce and remarriage, the *Candid
Friend* went under, although the court awarded her only £100. The last issue
was August 9, 1902.

Harris, as Shaw had suggested, turned to playwriting. *Shakespeare and His
Wife* (later *Shakespeare and His Love*) produced an option from Beerbohm Tree
for £500 but was not produced and was published only in 1910. *Black China*
would have the hero a thief, a role Tree refused to play. It was neither published
nor produced. Eventually there would be *The Bucket Shop*, given a Stage Society production at the Aldwych in 1914, and *Joan La Romée*, privately printed in

Nice in 1926, but Harris's career as playwright was, after *Mr and Mrs Daventry*, as futile as Shaw's was successful.

Turning again to magazines, Harris planned an *Automobile Review* which never published an issue. What resulted, however, was *Motorist and Traveller*, which he began editing in 1905 with backing from the Dunlop Tyre Company. The blend of gossip and travelogue, however, failed to hold together. When the venture ended in 1906, Harris's £500 annual salary ended with it. Quickly he turned to other friends and made £400 editing and peddling, to Macmillan, Winston Churchill's biography of his father.

With promises of borrowed money Harris then attempted to get back into magazine or newspaper publishing through the purchase of an existing organ. Among others, the proprietors of *The Times* declined the offers, but Harris did land the struggling *Vanity Fair*, producing his first issue early in 1907. To keep it from toppling into bankruptcy he even regally revisited the United States in search of funds and of copy. Only the latter materialized, and he published his accounts of the Far West in his own journal, later turning them into his purported memoirs of cowboy days, *On the Trail*. Chicago also produced the material for his novel about the 1886 Haymarket Riot, *The Bomb*. Meanwhile Harris cultivated lawsuits—on behalf of his shaky investments and alleged libels, piracies, and persecutions. A number of them added to his notoriety as blackmailer; some cost him money he did not have. *The Bomb*, which he wrote in two months of furious activity, was designed—but failed—to recoup his fortunes.

It was English hypocrisy and Philistinism that was bringing him down, he insisted, not the inability of Frank Harris to rein in his gift for self-destruction. And no help came from the pretty young Nellie O'Hara, who called herself Mrs. Harris all her life and had expensive tastes which kept Harris in debt. Only when the real (and long estranged) Mrs. Harris finally died at a great age in 1927 could Frank make an honest woman of Nellie, but Shaw through the years politely referred to her as if she and Harris were living together with full benefit of clergy; and termagant as she could be, she nevertheless tolerated Harris's indulgence of his sexual itch among servants, subeditors, and assorted females who wandered into his wide orbit. ("Sex," Harris assured his young assistant on *Modern Society*, the future novelist and playwright Enid Bagnold, "is the gateway to life," and she duly went through the gateway.)

Before Harris became a literary confidence man and let his journalistic hand falter, he possessed the confidence and aplomb of the successful late-Victorian man of letters. Yet there was a vulgarity about him which Shaw chose not to see. Harris had, Shaw wrote in his preface to *The Dark Lady of the Sonnets* in 1910, a "range of sympathy and understanding that extends from the ribaldry of a buccaneer to the shyest tenderness of the most sensitive poetry" and could be all things to all men. "To the Archbishop he is an atheist, to the atheist a Catholic mystic, to the Bismarckian Imperialist an Anacharsis Klootz,* to Anacharsis Klootz a [George] Washington, to Mrs Proudie a Don Juan, to Aspasia a John Knox: in short to everyone his complement rather than his counterpart, his antagonist rather than his fellow creature. Always provided, however, that the persons thus affronted are respectable persons."

---

*Jean Baptiste Klootz (or Clootz), who called himself Anacharsis, after the sixth-century B.C. Athenian friend of Solon, was a German revolutionary guillotined in Paris in 1794.

The lines explain much about the Shaw-Harris relationship. Shaw was cool, scrupulous, precise, generous, and humane. Beneath the post of self-advertising egoist he was a shy man; beneath the clown's motley he masked a philosophic mood; beneath the Bunyanesque preacher he was a sentimental Irish romantic. While Shaw's sexual temperature was low, the Irish-born Harris, who fancied himself a sentimental romantic, possessed a compulsion for lechery that, when he became impotent in later years, became transmuted into erotic "autobiography" which was more fantasy than fact.

Harris's finer feelings often did him credit, yet the real Harris he could never recognize in himself was more often unscrupulous and ungenerous. While Shaw was quick to own up to the "pantomime ostrich" he played, beneath the pose of Good Samaritan and altruist was a self-indulgent Frank Harris who saw himself only as a model human being. When he claimed that he had offered to help Oscar Wilde in his extremity, he really thought he had, although he had grossly exaggerated his assistance ex post facto. When in 1898 he had offered to assist Harold Frederic's mistress at her trial for manslaughter (she had treated Frederic's fatal stroke with Christian Science) and pay half the court costs, he actually did sit with her at the trial, and he even wrote a *Saturday Review* editorial defending her. That he stayed away at the end and failed to remember his offer to pay her legal bills never occurred to him as a flaw in his character. So it went through his life. "Frank Harris," Wilde concluded in his prison letter, "has no feelings. It is the secret of his success. Just as the fact that he thinks other people have none either is the secret of the failure that lies in wait for him somewhere on the way of Life."

Major Barbara's father in Shaw's play was always embarrassing his wife by doing the right thing for the wrong reasons, as Shaw might have done, while Harris was doing the wrong thing for the wrong reasons. Yet both might have claimed that they were somehow right and that each was following his own conscience. Perhaps Harris was an attractive personality to Shaw exactly because he was Shaw's complement rather than his counterpart, because there were qualities in him, exaggerated to be sure, that Shaw saw the lack of in himself. To Shaw, Harris was not "vulgar, mean, purblind, spiteful," which he was to other men—and women. And to Shaw, Harris lacked humor "because scorn overcomes the humor in him." Later, he would see a pathetic humor in Harris, but he contented himself in the *Dark Lady* preface with the prophetic line about his old friend: "Nobody ever dreamt of reproaching Milton's Lucifer for not seeing the comic side of his fall."

In Harris's dealings with others in person and in print Shaw often thought he saw a "capacity for pity," but it would become an obsessive self-pity when each attempt to recoup his fortunes would end in misfortune. Harris had immense capacities for bouncing back after defeat, but each resurrection required some help from his friends, and soon there were few who could stand the strain of such a friendship. The longest-standing friendship remained Shaw's, but it required lending no money and seeing Harris in person as little as possible while keeping Harris at arm's length via correspondence. Their exchanges of letters kept the relationship going, and at the level Shaw was willing to tolerate—not only for old times' sake. Harris was a walking melodrama, and Shaw enjoyed the roles he had created for the two of them, although Harris would regularly try to break out of his because he did not know that he was playing Frank

Harris. Had he known, his pride would not have permitted it. When Harris once objected to a jocularly accurate Shavian description of him, Shaw rose to the bait:

> You must not take my comments on your personal characteristics as sneers and disparagements. If you do you will find me an impossible man to have any relations with. I tell you you are a ruffian exactly as an oculist might tell you that you are astigmatic. I will tell you now more precisely what I mean—if I have done so already you have brought the reputation on yourself.
>
> Somebody in London society who likes interesting people meets you and invites you to dinner. He asks you to take in a bishop's wife. You entertain her with deep-voiced outpourings of your scorn for the hypocrisy and snobbery of the Church, finishing up with a touch of poetry about Mary Magdalene and her relations with Jesus. When the poor lady escapes to the drawing-room and you find yourself between the bishop and Edmund Gosse, you turn the conversation on to the [pornographic] genius of [Felicien] Rops, and probably produce a specimen of his work, broadening your language at the same time into that of the forecastle of a pirate sloop.
>
> And if you observe the least sign of restiveness or discomfort on the part of the twain, you redouble your energy of expression and barb it with open and angry scorn. When they escape upstairs in their turn, they condole with one another. Gosse says, "My God, what a man!" The Bishop says, "Oh, impossible; quite impossible!"
>
> Now though this particular picture is a fancy one, it is not founded on any lies that people have told me. I have seen and heard you do such things; I have been condoled with, and have had to admit that you are a monster, and that clever as you are, it is impossible to ask anyone to meet you unless they are prepared to stand anything that the utter-most freemasonry of the very freest thought and expression in the boldest circles can venture on. . . .

"You can't write to me or about me without calling me names," Harris complained with unfeigned concern. "I have never felt this inclination towards anyone and so cannot understand it in you. . . . What you call my 'ruffianism' is revolt against convention which you incarnated almost as strongly in London as I did. You . . . seem even more unconscious of it in yourself than I am." The "sex business" which he confessed he had trouble getting printers to print was as essential to his art as he knew it was to Shaw's, but somehow Shaw managed to tuck it safely between the lines. Harris did not have that alternative, he told Shaw, for "you cannot know a man without knowing his faith and practice in this respect; and I wanted to state them about the men I knew. . . . You, on the other hand, seem to have no difficulty in this matter."

Not seeing any possible relationship between Harris's principles and her husband's practice, Charlotte Shaw insisted that the first volume of Harris's notorious *My Life and Loves* be burned, page by page, in the fireplace; and she would tolerate neither another volume nor Harris. G.B.S. patiently indulged his old companion in arms of *Saturday Review* days, sometimes paying a heavy price for permitting the often-desperate Harris to exploit him. In part Shaw sincerely wanted to assist Harris, who was helpless to help himself; and since Shaw had been forced by his excess of public visibility to restrict the character of his benevolence, he wanted to furnish assistance within the confines he permitted himself. He would not write prefaces which might enable authors to peddle bad books. He would not recommend bad business bargains to London publishers on the strength of his name. He would not provide outright charity, which he felt broke the spirit. But he indulged Harris within characteristically

Shavian limits, permitting him to publish letters which had been composed as disguised articles or prefaces or afterwords, and when autograph Shaw letters began bringing substantial prices from collectors and Harris was even more down and out than usual, Shaw would carefully write a long, entertaining letter by hand rather than mail a typed letter that would bring less in the market-place. Yet this would happen only years later. (Shaw would tell him, honestly, after one begging letter, "I always hate the people I have to give money to; and they always—very properly—loathe me.")

Gaps in correspondence, especially between 1908 and 1915 suggest that some letters are missing. Yet Harris obviously saved all or most of Shaw's letters, and Shaw regularly filed his correspondence. Some letters may have been pilfered by secretaries or maids; some may yet be in private collections. It is clear, however, that these were years when the two had fallen out of sympathy and out of contact. Harris had moved from magazine to magazine, and Shaw had ceased furnishing him with copy as the journals became more gossip-ridden and scandalous and Harris's financial speculations leaned more and more over the edge of the law.

After Shaw had published his Shakespeare play, *The Dark Lady of the Son-nets* (1910), and Harris had accused him of pilfering from a Harris play about the Bard, *Shakespeare and His Love*, Shaw reviewed the book in the *Nation* (December 24, 1910), owning up to cribbing from everyone who had ever writ-ten on the subject, including Harris. But Harris's work was "impoverished by his determination not to crib from me. . . ." What was, to Shaw, most Harrisian was not the picture of Shakespeare as an Elizabethan Frank Harris but Harris's picture of himself as Shakespearean disciple:

> This remarkable portrait has every merit except that of resemblance to any Frank Harris known to me or to financial and journalistic London. I say not a word against finance and the founding of weekly journals; but if a man chooses to devote to them what was meant for literature, let him not blame me for his neglected opportunities. The book . . . with a preface accusing me of having trodden a struggling saint into darkness so that I may batten on his achieve-ments, might just as well have been published fifteen years ago. If they have been suppressed, it has been by Mr. Harris's own preoccupation with pursuits which, however energetic and honorable, can hardly be described as wrestling with angels in the desert in the capacity of one of "God's spies."

Harris's nonliterary activities (including amorous ones) had been sufficiently questionable to have provoked regular comment in the press, and Shaw did not need to detail them to his readers. "I have never disparaged his activities, knowing very little about them except that they seemed to me to be ultra-mun-dane; but I feel ill-used when a gentleman who has been warming both hands at the fire of life, and enjoying himself so vigorously that he has not had time to publish his plays and essays, suddenly seizes the occasion of a little *jeu d'esprit* of my own on the same subject . . . to hurl them, not into the market, but at my head. If he has been neglected, he has himself to thank." But Shaw was not finished. Dropping personalities, he concluded that if Harris wished "to keep in the middle of the stream of insult which constitutes fame for fine artists today," he had to furnish the public with "plenty of masterpieces to abuse" rather than a few desultory works "of the kind that our Philistine critics and advertisement managers do not understand even the need of reviewing. . . ."

Such sharp words, however witty and well meant, could only drive Harris farther apart from Shaw, but Shaw was in no mood to condone the fruits of Harris's Edwardian years. It would only be when both Shaw and Harris, for widely different reasons, found themselves in the wartime wilderness in 1915 that there was a reason for a rapprochement.

It took the war to initiate the interchange which would continue unabated until Harris's death. The beginning was not a letter from one to the other but Shaw's spirited defense of his old friend's war stance—which Shaw used to indirectly defend his own embattled position resulting from his iconoclastic supplement to the *New Statesman* the previous November, "Common Sense About the War." Harris, who had reemigrated to the United States shortly after the war began, had contributed a number of articles on the war to the New York *Sun* which were then revised and issued as a book, *England or Germany?* On June 19, 1915, although the book bore the imprint of a New York publisher, it was reviewed in the *New Statesman*, where both Harris and the book were condemned. Since Harris was considered an Englishman in America, the review declared, his "decidedly mischievous" anti-British writings were widely quoted. As a contribution to controversy the book was derided, but "as an event or symptom it has, by reason of the author's personality and career, a certain international significance." Harris's career was then recounted, including the seamy side. Between literary enterprises, the reviewer wrote, "Harris would appear in the courts in connection with cases of a curious shadiness; and about a year ago he closed his career in England with a short spell in a London prison. . . . It is extraordinary, we may agree, that a man like Frank Harris should be able in any circumstances to attain a position which invests with importance the things he does and says; but so it happens in this world of incalculable chance." Harris, it concluded, "a fugitive from England, is an advocate of German civilisation and German sins. There is, to be sure, nothing original in his articles or his book, except the impassioned denunciation of English law and the English prisons—product of a painful personal experience."

Shaw reacted in a letter to the editor of the *New Statesman*, published in the issue of June 19, 1915:

> To the Editor of The New Statesman.
> Sir,—Your article on Frank Harris gives me an excuse for a comment on his book and on himself which may perhaps supply a needed touch or two to the portrait of the man. I have just read the book, and am struck by its intense British feeling. It is a consistent and indignant attack on England, a plea for Germany, and an express repudiation of the author's connection with England (Frank declares himself a naturalized member of the United States Bar); and yet it all through expresses a sounded concern for England, and a high, if bitterly disappointed ideal of England, which, unreasonable as it may seem in its application to the war, makes it more bearable to seriously proud Englishmen than most of the professedly patriotic explosions with which so many of us are now relieving our feelings at the expense of making our country ridiculous, besides informing the enemy loudly of his mistakes, a service which, one would think, we might offer first to our own side.
> The book must be read with due discrimination. For instance, the chapters which deal with the author's personal misadventures in our courts must obviously be taken goodhumoredly as the petulances of a sensitive man who never could be got to understand that illiterate Philistines have rights as against men of genius. When Frank Harris really edited a paper, he edited it very well, as the

files of the *Fortnightly* and the *Saturday* shew. But when, preoccupied by more fascinating activities, he left the office boy to edit it, the results were disastrous. . . .

Harris lacked any vestige of a sense of humor but appreciated any defense whatever, and Shaw was his only public champion in England. The result would be a growing Harrisian dependence on a now-benevolent but cautious Shaw and a burgeoning correspondence which would end only with Harris's death in 1931.

World War I left Harris a shipwreck. He had barely escaped England ahead of his creditors and critics, the latter having multiplied because Harris, half out of bitterness with John Bull and half out of affection for the Germany he had known for several years as a student, had taken to observing publicly and often that England might be as war-guilty as Kaiserdom. In New York he struggled with yet another magazine, *Pearson's*, which he turned to socialism, sensationalism, and pro-Germanism and which survived only because whenever *Pearson's* was forbidden entry into the American mails, it received a new wave of publicity and Harris pocketed a few more handouts from supporters. Although he could no longer find publishers for his books in the United States or abroad, he nevertheless wrote volume after volume of reminiscences of the great men he had known (or, in some cases, read about), his *Contemporary Portraits*. They were not, Shaw told him in 1915, "like anybody else's attempts at the same kind of thing. They are really much more like what used to be called Characters than the sort of stuff we do nowadays. I doubt if any of our Savile Club scribes would venture to defend them." But, Shaw said in praise, "When you tackle a great man, you really do know the sort of animal you are dealing with. . . ." Among the less savory aspects of the "portraits" were not only Harris's pioneering emphasis (for reasons less historical than commercial) on his subjects' sex lives, but his suggestions, few with any validity, that he had more than a little to do with the biographee's success. Contemplating his own inevitable biography, Shaw tried to torpedo that treatment in advance with a letter which included a hilarious spoof, "How I Discovered Frank Harris," in which a penniless and starving Harris is discovered huddled on a bench on the Embankment and is catapulated to fame by an insistent G.B.S.

Harris nevertheless produced a portrait in which he was shown as actively involved in furthering Shaw's career. It concluded,

> I have always thought of him as Greatheart in Bunyan's allegory, a man so high-minded and courageous he will take the kingdom of heaven by storm and yet so full of the milk of human kindness that he suffers with all the disadvantages of the weak and all the disabilities of the dumb. He is the only man since William Blake who has enlarged our conception of English character; thanks to the Irish strain in him he encourages us to hope that English genius may yet become as free of insular taint as the vagrant air and as beneficent as sunshine.

To Shaw he wrote, in sending him a copy, "All I can say is, if you don't like it, your taste for sugar must be excessive for I have written it con amore." Clearly amused at the Harris blend of fulsomeness and egomania, Shaw followed it up with a lengthy self-portrait, "How Frank Ought to Have Done It," in which, in the third person, he parodied Harris's style, opening broadly:

> Before attempting to add Bernard Shaw to my collection of Contemporary Portraits, I find it necessary to secure myself in advance by the fullest admission of his extraordinary virtues. Without any cavilling over trifles I declare at once

that Shaw is the just man made perfect. I admit that in all his controversies, with me or anyone else, Shaw is, always has been, and always will be, right. I perceive that the common habit of abusing him is an ignorant and silly habit, and that the pretence of not taking him seriously is the ridiculous cover for an ignominious retreat from an encounter with him. If there is any other admission I can make, any other testmonial I can give, I am ready to give it and apologize for having omitted it. If it will help matters to say that Shaw is the greatest man that ever lived, I shall not hesitate for a moment. All the cases against him break down when they are probed to the bottom. All his prophecies come true. All his fantastic creations come to life within a generation. I have an uneasy sense that even now I am not doing him justice: that I am ungrateful, disloyal, disparaging. I can only repeat that if there is anything I have left out, all that is necessary is to call my attention to the oversight and it shall be remedied. If I cannot say that Shaw touches nothing that he does not adorn, I can at least testify that he touches nothing that he does not dust and polish and put back in its place much more carefully than the last man who handled it.

The parody was meant as fun and indeed contained some probing self-analysis as well as some jabs at Harris's approaches and style which would have deflated a less desperate man. Harris merely seized it, rushed it into print, and accepted the dollars it brought without embarrassment.

While the next decade saw Shaw's apotheosis with *Saint Joan* and a Nobel Prize, the 1920s were agonizing years for Harris. He left his American magazine, *Pearson's*, having sold the debt-ridden enterprise for $2,000—enough to get him and Nellie to Paris and then to the Riviera. Each succeeding volume of the half-imaginative *My Life and Loves* brought him as much legal and postal trouble as income, and at the last, racked by asthma and heart trouble, Harris proposed a full-length biography of Shaw. As negotiations proceeded, Shaw was alternately amused and concerned. Eventually he wrote to Harris,

> What a chap you are! You can of course compile a life of me as half a dozen other people have done—the sort of life that can be published whilst all the parties are still alive. . . . Also you can write an autobiography, as St Augustine did, as Rousseau did, as Casanova did, as you yourself have done. . . . A man cannot take a libel action against himself; and if he is prepared to face obloquy, and compromises no one except himself and the dead, he may even get a sort of Riviera circulation in highly priced top shelf volumes with George Moore and James Joyce. But you cannot write that way about other people. You have a right to make your own confessions, but not to make mine. If, disregarding this obvious limitation, you pick up what you can from gossip and from guesses at the extent to which my plays are founded on fact (in your Shakesperean manner), what will happen? Your publisher, believing me to be fabulously rich and an ill man to cross, will send me the MS and ask me whether I have any objection to it. . . . I will say that I have every possible objection. . . .

At the very last, Shaw had to rescue Harris, after some concern that he had confessed too much too explicitly to the old pirate, by permitting him to secure a large advance from an American publisher in order to concoct a G.B.S. biography largely out of Shaw's many autobiographical letters, texts of which Shaw censored and bowdlerized for publication, sometimes to Harris's great disappointment. But Harris made use of whatever he could, sometimes changing the first person to the third person and sometimes making no change at all. Yet even that turned out in the end to be not enough help to the failing Harris (who was beyond help) and his ghostwriter Frank Scully. When, in 1931, Harris died in the south of France, in self-exile from both England and America, Shaw felt that he had not only to complete the book but to rewrite it—in the pompous

Harrisian style—to pay for Harris's obsequies and provide for the ageing Nellie's uncertain future. Then he wrote a characteristically paradoxical postscript in his own name to give the book a further push.

It was a curiously appropriate end to a relationship that had been less than a friendship but undescribable by any other name. For a moment in time they had been valuable to each other professionally. After that the two flamboyant self-publicists were linked only by the conscious need of one for the propping up of a faltering ego and a fading reputation, and the unconscious desire of the other for basking in his hard-won self-esteem and for preening himself via his own memoir writings while helping a down-and-out colleague who had been unable to cope with his too-quick success. Grasping at straws at the end, the ill and increasingly desperate Harris even suggested, since he had preserved most of his letters from Shaw (who had earlier urged Harris to sell them while the market was right), that all their correspondence be published, as was Shaw's with Ellen Terry. Shaw was cool to the idea. "We have never had a correspondence in that sense," he explained to Harris on a postcard, and "my occasional attempts to persuade you that the world is not yet populated exclusively by Frank Harrises would not make a book even if they were fit for publication."

Piteously, Harris appealed: "Such a threat [to forbid quotation] is worse'than unfair. I have already months ago entered into a contract and received the money from the publisher for giving him my life of you and some of your own letters. Now 6 months afterwards you forbid me to use a word. Three months ago you wrote: 'I have written the information you want in my own hand; sell it and have a spree with Nellie.' And now you forbid and threaten me. . . . What am I to do? I cannot rewrite the whole book. . . . Do be sensible. You talk of [Archibald] Henderson's 600 pages as the only authorized biography. There is hardly a gleam of Shaw in the whole tome. . . . If you had put 'private' at the head of any letter I would have regarded it as an order. . . . You say you have 5 to 10 thousand £s a year—I have nothing. . . ."

Such a close to the affair, with Shaw teasing the hard-up and ailing Harris with the prospect of making his book from Shaw's letters and then alternately withdrawing and restoring permission to quote; censoring the mildly objectionable—and hardly Harrisian—parts after tantalizing the pathetic Harris with them at Harris's request; and finally (in an excess of guilt or self-protectiveness, or both) rewriting the book as well as seeing it through the press for Harris's widow, suggests an unsatisfactory side of Shaw. Perhaps it is an unappetizing aspect of all of us reflected in much of the Shavian side of the exchange. That for years he had been toying with his old friend while making efforts to help him suggests an element of unrecognized cruelty in the underside of benevolence. Yet it was Shaw who saw the relationship as that of the playwright and the pirate. In Harris's view it had been that of two old cronies (which they never were), who had shared a heyday before one fell upon bad luck. But they saw each other as each viewed his world—Harris as melodrama, Shaw as tragicomedy.

18 Shaw's Other Keegan: O'Casey and G.B.S.

In November 1919 Shaw received yet another request to write a preface to someone else's manuscript. His policy on such appeals from aspiring authors was clear, and he would eventually prepare a printed postcard which would inform disappointed applicants that they could not count upon an introduction by G.B.S. to boom their work. The newest entreaty came from an unknown writer in Dublin who was aware of Shaw's wartime writings on Irish questions and had put together a book of his own—*Three Shouts on a Hill*, on Irish labor, nationalism, and the Gaelic language—from articles he had produced for the *Irish Worker* and *Irish Opinion*.

Shaw had no idea that the "Shaun O'Casey" who signed the letter was an impecunious, self-taught union organizer and journalist already nearly forty. His kind response, nevertheless declining to write still another preface, suggested that he thought he was dealing with an earnest young man.

"I like the foreword and afterword much better," Shaw began, "than the shouts, which are prodigiously overwritten." Like other writers who wanted a Shavian preface to help get a book published, O'Casey received instead more questions than answers. Shaw wondered why O'Casey appeared ambiguous on labor issues and was impractical enough a nationalist to come out against the English language. "You ought to work out your position positively & definitely," he advised. "This objecting to everyone else is Irish, but useless." Besides, it was "out of the question" for O'Casey to assume that a preface by an established author would advance him as a writer. "You must go through the mill like the rest and get published for your own sake, not for mine."[1] Although O'Casey would carry the letter in his wallet for years, until it was frayed and cracked at the creases, the relationship appeared unlikely to prosper.

Shaw went on to produce *Heartbreak House*, which he had completed during the war, and to write his play cycle *Back to Methuselah* as well as *Saint Joan* before hearing of O'Casey again. Meanwhile O'Casey had been reading Shaw's plays as they were published and was now writing some of his own, offering them to a cautious Abbey Theatre management. The first three scripts, politely turned down, included *The Crimson in the Tri-Colour*, which Lady Gregory in November 1921 found "extremely interesting" but "disagreeable." Yeats proved "down on it," leaving no chance for O'Casey to bargain the play into production via revision.[2] It was, he recalled to Jack Carney twenty years later, "really 'a play of ideas' moulded on Shaw's style. It had a character posed on

A[rthur] Griffith, a Labour Leader, mean & despicable, posed on whomsoever you can guess, & the 'noble proletarian' in it was later 'The Covey' in the 'Plough and the Stars,' as was a carpenter who developed into 'Fluther' " (28 March 1942).

Eventually O'Casey's stylistic exuberance and colorful characterization would win over Lady Gregory's colleagues Lennox Robinson and W. B. Yeats, and by 1924 the Abbey had produced three, increasingly longer, O'Casey plays: *Kathleen Listens In, Shadow of a Gunman,* and *Juno and the Paycock.* He hoped, O'Casey wrote Lady Gregory, with whom he discussed Shaw's and Mark Twain's version of *Saint Joan* (Mark Twain's was a "supplement"), that Eamon de Valera would read *Back to Methuselah* and acquire broader vision. It was already clear from the published text of *Shadow of a Gunman* that year that O'Casey had also been reading the earlier Shaw. The self-styled "poet and poltroon" Donal Davoren, the first page of stage directions declare, has been "handicapped by an inherited self-developed devotion to 'the might of design, the mystery of colour, and the redemption of all things by beauty everlasting.' " O'Casey was quoting from the deathbed credo of Shaw's rogue artist Louis Dubedat in *The Doctor's Dilemma,* and Davoren's romantic idealism provides an ironic contrast to the amoral, courageous Dubedat. G.B.S., O'Casey confided to Mrs. Shaw years later, had been his "anamchara—soul-friend—as we say in Ireland" for many years before he "met him in the flesh."

That March, when *Juno and the Paycock* opened at the Abbey, gripping its audiences and turning O'Casey into a local hero, veteran playgoer Joseph Holloway had a chat with the new playwright in the theater vestibule. "He told me," Holloway noted in his diary, "that when he started to write plays he thought he was a second Shaw sent to express his views through his characters, and was conceited enough to think that his opinions were the only ones that mattered. It was Lady Gregory who advised him to cut out all expressions of self, and develop his peculiar aptness for character drawing."[3] O'Casey was rarely able to eliminate himself from the dialogue of his characters. The indebtedness to Shaw would be emerging in more ways than this misunderstanding of Shavian dialogue (based so much on debating technique), where even the Devil in *Don Juan in Hell*—or the Inquisitor in *Joan*—has to be given persuasive lines.

O'Casey's intentions may have been otherwise, but Juno herself is, in a number of her appeals, reading an O'Casey editorial, however eloquent. Yet echoes from Shaw were more apparent in *Juno and the Paycock* in the "paycock" figure of Captain Boyle, who may be O'Casey's genial parody of *Heartbreak House's* Captain Shotover, the aged and philosophic retired seaman who warns mankind of impending apocalypse. In *Juno* the dark vision is reduced to absurdity in Boyle's repeated declarations that "the whole worl's in a state o' chassis!" And Shotover's nostalgic recollections of living to the fullest demands of body and spirit as opposed to the softness he sees in the younger generation are again turned to absurdity by the lazy and unemployable Jacky Boyle and Joxer Daly, his parasite. "I was ten times happier on the bridge in the typhoon, or frozen into Arctic ice for months in darkness," Shaw's seafaring patriarch tells young Ellie Dunn. "At your age I looked for hardship, danger, horror, and death, that I might feel the life in me more intensely. I did not let the fear of death govern my life; and my reward was, I had my life."[4] Boyle, his wife Juno observes, had earned his "Captain" designation the easier way. He was only in the water "in an oul' collier from here to Liverpool, when anybody, to listen or look at you, ud take you for a second Christo For Columbus!" The sarcasm is quickly forgotten by Joxer and Boyle. Joxer recalls the "young days when you were steppin' the deck of a manly ship, with the win' blowin' a hurricane through the masts, an' the only sound you'd hear was 'Port your helm!' an' the only answer, 'Port it is, sir!'"

"Them was days, Joxer," says the Captain. "Nothin' was too hot or heavy for me then. Sailin' from the Gulf of Mexico to the Antanartic Ocean. . . . Ofen, an' ofen, when I was fixed to the wheel with a marlin-spike, an' the win's blowin' fierce an' the waves lashin' an' lashin', til you'd think every minute was goin' to be your last, an' it blowed, an' blowed—blew is the right word, Joxer, but blowed is what the sailors use. . . ."

For an audience familiar with *Heartbreak House*, the shiftless braggart Captain Boyle may have been meant to have special irony, reinforced when we recall that Shotover's "seventh degree of concentration" can be reached at his age only with the aid of rum. Jacky Boyle prefers to induce forgetfulness (rather than perception) with whiskey, and in the last scene, drunk, he mumbles something about "Irelan' sober . . . is Irelan' free" and recalls only that the world remains "in a terr . . . ible state o' . . . chassis!" The desolated flat which Juno and Boyle have occupied is O'Casey's first Irish version of Heartbreak House.*

In Boyle's romanticizing of tawdry reality—his philosophy as well as his religion come for him in a bottle—can be seen the symptoms identified in Larry Doyle's lament in *John Bull's Other Island*, that gentle satire of Irish ways apparently interpreted more harshly by O'Casey in play after play. "Oh, the dreaming! the dreaming!" Doyle observes,

> the torturing, heart-scalding, never satisfying dreaming, dreaming, dreaming, dreaming! No debauchery that ever coarsened and brutalized an Englishman can take the worth and usefulness out of him like that dreaming. An Irishman's imagination never lets him alone, never convinces him, never satisfies him; but it makes him [so] that he cant face reality nor deal with it nor handle it nor conquer it; he can only sneer at them that do, and be 'agreeable to strangers,' like a good-for-nothing woman of the streets. It's all dreaming, all imagination. He cant be religious. The inspired Churchman that teaches him the sanctity of life and the importance of conduct is sent away empty; while the poor village priest that gives him a miracle of a sentimental story of a saint, has cathedrals built for him out of the pennies of the poor. He cant be intelligently political; he dreams of what the Shan Van Vocht said in ninetyeight. If you want to interest him in Ireland you've got to call the unfortunate island Kathleen ni Houlihan and pretend she's a little old woman. It saves thinking. It saves working. It saves everything except imagination, imagination, imagination; and imagination's such a torture that you cant bear it without whisky.

In O'Casey's *The Plough and the Stars*, produced at the Abbey in 1926, we are reminded of the sardonic thrusts of *Major Barbara*. "I am rather interested in the Salvation Army," says Barbara's father, the armaments manufacturer Andrew Undershaft. "Its motto might be my own: Blood and Fire." Shocked, one of his prospective sons-in-law insists that it could not be "your sort of blood and fire, you know." "My sort of blood cleanses," insists Undershaft and "my sort of fire purifies."

O'Casey's play invokes the Irish Citizen Army, not the Salvation Army, when the shadowy figure of one of its ruthless officers is silhouetted and heard

---

*Later O'Casey would insist that *Heartbreak House* was Shaw's finest play, once arguing the point with Charlotte Shaw, who stood by *Saint Joan (Autobiographies,* VI, 248).

through the pub window. "It is a glorious thing to see arms in the hands of Irishmen," he exhorts the unseen crowd. "Bloodshed is a cleansing and sanctifying thing, and the nation that regards it as the final horror has lost its manhood. . . ."

Fluther's sentiments in the play, says critic Saros Cowasjee, have the ring of Shaw. "Fight fair!" Fluther asks about the Easter rising. "A few hundhreds scrawls o' chaps with a couple of guns an' Rosary beads, again' a hundhred thousand thrained men with horse, fut, an' artillery. . . an' he wants us to fight fair! [*To Sergeant*] D'ye want us to come out in our skins an' throw stones?" Shaw, Cowasjee reminds us, had published a protest against the British executions in May 1916, observing that the rebellion "was a fair fight in everything except the enormous odds my countrymen had to face."[5]

Although it would have been poor strategy for O'Casey to point to these apparent echoes of Shaw—even if he recognized them himself—he would, nevertheless, mention G.B.S. when precedents or examples were useful. When Lennox Robinson, then running the Abbey, objected, on behalf of actress Eileen Crowe, to allegedly indelicate language in *The Plough and the Stars*, O'Casey pointed out that Shaw had used "bastard" in *The Devil's Disciple*, which the Abbey had produced six years earlier. It was not Miss Crowe's only objection, and when she refused to speak her lines as written, she was replaced. O'Casey would have increasing difficulty with Irish prudes as well as with Irish patriots. The patriots, of course, objected to everything in *The Plough*, and in a letter to the *Irish Independent* the playwright again invoked the name of Shaw, who, he said, hated patriotic sham, pointing to the description of the supposedly heroic cavalry charge in *Arms and the Man* as "slinging a handful of peas against a window-pane."[6]

The author of *Gunman*, *Juno*, and *Plough* had read and seen all of Shaw he could encounter in Dublin but almost certainly thought that the only indebtedness to Shaw in his plays was his deliberate quotation from *The Doctor's Dilemma*. Irish productions of Shaw in the mid-1920s included *Saint Joan* and *Man and Superman*, both of which O'Casey attended. The *Man and Superman* presentation, he thought, was bad indeed, "a helter-skelter performance" in which "all the actors were subdued by the relentless enthusiasm" of F. J. McCormick, who played John Tanner. Thinking innocently that with the successes of his plays at the Abbey he was "among old friends," he spoke his mind. The reaction was a choked hush. Then McCormick, who had overheard, pushed close to O'Casey and warned, "I hear you've been criticising our rendering of Shaw's play. You've got a bit of a name now, and you must not say these things about an Abbey production. If you do, we'll have to report it to the directors; so try to keep your mouth shut."

O'Casey was bewildered by the crude blast but went home and naively wrote a long letter to the play's director, Michael J. Dolan, pointing out the flaws he thought he saw in the production, adding that the letter might be utilized in any way that could be helpful. "It's just like Sean," said Lennox Robinson. When the letter was posted on the Abbey's notice board, it ended O'Casey's access backstage. The next time he came by, Sean Barlow, a property man, asked what he was doing there. He was on his way to the Green Room, O'Casey explained. "There's none but the actors and officials allowed on the stage," said Barlow, "and we'd be glad if you came this way no more."

By the time O'Casey's next dispute with the Abbey and its public erupted, he was living in London, deliberately keeping his distance; and he had met Shaw, whose aid he soon needed in person. Shaw, in fact, seeing that O'Casey needed funds, quickly introduced him to Ivor Montagu, who was eager, G.B.S. said, to "experiment" on *Juno and the Paycock* as a film, and has his father's money to bankroll him. In the end it was Alfred Hitchcock who did the film—a reel of which was publicly burnt in the streets of Limerick in 1930. It did not solve O'Casey's chronic financial problems, which would be compounded by each new play. In the dispute over *The Silver Tassie*, Shaw would put in more writing time than any preface for another author would ever cost him.

To recount O'Casey's struggle with the Abbey management over *The Silver Tassie* in 1928 is unnecessary here. It permanently embittered the playwright's relations with the theater which most needed him, confirmed his estrangement from the soil which had inspired him, and left him without a regular audience or theater for his work thereafter. Shaw would not only come to his defense but help him find a producer in London.

O'Casey had sent a copy of the play to Shaw, who answered through Charlotte that both had read *The Silver Tassie* with *"deep interest"* and enthusiasm and wanted to have both Sean and Eileen to lunch to talk about it. As Shaw himself put it to O'Casey in a separate letter before the luncheon at Whitehall Court, "What a hell of a play! I wonder how it will hit the public." By then he knew how it had hit the directors of the Abbey. W. B. Yeats, Shaw explained, was "not a man of this world; and when you hurl an enormous smashing chunk of it at him he dodges it. . . ." Yeats had hectored O'Casey on writing about the Great War (in which neither had participated) rather than the Irish struggle, "You never stood on its battlefields or walked its hospitals, and so write [entirely] out of your opinions." "Was Shakespeare at Actium or Philippi?" O'Casey had countered. "Was G. B. Shaw in the boats with the French, or in the forts with the British when St. Joan and Dunois made the attack that relieved Orleans?"

To Lady Gregory, with whom Shaw interceded, the author of *Saint Joan* wrote that Yeats "should have submitted" to *The Silver Tassie* "as a calamity imposed on him by the Act of God, if he could not welcome it as another *Juno*." But the elderly Lady Gregory, who, Shaw told O'Casey, was really on his side, was in no position to countermand Yeats, Walter Starkie, and Lennox Robinson. "Playwriting," Shaw explained in a note on the back of another of O'Casey's letters, "is a desperate trade."

Despite the uproar, which had resulted in newspaper editorials and letters to the editor, Macmillan was willing to take its chances on publishing the play, and O'Casey secured Shaw's permission to use portions of his "hell of a play" letter on the jacket of the book—an unusual gesture for G.B.S. O'Casey then attempted to use the quote further, for a critic in the *Irish News* of Belfast had attacked the play he had not seen by observing, confidently, "Bernard Shaw would never have put his name to *The Silver Tassie*." But in effect Shaw had, came the O'Casey rejoinder, and he quoted the "hell of a play" paragraph from Shaw's letter. On July 7 the paper, staunchly Roman Catholic and nationalist, reported receipt of the letter and its inability to print it "unamended." There was a censorable word in the quotation from G.B.S., which the *News* took as another example of O'Casey's bad taste.

Hearing softened words from Yeats and Robinson, who needed a palatable O'Casey, Shaw urged conciliation, which O'Casey saw as impossible. The Abbey management, he insisted, had "turned a Playhouse into a silly little temple, darkened with figures past vitality. . . ." By this time Eileen was in contact with Charlotte Shaw, who agreed with her that it was a period when Sean "wants a lot of looking after" and offered G.B.S. as intermediary wherever useful. But Shaw's advice was not always heeded. After C. B. Cochran had lost money on a splendidly mounted production of *The Silver Tassie* and had warned O'Casey in Shavian fashion that he needed to write things which were not only fine but had some expectation of "material reward," O'Casey turned to political plays with no chance of commercial success and to a story which the English printer considered too immoral to set in type.

To Cochran, Shaw suggested that he had earned a place in a producer's Valhalla. The play would pass "into the classical repertory," he wrote, "and it was a magnificent gesture of yours to produce it. The Highbrows *should* have produced it: you, the Unpretentious Showman, *did*, as you have done so many other noble and rash things. . . . If only someone would build you a huge Woolworth theatre (all seats sixpence) to start with O'Casey and O'Neill, and no plays by men who have ever seen a five-pound note before they were thirty or been inside a school after they were thirteen, you would be buried in Westminster Abbey." The criteria didn't quite fit G.B.S. himself, yet it came close.

In 1932 Yeats decided that Ireland needed its own academy of letters and induced Shaw to become its first president (with Yeats himself as vice president). The first thirty-five writers invited to become founding members included O'Casey. But they also included, obviously, Yeats as well as the Abbey's impresario, Lennox Robinson. Bitter at the Abbey's treatment of him, for which he blamed Yeats, O'Casey found reasons to refuse admission, pointing to the dangers of implicit censorship through the approval or disapproval of the academy. Besides, he added in a letter to the *Irish Times*, the whole idea was a "literary cocktail" rather than anything truly useful for Ireland. That he saw Yeats as the evil genius behind the academy, he made no attempt to hide. That the invitation to join came over Shaw's signature made it, O'Casey later wrote in his memoirs, "the hardest refusal he had ever had to face," the "one favour" Shaw had ever asked him. A letter of refusal was sent to Shaw, O'Casey recalled, "but no answer came back." No such letter has turned up. Perhaps O'Casey had let his public statements stand for him and only imagined the letter later. In any case, Shaw knew what it would have cost O'Casey's pride to join something which had been Yeats's brainchild.

That year O'Casey was slipping deeper into debt. His income from minor journalism was not supplementing his meager royalties enough to arrest the slide. While preparing the prompt copies of his plays for Samuel French he received an offer from the publisher to purchase half the amateur rights to *Gunman*, *Juno*, and *Plough* for £300. He consulted Shaw, who warned him against the "absurdly bad bargain" and enclosed a loan of £100. "My advice," Shaw added, "is to let wife and child perish, and lay bricks for your last crust, sooner than part with an iota of your rights." O'Casey needed more than that but was reluctant to ask Shaw, who at about the same time was extricating his old friends Sidney and Beatrice Webb from assorted difficulties with a check for £1,000. O'Casey signed away his rights to French, only to discover later that the publisher was holding £350 in royalties for him, claiming that they had been unable at the time to locate his address. At least once Shaw would complain that O'Casey had repaid a loan, calling the gesture "Swank" in hopes the label would keep further repayments from occurring. "This is," Shaw insisted, "an improvident, extravagant . . . and entirely unnecessary proceeding, most inconsiderate to your wife and children."[7]

A rare opportunity for reciprocity came to O'Casey in the early 1930s. To Charlotte he had described Shaw's *Too True to Be Good* as a "rare title" and a "terrible (meaning terrifying) philosophy," and in the *Listener* he wrote a long review of *Too True* and *On the Rocks*, Shaw's next political-prophetic play. *Saint Joan*, he wrote, was easier to take, "like an illuminated Book of Hours that one can finger and fondle, and be amused by the quaint pictures, thanking God all the time that we are not as other men were." On the other hand, Shaw's apocalyptic plays set in the near present were "flames of courageous thought which some day, sooner or later, will burn to ashes the hay, straw, and stubble of god mercy and truth and righteousness and peace that find their vent in the singing of hymns, piling of law upon law, and the pampering of the useless and the unfit."[8] But O'Casey was not merely championing Shaw, he was pointing implicitly to his own increasingly uncommercial playwriting perspectives— visions of apocalypse in the present.

Within the Gates, an example of O'Casey's current method, had opened a month before his essay had appeared, and the playwright had brought Shaw to sit with him at the Royalty Theatre on opening night. The play, however, needed more than that. An essentially plotless, poetic, sentimental denunciation of hypocrisy and misery, it was Strindberg's *Dream Play* set in Hyde Park and peopled with contemporary types. What the public wanted was another *Juno* or *Plough*—Hibernian poetic realism rather than Strindbergian dream visions. He was not about to turn back, instead telling Shaw that he should write a play about the rebellion of Jack Cade. Shaw "could make a Communist St. Joan of him." O'Casey, rather, would begin a new symbolic play, *The Star Turns Red*, which would have no chance of either critical or commercial success. Having read it, Shaw found that a good reason to stay away from the opening, writing O'Casey afterward that the bad press "shewed up the illiteracy of the critics."

With little hope of burgeoning play royalties and with work on his "semi-autobiography" going slowly, O'Casey lived frugally and in debt. With his children growing into school age, he and Eileen[9] warmed to Shaw's suggestion that living away from the London area could be both inexpensive and valuable for schooling, especially if the O'Caseys could find a place near the modern Dartington Hall School in Devon. A spacious Victorian house in Totnes was available at £85 a year, very little by London standards, but the landlord (a dentist), seeing O'Casey and his brood, asked for a co-signer of the lease to guarantee his rent.

Not wanting to bother G.B.S. directly, O'Casey asked Charlotte, who invited him to the Whitehall Court flat to talk about it over lunch. Businesslike, she asked about the house, the rates, and if O'Casey was working on anything remunerative. O'Casey flushed at the means test, and G.B.S. barked, "Oh, give it to him!" The questioning halted, and everything seemed settled, but the landlord refused to accept a woman—even a millionairess—as guarantor. G.B.S. quickly obliged, writing O'Casey on October 17, 1938, "Your landlord, being a dentist, has developed an extractor complex. He proposed a lease in which I was not only to guarantee all your convenants, but indemnify him for all consequences." Since Shaw loved haggling over contracts and vetting other people's legal documents, nothing could have made him happier. "I said," Shaw told O'Casey, "[that] I did not know his character, but knew enough of yours to know that the consequences might include anything from murder to a European war; so I re-drafted the agreement. The lawyers, knowing that their man was only too lucky to get a gilt-edged (so they thought) security, and that his demands were absurd, made no resistance."

To Charlotte Shaw (G.B.S. was difficult to thank so directly) O'Casey wrote that he indeed needed the financial guarantee but—he took Shaw's joking remark literally—"I'm not going to ask anyone to guarantee my morals." Then he added, documenting what must have been the beginning of the Shavian impact upon him, "I have always had to fight like the devil for life; but you must blame your husband, G.B.S., for whatever sharpness and wit that have come into my fighting qualities; and [as well] my young Dublin comrade, member of the Fourth Order of Saint Francis, who first put the green-covered copy of *John Bull's Other Island* in my then reluctant hand."

"Read *John Bull's Other Island*," Kevin O'Loughlin had promised, "and the Ireland you think you know and love will vanish before your eyes."

"Well, that's a damn fine recommendation!" O'Casey had said skeptically, but when payday came, he had gone to Jason's bookshop and purchased the six-penny paper edition. By the time of his letter to Charlotte, *John Bull* had taken on an almost metaphorical quality to him.

By then, too, O'Casey was again a father (Shaw sent the infant Shivaun fifty pounds) and now working on a play which he hoped would combine what he wanted to do with what he hoped the public would accept. The result was the comic fantasy *Purple Dust*, a try at social criticism through a symbolic decaying country house and characters who might have come out of *Heartbreak House*. Saros Cowasjee, rather, sees a bond between *Purple Dust* and the play which had first turned O'Casey to Shaw a generation earlier. Still, as Cowasjee observes, Shaw had probed deeply into both Irish and English psyches, while O'Casey, who lived largely self-insulated from his surroundings, was unable to see profoundly into the English milieu. Shaw's characters can be absurd without being puppets or fools. In *Purple Dust*, O'Casey did not get beyond being cantankerous and colorful, but whether or not his inspiration had been *John Bull* or *Heartbreak House*, the result was one of his rare later plays which had some box-office success in his lifetime.

There are close resemblances in structure as well as theme to *John Bull's Other Island*, as Ronald Rollins notes. Both comedies utilize the device of English expeditions to a backward Ireland, a portion of which they propose to rehabilitate, and both expose fraudulent sentiment, spiritual torpidity, paralyzing class antagonisms, and consequent economic stagnation. "Excessive, neurotic fascination with imaginative splendors and/or glories of the past makes people, so Shaw and O'Casey suggest, inept participants in the present, rendering them victims and enemies of change, innovation, and progress."[10]

John Bull's Other Island reverberates through O'Casey's plays, although perhaps nowhere so much as in *Purple Dust*. Larry Doyle's penetrating analysis in *John Bull* of the Irishman's dreaming imagination, which "never lets him alone," permeates O'Casey's characters from Donal Davoren to the Irish dreamers of *Purple Dust*; and Cowasjee sees in both *John Bull* and *Purple Dust* the same portrayal of the "irresponsibility of the Irish, their sense of humor, their pride, their flattery of the English, the poetic brilliance of their speech and their queer love-making. . . ." The apocalyptic ending, however—a flood rather than a bombing—echoes *Heartbreak House*, and the warnings of imminent catastrophe are reminiscent of the prophecies of Shotover and Hector (and even echo the spoof of English respectability in *Caesar and Cleopatra*, about the dying of their bodies blue by Britannus and his confreres, so that even when stripped of their clothes they could not be robbed of their respectability). Says Philib of the English interlopers for whom he must work, reclaiming a dilapidated mansion on the edge of a river which regularly overflows its banks, "Hanmmerin' out handsome golden ornaments for flowin' cloak and tidy tunic we were, while you were busy gatherin' dhried grass, and dyin' it blue, to hide the consternation of your middle parts; decoratin' eminent books with glowin' colour an' audacious beauty were we . . . when you were still a hundred score o' years away from even hearin' of the alphabet. Fool? It's yourself's the fool, I'm sayin', settlin' down in a place that's only fit for the housin' o' dead men! . . . Wait till God sends the heavy rain, and the floods come!"

Later O'Casey would describe *Purple Dust* in *Heartbreak House* terms as without partisan politics—not an attack on England, "not even on any particular class in the country. . . . It is to some extent, a symbolic play, and unconsciously, a prophetic one too. The auld hoose, beloved by so many for so long, is in a bad way; old things are passing away, and new things are appearing in the sky, on the horizon, and right here in the middle of us. The house is falling, and we hardly know where to pick up the bits."

The move to Devon, prompted by Shaw, would prove to have the drawback for O'Casey that he was no longer in easy visiting distance.

"Sean missed him exceedingly," Eileen O'Casey remembered, as the war years, then beginning, were years of decreased mobility, because of wartime restrictions and O'Casey's increasingly failing eyesight. It would have been such a help, Eileen thought, if her husband "could have talked to somebody who really loved the theatre and who was in harmony with him." It was time, Shaw wrote O'Casey in 1943, that he produced a "money-spinner"; but written exhortations were the best that Shaw could do at eighty-seven, worn down himself with age and with care for Charlotte, who had died that year of a crippling bone ailment. O'Casey had received letters from Shaw just before Charlotte's death, he told Gabriel Fallon (April 3, 1945), "saying 'we are terribly lonely, & feel damnably old.'" As for money-spinners, O'Casey would write three volumes of what he would describe to Shaw, early in 1945, as "semi-biography." They would make up financially for the poor box office of such new plays as *Oak Leaves and Lavender*.

Loyally, in his fashion, O'Casey would refuse requests to write puffery for ninetieth birthday volumes planned for Shaw, which smacked of publishers' profit scheming to him. "If an article would lift 50 years off the 90," he assured G.B.S., "I'd do it quick." Beset by depression after Charlotte's passing and by an avalanche of mail in anticipation of the birthday, Shaw failed to respond to half a dozen O'Casey letters, and Sean wondered to George Jean Nathan whether he had said anything in the autobiographical books to offend. Finally, in 1948, there was a postcard. O'Casey had found the sure way to provoke one, asking Shaw to write a preface to an IRA memoir by Tom Barry, *Guerilla Days in Ireland*. He knew Shaw's attitude on prefaces. "So the postcard came," O'Casey wrote to Nathan, "saying he had written to the IRA author setting down reasons for refusal."

Shaw was writing fewer and fewer letters, which O'Casey blamed, in his own case, on Fritz Loewenstein, who had insinuated himself into Shaw's confidence and become his anointed bibliographer. He was really Shaw's "Iron Curtain," O'Casey told Nathan. Loewenstein "calls himself Shaw's Bibliographer and Remembrancer," O'Casey noted, seeing the role as a case of Shaw's weakness for self-publicity—something to which he also attributed Shaw's interest in photography, especially in pictures of himself. Yet soon O'Casey was writing to his publisher, Daniel Macmillan, about his friend Francis McCarthy, who had been a sergeant on a troop ship torpedoed in the Pacific by the Japanese. "He floated about for 26 hours before they picked him up, & sent him to Japan, where he was a prisoner until the war ended. He saved nothing but a photograph of Bernard Shaw that he had in an oilskin cover lying on his chest, & tied around his neck. A curious scapular!"

A variety of ailments, from heart trouble to near blindness, kept O'Casey at home in Devon, but at G.B.S.'s invitation, Eileen went to Ayot St. Lawrence early in 1950 to have tea with him. As the link between the two frail old Irishmen, Eileen did her job well, but pride would prevent her from doing what was clearly in the back of Shaw's mind. He would get no hint from her of the state of the O'Casey finances. "The old warrior," Sean reported to Nathan, "is as alive as ever; still gets indignant at stupidity; still has his cascading laugh; and takes an hour's walk every day in the garden, whatever the weather. And him goin' on for 94!" Shaw had greeted Mrs. O'Casey with, "Well, Eileen, you've still got your good looks." Irish diplomat John Dulanty, the friend who had driven Eileen to Ayot, recalled in a note on the meeting, "I wandered out of the room to give them the opportunity of a mild flirtation."

The revival of the relationship continued. Eileen had brought to Ayot a picture of the O'Casey family, and Shaw wrote that he had hung it on his wall. O'Casey was pleased and proud. In May 1950 Shaw told him that Irish Catholics were still sending him "medals of the Blessed Virgin, guaranteeing, if I say a novena, that she will give me anything I ask from her, to which I reply that the B V needs helpers and not beggars." While over the years Shaw had been generous in many ways to the O'Casey family, Sean himself had never begged anything after the abortive request for a preface, but the lease guarantee, which had cost G.B.S. nothing more than his signature. The genteel poverty in which the O'Casey's were surviving in Devon was something Shaw never realized, and in the immediate postwar years, when the self-styled Green Crow seemed to be turning out plays and polemics with regularity, Shaw had assumed the best, although O'Casey's cranky new comedies made little money. He would never find out otherwise.

After Shaw's fall at Ayot in July 1950, in which he broke a hip and became bedridden in his final months, Dulanty and Eileen returned at their first opportunity to see Shaw. It was October, and Shaw was frail and clearly failing, "caged now," as O'Casey would write, "in his own home." Privately, to Dulanty, Shaw asked how the O'Caseys were doing, and Dulanty confided that he did not think they were "all that good." When Shaw told him that he had heard, rather, that they were "in clover," Dulanty urged Eileen to tell him the truth. Afterward, as Shaw and Eileen talked of the children and the daily lives of the family, Shaw suddenly asked, "And how is Sean financially?" Unwilling to be a supplicant, she replied, as she recalls in her memoir, *Sean*, "Of course, we are perfectly all right." (Shaw "said he had heard we were in clover, and was relieved about it.") He went on to talk of his loneliness after the passing of so many friends and contemporaries, and Eileen felt that it was time to return to London, where she had been staying. It was the O'Caseys' last chance to be remembered in his will, and it had passed by.*

A few days later Shaw asked to see her. He opened his eyes when she walked in and said faintly, "I really think I am going to die." His musical voice, weakened to a whisper, was still clear. He was ready to go, he announced, for he was tired of dependence and especially disliked having to be minded by people he didn't know. He had willed his death, he said. "I want to go now; it is better to go now. It'll be interesting, anyway," he suggested, smiling, "to meet the Almighty."

"I'm sure," said Eileen, "that the two of you will get on splendidly together."

"I'll have a helluva lot of questions to ask Him," said Shaw.

"Take it calmly till Sean gets there, and then you can start a row."

"I'll find it hard to take it calmly, for I've always been a fighter."

He asked her to stroke his forehead, and—according to Sean—"he murmured that it was fine to feel the touch of a soft Irish hand & hear the soft sound of an Irish voice." When he fell asleep, Eileen strode out, but within ten minutes the sickroom bell rang. Shaw wanted to see Eileen again, to say good-bye. "I'm finished," he said, "and now it's up to Sean."

"No," she said, frankly, realizing that O'Casey was seventy and nearly sightless, "Sean is too old." At his request she kissed him good-bye, and he sank back into sleep. He died two days later, on November 2, 1950. O'Casey's tribute "to a Fighting Idealist" appeared in the first *New York Times Book Review* issue to be printed after Shaw's death.

In *Sunset and Evening Star* (1954), the sixth and last volume of his autobiographies, O'Casey would publish a long chapter he titled "Shaw's Corner," lovingly detailing his relationship with G.B.S. (Yet O'Casey had never been to "Shaw's Corner"—in Ayot St. Lawrence—having visited the Shaws only in London.) No one has been more eloquent or more persuasive about the poetic element in Shaw's plays (so often labeled as nonexistent). O'Casey saw poetry not only in Shaw's prose but in the Shavian theatrical imagination:

> Some critics say there is no poetry in Shaw's plays (how often have the Dublin bravos signed this in the air with a sawing hand!); and no emotion. There is poetry in the very description of the Syrian sky at the opening of *Caesar and Cleopatra*, in the way the Bucina calls, in the two great figures dwarfed between the paws of the Sphinx, in the rush of the Roman Legion into the Palace, halting to cry Hail, Caesar, when they see him sitting alone with the Queen of Egypt; poetry, and emotion, too. There is poetry and fine emotion in the scene on the banks of the Loire in the play of *Saint Joan*, and in the Saint's sorrow when she sees that while the world venerates her at a safe distance, the same world wants her no nearer; here is ironical emotion, shot with sadness stretching out to the day that is with us, for, with Christians now, it is not, Get thee behind me, Satan, but Get thee behind me, God. . . . There is poetry and emotion in *Candida*; poetry of a minor key in the way the doctors regard the thoughtlessness of the artist, Dubedat, rising into a major key at the death of the artist when the play is ending; it flashes through every scene of *Heartbreak House*; and stands dignified and alone in the character of Keegan in *John Bull's*

---

* Later, O'Casey, on his own deathbed in 1964, wept to Eileen that he was leaving her nearly penniless. "You could have married a millionaire," he said, remembering what a beauty she had been when he, at forty-seven, had married her thirty-seven years earlier. "If you hurry up," said Eileen gently, "I still can."

Other Island; the poetry and emotion gleams out in the revelation that God is close to Feemy Evans, the fallen woman of the camp, though the respectable humbugs wouldn't let her finger-tip touch the bible. The English critics are afraid to feel: Eton and Harrow seem to have groomed them against the destitute dignity of tears. . . .

O'Casey had been writing his memoirs since the early 1930s, and the third, *Drums under the Windows* (for which he had designed his own jacket, with the figure on the left, looking over a toy-town Dublin, meant to be Shaw),[11] had included nearly a dozen pages on the epiphany that was his encounter with *John Bull's Other Island*. "Near naked, Ireland stood, with the one jewel of [Father] Keegan's Dream occasionally seen sparkling in her tousled hair, attaching poverty to pride; a shameful figure, but noble still, though her story was hidden and her song unsung." The spurned O'Casey could identify readily with the reputedly mad, unfrocked Keegan, in O'Casey's words "banished from the altar, hinging himself more closely to his breviary than ever, torturing himself delightfully with the vision of a country where the state is the church and the church the people; three in one and one in three; where work is play and play is life; where the priest is the worshipper, and the worshipper the worshipped; three in one and one in three; carrying the vision around with him to pour it into the loneliness of a round tower: the dream of a madman, but the dream of an Irishman, too." In the mirror in O'Casey's house he could always confront the face of Father Keegan.

19 The Avant-Garde Shaw:
Too True to Be Good and Its Predecessors

I never burlesque anything; on the contrary; it is my business to find some
order and meaning in the apparently insane farce of life as it happens higgledy-
piggledy off the stage.
                              —Bernard Shaw, Preface to *Major Barbara* (1906)

In the first years of the present century, Shaw produced one play in which—
off stage—a squealing pig is transported, with enormous difficulty, in a motor car, and another play in which the second act opens with the stage filled by a
motor car under which appear the legs of a mechanic. They may have been the
earliest theatrical uses to which the new technology had been put.

A few years after that, in the infancy of the airplane, Shaw followed *John
Bull's Other Island* and *Man and Superman* with a play about an armaments
manufacturer—Major Barbara Undershaft's father—who, only two years after
the Wright brothers flew their motorized box kite, constructs "aerial battle-
ships." Several plays later, in *Misalliance*, Shaw would write in an airplane
crash just off stage, from which emerges the theater's first woman pilot. A decade beyond, in *Back to Methuselah* (1921), Shaw amused himself if not his audience by anticipating television, and even phonevision, in a farcical scene. Yet he
never fancied himself a theatrical H. G. Wells, and indeed has long been considered a playwright of ideas who put his new wine in old, Victorian, theatrical
bottles. He even fostered the notion, telling producer John Vedrenne that the
comic music-hall turns he wrote for his characters were the jam which made the
pill (of the message) go down and telling critic William Archer that he was a
"rather old fashioned stage manager."

The motor car in *Man and Superman*, Shaw confided, had been suggested to
him by actor Robert Loraine, who was soon to become addicted to fast cars and
airplanes. If so, Shaw was nevertheless quick to adopt the radical notion. One of
the last Victorians—he died in 1950—he was also avant-garde in the uses to
which he put the stage and the techniques he foresaw which would revolutionize
the staging of plays.

The only contribution that Shaw made to the modern drama, H. L. Mencken
once scoffed, was to state the obvious in terms of the scandalous. Yet in theory
as well as in practice, Shaw was an advanced playwright often a generation

ahead of his contemporaries. As far back as 1896, for example, Shaw, commenting as a working drama critic, rather than playwright, suggested that

> any play performed on a platform amidst the audience gets closer home to its hearers than when it is presented as a picture framed by a proscenium. Also, that we are less conscious of the artificiality of the stage when a few well-understood conventions, adroitly handled, are substituted for attempts at an impossible scenic verisimilitude. All the old-fashioned tale-of-adventure plays, with their frequent changes of scene, and all the new problem plays, with their intense intimacies, should be done in this way.[1]

Today we might consider Shaw's remarks as an anticipation of theater-in-the-round techniques. And his plays, when performed on the arena stage for which he never wrote, exhibit a high level of adaptability to the "new" method. What he thought the playhouse should look like is still largely an ideal. As he wrote in 1926, the "sort of theatre" his newer plays needed was one which had to "combine" the optics and acoustics of a first-rate lecture theater and a first-rate circus.

After his first decade as a dramatist Shaw had already outgrown Ibsenite realism—something which *Don Juan in Hell* makes sufficiently obvious. Soon he was objecting that to have props and settings "as real as in your drawing room at home" was actually unconvincing: "In fact, the more scenery you have the less illusion you produce." The charm of the earlier theater, even the theater of David Garrick, he thought, was "its makebelieve. It has that charm still, not only for the amateurs, who are happiest when they are most unnatural and impossible and absurd, but for audiences as well." Anticipating the way his own *Don Juan in Hell* would be performed after his death, he observed in 1900, before *Don Juan* was even written, "I saw Browning's 'Luria' performed in the lecture theatre of University College, London, with a pair of curtains for scenery and the performers in ordinary evening dress. It produced a hundred times more illusion," he thought, than a real-scenery, open-air performance of *As You Like It* which he had just seen. "A play that cannot do better without scenery than with hired trappings is not worth . . . attention."[2]

Those of Shaw's plays written in the Neanderthal era of films even anticipated the possibilities of that medium. A Shaw critic once observed that the treatment of the stage directions in *Caesar and Cleopatra*

> anticipates the technique of the movies with uncanny accuracy. It will be remembered that the play was written in 1898. The . . . film production in which Claude Rains and Vivien Leigh appeared followed precisely the 1898 stage direction:
> *The moonlight wanes: the horizon again shows black against the sky, broken only by the fantastic silhouette of the Sphinx. The sky itself vanishes in darkness, from which there is no relief until the gleam of a distant torch falls on great Egyptian pillars supporting the roof of a majestic corridor. At the further end of the corridor a Nubian slave appears carrying a torch. Caesar, still led by Cleopatra, follows him. They come down the corridor, Caesar peering keenly about at the strange architecture and the pillar shadows, between which, as the passing torch makes them hurry noiselessly backwards, figures of men with wings and hawks' heads, and vast black marble cats, seem to flit in and out of ambush. Further along, the wall turns a corner and makes a transept in which Caesar sees, on his right, a throne, and behind the throne, a door.*[3]

In 1898, of course, this could be done only with words, for readers.

Strangely enough, much of Shaw's modernism consists of his adapting to the modern stage, and his bringing back to life, theatrical conventions which had been discarded when naturalism and realism took hold in the theater. In order to make ideas behave dramatically, for example, he wanted his characters to be able to step out of their roles now and then to become bigger than life. Thus he made use of the prenaturalistic stage convention that characters may have written into their roles an artificial amount of self-consciousness. The device not only permitted the use of the ironic wit Shaw loved but made possible a clarity of expression in dialogue unavailable to a doctrinaire realist. Thus, of his characters in *Saint Joan*, Shaw wrote that

> it is the business of the stage to make the figures more intelligible to themselves than they would be in real life; for by no other means can they be made intelligible to the audience. . . . All I claim is that by this inevitable sacrifice of verisimilitude . . . the things I represent these three exponents of drama [in *Joan*] as saying are the things they actually would have said if they had known what they were really doing.

Shaw was never, he insisted, "a representation[al]ist or realist." Rather, he said, he

> was always in the classic tradition, recognizing that stage characters must be endowed by the author with a conscious self-knowledge and power of expression, and . . . a freedom of inhibitions, which in real life would make them monsters. . . . It is the power to do this that differentiates me (or Shakespear) from a gramophone and a camera. The representational part of the business is mere costume and scenery; and I would not give tuppence for any play that could not be acted in curtains and togas as effectively as in elaborately built stage drawing rooms and first-rate modern tailoring.[4]

Shavian characterization permitted non-realistic eloquence in places in the dialogue where it becomes necessary. This was justifiable not only on the grounds of psychological validity but because of its consistency with the self-consciousness of the role. Ibsen and others modified downward the level of dramatic language, Ibsen even commenting in a letter that writing "the genuine, plain language spoken in real life" was a "very much more difficult art" than writing poetic or pseudo-poetic lines for a character to speak. "My desire," Ibsen added, "was to depict human beings, and therefore I would not make them speak the language of the gods." Realist writers who attempted to represent life as it was accepted at first the limits of normal expression. If they were concerned with surface emotions, these limitations presented no difficulty; conversational resources for the discussion of meals or money or other basic needs remained adequate. But a dramatist could not express the whole range of human experience while committed to the language of probable conversation. To overcome this limitation, Shaw employed the player whose speech had a vitality beyond what would be normal for his role, using ordinary conversational speech throughout the play but shifting into intensified rhetoric (possibly poetic prose, or even verse) at the points of crisis. The technique is psychologically valid, for at times of crisis or peaks of emotion we all reach for another and more metaphorical level of language (at its lowest, that of the formerly unprintable variety). In some of the earlier plays the rhetorical heightening is formal, as in Caesar's apostrophe to the Sphinx, or the great impassioned speeches of Don Juan and the Devil. In some later plays the technique is still traditional. Joan, for example, has a great outburst which narrowly literal critics condemn as out of keeping with Joan's earthy, peasant intellect—her passionate, biblical-cadenced renunciation of her recantation.

In some of the earlier plays there is a foreshadowing of a nonrealistic Shavian technique to come, particularly in "mad" Father Keegan's chat with the grasshopper (*John Bull's Other Island*) and the Mayoress's great speech from the depth of a trance (*Getting Married*). In the later plays there is sometimes "a sudden shift to a patterned, semi-poetic, ritualistic speech [which] indicates a passionate intensity of perception or revelation which transcends the ordinary levels of the play." We see it in the darkness at the close of the first act of *Heartbreak House*, in the operatic trio of Captain Shotover, Hector, and Hesione. We see it in the quintet of Adam, Eve, Cain, and Serpent and Lilith as they vanish one by one to end the last scene of *Back to Methuselah*. We see it in the chanting praise, and agonized rejection, of Joan in the epilogue to *Saint Joan*. We see it again in such allegorical and extravagant plays of the 1930s as *Too True to Be Good* and *The Simpleton of the Unexpected Isles*. Scenes and speeches such as these do not escape from a commitment to reality—they provide for Shaw and later dramatists who use this device opportunities for creating a reality of ideas and emotions which goes beyond a commitment to external details.

A logical step beyond is Shaw's player who is both actor and character in the same person—the self-conscious character, or actor directly aware of his audience. This was a Shavian anti-illusionary device used as early as the turn of the century in "Don Juan in Hell" yet still considered in current playwrights the epitome of modernity. Shaw had combined two of the most primitive, yet most basic, elements of the self-conscious theater in his work; the platform of the philosopher and the stage of the clown. Perhaps he was only as avant-garde as Aristophanes. "Theatre technique," Shaw observed, "begins with the circus clown and ringmaster and the Greek tribune, which is a glorified development of the pitch from which the poet of the market place declaims his verses. . . ." He might have added that Shavian theater techniques include the amusement park's distorting mirrors held up to human nature, the old-fashioned yet timeless routines of burlesque and the music hall, and the exhortations of what Shaw called "the roofless pavement orator." In post-Shavian refinements these are the techniques of *Waiting for Godot*, Ionesco's *The Chairs*, or Genet's *The Balcony* and the techniques, too, of Bertolt Brecht. By destroying stage illusion and by inhibiting the possibilities of empathic identification between audience and characters, the playwright, theoretically at least, creates a distance which forces the spectator to look at the action on stage in a detached and critical spirit: what Brecht called, years later, his "alienation effect." The playful shifting in and out of illusion enlivens not only the later works, however. We see it in the earlier comedies as well, as when the amoral artist Louis Dubedat in *The Doctor's Dilemma* confides that he is a disciple of Bernard Shaw or when the critics who attend the premiere of *Fanny's First Play* (a play within the frame of the critics' dialogue) declare that while the play is too good to really be by Fanny O'Dowda, one had to eliminate Shaw from the possibilities. "I've repeatedly proved that Shaw is physiologically incapable of the note of passion," says one. The others also eliminate Shaw:

> VAUGHAN. Well, at all events, you cant deny that the characters in this play are quite distinguishable from one another. That proves it's not by Shaw, because all Shaw's characters are himself: mere puppets stuck up to spout Shaw. It's only the actors that make them seem different.
> BANNAL. There can be no doubt of that: everybody knows it. But Shaw doesnt

> write his plays as plays. All he wants to do is to insult everybody all round and set us talking about him.
> TROTTER [*wearily*] And naturally, here we are all talking about him. For heaven's sake, let us change the subject.

The audience, then, is given little opportunity to absorb itself imaginatively into the play, for the playwright jests directly with his audience. Again, Shaw in *Misalliance*, realizing that his audience knows very well indeed that he is the author of *Man and Superman*, has his book-mad character John Tarleton, who is constantly advising people to read this and that, observe:

> Still, you know, the superman may come. The superman's an idea. I believe in ideas. Read Whatshisname.

No one in a Shaw audience could possibly mistake the reference, and each one is thus taken out of the play and into the playwright's confidence. Similarly, when Private Meek in *Too True to Be Good* turns out to be messenger, translator, intelligence officer, and almost every other military specialist wrapped up in one, we find this out through cross-talk reminiscent of traditional music-hall sketches, and the absurdity reinforces the nonrealism while making the obvious point that the system and the setting are equally absurd. It does not surprise us that the sergeant is a disciple of John Bunyan, only that the zany Private Meek is not another self-confessed disciple of Bernard Shaw.

"To call Shaw's plays forerunners of the theatre of the absurd," says one of the better Shaw critics, "would be indeed farfetched."[5] Yet eighteen pages later the critic writes, quite accurately, "In *Too True to Be Good*, more than in any of his other plays, Shaw dramatizes the absurdity of the human condition." Among the numerous irrational and absurd speeches and happenings pointed to is that of the Doctor and the Microbe, with the latter insisting that he did not give the Patient measles but rather that she gave it to him; the following lines are quoted:

> THE DOCTOR. The microbe of measles has never been discovered. If there is a microbe it cannot be measles: it must be parameasles.
> THE MONSTER. Great Heavens! what are parameasles?
> THE DOCTOR. Something so like measles that nobody can see any difference.

"Irrational dialogue," says the critic, forgetting his earlier words, "suggests an irrational universe," and he observes in a footnote that "This particular dialogue, anticipating dialogue in absurdist plays, differs little from the lecture on Spanish and neo-Spanish in Ionesco's *The Lesson*." Yet a much earlier play, a one-act farce produced in July 1905, *Passion, Poison and Petrifaction*, anticipates Ionesco's *The Bald Soprano* (with its "English clock" striking "seventeen English strokes") by nearly half a century. It begins with the bedroom clock striking sixteen:

> THE LADY. How much did the clock strike, Phyllis?
> PHYLLIS. Sixteen, my lady.
> THE LADY. That means eleven o'clock, does it not?
> PHYLLIS. Eleven at night, my lady. In the morning it means half-past two; so if you hear it strike sixteen during your slumbers, do not rise.

In this play, as in others by Shaw, it is not that the stage is all the world but rather that all the world is the stage:

PHYLLIS. Will your ladyship not undress?

THE LADY. Not tonight, Phyllis. [*Glancing through where the fourth wall is missing*] Not under the circumstances.

Later someone is poisoned, and an antidote is suggested "if an antidote would not be too much of anticlimax." Adolphus, the victim, declares, "Anticlimax be blowed! Do you think I am going to die to please the critics? Out with your antidote. Quick!" And Adolphus then eats the plaster ceiling for the lime in it.

Shaw, who in the subtitle calls this farce a "tragedy," is thinking along the lines of the later Ionesco, who spoke of "the tragedy of language." Throughout the play the dialogue is no more real than the action, for the dialogue communicates the absurdity of the society Shaw shows in his distorting mirror. There is a thunderstorm, and maid and mistress anticipate the worst:

LADY MAGNESIA. In case we should never again meet in this world, let us take a last farewell.

PHYLLIS [*embracing her with tears*] My poor murdered angel mistress!

LADY MAGNESIA. In case we should meet again, call me at half-past eleven.

It is difficult to keep in mind that this was written in 1905, in the comfortable years of Edward VII. But Shaw's sense of the absurd would keep surfacing until it became the dominant mood of his plays in the 1930s, where the duologues in one of his playlets of the period, *Village Wooing*, are between "A" and "Z" and where the conversation has the most vitality it anticipates the playwrights of a later generation in using clichés in cross-talk as an assault on human reason.

Z. Excuse me. Could you tell me the time?

A. [*curtly*] Eleven.

Z. My watch makes it half past ten.

A. The clocks were put on half an hour last night. We are going east.

Z. I always think it adds to the interest of a voyage having to put on your watch.

A. I am glad you are so easily interested [*he resumes his writing pointedly*].

Z. I never cared much for geography. Where are we now?

A. We are on the Red Sea.

Z. But it's blue.

A. What did you expect it to be?

Z. Well, I didnt know what color the sea might be in these parts. I always thought the Red Sea would be red.

A. Well, it isnt.

Z. And isnt the Black Sea black?

A. It is precisely the color of the sea at Margate.

Z. [*eagerly*] Oh, I am so glad you know Margate. Theres no place like it in the season, is there?

A. I dont know: I have never been there.

Z. [*disappointed*] Oh, you ought to go. You could write a book about it.

A. [*shudders, sighs, and pretends to write very hard!*]

[*A pause.*]

Z. I wonder why they call it the Red Sea.

A. Because their fathers did. Why do you call America America?

Z. Well, because it is America. What else would you call it?

When Noel Coward would write such uncommunicative absurdities in *Private Lives*, it would be considered ultrasmart; when Pinter would put together such talk in *The Caretaker* and other plays in the postwar theater, critics would talk of his breaking new ground. But *Village Wooing* was the play Shaw wrote after *Too True to Be Good*, in the very early 1930s.

As an aside, it is worth mentioning another anticipation of midcentury playwrights, this one from *Heartbreak House*:

> RANDALL. Really, Hushabye, I think a man may be allowed to be a gentleman without being accused of posing.
> HECTOR. It is a pose like any other. In this house we know all the poses: our game is to find out the man under the pose. . . .
> RANDALL. Some of the games in this house are damned annoying, let me tell you.
> HECTOR. Yes, I've been their victim for years. I used to writhe under them at first, but I became accustomed to them. At least I learned to play them.
> RANDALL. If it's all the same to you, I'd rather you didn't play them on me. . . .

More than a generation later, Edward Albee would pick this up in having his characters talk about game playing in *Who's Afraid of Virginia Woolf?*, and Pinter and Osborne in England would do much the same thing.

Even the ancient world was a stage for Shaw, who begins *Caesar and Cleopatra* with an old-fashioned, prenaturalistic prologue. Spoken by the Egyptian god Ra, it is a lecture which makes the audience well aware that it *is* an audience and that the play is a play:

> (. . . *He surveys the modern audience with great contempt; and finally speaks the following words to them.*) Peace! Be silent and hearken to me, ye quaint little islanders. . . . I ask you not for worship but for silence. Let not your men speak, or your women cough; for I am come to draw you back over the graves of sixty generations. . . . Are ye impatient with me? Do you crave for a story of an unchaste woman? Hath the name of Cleopatra tempted ye hither? . . .

In similar spirit, after the improbable incidents of the first act of Shaw's *Too True to Be Good*, the act ends with the announcement by one of the cast: "The play is now virtually over; but the characters will discuss it at great length for two acts more. The exit doors are all in order. Goodnight." The play ends with the impassioned but interminable oration of a young man which goes on while the other characters exit, leaving him to preach in solitude; at last he is enveloped in fog and darkness. In the opening words of Shaw's last stage direction, *The audience disperses. . . .*" It has become part of the play. We will return to this scene.

After his first few plays satisfied his commitment to Ibsen, Shaw was always

> ready to stop the overt action for a good discussion or good lecture, or even step out of the proscenium frame to harangue the audience in behalf of a relevant philosophy or sociology which is beyond, if not indeed antithetical to, the illusion achieved by plodding realists and the designers who provide scenic realism.

Since the 1890s this had been Shaw's principle as well as his practice. His early plays as well as the concluding chapters of *The Quintessence of Ibsenism* show that he rapidly outgrew the confines of realism, and if Shaw's later plays belong at all

> to the genre of realism it is by virtue of their engagement to reality, chiefly by comprising a conflict of ideas, principles, ways of thinking, and ways of living. For the sake of reality, Shaw was always prepared to violate realistic structure and verisimilitude, to turn somersaults of the most farcical or fantastic kind, and to be arbitrary with his plot or discard plot altogether.[6]

A playwright who often directed and cast his own plays, Shaw was as much interested in the problems of staging as he was in the intellectual and emotional climate he was writing into his plays. Because they became for him aspects of the same problem, he experimented not only with new theoretical wine in famil- iar bottles, and finely aged wine in new and unfamiliar bottles, but with the indivisibility of technique and theme. The result was often a play which by or- thodox, contemporary standards only baffled orthodox contemporary critics. Max Beerbohm in 1903 was convinced that *Man and Superman*, particularly the "Don Juan in Hell" interlude, was a "peculiar article" and "of course, not a play at all." Paradoxically, Max added, "It is 'as good as a play'—infinitely bet- ter, to my peculiar taste, than any play I have ever read or seen enacted. But a play it is not."[7] Within two years Max had recanted, admitting that the failure had been his own—his own narrowness of theatrical imagination.

Sometimes the complaints about Shaw's playcrafting were really expressions of frustration at not finding a conventional plot and predictable characters moving within it. When Shaw was ninety-four he observed that this was an old story:

> Now it is quite true that my plays are all talk, just as Raphael's pictures are all paint, Michael Angelo's statues all marble, Beethoven's symphonies all noise.[8]

In 1908, when a fictitious interviewer from the *Daily Telegraph* had prodded G.B.S. for "some notion of the plot" of *Getting Married*, which proved to be one of Shaw's most talky dramas, the author, with jesting truthfulness, responded:

> MR. SHAW: The play has no plot. Surely nobody expects a play by me to have a plot. I am a dramatic poet, not a plot-monger.
> INTERVIEWER: But at least there is a story.
> MR. SHAW. Not at all. If you look at any of the old editions of our classical plays, you will see that the description of the play is not called a plot or story but an argument—an argument lasting three hours, and carried on with unflagging cerebration by twelve people and a beadle.[9]

Unprepared by conventional drama for this genre of theater, a later critic wrote of *The Apple Cart*:

> Here is the final exaggeration of all of Shaw's tendencies as a dramatist. Action has totally disappeared and all the characters sit on chairs, hour in and hour out. And in the place of human emotion is the brain of Shaw, bulging larger and larger, filling the stage, hard and brilliant, glittering like a jewel.[10]

The cerebral fantasies and dramatic debates—Shavian plays of passionate ideas—were to come to life in a variety of symbolic or naturalistic settings. When Shaw's plays after World War I were inaugurated by *Heartbreak House*, one unsung Shaw commentator noted that Shaw's "was a grave message: it would issue gravely if it were not for the instinct for absurdity which has never deserted him." But it caused his public, unready for this approach to drama, to desert him when *Heartbreak House* was first staged in 1920. It played to nearly empty houses, and even a return look arranged for the London reviewers failed to convince any of them that they had been wrong the first time. After sixty- three performances it had to close. No one could make head or tail of it, Shaw explained. "The house is not Heartbreak House at first: the fly walks into the parlour with the happiest anticipations, and is kept amused until it gets fixed there as by a spell. Then the heartbreak begins, and gets worse until the house breaks out through the windows, and becomes all England with all England's heart broken. In vain do the tortured spectators beg for the house without the heartbreak, or to be at least allowed to go home. They are held ruthlessly on the rack until the limit of human endurance is reached after three hours of torment. . . .'' In description Shaw made the play sound more like *The Ghost Sonata* of Strindberg than a play by G.B.S.—but what he had written was a play of a nature almost unique to himself at the time: "serious farce," almost a contradiction in terms.* Like some of the later plays of Strindberg, it had the disconnected quality of a dream.

It is just possible, in fact, that the play is largely the dream of Ellie Dunn, who falls asleep in the Hushabye (Heartbreak) House before the play is two pages old. Similarly, a later Shavian play in which the *Heartbreak House* techniques and themes are extended, *Too True to Be Good*, may also be largely the dream fantasy of a woman, ill and delirious, who fantasizes her recovery and escape from her sickbed. Shaw doesn't even make a distinction between sleeping and waking consciousness; the Patient insists in Act III as she had in Act I that what happens is contained in her dream. If she belongs to both fantasy and reality, however, do the other characters also?

A number of twentieth-century critics have pointed out that although medieval and renaissance drama sometimes used the device of a dream, it is only modern drama that uses dream structure and dream imagery significantly. Here again Shaw's contribution is significant. One of the earliest twentieth-century plays to combine both approaches was Shaw's *Man and Superman*, which combines what is apparently a conventional play with a dream vision in which grand, representative figures of myth parallel characters in the play. Martin Esslin, in *The Theatre of the Absurd*, suggests that "the first to put on the stage a dream world in the spirit of modern psychological thinking was August Strindberg. The three parts of *To Damascus* (1898-1904), *A Dream Play* (1902), and *The Ghost Sonata* (1907) are masterly transcriptions of dreams and obsessions, and direct sources of the theatre of the Absurd.'' Strindberg himself wrote of his aims in his introductory note to *A Dream Play*.

> In this dream play. . . the author has sought to reproduce the disconnected but apparently logical form of a dream. Anything can happen; everything is possible and probable. Time and space do not exist. On a slight groundwork of reality, imagination spins and weaves new patterns made up of memories, experiences, unfettered fancies, absurdities, and improvisations. The characters are split, double and multiply; they evaporate, crystallize, scatter and converge. But a single consciousness holds sway over them all—that of the dreamer. . . .

Concurrently, and differently, Shaw was using the concept of the dream vision, uninfluenced by Strindberg. The concepts with which they were working were part of the then-current intellectual climate, and each, according to his nature, had put these ideas into his playwriting. Shaw, in the "Don Juan in Hell" episode in *Man and Superman*, had projected into his art a momentary vision of bodiless intelligences who manifest themselves by willing ghostly forms and engage in a Shavio-Mozartian quartet without time, space, or dimen-

---

*A curious anticipation of the term occurs in Shaw's draft press release for the first production of *The Doctor's Dilemma* in 1907. The play "will probably be called a *farce macabre*," he prophesied, adding, "The death scene is an unprecedented mixture of fanciful poetry and pathos with ludicrous realism and biting irony." (Berg Collection, New York Public Library)

sion. Here is Shaw's own description of his aims, from the program notes for the 1907 production at the Royal Court Theatre:

> The scene, an abysmal void, represents hell; and the persons of the drama speak of hell, heaven and earth as if they were separate localities, like "the heavens above, the earth beneath, and the waters under the earth." It must be remembered that such localizations are purely figurative, like our fashion of calling a treble voice "high" and a bass voice "low." Modern theology conceives heaven and hell, not as places, but as states of the soul; and by the soul it means, not an organ like the liver, but the divine element common to all life, which causes us "to do the will of God" in addition to looking after our individual interests, and to honor one another solely for our divine activities and not at all for our selfish activities.
>
> Hell is popularly conceived not only as a place, but as a place of cruelty and punishment, and heaven as a paradise of idle pleasure. These legends are discarded by the higher theology, which holds that this world, or any other, may be made a hell by a society in a state of damnation: that is, a society so lacking in the higher orders of energy that it is given wholly to the pursuit of immediate individual pleasure, and cannot even conceive the passion of the divine will. Also that any world can be made a heaven by a society of persons in whom that passion is the master passion—a "communion of saints" in fact.
>
> In the scene presented to-day hell is this state of damnation. . . .

Continuing to use elements of dream and of myth, Shaw often combined the two, as in *Androcles and the Lion, Pygmalion, Back to Methuselah,* and *Saint Joan.* One critic remarked that Shaw

> would have furiously protested against our ascribing to him any such notion as that life is a dream. But when we look at some of his finest works this is what they say. Take such a masterpiece as *Pygmalion,* for example. Here we have the complete transformation of a vulgar, dirty and illiterate girl into a dazzling lady, brought about by cleansing her, dressing her, and altering her diction. The play is incidentally a Cinderella story.[11]

The critic might have added that Shaw, in a realistic setting, had utilized the myths of both Pygmalion and Cinderella and, as dreams do, inverted elements of them. *Saint Joan,* too, uses a figure about which an entire mythos has grown up. Shaw presents her story as a realistic chronicle and then concludes with a dream fantasy apparently no less real than the earlier reality yet one which wrenches the audience, moved by Joan's death, back into a more objective frame of mind, its humor leaving the audience nonetheless "guilty creatures sitting at a play." An alert audience, watching the epilogue, would realize that the appearance of the clerical gentleman from the Vatican, in 1920 costume, breaks the illusion of the dream, just as when the "Dream in Hell" interlude in *Man and Superman* closes, we have the following lines in the transitional scene:

MENDOZA: Did you dream?
TANNER: Damnably. Did you?
MENDOZA: Yes. I forget what. You were in it.
TANNER: So were you. Amazing.

Shattering illusions, even the stage illusion of the dream, was always basic to Shaw's techniques, as it was to his themes. But one final illusion remains to be shattered—the very absurdity of the conclusion of *Too True to Be Good,* in which Aubrey Bagot, the burglar turned preacher, exhorts the audience in a speech of conspicuous absurdity as (in Shaw's stage directions) the lights go on in the auditorium, the audience begins to disperse, and the curtain goes down on the still-preaching protagonist. Shaw wrote to the producer, H. K. Ayliff, while the play was in rehearsal, to confide that he was both theatrically stupid and inconsiderate to the actor to leave the speech at the curtain incomplete and depend upon a backstage technician to drop it at the right instant. Since any delay whatever would ruin the effect, Shaw promised to send Cedric Hardwicke, the Aubrey Bagot of the production, a peroration which could close the play even if the curtain failed utterly to descend. Then, to Hardwicke, he offered

> apologies for the indelicacy of leaving you with an uncompleted thought, and the blunder of placing you at the mercy of the curtain dropper, who is always late. I enclose a complete peroration which will see you through even if the stage hands do a lightning strike and the curtain does not come down at all. If and when it does fall, go on at full pitch for a word or so after it touches the ground. Then turn your back to it and walk up stage and off through the centre opening, preaching away *fortissimo* all the time to the end. They will hear you in front *after the fall of the curtain*—which is essential—and hear your voice away into silence quite naturally. I have attached a typed copy which will fit into your book. Paste it in. . . .[12]

Shaw did not tell Hardwicke (who was to speak the lines), as he told Ayliff,[13] that the words, although indistinct to the audience, should give the impression of meaning something. They didn't, he confessed, but they would serve their purpose.

The eloquent final lines, then, were the ultimate absurdity. If Aubrey Bagot's reactions were to a world he conceived as absurd, Shaw had, for the wrong reasons, kept him in character to the end. Yet the very absurdity of the finale was itself absurd. The lines were written only to gain time to get the curtain down.

Notes

3   The Novelist in Spite of Himself

[1]Shaw to Arnold White, October 5, 1879, in Dan H. Laurence, ed., *Bernard Shaw: Collected Letters* (London, 1965) I, 23. Further letters will be referred to as *CL*.

[2]Quoted in Charles Morgan, *The House of Macmillan* (London: Macmillan, 1943), pp. 119–20.

[3]Shaw to Macmillan & Co., February 1, 1880. In *CL*, I, 27.

[4]Shaw to Richard Bentley & Son, February 18, 1882. In *CL*, I, 48.

[5]Shaw to Kegan Paul, Trench & Co., December 18, 1883. In *CL*, I, 78.

[6]Letter to Maurice Holmes in *Some Bibliographic Notes on the Novels of George Bernard Shaw* (London, 1929), pp. 5–6.

[7]Quoted in May Morris, *William Morris* (Oxford, 1936), II, 244.

[8]Ibid., 244n.

[9]Quoted in F.E. Loewenstein, *The History of a Famous Novel* (London, 1946), pp. 14–15.

[10]Fanny Stevenson, letter to Mrs. William Archer, February 1888, in C. Archer, *William Archer, Life, Work, and Friendships* (New Haven, Conn., 1931), pp. 146–47.

[11]R. L. Stevenson, letter to William Archer, February 1888. In *Letters of Robert Louis Stevenson*, Sydney Colvin, ed. (New York, 1921), III, 51.

[12]Shaw, "My Mother and Her Relatives," in *Sixteen Self Sketches* (London, 1949), p. 16.

[13]Doris Langley Moore, *E. Nesbit. A Biography* (Philadelphia, 1966), p. 84.

[14]St. John Ervine, *Bernard Shaw, His Life, Work and Friends* (London, 1956), pp. 155–156.

4   G.B.S., Pugilist and Playwright

[1]Letter to Frank Harris, March 10, 1919, in S. Weintraub, ed., *Bernard Shaw and Frank Harris: A Correspondence, 1895–1930* (University Park: Penn State Press, 1982).

[2]The verses to Paquito are in the Humanities Research Center, University of Texas at Austin.

[3]Preface (1901) to a reprint of *Cashel Byron's Profession*.

[4]"Note on Modern Prizefighting," appendix to the 1901 reprint of *Cashel Byron*.

[5]References to Shaw's shorthand diary of 1885–1879 at the LSE (London School of Economics) are from the Stanley Rypins translation.

[6]"Note on Modern Prizefighting."

[7]Shaw's correspondence with Tunney, and the stage history of *Cashel Byron*, are amusingly related in Benny Green's *Shaw's Companions. G.B.S. and Prizefighting from Cashel Byron to Gene Tunney* (London, 1978); however, Green was unaware of Shaw's boxing verses (in manuscript at the University of Texas), Shaw's involvement in the 1883 competition, his use of boxing in his later plays, and his 1929 appearance at Holborn.

[8]*CL*, I, 560 (September 17, 1895).

[9]Quoted in Bernard F. Dukore's introduction to his *Collected Screenplays of Bernard Shaw* (Athens: University of Georgia Press, 1980), p. 23.

[10]*Major Barbara* screenplay, in Dukore, op. cit., p. 308.

5   Bernard Shaw, Actor

[1]Preface to *The Irrational Knot* (New York, 1905), p. xxv.

[2]Shaw to Mary Grace Walker (Mrs. Emery Walker) January 23, 1885. In *CL*, I, 114–15.

[3]Shaw's shorthand diaries of the period are at the LSE. The Englishing is by the late Stanley Rypins.

[4]"Ibsen in England," *Dramatic Review*, April 4, 1885; review of the March 28, 1885, production of *Nora* at the School of Dramatic Art.

[5]Eleanor Marx to Shaw, June 2, 1885. Quoted in Chuschichi Tsuzuki, *The Life of Eleanor Marx* (Oxford, 1967), p. 165.

[6]May Morris would marry Sparling, her father's assistant, after giving up hope that Shaw would propose. The marriage was not a success, at least partly because at May's invitation, Shaw, recuperating from an illness, moved in with the newlyweds to convalesce. There was a divorce, but Shaw remained unmarried until captured by Charlotte Payne-Townshend in 1898.

[7]Shaw describes the production in "William Morris as Actor and Dramatist," *Saturday Review*, October 10, 1896. Reprinted in *Our Theatres in the Nineties*, II.

[8]A copy of the playbill survives at the Humanities Research Center, University of Texas at Austin. For "Garrick," see British Library Shaw archive, vol. 50, 701.

[9]Shaw to Ellen Terry, July 5, 1896. In *CL*, I, 634–35.

[10]"G.B.S. at Rehearsal," in Mander and Mitchenson's *Theatrical Companion to Shaw*, (London: Rockliff, 1955), p. 17.

[11]Item 395, ascribed to April 20, 1932, in Catalogue Number Six, *Literary Autographs: Letters and Manuscripts* (Maurice F. Neville Rare Books, Santa Barbara, Calif.).

6 Exploiting Art: Shaw in the Picture Galleries and the Picture Galleries in Shaw's Plays

[1]*Collected Letters, 1874–1897*, Dan H. Laurence, ed. (London, 1965), I, 145–47 (Shaw to Archer, December 12, 1885, and December 14, 1885). Unless otherwise indicated, all letters are quoted from this volume or its companion, *Collected Letters, 1898–1910* (London, 1972).

[2]*World*, July 6, 1892. Reprinted in *Music in London*, II.

[3]*Everybody's Political What's What?* (London, 1944), 179–80.

[4]"Art Corner," *Our Corner*, May 1886, p. 310. (Where not otherwise noted, quotations from Shaw's art criticism are from his "In the Picture-Galleries" columns in the *World*.)

[5]Barnard, known to his contemporaries as "the Charles Dickens among black-and-white artists," did many of the illustrations in the (London) Household Edition of Dickens, including *A Tale of Two Cities*. He also published three sets of six-lithograph depictions of Dickensian characters as "Character Sketches from Dickens," each afterward issued as a 20 by 14½-inch one-guinea photogravure. The first set (1879) included a Sydney Carton.

[6]Shaw to Ian Robertson, c. May 23, 1900. In *CL*, II, 167.

[7]British Library Ms. 50603.

[8]Shaw to Ellen Terry, April 6, 1896; Shaw to Janet Achurch, March 20, 1895. In *CL*, I.

[9]Shaw to Ashley Dukes, April 6, 1927. ALS, Burgunder Collection, Cornell University Library.

[10]Shaw to Ellen Terry, August 8, 1899. In *CL*, II. Sargent had painted a portrait of Ellen Terry as Lady Macbeth in 1888.

[11]Shaw in the *Daily Chronicle* (London), March 5, 1917. Reprinted as "Joy Riding at the Front," in *What I Wrote About the War* (London, 1931), p. 255.

[12]Shaw to Siegfried Trebitsch, August 16, 1903. In *CL*, II, 345.

[13]Martin Meisel, "Cleopatra and 'The Flight into Egypt,'" *Shaw Review* (1964), 62–63.

[14]George W. Whiting, "The Cleopatra Rug Scene: Another Source," *Shaw Review* (1960), 15–17.

[15]Thomas Rice Holmes, *Caesar's Conquest of Gaul* (London: Macmillan, 1903), p. xxvi.

[16]Shaw derived his characterization of Burgoyne from De Fonblanque's biography of 1876.

[17]Shaw to Reginald Golding Bright, November 2, 1900. In E. J. West, ed., *Advice to a Young Critic and Other Letters* (New York, 1955). The book was the Grant Richards edition of 1901.

[18]Manuscript pages in the Humanities Research Center, University of Texas. Quoted in *Shaw: An Exhibition*, by Dan H. Laurence (Austin, 1977), as catalogue item 280.

[19]"Mr. Shaw's Roderick Hudson," *Saturday Review*, November 24, 1906.

[20]Preface to *Immaturity* (London, 1930).

[21]Preface to *Saint Joan*.

[22]Shaw to Mrs. Campbell, September 8, 1931. In Alan Dent, ed., *Bernard Shaw and Mrs Patrick Campbell: Their Correspondence* (New York, 1952).

[23]Preface to *Saint Joan*.

[24]*Daily Chronicle*, March 5, 1917.

[25]Shaw may also have known painter William Hilton's *The Citizens of Calais Delivering Their Keys to King Edward III* (1810), an early-nineteenth-century favorite.

[26]Shaw, "How Shaw and Russell Met," *Pearson's Magazine*, July 1921.

[27]Shaw, "Chestertonism and the War," *New Statesman*, January 23, 1915.

[28]Shaw to T. T. Crowe, London, December 9, 1920. Quoted in the Paul C. Richards catalog 121 (1979) as item 46.

[29]*Letters to Molly Tompkins*, Peter Tompkins, ed. (New York, 1960), p. 140.

[30]Shaw to G. S. Sandilands, London, May 4, 1932. Reproduced in facsimile in Paul Richards catalog 121 (1979) as item 57.

[31]F. R. Rattray, *Bernard Shaw: A Chronicle* (London, 1951), p. 283.

[32]"Rodin," *Nation*, November 9, 1912. Reprinted in *Pen Portraits and Reviews* (London, 1931), pp. 226–31.

[33]*Table Talk of George Bernard Shaw*, Archibald Henderson, ed. (London, 1925), pp. 90–91.

[34]Quoted from Epstein in Richard Buckle, *Jacob Epstein, Sculptor* (London, 1963), p. 210.

[35]Shaw, preface to the catalogue of the exhibition of Sigismond de Strobl's sculptures (London, 1935).

[36]Letter to Epstein, quoted in Buckle, op. cit., p. 211.

[37]Shaw to Curtis Freshel, tls, November 27, 1936, Southern Historical Collection at the University of North Carolina Library, Chapel Hill, North Carolina.

[38]Michael Holroyd, *Augustus John* (New York and London, 1975), p. 436.

[39]Harold Nicolson, diary entry for December 11, 1950. In *Harold Nicolson: Diaries and Letters: The Later Years*, Nigel Nicolson, ed. (New York and London, 1968).

7   G.B.S. Borrows from Sarah Grand: *The Heavenly Twins* and *You Never Can Tell*

[1]All quotations from the novel are from the first edition, 3 vols., London, 1893.

[2]British Library Add. Ms. 50603B, folio 15.

[3]Whistler recalled once meeting Sarah Grand at a dinner party after she had returned from some weeks in France—where Madame Grand started the evening by complaining that Frenchmen could never forget that women are women. She liked to meet men as comrades—without their constant awareness of her sex. Whistler's comment—he reported—was, "Certainly the Englishwoman succeeds, as no others can, in obliging men to forget their sex" (*Whistler Journal* [Philadelphia, 1921], pp. 190–91). Shaw's Mrs. Clandon of *You Never Can Tell* dresses in "as businesslike a

way as she can without making a guy of herself, ruling out all attempt at sex attraction and imposing respect on frivolous mankind and fashionable womankind" (679).

[4]Bernard Shaw, *Collected Letters 1874-1897*, Dan H. Laurence, ed. (New York, 1965), p. 461.

[5]Bernard Shaw, *Our Theatres in the Nineties*, 3 vols. (London, 1932), I, 20–21.

[6]*Our Theatres*, I, 108.

[7]*Our Theatres*, II, 170.

[8]*Our Theatres*, III, 49–50.

[9]British Library Add. Ms. 50605A (December 1895).

[10]Bernard Shaw, *You Never Can Tell* (1897); text from the *Bodley Head Bernard Shaw*, I, 675 (London, 1970). Further quotations are from this edition.

[11]R. F. Rattray, *Bernard Shaw: A Chronicle* (New York, 1951), p. 115.

8 Shaw's Lady Cicely and Mary Kingsley

[1]Bernard Shaw, *Captain Brassbound's Conversion*. All quotations from preface, play, appendix, and program notes are from the *Bodley Head Bernard Shaw*, II (London, 1971).

[2]Hesketh Pearson, *Bernard Shaw* (New York, 1963), p. 211.

[3]Roland Duerksen, "Shelleyan Witchcraft: The Unbinding of Brassbound," *Shaw Review*, XV (1972), 21–25.

[4]Mary Kingsley, *Travels in West Africa* (London, 1897). All quotations from Miss Kingsley are from this edition.

[5]Christopher St John, ed., *Ellen Terry and Bernard Shaw: A Correspondence* (New York, 1932), p. 245 (August 3, 1899); 241 (July 12, 1899).

[6]Dan H. Laurence, ed., *Collected Letters of Bernard Shaw* (London, 1972), II, 98-99. Privately too, Shaw later repeated his Mary Kingsley reference to William Archer (February 18, 1901, *Collected Letters*, II, 218).

[7]Olwen Campbell, *Mary Kingsley* (London, 1957), p. 15.

[8]*Bodley Head Bernard Shaw*, II.

[9]Campbell, op. cit., p. 179.

[10]Campbell, op. cit., pp. 179–80.

9 Shaw's Mommsenite Caesar

[1]Program of performance, special matinee, March 15, 1889, Theatre Royal, Newcastle-on-Tyne, with notes by Shaw. Reprinted by Archibald Henderson, *George Bernard Shaw: Man of the Century* (New York: Appleton-Century-Crofts, 1956), p. 555.

[2]Theodor Mommsen, *The History of Rome*, tr. William Purdie Dickson, 5 vols. (New York, 1903); edition hereinafter cited.

[3]Emery Neff, *The Poetry of History* (New York, 1947), pp. 192–93.

[4]Quoted by Neff, op. cit., p. 193.

[5]Eric Bentley, *Bernard Shaw* (London, 1950), p. 135.

[6]Quoted by Neff, op. cit., p. 193.

[7]Bernard Shaw, letter to Hesketh Pearson, 1918. Quoted by Pearson in *G.B.S.: A Full Length Portrait* (New York, 1942), p. 187.

[8]Quoted by Gordon W. Couchman in "Here Was a Caesar: Shaw's Comedy Today," *PMLA* LXXII (March 1957), 274.

[9]Ibid.

[10]Bernard Shaw, Notes to *Caesar and Cleopatra* in *Bodley Head Shaw*, II.

[11]Bernard Shaw, Preface to *Three Plays for Puritans* in *Bodley Head Shaw*, II.

[12]Bernard Shaw, "Tappertit on Caesar," *Saturday Review* (London), January 29, 1898. Reprinted in *Our Theatres in the Nineties* (London, 1932), III, 298.

[13]*Our Theatres in the Nineties*, III, 298–99.

[14]The unfrocked priest in *John Bull's Other Island*.

[15]Quoted by St. John Ervine in *Bernard Shaw: His Life, Work and Friends* (London, 1956), p. 334.

[16]Ibid.

[17]John Mason Brown, "Seeing Things: Hail Caesar—and Cleopatra," *Saturday Review of Literature*, January 4, 1950, pp. 26–27.

[18]Couchman op. cit., p. 278.

[19]Brown, op. cit., p. 26.

[20]*Lives*, tr. Bernadotte Perrin (Loeb Classical Library, 11 vols.: Cambridge, Mass., 1919), VII, 561.

[21]Shaw, for example, probably took from Plutarch the episode in which Cleopatra is brought to Caesar in a rug. He found no mention of it (but no rejection of it, either) in Mommsen and apparently liked it well enough to adopt it.

[22]Couchman, op. cit., p. 275.

[23]Quoted from "Bernard Shaw and the Heroic Actor" by Archibald Henderson in *Bernard Shaw, Playboy and Prophet* (New York, 1932), p. 193.

[24]Ibid., p. 494.

[25]Julius Bab, *Bernard Shaw* (Berlin, 1926), p. 217.

[26]H. W. Massingham, "Mr. Shaw's Caesar," *Nation* (London), April 19, 1913.

[27]Eric Bentley, *A Century of Hero-Worship* (Philadelphia, 1944), p. 190.

[28]A reviewer of a modern abridgement of *The History of Rome* has commented (*TLS*, May 8, 1959, p. 275): "It is time that we admitted, quite openly, how pernicious a book in many ways the *History of Rome* is. Here Mommsen was the victim of his nationality, class and age, and fell headlong into all the traps he managed to avoid in more specialized work. His present editors are uneasily aware of this. . . . They are vaguely apologetic over the old Prussian's obsessional Caesar-worship, his disgusting cant about the heroic agent of destiny and Necessity's iron laws, his Junker's loathing for the civilian Cicero, his belief in a Roman 'democratic' party along modern lines.

"Still . . . there is a sweep and vigour and narrative power about Mommsen's work that are sadly to seek in many modern historians."

10   The Social Critic as Literary Critic

[1]In his Collected Edition, the volume *Pen Portraits and Reviews* included reprints of some of his literary essays, but—as the title indicates—it put more emphasis upon memoir pieces than literary ones.

[2]Eleven years later Shaw had more to say about Browning's poem, in a review of Max Nordau's book *Degeneration* which he wrote for the American magazine *Liberty* and afterward expanded into *The Sanity of Art:*

> Passion is the steam in the engine of all religious and moral systems. In so far as it is malevolent, the religious are malevolent too, and insist on human sacrifices, on hell, wrath, and vengeance. You cannot read Browning's Caliban upon Setebos (Natural Theology in The Island) without admitting that all our religions have been made as Caliban made his, and that the difference between Caliban and Prospero is not that Prospero had killed passion in himself whilst Caliban has yielded to it, but that Prospero is mastered by holier passions than Caliban's. Abstract principles of conduct break down in practice because kindness and truth and justice are not duties founded on abstract principles external to man, but human passions, which have, in their time, conflicted with higher passions as well as with lower ones.

[3]The longhand draft of the unfinished article is British Library Add. Ms. 50693, folios 201–222.

[4]Ironically, it was George Moore who was the chief enemy of the Mudie and Smith censorship, prefacing a Zola translation with the declaration, "We judge a pudding by the eating, and I judge Messrs. Mudie and Smith by what they have produced; for they. . . are the authors of our fiction." In an 1885 pamphlet, *Literature at Nurse, or Circulating Morals*, Moore had censured Mudie for hypocrisy, quoting at length from novels he had passed, and urged the public to withdraw its patronage from libraries which failed to furnish the books it wanted. Eventually cheap editions, including Moore's, rather than polemics, defeated the library censorship.

[5]Mary Louise de la Ramée (1839–1908).

[6]Joyce had written to his prospective publisher of *Dubliners* that the book, written with "scrupulous meanness," was intended as a "chapter of the moral history of my country" and a "first step toward the spiritual liberation of my country."

[7]Reports survive of two other literary lectures during that decade: one on drama at Oxford just before the war, and the other on fiction to a Fabian summer school session during the war.

[8]Noddy Boffin, the dustman who inherits a fortune from the miserly dust-removal contractor Harmon and is immediately beset by selfish merchants, begging relatives, and rapacious charities, is a clear precursor of Shaw's Alfred Doolittle in *Pygmalion*.

[9]Yet Shaw also saw in Keats something rare among "lyrical genius of the first order"— the quality of "geniality," generally missing from artists who took themselves and their work seriously. Keats "could not only carry his splendid burthen of genius, but swing it round, toss it up and catch it again, and whistle a tune as he strode along."

[10]As Shaw put it in his Ruskin lecture, " You may aim at making a man cultured and religious, but you must feed him first. . . . Unless you build on that, all your [cultural and social] superstructure will be rotten." Shaw had made this point as early as his music-critic days, and it would become Barbara Undershaft's epiphany in the closing scene of *Major Barbara*.

11   The Royal Court Theatre and The Shavian Revolution

[1]*At the Royal Court*, Richard Findlater, ed. (New York and London, 1981), tells the story of the 1956 resurgence of the Court in essays by the principals about the metamorphosis from 1956 through 1981.

[2]Sloane Square Station is now a stop on the Circle Line in the London Transport system.

[3]According to Hesketh Pearson's *George Bernard Shaw* (1942), G.B.S. was gone by the time his admirers arrived. This is confirmed by Theodore Stier (see below, note 7).

[4]Shaw to Iden Payne, February 3, 1911, in *University of Buffalo Studies*, XVI (September 1939), 126.

[5]Shaw to Reginald Golding Bright, October 27, 1904, in *Advice to a Young Critic*, E. J. West, ed. (New York, 1963), p. 155.

[6]A. E. Wilson, *Edwardian Theatre* (London, Arthur Barker, 1951), pp. 173–74.

[7]Theodore Stier, *With Pavlova Round the World* (London, n.d.). Reprinted in "Barker and Shaw at the Court Theatre: A View from the Pit," *Shaw Review*, X (1967), 20–21. Stier conducted the pit orchestra at the Court.

[8]Masefield had first shown up at the Court to whistle some sea chanty tunes to Barker, who was thinking of using sea chanties in the second act of a revival of Shaw's *Captain Brassbound's Conversion*. Masefield had composed them himself while serving on an ancient wooden sailing ship.

[9]Yet Shaw only three months afterward (July 27, 1907) would offer to back their Savoy Theatre venture to the tune of £2,000. Obviously, he found some saving merit in the Court system and management.

[10]C. B. Purdom, *Harley Granville Barker* (Cambridge, Mass., 1956), p. 65.

[11]MacCarthy, later Sir Desmond (1878–1952), began to write on the theater in 1904, the year of the first Court season, when he joined the staff of the *Speaker*. In 1913 he

moved (as "Affable Hawk") to the *New Statesman*—just in time to do memorable reviews of the first English productions of Shaw's *Androcles and the Lion* and Chekhov's *Uncle Vanya*. Later he succeeded Sir Edmund Gosse as the leading critic of the London *Sunday Times*. A member of the famous Bloomsbury Group, he was a friend of Leonard and Virginia Woolf, Clive and Vanessa Bell, Roger Fry, E. M. Forster, Lytton Strachey, and John Maynard Keynes. Virginia Woolf drew him as Bernard in *The Waves* (London, 1831).

[12]Beerbohm published a selection of his critiques for the *Saturday Review* from 1898 through 1910 as *Around Theatres* (1924 and other reprintings since). The remainder were published after his death by Rupert Hart-Davis as *More Theatres* and *Last Theatres*.

[13]His partner at the Court and later ventures, Vedrenne, worked with him until March 1911, when the management ended in debt—and G.B.S. underwrote the losses. Vedrenne continued in theater management, making a fortune in a partnership which produced the Arnold Bennett–Edward Knoblock long-running *Milestones* (1912). He died in 1930, sixteen years before Barker.

[14]Preface to *Back to Methuselah*, 1921.

12   Four Fathers for Barbara

[1]Shaw to Elinor Robson, July 4, 1905, in Elinor Robson, *The Fabric of Memory* (New York: Farrar, Straus and Cudahy, 1957), p. 39.

[2]Archibald Henderson, *George Bernard Shaw* (Cincinnati, Stewart and Kidd, 1911), p. 380.

[3]Louis Crompton, *Shaw the Dramatist* (Lincoln: University of Nebraska Press, 1969), pp. 115–16.

[4]William Manchester, *The Arms of Krupp* (Boston: Little, Brown, 1968), p. 179.

[5]Manchester, op. cit., p. 206.

[6]Ibid., p. 249.

[7]David Bowman, "Shaw, Stead and the Undershaft Tradition," *Shaw Review*, XIV (January 1971), 29.

[8]Ibid., 29–32.

[9]Ms. draft of article, probably 1880s (Texas).

[10]*John Bull's Other Island*, Act I.

[11]John Stow, *A Survey of London* (1658), Henry Morley, ed. (London, 1890), p. 163. The first time attention was called to Stow's account was in S. Weintraub, *Shaw Review*, II (1958), 22.

[12]Ibid.

[13]Joseph Frank, "*Major Barbara:* Shaw's *Divine Comedy*," *PMLA*, LXXI (1956), 61–74.

[14]Preface, *Back to Methuselah*.

13   Brogue-Shock: The Evolution of an Irish Patriot

[1]Shaw, *The Matter with Ireland*, Dan H. Laurence and David H. Greene, eds. (London, 1962), pp. 86–87.

[2]Shaw to Mabel Fitzgerald, December 1, 1914. In *Memoirs of Desmond Fitzgerald* (London, 1968), pp. 185–87.

[3]Ibid., pp. 194–96.

[4]Ibid., pp. 197–98.

[5]Harold Owen, *Common Sense About the Shaw* (London, 1915).

[6]Shaw to Mrs. Patrick Campbell, May 15, 1915. In Alan Dent, ed., *Bernard Shaw and Mrs. Patrick Campbell: Their Correspondence* (New York, 1952), p. 196.

[7]Preface to *O'Flaherty, V.C.* (London, 1919).

[8]*O'Flaherty, V.C.*

[9]Quoted by Blanche Patch in *Thirty Years with G.B.S.* (London, 1951), p. 19.

[10]St. John Ervine, *Bernard Shaw* (London, 1956), p. 471.

[11]Horace Plunkett to Shaw, a.l.s. November 15, 1915. British Museum Add. Ms. 50547.

[12]Lucy Shaw to Ann Elder, May 25, 1916. In Henry George Farmer, *Bernard Shaw's Sister and Her Friends* (London, 1959), p. 231.

[13]Archibald Henderson, *George Bernard Shaw* (New York, 1956), p. 623.

[14]The *New Age*, May 18, 1916.

[15]James Stephens, *The Insurrection in Dublin* (New York, 1916), p. 4.

[16]James Camlin Beckett, *The Making of Modern Ireland* (New York, 1966), p. 441. Beckett also points to the importance of Shaw's letter of warning to the British authorities in the *Daily News*.

[17]Sydney Cockerell, manuscript diary entry for May 12, 1916. British Museum.

[18]Shaw to Mrs. Campbell, May 14, 1916. In Alan Dent, ed., *Bernard Shaw and Mrs. Patrick Campbell: Their Correspondence* (New York: Knopf, 1952), p. 209.

[19]Charlotte Shaw to T. E. Lawrence, September 15-16, 1927. In Janet Dunbar, *Mrs. G.B.S.* (New York, 1963), pp. 254-56. Shaw, letter to the editor, *Irish Press* (Dublin, March 15, 1937). In *The Matter with Ireland*, pp. 134-35.

[20]Beatrice Webb, *Diary 1912-1924*, Margaret Cole, ed. (New York, 1952), pp. 62-63.

[21]Shaw, *A Discarded Defense of Roger Casement* and prefatory note, privately printed by Clement Shorter in 1922. Reprinted in *Matter with Ireland*, pp. 114-23.

[22]*Matter with Ireland*, p. 123.

[23]Both appeals were reprinted in *Matter with Ireland*, pp. 125-31.

[24]J. M. Hone, "Mr. Shaw in Ireland," *New Statesman*, March 17, 1917, p. 568.

[25]Robert Hogan and Michael J. O'Neill, eds., *Joseph Holloway's Abbey Theatre* (Carbondale, Ill., 1967), entries for March 25 and May 9, 1917, pp. 191-93.

[26]Lady Gregory to Shaw, Coole, August 12, 1916. In Daniel J. Murphy, "The Lady Gregory Letters to G. B. Shaw," *Modern Drama*, X (February 1968), 342.

[27]"Brogue-Shock" *Nation*, March 24, 1917. Reprinted in *Matter with Ireland*, pp. 135-40.

[28]Shaw to Johanna Collins. In John Lavery, *The Life of a Painter* (London, 1940). Reprinted in *Matter with Ireland*, p. 258.

14 Shaw's *Lear*

[1]Bernard Shaw, *World*, May 3, 1893. Reprinted in *Music in London 1890-94*, II, pp. 299-300.

[2]Shaw to Gilbert Murray, October 1, 1905. In Dan Laurence, ed., *Bernard Shaw: Collected Letters 1898-1910*, (London, 1972), p. 564. Further letters will be referred to as *CL*.

[3]R. F. Rattray, *Bernard Shaw: A Chronicle* (London, 1951), p. 201.

[4]Paul Green in an interview with Shaw, *Dramatic Heritage* (New York, 1953), p. 127.

[5]Shaw to Lillah McCarthy, a.l.s. August 10, 1917 (courtesy the Academic Center Library, University of Texas, Austin).

[6]*George Bernard Shaw: His Life & Personality* (New York, 1963), pp. 362-363.

[7]Lillah McCarthy, *Myself and My Friends* (London, 1933), p. 207.

[8]"That Shakespeare's soul was damned (I really know no other way of expressing it) by a barren pessimism is undeniable; but even when it drove him to the blasphemous despair of Lear and the Nihilism of Macbeth, it did not break him. He was not crushed by it: he wielded it Titanically, and made it a sublime quality in his plays. He almost delighted in it: it never made him bitter: to the end there was mighty

music in him, and outrageous gaiety." (Shaw, "Frank Harris's Shakespeare," reprinted from *Nation*, December 24, 1910, in *Pen Portraits and Reviews*, London, 1932.)

[9]Preface to *Back to Methuselah* (London, 1921), p. lxxxvi.

[10]Shaw to Lady Gregory, August 19, 1909. In *CL*, 858–859. The minor misquotation is Shaw's.

[11]Shaw, *Heartbreak House*, typewritten transcription of original shorthand draft, May 1917, with manuscript additions and cancelations, leaves 8, 43, and 60. Add. Ms. 59901, British Library.

[12]Shaw to Robert Loraine, July 25, 1918. In Winifred Loraine, *Robert Loraine* (New York, 1936), p. 242. Shaw misquotes slightly from memory.

[13]From Shaw's observations on his dramatic technique written at the request of Archibald Henderson and quoted in his *George Bernard Shaw* (New York, 1956), p. 741.

[14]*Heartbreak House* has several "storm trios" involving fools and sham madmen.

[15]*Shakespeare Our Contemporary* (New York, 1964), pp. 127–168.

[16]*"King Lear* and the Comedy of the Grotesque," *The Wheel of Fire* (London, 1965), p. 163.

[17]J. I. M. Stewart, *Eight Modern Writers* (New York and London, 1963), p. 171.

[18]Martin Meisel, *Shaw and the Nineteenth Century Theatre* (Princeton, 1963), pp. 316–317.

[19]Stewart, op. cit., p. 171.

[20]The suggestion is that of Robert Chapman.

[21]Shaw might also have been remembering, although at ninety-two he did not recognize the fact, a painting he had written about some sixty years before, the Pre-Raphaelite Ford Madox Brown's *Lear and Cordelia* (see *Music in London*, II, p. 15).

[22]Meisel, op. cit., p. 317n.

[23]Later, in *The Simpleton of the Unexpected Isles* (1935), Shaw revived an idea he had been mentioning for a generation—that a future society might require individuals to justify their existence or lose it. In *The Simpleton* the Day of Judgment comes and most Members of Parliament disappear, as well as most physicians, lawyers, and other professionals.

[24]Audrey Williamson, *Bernard Shaw, Man and Writer* (New York, 1963), p. 172.

[25]Peter Brook, *The Empty Space* (New York, 1968), p. 93.

[26]Arthur M. Eastman, *A Short History of Shakespearean Criticism* (New York, 1968), pp. 172–173. "Between the vision of Shakespeare's characters and the vision of Shakespeare himself," says Eastman, "Shaw fails to discriminate." But Eastman fails to indicate the practical possibilities of such discrimination.

[27]*Saturday Review*, January 2, 1897.

[28]*Saturday Review*, May 29, 1897.

[29]Meisel sees "the wife-dominated Hector, the [unseen but] bamboo-wielding Utterword" as "reminiscent of Albany and Cornwall," and it is true, as he notes, that Hector even echoes Albany. Margery Morgan in *The Shavian Playground* (London, 1972), pp. 211–214, sees relationships to *The Tempest* and *A Midsummer Night's Dream* as well as to *Lear*. Richard Hornby sees, "Reminiscent of the extensive animal imagery in *Lear* . . . references in Act III [of *Heartbreak House*] to *animals, horses, dogs, cat and mouse, jellyfish, flying fish, birds, rats* (twice) and *moths*" "The Symbolic Action of *Heartbreak House*," *Drama Survey* 7 [Winter 1968–1969], p. 19.

16   The "Unknown Soldier": Shaw's Unwritten Play

[1]Michael Holroyd and Robert Skidelsky, eds., introduction to William Gerhardie, *God's Fifth Column* (New York: Simon & Schuster, 1981), pp. 17–18.

[2]Undated August issue of *Reichsbote* quoted in *The Times*, 23 August 1918.

[3]Reproduced as item 663 in *Shaw: An Exhibit,* Dan H. Laurence, ed. (Austin, Texas, Humanities Research Center, 1977).

[4]Quoted in Jeffrey Holmesdale, "Rating and Cut-Rating" (a column of theater gossip), *World* (New York), November 18, 1928, p. 2M.

[5]From the three-page typescript, with autograph corrections and annotations by Shaw, dated April 14, 1930, in a private collection. Permission to publish the previously unpublished Shaw quotations has been granted by the Society of Authors on behalf of the Bernard Shaw Estate.

[6]Ibid.

[7]Paul Green, *Dramatic Heritage* (New York, 1953), pp. 130–31.

[8]Mary Anderson Navarro, *More Memories* (London, 1936), pp. 218–19.

[9]Cedric Hardwicke as told to James Brough in *A Victorian in Orbit* (New York, 1961), p. 107.

[10]Charlotte Shaw to Sean O'Casey, August 27, 1931, in David Krause, ed., *The Letters of Sean O'Casey, 1910–1941* (New York: Macmillan, 1975), p. 433.

17   The Playwright and the Pirate

[1]The annotated texts of both sides of the correspondence between Shaw and Harris, 1895–1931, appear in S. Weintraub, ed., *The Playwright and the Pirate. Bernard Shaw and Frank Harris: A Correspondence* (University Park: The Pennsylvania State University Press, 1982). It also includes substantial extracts from Harris's "Contemporary Portraits" biography of Shaw, and Shaw's spoof-rejoinder.

18   Shaw's Other Keegan: Sean O'Casey and G.B.S.

[1]Shaw's letters are quoted from the notes to David Krause, ed., *The Letters of Sean O'Casey,* I, 1910–41 (London and New York, 1975), II, 1942–1954 (London and New York, 1980), and from Eileen O'Casey, *Sean* (New York, 1972).

[2]David Krause, ed., *The Letters of Sean O'Casey,* I, 96, quoting Lady Gregory's analysis.

[3]Robert Hogan and Michael J. O'Neill, *Joseph Holloway's Abbey Theatre* (Carbondale, Ill., 1967), entry for March 18, 1924, p. 227.

[4]Shaw's plays are quoted from the *Bodley Head Bernard Shaw* (London, 7 vols., 1970–74).

[5]Saros Cowasjee, *Sean O'Casey: The Man Behind the Plays* (London, 1963), pp. 77–78.

[6]O'Casey's letters are quoted from Krause.

[7]Shaw to O'Casey, July 4, 1935, quoted in Sotheby catalogue of the 29–30 June, 1982 sale, item 593, p. 252.

[8]"G.B.S. Speaks Out of the Whirlwind," *Listener,* March 7, 1934, Supplement III-IV.

[9]Eileen's memories hereafter supplement the *Letters* and O'Casey's own autobiographies; *Mirror in My House* (New York, 1956).

[10]Ronald G. Rollins, "Shaw and O'Casey: John Bull and His Other Island," *Shaw Review,* X (1967), 60–69.

[11]Ronald Ayling and Michael J. Durkan, *Sean O'Casey: A Bibliography* (London, 1978), pp. 71–72.

19   The Avant-Garde Shaw: *Too True to Be Good* and its Predecessors

[1]*Our Theatres in the Nineties*, II, 84. As a futurist Bernard Shaw was no H. G. Wells, yet it is interesting to note that Shaw seems to have anticipated other playwrights in

practice as well as in theory. A long list of stage "firsts" can be assigned to Shavian drama. The first automobile on stage appears in *Man and Superman* (1903), and the first airplane makes its entrance (via an off-stage crash) in *Misalliance* seven years later—along with the first aviatrix. The first Zeppelin appears in *Heartbreak House* (1917), and the first robot in *Back to Methuselah* (1920), where one also conducts telephone conversations via a television screen.

[2]"On the University Dramatic Society," a G.B.S. lecture published in the *University College of Wales Magazine*, XXII (January 1900), 167-68.

[3]Homer Woodbridge, *G. B. Shaw: Creative Artist* (Carbondale, Ill., 1963), p. 52.

[4]Shaw in a letter to Alexander Bakshy, June 12, 1927. In *The Theatre Unbound*, by Cecil Palmer. Reprinted in E. J. West, ed., *Shaw on Theatre* (New York, 1958), p. 185.

[5]Bernard F. Dukore, *Bernard Shaw, Playwright* (Columbia, Mo., 1973), p. 218.

[6]John Gassner, "Bernard Shaw and the Making of the Modern Mind," *Dramatic Soundings* (New York, 1968), p. 635.

[7]Max Beerbohm in the *Saturday Review*. Reprinted in his *Around Theatres* (New York, 1954), pp. 268-72.

[8]Shaw, "The Play of Ideas," *New Statesman*, May 6, 1950. Reprinted in West, op. cit., p. 290.

[9]Reprinted in the *Bodley Head Bernard Shaw* (London, 1971), III, 667-68. This was a Shavian self-interview.

[10]Francis R. Bellamy, review of *The Apple Cart*, *Outlook*, March 12, 1930, p. 429.

[11]Lionel Abel, *Metatheatre: A New View of Dramatic Form* (New York, 1963), p. 106.

[12]Undated but described as written the day after the play opened at Malvern in 1932. Quoted in Cedric Hardwicke, *A Victorian in Orbit* (New York, 1961), pp. 183-84.

[13]Shaw to H. K. Ayliff, tls, August 8, 1932. Hofstra University Library.

Acknowledgments

Portions of this book have appeared before, in earlier stages of development and often under other titles. I am indebted to the original publishers for the opportunity to have tried out my ideas in their pages as noted below:

"Everybody's Shaw"—in *Modern British Dramatists, 1900–1945*, Dictionary of Literary Biography, vol. 10, ed. S. Weintraub (Detroit: Gale Research Co., 1982).

"Sketches for a Self-Portrait"—Preface to *Shaw: An Autobiography 1856–1989*, ed. S. Weintraub (New York: Weybright & Talley, 1969).

"The Novelist in Spite of Himself"—Preface to *An Unfinished Novel by Bernard Shaw*, ed. S. Weintraub (London: Constable; New York: Dodd, Mead, 1958).

"G.B.S., Pugilist and Playwright"—as "A Passion for Pugilism," *The Times Literary Supplement*, London, May 5, 1978.

"Bernard Shaw, Actor"—in *Theatre Arts*, October 1960.

"Exploiting Art: Shaw in the Picture Galleries and the Picture Galleries in Shaw's Plays"—as "In the Picture Galleries," in *The Genius of Shaw* ed. Michael Holroyd, (New York: Holt, Rinehart & Winston, 1979).

"G.B.S. Borrows from Sarah Grand: *The Heavenly Twins* and *You Never Can Tell*," *Modern Drama*, December 1971.

"Shaw's Lady Cicely and Mary Kingsley"—in *Fabian Feminist*, ed. Rodelle Weintraub (University Park: Penn State Press, 1977).

"Shaw's Mommsenite Caesar"—in *Anglo-German and American-German Crosscurrents*, eds. P. A. Shelley and A. O. Lewis (Chapel Hill: University of North Carolina Press, 1962).

"The Social Critic as Literary Critic"—Preface to *Nondramatic Literary Criticism of Bernard Shaw*, ed. S. Weintraub (Lincoln: University of Nebraska Press, 1972).

"The Royal Court Theatre and the Shavian Revolution"—Preface to reprint edition of Desmond McCarthy's *The Royal Court Theatre* (Coral Gables: University of Miami Press, 1966).

"Four Fathers for Barbara"—in *Directions in Literary Criticism*, eds. S. Weintraub and P. Young (University Park: Penn State Press, 1973).

"Brogue-Shock: The Evolution of an Irish Patriot"—as "The Making of an Irish Patriot," in *Eire-Ireland*, Winter 1970.

"Shaw's *Lear*"—as "*Heartbreak House*: Shaw's *Lear*," in *Modern Drama*, December 1972.

"The Genesis of *Joan*"—Preface to the Bobbs-Merrill *Saint Joan* (Indianapolis: Bobbs-Merrill, 1971).

"*The Unknown Soldier:* Shaw's Unwritten Play"—as "Bernard Shaw and the Unknown Soldier" in *The Times Literary Supplement*, November 13, 1981.

"The Playwright and the Pirate: Bernard Shaw and Frank Harris"—Preface to *The Playwright and the Pirate. Bernard Shaw and Frank Harris: A Correspondence*, ed. S. Weintraub (University Park: Penn State Press; Gerrard's Cross: Colin Smythe, 1982).

"Shaw's Other Keegan: Sean O'Casey and G.B.S."—in *Sean O'Casey Centenary Essays*, ed. Robert Lowry (Gerrard's Cross: Colin Smythe; New York: Barnes and Noble, 1980).

"The Avant-Garde Shaw: *Too True to Be Good* and Its Predecessors"—as "The Avant-Garde Shaw" in *Shaw Seminar Papers* (Toronto: Copp Clark, 1966).

Index

[For Shaw titles, see under *Shaw, Bernard*; all other titles are indexed alphabetically.]